D0948683

ANTHROPOLOGY OF LAW
A COMPARATIVE THEORY

ANTHROPOLOGY
OF
LAW
A
COMPARATIVE
THEORY

Leopold Pospíšil
Yale University

Harper & Row, Publishers
New York, Evanston, San Francisco, London

to my father and my mother

K

CONTENTS

PREFACE

Law has traditionally been regarded as the property of only the "higher" cultures and civilizations. It has often been claimed that law does not exist among the more primitive agricultural tribal societies, especially the hunters and gatherers. As "proof" of these claims some students of jurisprudence, political science, and sociology have used a Western-biased definition of law that indeed leaves no room for consideration of any but the law of western Europe and countries colonized by Europeans. We read, for example, that "unless there are official agencies to decide disputes by interpreting and applying legal rules to given situations—that is, unless there are courts—there is no law as defined here" (Davis *et al.* 1962: p. 45). The interesting thing is that this definition not only excludes tribal societies from the benefits of law, but it also denies the existence of law in many non-European and even in some ancient European civilizations. Prior to the establishment of Communism, Chinese magistrates, for example, were not concerned with "interpreting and applying legal rules" to actual cases of conflict, but rather used the rules only as guides—helpful models which in a concrete case need not be followed. Law, as conceived by Davis and colleagues can hardly apply even to the formal legal controls used in ancient Greece and Rome. The main source of law there were the contemplations of judges (*themistes*) preceding legal decisions, or the opinions of jurisconsults; disputes were not adjudicated on the basis of the relatively few rules that were codified (e.g., *Lex Duodecim Tabularum*) and that judges could "interpret and apply to a given situation." But even the most orthodox legal scholar of the West would be shocked by a claim that ancient Rome had no law.

Anthropology or law avoids (with very rare exceptions) such ethnocentric bias and has several advantages over such disciplines as jurisprudence, political science, and sociology. First, it is not culture bound. It studies societies comparatively, no matter how "primitive" or "civilized," and does not, as a rule, discriminate qualitatively in favor of

one type of human society against another. Second, in contrast to some
of the other social sciences, it does not arbitrarily carve out from human
culture a segment such as the economy, political structure, law,
personality structure, or "social relations," but conceives and studies
human culture as an interrelated whole. In other words, an
anthropologist does not (or at least should not) go to the field and there
concentrate his attention solely upon what he conceives law to be,
excluding the rest of the "nonrelevant" culture. Law should be studied
as an integral part of the cultural whole, not regarded as an autonomous
institution. Third, modern anthropology does not concentrate upon the
study of "social forces" and the "superorganic" to the exclusion of the
role of the individual. Both are taken into consideration. Fourth, society
is no longer viewed as in a static social equilibrium, which is "disturbed"
by delicts. Rather, it is conceived as a dynamic phenomenon, so that the
social role of law is not limited solely to maintaining the status quo. As a
consequence, the claim is not made that *all* law has to be supported by
public sentiment or that it emanates from an inevitable course of social
change that an authority—lawyer or tribal chief—can interpret but not
alter. Anthropology of law does not, in Stone's words, subscribe to
"legislative impotence" (1950: p. 444). Fifth, anthropology of law is a
science of law and therefore empirical. Theories should be supported by
all relevant facts or at least a representative sample of all facts (meaning
phenomena perceived by our senses) available. Scientific theories should
be distinguished from scientific hypotheses and presented as ideas that
can be ultimately proved by empirical methods. All of these, in turn,
should be dissociated from pure speculation, from intellectual pagodas
built on the basis of "pure logic" or sometimes even on emotion or
sheer fantasy.

     In this book I have tried to distinguish these categories and follow
the maxims stated here. If I have failed generally or at some point, it
does not mean, of course, that a rigorous science of law is impossible or
that it is wishful thinking. It can only mean that either my method or
data, or both, were inadequate.

     Until the Marxian evolutionary dogmas of the nineteenth century
made their inroads into anthropological theory, it was generally believed
that law was indispensable for any kind of society. It is no accident that
many of the anthropological giants of the nineteenth century were
trained lawyers. Also, and it is no surprise to read on the jacket of
Lloyd's most interesting book *The Idea of Law*, "Like it or not—and
many from Plato to Marx have disliked it—law is a central concept in
human society: without it, indeed, there would be no society" (1966).
Similarly, Gluckman concludes that African law incorporates the same
fundamental conceptions as does our own (1967: p. 96), obviously
implying universality of law in human societies. The same implication is
derived from Llewellyn and Hoebel's discussion of the basic elements

that give rise to law; all these, such as the social group, joined and continuing activity, patterned behavior and degree of its predictability, divergent motives of individuals and their occasional conflicting claims, are decidedly present in all human societies, forming the prerequisites for law and leading to its universal emergence (1961: pp. 273–274).

It is therefore surprising that American anthropologists and social scientists in general, in spite of this legal-anthropological tradition and an epoch-making legal masterpiece, *The Cheyenne Way* (Llewellyn and Hoebel: 1961; originally published in 1941 by two American scholars, a lawyer and an anthropologist), shunned analyses of law until very recently. In general we do not find a chapter on law in ethnographies by Americans, in spite of the fact that law, with its sanctions, controls such important institutions as marriage, incest, inheritance, offenses against religion, and so forth, all topics central to anthropological investigation. It might be said that this neglect results from a narrow conceptualization which holds that law is applicable only to the social controls of civilized societies. This book attempts, then, to help broaden the study of law in American anthropology and to contribute to the recent corrective trend represented by such scholars as Hoebel, Bohannan, Roberts, Smith, Nader, Kay, Moore, and others.

The theory around which this book is organized is the result of a prolonged study that began at the law school of Charles University in Prague. At that time I was impressed by the beautiful, systematic, logic of Roman law, brilliantly analyzed in the writings of Professor Otakar Sommer (esp. 1933, 1935). My original legalistic orientation to the study of law and legal theory began to change after I arrived in the United States, where I studied sociology at Willamette University in Oregon and followed that by study toward a Master's degree in anthropology at the University of Oregon. At that time Professor H. G. Barnett suggested law as a topic for my thesis. Under the advisory supervision of Professor W. S. Laughlin, I was exposed for the first time to *The Cheyenne Way,* a book that changed my orientation and which, next to the writings on Roman law, has been the most influential force in shaping my thinking. That is not to say, of course, that I uncritically accepted the theories of Hoebel and Llewellyn. I am sure that neither of them would have appreciated that. However, I do mean that the book influenced my thoughts and that some of my ideas originated either as an elaboration of the authors' statements or as a positive or negative reaction to them. In order to balance this anthropological influence, and to acquire some historical perspective in legal theory, I immersed myself simultaneously in the writings of Professor Julius Stone. These three sources then—the Roman juridical, the anthropological, and the jurisprudential—form the basic background against which many of my thoughts should be projected.

The major theoretical orientation of this book, as well as some of its specific topics, took its preliminary form in my Master's thesis, "Nature of Law," submitted to the Department of Anthropology at the University of Oregon (Pospisil: 1952). This study was based strictly on comparative library research and was subsequently tested during my first field work among the Hopi Indians in Arizona in the summer of 1952. Further research at Yale University brought the number of intensively studied cultures to thirty-two and was supported by a survey of an sixty-three additional societies. The cultures in that sample ranged from very simple ones like those of the Bushmen and the Yaghan to the complex civilizations of the Romans, Incas, and Chinese. The developing theory underwent a real test during my prolonged research among the Kapauku Papuans of West New Guinea, where I studied a political confederacy of lineages of the yet unpacified Kamu Valley (the original research of 1954–1955 was followed by two summer research periods in 1959 and 1962). The results of this research were incorporated into my doctoral dissertation and have been published in three books and a series of articles. In 1957 I added the Nunamiut Eskimo of Alaska to my investigated societies and since 1962 I have continued my legal researches in the Tirol of Austria.

These four cultures have given me an opportunity to study law and social control in societies of varied types and complexity. The Nunamiut are nomadic hunters and gatherers with weakly defined political leadership; the Kapauku are a sedentary people with more formalized leadership; they practice shifting cultivation. It has been claimed that law is absent in both these societies. The Hopi Indians of Arizona can be regarded as transitional between a farming tribal society and an emerging civilization with incipient towns, governed by formal chiefs. The Tiroleans, with their traditional civilization, are simultaneously exposed to two types of social control: the informal settlement of conflicts by the community's authorities (mayor, priest, schoolteacher, etc.) and the adjudication of disputes by the Austrian courts of law.

I have investigated two of the societies over a long period of time, and I not only concentrated on their legal systems in a static way, but I also studied their cultural and legal change. Among the Kapauku Papuans, acculturation changes were rapidly effected by construction of an airstrip in the Kamu Valley, still a basically Stone Age area in 1954–1955; in the Tirol, the fast urbanization of the formerly secluded and traditional Obernberg Valley was initiated by other means—the first paved road into the valley and an adjacent exit from the *Autobahn*. Of the four societies, the Tirol provided me with the most voluminous material. Since this research is still in progress, most of the data have not yet been quantitatively analyzed, but the qualitative results and a formal analysis of the Tirolean laws of inheritance have been concluded and are incorporated into this volume. To balance the sample of the studied peoples, I still hope to do major research in an African society with formal chiefs and court procedures.

The book, after this brief introduction, presents a systematic theory of law (of "procedure") and my first theoretical attempts to analyze substantive law by a method of potential cross-cultural applicability. In the chapter "Changes of Legal Systems," the legal topic to which almost every legal philosopher addresses himself, I have made no contribution of my own, being satisfied with a historically oriented survey of other people's theories. Faced with inadequate data on one hand, and the purely speculative or vague theoretical results of other writers, I leave this field to more imaginative anthropologists.

Studies among the Kapauku Papuans of West New Guinea were generously financed by the Ford Foundation, Social Science Research Council, and the American Philosophical Society. My investigation of the Nunamiut Eskimos was sponsored by the Arctic Institute of North America, and my long fieldwork in the Tirol has been supported by the National Science Foundation and one field session by the Social Science Research Council. None of these foundations and organizations, however, is to be understood as approving by virtue of its grant any of the statements made or the views expressed in this book.

I express my thanks for the assistance of many individuals: Ijaaj Jokagaibo and Ijaaj Awiitigaaj of New Guinea, Homer Mekiana of Alaska, Faye Avatchoya of the Hano Pueblo, and Stefan and Stefanie Hammer, Alfred and Michael Larcher, and Elisabeth Riedl, all from Obernberg in Tirol, for serving as my best informants; Ijaaj Akaawoogi and my forty-seven other adopted sons of New Guinea, Joe Mekiana of Alaska, Karl and Heinz Kopeitka of Tirol, and my father, Dr. Leopold Pospíšil, for helping me as my field assistants; Professor E. Adamson Hoebel, G. P. Murdock, Cornelius Dsgood, Floyd Lounsbury, Paul Bohannan, Max Gluckman, Harold Conklin, W. S. Laughlin, Laura Nader, and Theodore Stern for helpful advice and criticisms; Mrs. Anne Wilde for editing the manuscript; R. Farren and J. Fredrick for help as research assistants; Mrs. Josephine Williams, Adele Shapiro, Marcia Ezra, and Cecilia Rivera for their editorial help and secretarial services.

Finally, I wish to thank my father for awakening my interest in social problems, for introducing me to law, and for helping me with my research in the Tirol. I also wish to thank him for making me understand that law is nothing but a tool for effecting justice, and that personal courage and integrity are worth more than a sheltered life as a conformist or a slave.

New Haven, 1971   Leopold Pospíšil

CHAPTER
ONE
INTRODUCTION

THREE LEGAL DICHOTOMIES

Before I discuss the different types of violence in human societies, which will constitute the second part of this introduction, I would like to clarify some basic legal ideas and concepts that might be misunderstood. They constitute three dichotomies. The first distinguishes between substantive and procedural law. The law of substance sets limits to permissible behavior and deals chiefly with the content of legal precepts, such as kinds of crimes and torts and their punishment, types of contracts, and rights to things and ways of disposing of inheritance, as well as legally recognized family relationships. The law of procedure, on the contrary, deals with the process of law, e.g., with the problems of jurisdiction, allocation of authority, nature and administration of sanctions, court proceedings, and the question of justice. The law of procedure is the subject of most of my theoretical attention in this book.

The second dichotomy deals with the principles of the territoriality and of the personality of law. This problem focuses mainly on jurisdiction. In modern civilized nations we are confronted with a principle according to which law is enforced within a territory, irrespective of the identity and status of the persons involved in the litigation. The personality principle of law, on the other hand, declares that the jurisdiction and application of a legal system is determined exactly by the identity and status of the litigants, irrespective of the territory where they commenced their litigation, or where a crime or tort was committed. As the anthropologist may remember, this personality (or status) principle of law has often been erroneously attributed to tribal societies only, while, in contradistinction, all civilizations were supposed to have legal systems employing the territoriality principle. Of course, this simplistic dichotomization does not stand the test of empiricism. For example, the famed Roman civil law was based upon the personality principle. As a consequence, no matter where he entered into a litigation (in Rome, in a province, or abroad) a Roman was subject to *ius civile,* but a foreigner was not entitled to the provisions of this law even in Rome. As a consequence, for example, a Roman who married a foreign woman was not considered married, according to *ius civile;* his family was not *familia* in the Roman sense and, of course, laws of inheritance did not apply (Sommer 1933: p. 13). In contrast the Nunamiut Eskimos of the old tribal days would apply their law to foreigners without hesitation.

The last dichotomy deals with the difference between the Latin terms *ius* (*Recht* in German, *pravo* in Czech and Russian, *droit* in French, etc.) and *lex* (*Gesetz* in German, *zákon* in Czech and Russian, *loi* in French, etc.). Unfortunately, both these terms are translated into English as "law." While *ius* means law in terms of the principles implied in precedents or rules (statutes), *lex* means an abstract rule, usually made explicit in a legal code (as a statute). Consequently, legislation creates *leges* (plural of *lex*), which incorporate principles that are termed *ius*. Thus *ius* is more fundamental than *lex,* the latter being only one of the forms (a formalized and explicit one) of *ius.* Misunderstanding of the precise meanings of these terms has led some theoreticians, working with translations or with foreign texts, into errors. From the statements of Stanley Moore in his article, "Marxian Theories of Law in Primitive Society" (1960), he appears to have committed this error in his argument about a radical difference between Marx and Engels' and Lenin's versions of Marxism as far as the evolution of law is concerned. He concluded that while Marx and Engels argued for an existence of law in a tribal society, Lenin denied law in this evolutionary stage and asserted that law required a class society, the state, for its existence. Translated into English, the sources certainly substantiate this finding, but an understanding of the original text reveals the basic difference between the two concepts. While Marx and Engels chiefly discuss *Recht* (*ius*) in the tribal societies (see esp. Moore 1960: pp. 645–646; also "Marxism" in Chapter Five of this book), Lenin is talking about *zákon* (*lex*) when he argues that it exists exclusively in the state, where it is used to oppress the lower classes (esp. Moore 1960: p. 653). It will be *ius* then that is the subject of my theorizing and which I shall translate as "law"; I shall call *lex* "abstract rule" or "statute."

FEUD

In some anthropological reports and ethnographies the concept of law (*ius*) has been identified with feud. Several well-known anthropologists and legal scholars have claimed that feud constitutes the form that law assumes in some tribal societies. Since feud has been so frequently regarded as a tool of law and because it is obvious that the most striking common feature of feud and law is violence, I feel compelled, first, to discuss the nature of feud and its relation to law and, second, to make a brief survey and rough classification of the violence which one encounters in human societies.

Thus, as a preamble to the analysis of legal phenomena, the reader will be acquainted with the position of law within the broader field of human violence and its relation to the various types of the latter.[1]

Feud has been defined by Lasswell as "relations of mutual animosity among intimate groups in which a resort to violence is anticipated on both sides" (1931: p. 220). This definition includes two important concepts—"violence" and "intimate [or related] groups"—that require amplification.

Nature of Violence

Concerning the concept of violence, the question arises: Is any type of violence between intimate groups a feud, or are there specific characteristics that denote the violence of a feud? The concept is commonly refined, in terms of intensity and duration. Thus, there appears to be general agreement that the violence typical of a feud may range from beating, which leaves only slight injuries, to killing several members of the opposite group. A feud involves prolonged and intermittent hostilities. As a logical consequence, a single fight or a single killing cannot be defined as a feud. Long intervals of relative peace sometimes elapse between the fights and slayings (Lowie 1920: p. 414). Bohannan says that "feud occurs when the principle of self-help gets out of hand" (1963: p. 290), implying that if an injury is redressed through violence and the self-redress is final and more or less accepted by the other party, such violence does not merit the term "feud." Lasswell states that feuds often continue so long after they begin that the precipitating episodes are even forgotten (1931: p. 221). Evans-Pritchard (1940b: p. 293) agrees with the criterion of prolonged violence. However, he points out that a feud cannot go on indefinitely; otherwise the relationship of the fighting groups (among the Nuer, their membership in the same tribe) would be severed, and further hostilities, not occurring between related groups, could no longer by implication be called feud (1940b: pp. 279, 283).

We may conclude, then, that feud involves prolonged, often intermittent violence which must end at some point short of the obliteration of the second criterion of feud—the intimate relationship of the feuding groups. Of course, concluding a feud does not necessarily mean that mutual hostility is transformed into indifference or friendship. A new feuding cycle most likely erupts between the old combatants any time that a new crime or injury is committed by an individual against a member of the other side.

The chain of violent acts that marks the feud is initiated in order "to secure revenge, reprisal, or glory for a particular individual or family within the group" (Wright 1959: p. 90). Another common characteristic of the

---

[1]The following section is reprinted with minor changes from "Feud" by Leopold Pospisil. Reprinted with permission of the publisher from *International Encyclopedia of the Social Sciences,* David L. Sills, ed., vol. 5, pp. 389–393. Copyright © 1968 by Crowell Collier and Macmillan, Inc.

violence that may be classified as feud is the claim that the actual acts of hostility are regulated by customs shared by the two fighting groups (Radcliffe-Brown 1952: p. 215). In other words, the hostilities of the two groups are patterned upon, and subject to, rules which both sides observe. Furthermore, the initial act of violence is regarded as injury to the whole group to which the victim belongs (family, clan, or village), and the members consequently stand under an obligation to avenge the injustice (Radcliffe-Brown 1952: p. 215; 1940: p. xx; Nadel 1947: p. 151). Paraphrasing Durkheim, Radcliffe-Brown calls their duty an expression of "collective solidarity." However, this principle works also with regard to the opposite party, where it produces a group liability, with the effect that any member of the offender's group may be slain for the crime of his relative, his friend, or a coresident (Radcliffe-Brown 1952: p. 215; Nadel 1947: p. 151).

According to Radcliffe-Brown (1952: p. 215; 1940: p. xx), another aspect of the violence of feuds is that it is justified by "public sentiment." Unfortunately, he fails to specify whether this public sentiment pertains to the group of avengers, to both of the groups in conflict, or to the society at large. If we recall his statement that the acts of violence are regulated by custom, we may conclude that this public sentiment pertains to the larger society of which the two fighting groups are constituent segments. Not all acts of violence justify development of such a sentiment: in order that a violent revenge be considered a justifiable act, its magnitude should be valued as an equivalent to the injury suffered (Radcliffe-Brown 1952: p. 215; 1940: p. xx; Nadel 1947: p. 151). Who, however, determines the equivalent? Implied in the writings of Radcliffe-Brown and Nadel is the notion that the criteria for equivalence are sufficiently objective, i.e., part of a general custom known to all, so that it is often unnecessary for a specified authority to deliver an opinion on the balance between the injury and revenge. Among the Nuba, for example, "equivalence" is so specific that not only must a man be killed for a man and a woman for a woman, but the age of the person killed in revenge should approximate that of the original victim. For death in excess of requirement a compensation must be offered in the form of a person who is adopted into the offended clan (Nadel 1947: pp. 151–152). In most other primitive societies such compensation is usually tendered in payment known in the literature as "blood money." Bearing in mind Bohannan's important point that feud occurs when "self-help gets out of hand," Radcliffe-Brown's and Nadel's principle of equivalence of revenge applies to feud only when such equivalence is not achieved by the first retaliation of the injured party. There have to be more than two acts of violence to justify the application of the term feud.

The characteristics of violence that form one of the two major criteria of feud may be summed up as follows: (1) the violence of a feud ranges in intensity from injury to killing; (2) it is initiated on behalf of a particular individual or family that is a member of the more inclusive "injured group";

and (3) it is of long duration, involving at least three instances of violence —injury, revenge, and counterrevenge. Hostile acts consisting of an injury and of an equivalent revenge that is accepted as final by both parties do not merit the term feud and should more properly be called self-redress. The nature of self-redress is, in most cases, basically different from the prolonged violence called feud.

Nature of Feuding Groups

The second major criterion of feud, which requires the committed violence to occur between two "intimate [or related] groups," is far more important and complex (Lasswell 1931: p. 221). It is almost generally agreed that the two groups fighting each other must be related in order to qualify such hostilities as a feud. However, various authors differ in their explanation of the nature of this relationship. An imprecise position is assumed, for example, by Wright, who states that

> *"most primitive groups observe different war practices toward a related group with which friendship normally exists and toward a wholly alien group. Hostilities of the first type, although group sanctioned, are usually of the nature of a feud to secure revenge, reprisal, or glory for a particular individual or family within the group." (1959: p. 90)*

Others who have studied feuds—for example, Malinowski (1964: p. 261)— go further, claiming that relationship between the two groups obtains from the fact that they both belong to "the same larger cultural unit." Similarly, those who use the phrase "members of the same society" do not necessarily identify the political unit involved. For example, Max Gluckman (1940: p. 41) speaks of a type of intertribal feud within a larger nation, while Hobhouse and his associates restrict the relationship of feuding groups to membership in the same tribe: "Feuds would thus also be the appropriate name for reprisals exercised by one branch of a community upon another, e.g., as between two clans or two local groups within a tribe" (Hobhouse, Wheeler, and Ginsberg: 1930: p. 228). Besides this type of an "internal self-redress" called feud, these authors recognize another type of redress which exists between two segments of otherwise unrelated communities and is labeled "external self-redress." A similar limitation of the application of the concept of feud to the fighting done by groupings that belong to the same tribe is upheld quite explicitly by Evans-Pritchard. He contrasts these hostilities with the intertribally organized violence which he calls war: "Thus, if a man of one tribe kills a man of another tribe, retribution can only take the form of intertribal warfare" (1940b: p. 278). "Between segments of the same tribe, opposition is expressed by the institution of the feud" (1940b: p. 283).

Some authors theorize that marriage ties constitute the link between the two feuding groups. Accordingly, hostilities in a society with exogamous subgroups such as clans, lineages, or local communities are all regarded as feuds and not as wars (Schneider 1964: p. 282; also implied by Colson 1962: p. 120).

The relationship between the hostile groups is far less nebulous and more related to the feuding itself than the marriage-tie hypothesis would imply. Evans-Pritchard has the following to say about those Nuer who engage in intratribal fighting:

> "Then either the contradiction of feuds is felt and they are settled, the unity of the tribe being maintained thereby, or they remain so long unsettled that people give up all hope and intention of ever concluding them and finally cease to feel that they ought to be concluded, so that the tribe tends to split and two new tribes come into being." (1940b: p. 279)

This statement suggests that the nature of the relationship of two feuding groups lies in the fact that the more inclusive group of which the two are members is, at least to some degree, politically organized. The political organization may mean that there exists a formally designated authority with jurisdiction over both feuding groups; in other cases it may consist of only the most informal arbiters or go-betweens, who customarily settle internal political problems. Gluckman (1959: p. 20) went so far as to claim that feuding, by creating a necessity for the existence of such go-betweens, tends to unite the members of the larger grouping. There are good examples of formal political authority terminating feuds between subgroups by the use of force, in the event that the customary exchange has failed. I would hesitate to designate as a feud fighting that occurs between politically unrelated groupings and would criticize Wagner (1940: p. 223) and Schneider (1964: p. 279) for holding that an overall political organization is not necessary to qualify a condition of strife as a feud. Wherever feuds do occur, there exists a politically influential authority (a formal chief, an informal headman, a council of important men, or an individual of very limited power, such as a go-between), who is usually too weak or disinterested in controlling his constituents, with the result that prolonged fighting is not prevented. The weaker the political control, the longer the feuds last and the harder it is to conclude them (see esp. Evans-Pritchard 1940b: pp. 278–279; and Gluckman 1959: p. 19).

Feud and War
The criterion of an over-all political organization that relates the two feuding groups may also be used to mark the boundary between feud and war. Whereas feuds can occur only within a politically organized whole, war occurs beyond such an organization and always involves two groups that are politically unrelated (Nadel 1947: p. 301). One should not, however, go to the extreme and claim that it would be "advisable to include all external,

group-sanctioned violence against other human beings in the conception of primitive war" (Schneider 1964: p. 276). There seem to be two kinds of hostility external to politically organized groupings: hostility which is "exercised by a part of a community only upon members of another community" and which should properly be called "external self-redress," or retaliation; and hostility which means "an operation conducted in the name of the community as a whole," and which thus deserves to be regarded as war (Hobhouse, Wheeler, and Ginsberg 1930: p. 228).

These structural criteria that distinguish feud, external redress, and war appear to be more politically relevant and suitable than the following, which are of only circumstantial nature. For example, the claim that only publicly initiated hostilities should be called war, while the privately initiated ones should be labeled feuds, constitutes a most impractical criterion. However, Schneider's criticism of anthropologists for misusing the term "war" is erroneous; it is based on his contention that hostilities within a society that is segmented into exogamous groups (such as clans, lineages, or communities) cannot be called war (Schneider 1964: pp. 279, 282). He disregards the fact that exogamy is a social-structural feature and war is a political phenomenon and that, therefore, presence or absence of exogamy is irrelevant to this problem. To make the term "war" cross-culturally applicable and meaningful, one should define it in terms of political-structural features. Data on the Kapauku Papuans of New Guinea bear out the fallacy of such an analysis (Pospisil 1958a: pp. 74–88). These Papuans live in localized exogamous lineages. Several lineages, belonging to different sibs, unite for defense purposes into a political confederacy. Beyond this unit no political organization exists. Interconfederational strife, which is true war, is marked by organization, by participation of whole confederacies as units in the fighting, and by ferocity involving slaughter, arson, rape, and so forth. On the contrary, fighting within a confederacy is done, as a rule, with sticks, not with bows and arrows, and does not result in death. No raping of women, burning of houses, killing of pigs, or destruction of gardens accompanies these internal hostilities. To consider both types of fighting as feud would be to obscure rather than clarify the ethnological reality. Bearing the political-structural criteria of feud and war in mind, one can readily see how erroneous are the claims that war is uncommon or nonexistent in "the lowest stages" of social development (Hobhouse Wheeler, and Ginsberg 1930: p. 228) and that it requires for its existence a "certain development of social organization." Indeed, it is the feud that requires a complex social development—a large social entity with an overall political organization that is segmented into subgroups.

Feud and Law

The fact that feuds are fought between subgroups of a more inclusive grouping possessing an overall network of political relations has led to the conclusion that feud is a primitive juridical mechanism and that it is an expression, or manifestation, of primitive law. Accordingly, Malinowski writes, "Fighting, collective and organized, is a juridical mechanism for the adjustment of differences between constituent groups of the same larger cultural unit" (1964: p. 261). Spencer contends that after a north Alaskan Eskimo was killed, "his own kin became embroiled and the legal mechanism of the feud was put into motion" (1959: p. 161). The notion that feuding is a manifestation of primitive law led Lasswell to the conclusion that there must be two types of feuds: "While the blood vengeance feud was itself the expression of primitive law, the modern feud is at least formally illegal and characteristically fills the interstices left in the functioning of the prevailing system of legal organization" (1931: p. 220). Many anthropologists have disagreed with the idea that feud is the expression of primitive law and have proposed or implied a unitary definition of feud. Hoebel (1949b: p. 3) considers that feud lies outside the sphere of law. He bases this distinction on the fact that the counterkillings do not stop and that there is nothing one may regard as a mutually recognized coercive sanction against the killer and his group. Similarly, Bohannan (1963: p. 290) calls feud "a faulty jural mechanism" because it does not lead to a final settlement—to peace and rectitude. Radcliffe-Brown, on the other hand, refuses to regard feud as law, not because of its functional aspect but because it lacks "the exercise of recognized authority in settling disputes" (1940: p. xx).

I have defined law (1956: pp. 748–751) by means of four criteria, none of which is inherent in the phenomena of feuds: (1) law is manifested in a decision made by a political authority; (2) it contains a definition of the relation between the two parties to the dispute (obligatio); (3) it has a regularity of application (intention of universal application); (4) it is provided with a sanction. Law, which is characterized by these four criteria, is present in all societies—indeed, in every functioning group or subgroup of people —that I have investigated. In the primitive societies in which feud is endemic, law exists in those subgroups which have developed leadership, thus coexisting with feuds without incorporating them into the jural mechanism. Whereas law presupposes decisions passed by an authority holding jurisdiction over both litigants and regular respect for, and compliance with, these decisions by the parties to the dispute, a feud represents an intergroup fight in which all the participants ignore and even defy the jurisdiction of the overall political authority, which is usually weak or uninterested. Consequently, whereas law is a means of intragroup settlement of disputes, a feud —because of the feuding parties' defiance of the superordinated political structure—is basically an intergroup phenomenon, although it occurs within a more inclusive, politically organized unit. The difference between law and feud is again of political-structural nature, as are the differences among feud, war, and external redress. That law stands in opposition to feud and that the latter is actually the antithesis of the former rather than its manifestation is well documented in those societies in which feuds are stopped by legal decisions of the overall authority, who either has enough power to enforce his will or possesses the skill to persuade the quarreling parties to accept his solutions (see esp. Nadel 1947: p. 154; Evans-Pritchard 1940b: pp. 278–279).

Finally, it should be pointed out that not every case of "internal self-redress" constitutes a feud. When a counterkilling is accepted by the overall political authority as a just punishment of the culprit or of his subgroup and the subgroup of the defender is induced or forced to accept such a verdict and to refrain from further counterkillings, the sanctioned reprisal constitutes a case of legal self-redress that is true law (Hoebel 1949b: p. 3; Pospisil 1958a: p. 256; Bohannan 1963: p. 290). Hoebel, for example, writes, "If the kin group of the original killer customarily accepts the action of the avengers as just, and stays its hands from further counterkilling, then we have legal law" (1949b: p. 3).

We can now summarize the salient features of feud and set it off from the related concepts of law, war, external self-redress and legal (or internal) self-redress. The essence of feud has been found to be a series (at least three instances) of acts of violence, usually involving killings, committed by members of two groups related to each other by superimposed political-structural features (often involving the existence of an overall political authority) and acting on the basis of group solidarity (a common duty to avenge and a common liability). This definition sets feud apart from war and external self-redress because the last two terms refer to acts of violence committed by members of politically unrelated groups: In war both combat groups act as units in the organized fighting; in external self-redress members of two subgroups only, each belonging to a different, politically unrelated group, participate in the hostilities. It also distinguishes feud from law. Feud is an internal affair, conducted, however, by members of the subgroups of an overall political organization who ignore or even defy its political authority; it refers to intergroup phenomena. Law, on the contrary, is an intragroup affair in the full sense of the term: A decision of the authority who holds jurisdiction over both parties to the dispute is passed, and both disputing parties are induced or forced to comply with its provisions.

Internal self-redress and crime are also types of intragroup violence. Although both initiated and conducted without the support of the pertinent legal authority, internal self-redress as a rule conforms to legal provisions and receives subsequent authorization, while crime (or any other delict that uses violence), whether organized, or committed by an individual, is antithetical to law and is punished by it instead of receiving subsequent approval. The relationship of the various types of violence are shown in Figure 1, which is self-explanatory:

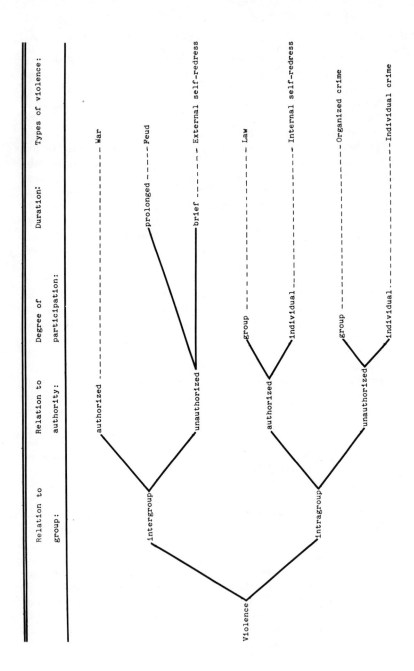

FIGURE 1. Classification of Violence

CHAPTER
TWO
FORM
OF
LAW

Aurea prima sata est aetas quae vindice nullo
Sponte sua, sine lege fidem rectumque colebat.
Poena metusque aberant nec verba minantia fixo
Aere legebantur nec supplex turba timebat
Iudicis ora sui, sed erant sine vindice tuti.

     —Ovid, *Metamorphoses*[1]

  These words of Ovid, written almost 2,000 years ago, still characterize in some specific aspects the thinking of some social scholars who deal
with the problem of law in primitive societies. According to these authors,

> The golden age was first; when man, yet new,
> No rules but uncorrupted reason knew:
> And, with a native bond, did good pursue,
> Unforc'd by punishment, unaw'd by fear,
> His words were simple, and his soul sincere;
> Needless was written law, where none opprest:
> The law of man was written in his breast:
> No suppliant crowds before the judge appear'd
> No court erected yet, nor cause was heard:
> But all was safe for conscience was their guard.

     —Ovid, *Metamorphoses,* 1815, p. 4

  This chapter is reprinted here with minor changes from Leopold Pospisil, "Law
and Order," in James A. Clifton (ed.), *Introduction to Cultural Anthropology: Essays
in the Scope and Methods of the Science of Man* (Boston, Houghton Mifflin Co.,
1968), pp. 201–222, with the kind permission of the publisher.

conformity with basic values and general order in such societies are maintained not through an application of law in authoritative decisions, formally or informally rendered by the societies' judges, chiefs, headmen, or other important men, but by the power of custom, which is well known to everyone and needs little restatement, determination, or elucidation by an individual or a body of individuals endowed by the society with judicial powers. This position was assumed by many early anthropologists and sociologists, leading them to conclude that an absence of law is a special characteristic of primitive societies.

Sidney Hartland expressed this position quite well by portraying primitive man as "hemmed in on every side by the customs of his people . . . bound in the chains of immemorial tradition . . . whose fetters are accepted by him as a matter of course; he never seeks to break forth" (1924: p. 138). The law to him would be equal to "the totality of the customs of the tribe" (1924: p. 85).

W. H. R. Rivers identified the force that accounts for conformity and order in primitive societies in Durkheimean terms, calling it a "group sentiment which makes unnecessary any definite social machinery for the exertion of authority"; people conform because of the presence of "the spontaneous, or, as it might be called, intuitive mode of inflicting punishment" (1924: p. 169). Similarly, Hobhouse concluded that "in quite the lowest races there is, as we have seen, scarcely anything that is strictly to be called the administration of justice" (1906: p. 80).

This tradition of regarding the primitive societies as being regulated by omnipotent custom known to everyone, as existing without a need for even the most informal leaders who would restate, determine, and mold the custom in their advice or decisions pertaining to settlements of disputes, did not perish with the early generations of anthropologists, who were affected by the Durkheimean jargon of generalities and the speculative stages of unilineal evolutionism. Indeed, it is being continued today by some contemporary authors who in their fieldwork have failed to recognize the subtlety of informal authority and who insist upon a virtual absence of leadership in the groups they investigate. Accordingly, Meggitt describes a leaderless society when he writes of the Walbiri of Australia: "In short, the community had no recognized political leaders, no formal hierarchy of government. People's behavior in joint activities was initiated and guided largely by their own knowledge and acceptance of established norms" (1962: p. 250). As far as the mechanism of social control is concerned, Meggitt observes that "there are explicit social rules, which, by and large, everybody obeys; and the people freely characterize each other's behavior insofar as it conforms to the rules or deviates from them. The totality of the rules expresses the law. . . ." (1962: p. 251). Strangely enough, several pages later one reads that in this "leaderless" society with rules that by and large everybody obeys, the effective punishment of lawbreakers involves a person knowledgeable of custom who passes a decision as to the guilt of the offender and his proper punishment (1962: p. 255). Of these two statements, which seem to contradict each other, I regard as more accurate the more specific latter one. Consequently, when one looks more closely at the social reality, abandons such generalities as "public opinion" (Meggitt 1962: p. 254), and does not insist upon a legal authority as having "permanent and clearly defined legislative and judicial functions" (Meggitt 1962: p. 251), one finds that justice is not expressed spontaneously by an expression of mystifying "public opinion," but that its administration is usually vested in the decision-making activity (irrespective of its informality or subtlety) of an individual or a group of individuals of influence.

As a reaction to this trend of dissolving law into the mass of omnipotent custom (or "norms of behavior") which is relatively static, known to every member of the primitive society, and to which most or even all the natives conform without the need of inducement through decisions of a leader, there emerged another set of anthropologists who tried to define law rigorously, to make it a useful ethnographic tool. These authors did not try to derive their concepts of law from comparative studies of various societies but, influenced by Western legalistic tradition in general or by some legal scholars in particular, conceptualized law too narrowly, so the concept was inapplicable to many primitive societies. In other words, they concluded that some societies were simply lawless.

The early representative of this trend of anthropological thought was Radcliffe-Brown. He accepted Pound's definition of law and confined the term to "social control through the systematic application of the force of politically organized society" (Radcliffe-Brown 1952: p. 212). This narrow definition inevitably led him to the conclusion that "some simple societies have no law, although all have customs which are supported by sanctions" (1952: p. 212). Accordingly, the Yurok of California and Ifugao of Luzon, as examples, were judged to lack law (1952: pp. 216–217). Along with the theories of the first group of anthropologists, the trend of thought of the second group continues to be manifest in the writings of many contemporary authors. We shall consider here two recent examples of the second type of legalistic thinking.

In his recent book (1962), Van den Steenhoven, writing on the law of the Caribou and Netsilik Eskimo of Canada, states a certainly acceptable and praiseworthy premise: "Firstly, we should avoid the adoption of a law concept which, though perhaps it may be useful for application to one or more simple societies, will be unfit for utilization in the study of all societies" (1962: p. 100). Bearing this claim in mind the reader would expect a definition of law based on a broad, cross-cultural research and applicable at least to those societies well covered in the anthropological literature. This modest expectation is not fulfilled and, incredibly, the author defines law in such a way that it does not even apply to the society whose analysis constitutes the content of his book. His intuitive, arbitrary, and narrow definition of law leads him to the following conclusion in his work, *Leadership and Law Among the Eskimos of the Keewatin District, Northwest Territories:* "The conclusions to be drawn from the evidence presented seems undeniably negative as regards the (threat of) physical force, the 'official' authority, the regularity of application and the non-spontaneity of community response which in this study are used as the elements to identify law" (1962: p. 112).

The claim of an absence of law among these Eskimos is a consequence of a definition of law based on several misconceptions about the nature and function of those phenomena of social control which usually are called "law." First, in common with many authors of books on law, Van den Steenhoven seems not to be quite sure whether law is a concept (1962: pp. 103, 112) or a phenomenon (1962: pp. 100, 101, 112). One almost gains the impression that he uses the two terms interchangeably. Second, following the suggestion of Hoebel, he unduly stresses (unlike Hoebel) the importance of physical sanction as a criterion of law to such an extent that he neglects the most devastating sanctions in the Eskimo society—which are psychological (ostracism, ridicule, name calling, and the like)—and his emphasis upon physical violence causes him to select only those cases for consideration that in our law would be termed "criminal." Consequently, disputes that a Western lawyer would call "civil" are not touched upon at all. Third, in his emphasis on violence Van den Steenhoven identifies legal authority with agents who mete out physical punishment (1962: pp. 103, 108, 111). He fails to recognize that the essence of the legal procedure is the decision-making process and that even in Western society the legal authorities (judges, juries) relegate the execution of their verdicts to the executive organs of the state (e.g., police, prison wardens, guards, executioners, and so on). Fourth, the author makes the existence of law dependent upon an ambiguous, vague, and elusive criterion that he calls "nonspontaneity" (1962: pp. 103, 104), which postulates that law exists only where a "spontaneous" reaction of a group of people may be absent. Aside from the very vague and undefined nature of this criterion, I fail to understand how, after a research lasting only six weeks, without a knowledge of the native language, and using only cases of past history interpreted for him by a missionary, Van den Steenhoven could determine whether the group in question "reacted spontaneously" or acted upon the decision, advice, or informal and subtle inducement of the native leaders.

In a joint account with three other scholars, called *Society and the Law,* F. James Davis, a sociologist, defines law as *"the formal means of social control that involves the use of rules that are interpreted, and are enforceable, by the courts of a political community"* (1962: p. 41). This definition, then, is assumed to have universal validity and to be applicable to all societies in the world. However, by designing a Western-biased definition, which makes interpretation of abstract rules as well as existence of formal courts of law prerequisites for the presence of law in a given culture, Davis has excluded most primitive societies from his consideration of law. Furthermore, this narrow concept of law is not only impractical from the anthropological point of view but it unfortunately also eliminates some non-European civilizations from the legal scene. For example, the ancient Chinese civilization is clearly excluded by the author's insistence upon the Western conceptualization of legal process which is made explicit by the following statement: "Unless there are official agencies to decide disputes by interpreting and applying legal rules to given situations—that is, unless there are courts—there is no law as defined here" (Davis *et al.,* 1962: p. 45). Chinese magistrates were not concerned with "interpreting and applying legal rules" in their settlements, but used the rules only as advice, as helpful models, which they had no obligation to follow in their adjudication of cases. The deficiency of this definition can be made even more dramatic by applying it to those European societies to which we traditionally impute the existence of law. Since neither the Greek nor the Roman civilizations forced their judges to follow abstract rules and to "interpret and apply [them] to a given situation," their law being basically casuistic, the social controls in these two ancient civilizations would not qualify by Davis' definition as "law." To claim that ancient Rome had no law would be difficult even for the most ethnocentric, narrow-minded, and traditionalist Western lawyer to accept.

As a reaction to this narrow, ethnocentric approach to the question of the concept of law, a third trend in legal thinking has arisen, which, while castigating ethnocentricity in anthropological and sociological jurisprudence, tries to comprehend legal phenomena through the frame of thought of the members of the particular society whose legal structure and content are being investigated. Bohannan characterizes the objectives of this endeavor as follows: "Obviously, the human beings who participate in social events interpret them: they created meaningful systems out of the social relationships in which they are involved. Such a system I am going to call a 'folk system' of interpretation, by analogy with 'folk etymology' " (1957: p. 4). Although Bohannan very meaningfully distinguished this kind of system from the analytical system "which sociologists and social anthropologists create by more or less scientific methods" (1957: p. 5), in his book, *Justice and Judgement Among the Tiv,* he almost exclusively concentrates upon the "folk systems." Thus his work presents a description of the Tiv conceptualization of this system, but not with broader theoretical considerations ("analytical systems," in Bohannan's terms). While I certainly agree with Bohannan that a good *ethnographer* "should also give the folk system," I have to add very emphatically that a good *ethnologist* (as distinguished from a purely descriptive ethnographer) should also work with an analytical system.

However, Bohannan's actual presentation of the Tiv folk system seems to contradict his more abstract statements. In the introduction to his book, for example, he makes the following statement concerning the Tiv folk system: "But I have tried *not* to 'explain' it *in terms* of our own system of 'law,' which would do violence to the Tiv ideas and folk system" (1957: pp. 5–6). Yet he uses Western legalistic terms which even some notoriously ethnocentric writers on non-European legal systems have not dared to use. Accordingly, Bohannan classifies Tiv cases as "criminal" and "civil." He tries to justify this obvious violence to his principles by the fact that a scribe of Mba Duka *jir* (a native court) used these terms himself (1957: p. 113). It is my strong suspicion that this Western dichotomy, despite the native scribe's use, is a poor expression of the actual native conceptualization.

In their discussion with the white man the Kapauku Papuans, whom I investigated, refer to their *tonowi* (informal headman) with the Malay term *kapala,* which in Indonesia stands for a strongly formalized type of leadership, an appointed head of a locality. In spite of the Kapauku "translation" of their folk concept of a rich informal headman (who is actually not a village leader but a leader of a lineage or confederacy of lineages) by the term *kapala,* I would reject such a misleading usage in my writings and would rebuke the native informant for misinterpreting his society's "folk reality." In conclusion I would say that Bohannan's theoretical statements concerning the "folk and analytical systems" are certainly very sound, but he can be criticized for neglecting the analytical approach and for possibly violating the principles he set for presenting his folk system.

Bohannan's sound theoretical differentiation between folk systems and analytical systems was seriously misinterpreted by S. J. L. Zake, one of his students. Instead of understanding this conceptual dichotomy, Zake embraced the folk definition of law as the only proper approach to the problem of law, disregarding the analytical approach altogether. In his thesis he claims that definitions of law should change with time and provenience, where phenomena regarded as legal are to be found (1962: pp. 66–67). As a consequence, he himself refuses to define law (1962: p. 67) and on the basis of library research alone attacks most anthropologists who have written about law (except Bohannan), criticizes them for their theoretical attempts to arrive at a cross-culturally valid definition of law, labels them ethnocentric, and lectures them on what the legal systems of the Cheyenne, Barotse, Kapauku, and others are really like. I shall not deal here with Zake's misinterpretations of factual material, but will concentrate upon his theoretical misinterpretations that are of general importance and that affect less dogmatic and more concrete writers on law, who have based their publications on fieldwork.

First, Zake's most serious mistake is that he does not realize clearly that "law" is a term applied to a concept, not a phenomenon (1962: esp. pp. 67, 68, 157, 158). He does not seem to understand that law is a concept whose justification lies in its heuristic value, in its efficiency as an analytical tool in the hands of an ethnologist (and not necessarily of a descriptive ethnographer). Second, Zake does not differentiate between social control in general and law as one of its specialized and institutionalized forms (1962: esp. p. 165). Had he understood this difference he would not have insisted that law accounts for practically all conformity within a culture. Third, Zake does not understand what Bohannan meant by the term "analytical system," a notion that reaches to the fundamental conception of science.

What Zake talked about in his dissertation were "folk systems" of law —descriptions of native laws with the natives' conceptualization pertaining to their own legal systems. As Bohannan correctly pointed out, inquiry into this subject is an important step in the research procedure every ethnographer must undertake. Indeed, Gluckman, Hoebel, Bohannan, Schapera, and other anthropologists including myself have discussed the concepts of natives pertaining to their law. However, Zake does not seem to have realized that this is but the first and, even in Bohannan's implied terminology, only a descriptive step. The second, and much more important step for anthropology of law as a science, is a conceptualization of an analytical system (to use Bohannan's expression) or, better, the formation of an analytical and cross-culturally applicable concept and theory of law. Zake failed to discuss this in his work and, consequently, it is not surprising that he could not understand Hoebel's statement of fundamental importance: "acceptance of everyone's folk system as an end in itself—an insufficient stultifying end . . . this would preclude the development of any useful theory of anthropological jurisprudence" (1961: p. 432).

In his dissertation Zake labeled virtually all legal anthropologists as "ethnocentrists." He criticized their "analytical conceptualizations in the field of law" for not conforming to the first concept of Bohannan's dichotomy—"the folk legal system." A cross-cultural theory of law cannot be composed of a mishmash of contradictory concepts derived from the various cultures whose only common denominator and virtue (in Zake's opinion) would be their "folk system origin." His insistence and fixation upon folk systems leads him to fantastic claims about anthropology in general that make it doubtful that he has grasped the very basic principles of the science he studies:

> There is, therefore, no substitute for using the terminology of a nonliterate society. In studying other aspects of the culture in nonliterate societies, like religion or social organization or authority systems, this is what has in fact been done and there is no reason why the same principle should not be followed in the sphere of legal research. (1962: p. 165)

To this statement I have only to add my strong doubt that descent, genealogy, Crow or Omaha kinship systems, reduction rules, avunculocal residence, and so on are concepts that belong in any of the world's folk systems (with the exception of the Western anthropological). To conclude my reaction to this "hypononethnocentric (or hypofolk) trend of thought" I restate the position I have already expressed in "Kapauku Papuan Laws of Land Tenure" (1965a). Scientific inquiry uses as its tools concepts, categories, apparatus, and procedures designed or selected by the scientist and not by the subjects he studies. Even if the purpose of the study is cognitive (or folk-oriented), one studies the native categories and cognitive processes as facts, as phenomena presented by the native informants. One does not necessarily adopt these categories for one's own cognition or for cross-culturally valid theories (unless they are of a cross-cultural validity). To analyze Kapauku, Cheyenne, Barotse, or any other people's thinking and their cognitive categories one does not have to think and speak as these people do.

THE MANIFESTATION OF LAW:
A Threefold Possibility

I have discussed above three traditions in legal-anthropological thinking concerned with the problem of the definition of law. The first tradition, which identified law with custom or norms that are somehow automatically observed without requiring leadership, legal authority, and adjudication, made the term "law" obsolete by identifiying it with prescribed behavior and divorcing it from the decision-making process of authority (or group leaders). The second tradition represents a reaction to the first in attempting to define law by rigorous criteria, thus dissociating it from the body of prescriptive customs and making it an analytically meaningful concept. The failure of this tradition lies in the fact that law has been defined, not on the basis of extensive cross-cultural research and experience, but in ethnocentric, narrow terms in the legal tradition of Western civilization. The third tradition, the most recent, tries to correct the extreme of ethnocentricity by moving to another extreme, that of cultural relativity. As a result, no analytical definition of law is given: only dogmatic statements concerning folk classifications and criticisms (often unjustified) of anthropologists who have designed analytical legal definitions are offered to the puzzled reader (see esp. Zake 1962). In the subsequent discussion we shall concentrate upon efforts that deal more realistically with the problem of an analytical definition of law. Folk classifications and folk semantics have their place in a chapter in particular ethnographies but not in a chapter on law as a theoretical-analytical device.

Since in their ethnographic accounts several recent authors have regarded the concept of law as a "phenomenon" (esp. Zake 1962: pp. 67–68, 157–158; Van den Steenhoven 1962: pp. 100–101, 112), I am forced to state a premise which most anthropologists will regard as needless, superfluous, or obvious. I have to stress that Law as a theoretical and analytical device is a concept which embraces a category of phenomena (ethnographic facts) selected according to the criteria the concept specifies. Although it is composed of a set of individual phenomena, the category itself is not a phenomenon—it does not exist in the outer world. The term "law," consequently, is applied to a construct of the human mind made for the sake of convenience. The justification for a concept of law does not reside in its existence outside the human mind, but in its value as an analytic, heuristic device. Since phenomena of social control often represent a continuum rather than qualitative clusters with clearly defined gaps between them, there cannot be sharp divisions between the categories of the various types of social control. Instead, one must conceive of transitional zones between the categories, wherein the criteria of the neighboring categories overlap and, consequently, where it is difficult to determine which ones dominate the field. The blending of the phenomena of one category of social control into those of another does not invalidate the justification for those categories, for the same reason that we keep the concepts of, for example, the colors orange and red. Although there is a transition rather than a sharp dividing line between the elements in both instances, most of the pertinent phenomena can safely be placed within the boundaries of the categories. Furthermore, unlike colors phenomena of social control are categorized into law, custom, political decisions, religious taboos, and so on, each on the basis of a different set of criteria (rather than on the basis of a different quantity of the same criterion, as is the case with different colors). Consequently, I refuse to be intimidated by those followers of Radin who adhere to his creed that law is an undefinable concept. (1938: p. 1145).

In the following discussion I shall restate my definition of law originally arrived at through an intensive cross-cultural study of 32 cultures and a survey of an additional 63, and subsequently tested in three societies: the Nunamiut Eskimo hunters of Alaska, the Kapauku Papuan horticulturalists of West New Guinea, and the Tirolean peasants of Austria. Instead of concentrating upon the analytical attributes of law, which I shall discuss in Chapter Three, I shall deal here with the basic methodological problem of the form in which the legal phenomena are manifested, a problem that confronts every fieldworker interested in the subject of institutionalized social control.

In their book *The Cheyenne Way* Llewellyn and Hoebel identified three main "roads into exploration of the law-stuff of a culture" (1941: p. 20). These roads constitute three possible ways one may conceive of manifestations (or form) of law: first, as abstract rules that either form the content of legal codifications in literate societies or are found as a set of verbalized ideals in the repository of the minds of knowledgeable individuals in a nonliterate society; second, as patterns of actual behavior of members of a society; and third, as principles abstracted from decisions of legal authorities passed while solving disputes within their groups. To be sure, there are other possibilities of conceiving of the form of law. However, most of the theories of social scientists have tended to follow one of the three roads identified above.

It may be argued that all three categories of the phenomena are so important for the investigation of institutionalized social control that the term "law" should apply to them all. Although it is imperative that a student of law investigate all three bodies of data, the term "law," as we shall see, cannot be applied to all of them, because not all three instances would necessarily relate to social control, which constitutes the core of the law concept—the institutionalized social control. Furthermore, this use of the term would make "law" coterminous with ideals, and, at the same time, with the concept of custom. Consequently, a concept of law so conceived would become so broad and all-comprising as to preclude any effective analytical application of it.

Abstract Rules

The legal thought that regards abstract rules, embodied within the coded law of civilized peoples or in the memory or preliterate peoples, as the proper and exclusive manifestation of law, represents the major legal tradition in western Europe, especially on the Continent. Because of its paramount importance and general acceptance there, one may regard this as Europe's "folk category of law." The origin of the emphasis on abstract rules in the legal sphere has a long cultural history and dates back to the Babylonia of Hammurabi and to the origin of the notion of natural law (c. 2,000 B.C.), a conception of law which was considered universally applicable and an abstract divine command to all mankind (Needham 1956: p. 533).

Although Heraclitus (c. 500 B.C.) had already made a claim that divine law nourishes all human laws, the idea that all of nature and, consequently, man's behavior is also subject to a universal law was firmly embodied in Greek philosophy with the Stoic School about two centuries later. According to Needham, this idea was a consequence of a direct diffusion of thought from Mesopotamia (1956: p. 534). Through the Greek settlements in southern Italy and on Sicily, the Stoic ideas influenced Rome, as witnessed in Cicero's work *De Legibus,* in which he claimed that "human life is subject to the decrees of the Supreme Law" (1928: p. 461). Old Roman Law, true enough, had its base in the *Lex Duodecim Tabularum* (Law of the Twelve Tables) which consisted of sets of abstract principles. However, these principles did not mechanically bind the Roman *jurisconsults* (lawyers) or magistrates; they were treated as a framework to be interpreted and adjusted to the problems arising from actual disputes. They were guides, not to be blindly followed by the jurist, but to help him write his *responsa prudentium,* advice to the parties of a dispute (Sommer 1933: p. 15; Maine 1963: p. 33). Because the Roman magistrate, the *praetor urbanus,* was often a political appointee, he relied heavily on the writings of these jurisconsults in his adjudication of cases. Thus these lawyers' opinions, written in response to particular cases, were the actual source of Roman law, which thus became a law of cases rather than a law based exclusively upon abstract rules. When the Stoic philosophy began to be studied in Rome, the casuistic nature of ancient Roman law was slowly influenced by the Eastern emphasis on abstract rules. Accordingly, as the Roman Republic approached its end, the responses of the jurisconsults were reduced to systematized compendiums reflecting the praetor's edict. The edict, originally an annual proclamation of policy of that Roman republican magistrate, gradually incorporated more and more abstract legal precepts which became further sources of Roman law (Maine 1963: p. 39).

With the advent of the Roman Empire abstract statutes (*constitutiones*) promulgated by the emperors slowly accrued importance. Because the praetors incorporated the contents of previous edicts into their annual statements, the praetorian annual edict itself developed into an *edictum perpetuum,* a perpetual edict adopted mechanically by succeeding praetors from the time of Hadrian (Maine 1963: p. 61). The edict thus lost its function as a dynamic mechanism of Roman law. Finally, dating from Emperor Alexander Severus, Roman law became the exclusive domain of imperial *constitutiones* (statutes). There were periodic attempts to codify the body of existing law. The evolution of Roman law ends with the reign of Justinian and his successful codification known nowadays as *Corpus Iuris Civilis* (c. A.D. 533). Thus the originally casuistic law of Rome evolved into a legal system which relied on abstract rules and their codification.

After being forgotten for several centuries this codified Roman Law was resurrected and "received" in northern Italy. Although this process started in the eleventh century, it was not until well over half a century later with the renewal of the studies of Roman law at Bologna that the Western world regained firm possession of its lost legal treasure. Because of its consistency, its admirable and precise juristic logic, and its systematic treatment of legal matter, Roman law rapidly gained tremendous prestige and became a subsidiary law in the legal systems in Italy and central Europe. For political reasons the German emperors accepted Roman law as valid in their Holy Roman Empire: they thus tried to strengthen the fiction of the continuity of the German Empire with the Old Roman Empire (Sommer 1932: pp. 12–13). The prestige of the abstract tenets of the Roman law was so high that it became a subject of studies in a succession of several "juristic schools," such as Glossators (thirteenth century), Commentators (thirteenth and fourteenth centuries), Humanists (sixteenth century), and Romanists-Pandectists (nineteenth century) (Stone 1950: pp. 424–427). At the close of the eighteenth and the beginning of the nineteenth century, when there was an era of widespread codification of European legal systems, Roman law was invariably incorporated into them as a "spiritual backbone." Most of these codes are still in force on the Continent.

From the cultural point of view this historical sequence of events resulted in a type of legal philosophy and practice that is usually termed "legalism." In essence, legalism is an extreme emphasis upon abstract rules, which are regarded as the objective revelation of the legislator's will, as the exclusive manifestation and source of law. The individual rules themselves are seen as the exclusive and concrete answers (solutions) to particular disputes. Parties to disputes are viewed by the legalists as playing a single role, namely, that specified in the rules. Consequently, unlike many non-European societies, the total status of the litigants is dismissed from the court proceedings as irrelevant. Furthermore, all evidence that may be actually related in various degrees to the case but that fails to illuminate the specific points stressed by the pertinent rule is ruled inadmissible. The juristic method of legalism, ideally speaking, relieves the judge of all legal creativity. His function consists essentially in extrapolating from a given legal case the essential, "legally relevant" features, and equating the resultant legal situation with a similar situation in the codified rules which in its essential features comes closest to it. What follows is basically a fiction by which two situations are literally held identical, with the consequence that the rule's provision (judgment and sanction) is mechanically applied to the case. Because the "letter of the law" is held by "legalistic" lawyers to be sacrosanct, flagrant injustice may sometimes ensue as the result of "legal technicalities."

However, law is a category of social (rather than purely philosophical) phenomena and, consequently, it changes with time. Furthermore, because of the complexity of social life the legalists' assumption that coded rules can encompass the totality of social relations and behavior remains a myth. In order legally to accommodate disputes involving relations and claims obviously absent from the inventory of rules, and at the same time to keep alive the myth (and dogma) of the full adequacy of the code of rules, the legalists resorted to further methodological fictions which they called "analogies." Essentially two types of these fictions have been distinguished: *analogia legis* (analogy of a rule), which consists of solving a legal problem not mentioned in the codification by deciding the case on the basis of a principle contained in a rule dealing with a "similar" problem, and *analogia iuris* (analogy of law) which helps to solve legal problems not resembling any of those solved in specific rules by applying to them principles which are thought to permeate the legal system as a whole (Sommer 1933: p. 20).

This legalistic thinking was not limited to the legalistic schools that were preoccupied with the reception of Roman law. Through its domination of the legal philosophy of Continental European law schools as well as courts of law, it affected to a greater or lesser degree most of the legal thinking of such authors as John Austin, Ernst Roguin, Hans Kelsen, Josef Kohler, and others. Further, the influence of legalism and its emphasis on abstract rules affected Durkheim and, through him, the Western social sciences, especially modern sociology (see, for example, Max Weber 1967: p. 5). An outstanding recent American example of this influence is presented by F. James Davis in his definition of law, cited above, according to which not only do most nonliterate peoples have no law, but even the ancient Chinese as well as casuistic ancient Rome have to be regarded as without "law." Thus the reception of Roman law and the attitude toward it expressed in the teaching and practice of legalistic scholars have provided Western civilization with a folk category of law whose component parts are abstract rules, preferably organized in a code.

Law conceived of as a system of abstract rules, codified or remembered, has been used by legalists, and contemporary scholars who have been influenced by legalists, as an analytical device intended to be applicable cross-culturally. The problem with studies that assign such an analytical value to abstract rules lies in the fact that this legal category has not been selected on the basis of its heuristic value in a comparative research involving several non-European cultures, but has been dogmatically adopted because it was the "folk category" of the writer. Unlike Zake (1962: pp. 66–67), I have no objection to the use of a writer's folk concept as an analytical device in his investigation of other cultures, as long as the cross-cultural analytical value of such a concept is positively established. Consequently, I shall argue against the use of the legalistic conception of law (as a set of abstract rules) purely on the basis of its value as an analytical tool and will try to demonstrate, logically as well as empirically, its inapplicability in cross-cultural research.

Probably the best opening for my argument is to state the simple fact that, if abstractly worded rules are regarded as the manifestation of law, because of a virtual lack of rules in many tribal societies, there would be many "lawless" peoples. Law would cease to be a universally usable concept, being limited in its applicability only to those societies which have either written legal codes or sets of rules deposited in the memories of their "wise men." As a consequence of this definition of law, people like the Cheyenne (Llewellyn and Hoebel 1941: p. 313), Comanche (Hoebel 1940: p. 6), and the Barama River Carib (Gillin 1934: p. 331), because they lacked systems of abstract rules, would have to be regarded as societies without law, and the three authors as having written their legal books and essays on chimeras.

The second argument centers around the incidence of legalistic ideas outside the sphere of Western civilization. To my knowledge there has been just one non-European parallel to Western legalism in the whole world. A legalistic philosophy developed independent of the West and became the dominant doctrine in the juristic thinking and legal practice in China during the rule of the Ch'in dynasty (221–206 B.C.). Although this school of thought had already developed in the northeastern state of Ch'in at the close of the fifth century B.C., its doctrine did not become the leading philosophy of China as a whole until the third century B.C., when policies based upon it enabled the Ch'in dynasty to assume power over the whole country, and its last prince "to become the first emperor of a unified China" (Needham 1956: p. 204). The tenets of Chinese legalism, so radically different from the traditional Chinese Confucian philosophy, were determined and elaborated by several Chinese scholars, of whom Han-Fei Tzu and Kung-sun Yang supplied the most significant contributions.

These tenets of Chinese legalism, closely paralleling those of legalistic Europe, could be very briefly summarized as follows: The exclusive form of law was *fa,* a positive law consisting of abstract rules promulgated by the emperor. These rules were required to be definitive (no exceptions allowed), public, logically consistent, universal to all peoples in China, and binding not only the subjects but also the emperor himself. This type of law could not be questioned because its validity was considered to be derived from the authority's consent (promulgation) and not from morality. The judges were forbidden to change or adjust the law with regard to special circumstances of particular cases; they were expected to apply the pertinent rules mechanically. The abstract rules were believed capable of solving concrete problems arising from any type of relationship that might be present. Because of its radical and rather abrupt departure from Confucian thought, legalism died in China with the fall of the Ch'in dynasty. In the twentieth century a European brand of legalism was introduced there, after about two millennia of Confucianism. Rather than supporting the legalistic conception of law and the notion that abstract rule is the form or source of law, the Chinese exception confirms the inapplicability of this conception of law on a cross-cultural basis.

If we turn our attention from the societies having no rules to those that do have abstract rules, I will still argue that even in these societies the conception of law as a body of abstract rules is untenable. My argument here may well start with the observation that almost all authors of treatises dealing with law have agreed upon one basic characteristic of the phenomena that should belong to this conceptual category, namely, that they should be a form of institutionalized social control. Consequently, those phenomena that do not exercise social control, that cannot be regarded as containing principles of behavior which are to some degree binding by being enforced, cannot be called law. It is often tacitly assumed that the sole existence of abstract legal rules in a society constitutes by itself an evidence that they exercise social control by being rigorously enforced by the authorities. Unfortunately, hardly anything can be farther from truth than such an assumption. In many societies in the world abstract rules play a different role from that which the Western legal scholar would expect. There were and are societies in which abstract rules are not expected to be enforced, where these are not regarded as inflexible orders to the judges.

An excellent example of a society with a radically "non-Western" conception of the role of abstract rules is Imperial China. Throughout its history, excepting the brief legalistic interlude discussed above, the Chinese legal sphere was dominated by Confucian ideals. These did not place *fa,* the positive law of abstract rules of the numerous dynastic legal codices, at the apex of legal importance. On the contrary, *fa* was much inferior in prestige (and consequently also in the judicial practice) to *I* and *Li.* While *I* may be briefly defined as the spiritual justification of *Li,* which in some instances may be compared with the Western idea of equity, *Li* consisted of ethical principles contained in social customs. However, unlike the West, the Chinese did not make sharp distinction between social laws and those of nature, with the consequence that they regarded man's social world as closely interrelated with the natural world. This interrelatedness was considered to be so close that human actions were believed to affect nature: good behavior had a positive effect; crimes, on the contrary, caused natural catastrophes, such as drought, floods, and famine. *Li,* then, were ethical principles permeating the whole universe—that of man as well as nature. The effect of this conceptualization upon Chinese law was well stated by Needham:

> *If, then, all crimes and disputes were looked upon in ancient China, not primarily as infractions of a purely human, though imperial, legal code, but rather as ominous disturbances in the complex network of causal filaments by which mankind was connected on all sides with surrounding Nature, it was perhaps the very subtlety of these which make positive law seem so unsatisfactory. (Needham 1956: p. 528)*

The knowledge of *Li,* of the uniform ethical principles regulating nature as well as human society, meant title to power. Since the emperor had most of the power, he was expected to know *Li* well. His statutes (*fa*) were expected to reflect *Li* and were regarded as binding only as long as the magistrates could see a basic correspondence between the two. This philosophy allowed the possibility that a wise judge might know *Li* in a given case better than the emperor, thus allowing him legally to disregard the statutes. Essentially, abstract rules of Chinese legal codifications were just models the judges might use for formulating their decisions in specific cases. However, the rules were never binding; a decision contrary to the rule was very often the case. In accordance with this conclusion Jean Escarra stated "Finally, the legal rule, being nothing but a model, a model to which an individual is asked to approximate as far as possible without necessarily requiring that he conform entirely to it, the sanction by its required severity has an ideal and theoretical character" (Escarra 1936: p. 74).[2]

Van der Valk arrived at a similar conclusion when he observed:

---

[2]Translated by Pospisil. "Enfin, la loi n'étant qu'un modèle, un modèle dont on demande à l'individu de s'approcher le plus possible sans toutefois exiger qu'il s'y conforme intégralement, la sanction, par sa sévérité voulue, garde un caractère idéal et théorique."

The law was always considered as a model according to which other cases might be solved. Therefore the rule nullum crimen sine praevia lege poenali *could not exist. This idea moreover involved that the written law was not necessarily always implied. It was only a model to be followed under certain circumstances and had no binding force as such. (1939: p. 11)*

The role of abstract codified rules in Imperial China therefore was, from the point of view of actual social control, relatively unimportant, and the study of the Chinese codices alone would tell little about the judicial practice and law, if by the latter was meant behavioral principles which are actually enforced.

The legalistic doctrine which considers the exclusive source of law to be a set of abstract rules is applicable equally to ancient Rome. True enough, the *Lex Duodecim Tabularum* was already in existence during the republic as a form of codified law, but some of the statements of this codex were expressed in a casuistic form (as decisions of concrete cases, functioning here as do our modern "precedents"), referring to specific legal decisions rather than to abstract principles (Sommer 1932: p. 51). Furthermore, the codex, as in Imperial China, did not bind the Roman magistrates, who possessed the explicit power to formulate their own law. Sometimes their decisions clearly contradicted it (Sommer 1933: p. 15). One may go even further and argue that ancient Roman law (until the onset of absolutistic empire) was by nature casuistic rather than legalistic. It relied primarily upon the *responsa prudentium,* which were in essence opinions written by Roman *iurisprudentia* (lawyers) for the parties to particular disputes. These opinions became, in effect, the main source of Roman law by which actual disputes were adjudicated. Although they were regarded as "interpretations" of the principles and of the thoughts contained in the codex adjusted to concrete cases, in actuality they became the primary source of the law, objectively rather independent from *Lex Duodecim Tabularum* (Sommer 1933: p. 15). As a consequence, Rome was another civilization with a legal code whose abstract rules were not rigorously enforced (as we understand enforcement nowadays): in some cases they were even utterly disregarded. Here, too, one would not gain too much of an insight into actual Roman judicial practice or into the behavior that was actually enforced in Rome by studying the Twelve Tables alone.

The case for abstract rules as the source of law does not look much better if we turn to societies in which it has been assumed that the provisions of the codified law (written or memorized) are actually enforced. The first obstacles encountered are the so-called "dead rules." These are abstract norms, usually but not always outdated, whose provisions are tacitly disregarded in practice, the judiciary deciding legal cases as though these rules did not exist. As a consequence, all pertinent decisions contradict this kind of abstract rule. In European collections of statutes they are so notorious that one need not bother with examples. However, it would be a mistake to believe that they are a specialty of European legal systems. For example, in the Quechua region of Peru, "The haciendas are required by law to maintain schools for their peones, but Government educational officers whom we met admitted that this law was largely a dead letter and that the majority of the estates did not even pretend to observe it" (Rycroff 1946: p. 79). Similarly, in Republican China the Civil Code of 1931, Article 1144, stated; "Each spouse has the right to inherit the property of the other and his or her successional portion is determined according to the following provisions . . ." (Ching Lin Hsia *et al.* 1931: p. 50). This rule belonged to a group of several that may be regarded as dead and of which Marion Levy said, "Again it must be observed that these laws are not enforced" (1949: p. 332). Even in some of the nonliterate societies, we find, with amazement, that those having abstract "mental codifications" also have dead rules. Among the Kapauku of Western New Guinea, who have a rather sophisticated system of abstract remembered rules, we find several that are not enforced, although they are recited verbatim by the informants as the "ideal." One of the rules regulating incest clearly states *keneka bukii daa* (it is prohibited to marry a sibmate). Yet in the Ijaaj-Pigome political confederacy of the southeastern corner of the Kamu Valley this rule is disregarded, and incestuous relations, which should be punished by death, are not only condoned by the local headman but even advocated as correct (for detail see Chapter Six). Another rule of this confederacy specifies that an adulterous wife should be executed. However, in actual cases of adultery the Kapauku *tonowi* (headman) requests that the woman should only be beaten, and the husband is threatened with prosecution and punishment should he kill or even attempt to kill his spouse. Another such rule clearly calls for a full indemnity payable by a garden owner to the owner of a domesticated pig which is killed by a spiked trap set for a wild boar. This provision may be considered "dead," because in the headmen's decisions it became customary to request from the trapper a payment of only half the value of the killed animal, and to permit him to keep that quarter of the pig's carcass that was pierced by the spikes (Pospisil, 1958a: p. 252).

But even if we ignore these cases we face a much broader problem pertaining to the enforcement of abstract rules: the rules are usually not enforced in the form in which they appear in the codes owing to various circumstances and factors. In other words, here too a study of the abstract rules alone would tell little about social control in the group. For example, of the 176 trouble cases reported for the Kapauku Papuans, only 87, or less than 50 percent, conformed to the provisions of the pertinent rules (for the various reasons for these discrepancies, see Pospisil 1958a: pp. 250–251).

There are many other arguments against the form of law conceived of as abstract rules. One may point out that such rules cannot exercise proper social control because they are known to relatively few people in a society (judges in the West, headmen and old wise men among the Kapauku). Another objection claims that it is not the provision of the rule that is important, but what the judges actually decide. Even if they try to follow the "letter of the law," their decisions will differ, due to individual variations in interpretation and semantic understanding.

Some words in Western codes or rules are often deliberately vague in order to encourage the individual judge to "legislate" in a given case. Expressions like "due care," "due respect," "reasonable doubt," "reasonable person," "in due time," and "criminal negligence" almost beg for variations among the judges and for discrepancies among the interpretations at different times of history: while the written word remains unaltered, its semantics changes in time. These changes can be detected and ascertained in the actual decisions, but never in the rules themselves. To pretend legalistically that one is, for example, detecting the "intent of the legislator" in a rule which is 200 years old often amounts to conscious self-deception.

Abstracts from Actual Behavior

The limitations and ethnocentric bias of the theoretical position that equated law with abstract rules were clearly realized by Eugen Ehrlich during his stay in Galicia. There he had an opportunity to discover that the "law" expressed in the Austrian legal codification of 1811 was an element completely foreign to the natives of the Austrian province upon which it was rather ruthlessly imposed by the government. Ehrlich, being a most perceptive man, noticed that the life of the peasants, that is, their behavior, followed very different canons from those contained in the official codex. He called these principles of actual behavior "living law," thus introducing a second path for legal thought that regards law as the principles abstracted from the actual behavior of members of the society (Ehrlich 1936: esp. pp. 493–497, 502). This kind of "living law" he contrasted with "norms for decisions"—actually abstracts from actual court decisions (1936: p. 175)—and "legal propositions" (statutes). The latter he regarded as the basic principles abstracted from the norms for decisions, "couched in words, proclaimed authoritatively with a claim to universal validity" (1936: p. 174).[3] Thus to Ehrlich the living law was "the law which dominates life itself even though it has not been posited in legal propositions" (1936: p. 493).[4] Over and over again he stressed the behavioral attribute of his living law: "The living law is not the part of the content of the document that the courts

[3]". . . in Worte gefasst, mit dem Anspruch auf Allgemeingültigkeit autoritativ verkündet. . . ." (Ehrlich 1913: pp. 140–141)
[4]". . . das nicht in Rechtssätzen festgelegte Recht, das aber doch das Leben beherrscht." (Ehrlich 1913: p. 399)

recognize as binding when they decide a legal controversy, but only that part which the parties actually observe in life" (1936: p. 497).[5] He suggested that to acquire the knowledge of this law one should study its provisions "quite independently of the question whether they have already found expression in a judicial decision or in a statute or whether they will ever find it" (1936: p. 502).[6]

It should be mentioned that Ehrlich's position has sometimes been misinterpreted. Preoccupied with the notion that actual behavior of people is controlled and guided by the various leading philosophies of the nations, Northrop implicitly equated Ehrlich's living law with these philosophies. He concluded that to understand, for example, the Chinese living law, one would have to study Confucian philosophy, while to understand modern Russian living law one must turn to Marx-Leninism (1951: p. 111). Besides the fact that an overwhelming majority of the Chinese were Taoists and Buddhists and ignorant of the official Confucian philosophy, nothing can be farther from Ehrlich's living law than principles of well-formulated scholarly philosophies which usually are the property of very few in a given society; "living law" derives from the actual behavior of people, not from officially recognized theories posited in scholarly treaties.

In his conception of law, Bronislaw Malinowski came very close to Ehrlich's concept. Although in his writings he used the term "rules" when referring to the nature of law, to a careful reader it soon becomes obvious that Malinowski's rule has little in common with abstract rules (written or memorized) aimed at adjudication or informal settlements of disputes. What Malinowski had actually in mind were rules of conduct of members of the society as seen in (or abstracted from) the actual behavior and dictated by belief in their efficiency. Thus legal phenomena "do not consist in any independent institutions" (1959: p. 59), such as codified abstract rules used by the courts, for example. Among the Melanesians "Law represents rather an aspect of their tribal life, one side of their structure, than any independent, self-contained social arrangements. Law dwells not in a special system of decrees, which foresee and define possible forms of non-fulfillment and provide appropriate barriers and remedies" (1959: p. 59). Rather than a decree,

> the positive law governing all the phases of tribal life, consists
> then of a body of binding obligations, regarded as a right by one
> party and acknowledged as a duty by the other, kept in force by

---

[5]"Lebendes Recht ist vom Urkundeninhalte nicht das, was etwa die Gerichte bei der Entscheidung eines Rechtsstreites als verbindlich anerkennen, sondern nur das, woran sich die Parteien im Leben halten." (Ehrlich 1913: p. 401)

[6]". . . ganz unabhängig davon, ob sie in einer Entscheidung oder in einem Gesetze bereits Ausdruck gefunden haben oder je darin Eingang finden würden." (Ehrlich 1913: p. 406)

a specific mechanism of reciprocity and publicity inherent in the structure of their society. (1959: p. 58)

According to Malinowski the nature of the mechanism of reciprocity that exercises control over the behavior lies in what I would term "superrational behavior" of the people: "The tribesman discharges his duty towards his neighbor, however painful or onerous it may be, with a long-range view of the situation. He anticipates and balances rewards quite as much as penalties, approval as well as condemnation" (1961: pp. xxxv–xxxvi). In my own experience, in full honesty, I could hardly point out one Eskimo, Kapauku Papuan, Austrian peasant, or even a European city dweller with such a rational approach toward his behavior. I am far from denying that consideration of reciprocity motivates some behavior. However, the assumption that it motivates all behavior, and of every person, I must reject as highly unrealistic.

The basic premise for an adequate concept of law, advanced in this chapter and reflecting an almost general agreement among lawyers and social scientists, has been the requirement that the phenomena included in this concept constitute some form (usually institutionalized) of social control. In this respect rules and principles abstracted from the actual behavior of the people present several difficulties. First, the behavior of different people varies; its supposed identity is only a fiction used for ease of presentation by various authors. In every society, moreover, and in every subgroup, there are individuals whose behavior is considered more important than that of other members. To speak of law as an "average behavior" computed by the research worker would be equally futile because people are unaware of "averages." To "follow" averages as an ideal would often be impossible; imagine a "law" stating that "five and a half persons, on the average, form a household group among the Kapauku." Furthermore, the actual behavior of all the members of a social group lacks the ideal attribute, which is so important in making people conform and so essential for the concept of law. After all, if law were identified with behavioral patterns, then the concept of law would become utterly meaningless and superfluous.

Finally, I must insist that law often differs from actual behavior (a statement that may come as a shock to Durkheimean-minded sociologists and anthropologists). For example, Timasheff presented a well-taken criticism of Malinowski's conception of law. He argued that if obligation were the essential criterion of law, then a challenge to a duel and its acceptance, which certainly was a generally recognized obligation in eighteenth-century France, should have been law. Actually, however, according to the state law, dueling was illegal and punishable by imprisonment (Timasheff, 1938: p. 871). There are many so-called "authoritarian laws," imposed ruthlessly upon whole populations against their will by a ruling minority (sometimes amounting only to a clique). They certainly not only fail to constitute abstractions from the "actual behavior" of the people, but often are diametrically opposed to it. During World War II most of the Nazi laws imposed upon the Czechs in Bohemia and Moravia were antithetical to actual behavior, and, in spite of Draconic penalties, were not obeyed by the Czechs. Most of the Czechs listened to broadcasts from London, although this transgression, if detected, was punishable by death.

For a last argument, I will turn to a situation in a primitive society. The Kapauku Papuans of West New Guinea steal whenever the opportunity presents itself. Thus a "living law" would necessarily state that the law concerning theft indicates stealing whenever the chances are good that it will go undetected. Such a "legal norm," in addition to its absurdity and neglect of the Kapauku ideal rule, *oma peu, oma daa* (theft is bad, theft is prohibited), would completely ignore the numerous trials and wide range of institutionalized punishments for thieves for which this society is famous.

Principles Upheld by Legal Decisions
The third path to a definition of the form of law leads, according to Llewellyn and Hoebel, toward investigation of cases of conflict, toward the identification of law with principles of social control that are actually upheld in legal decisions. To be sure, although Llewellyn became one of the most effective and eloquent advocates of this path, the conviction that legal decisions offer the best way to investigate law (viewed as principles abstracted from judicial decisions) did not originate in his writings. It was Oliver Wendell Holmes who, in his work *Path of Law,* pointed out this approach toward investigation and conceptualization of law. He stated his concept of law quite bluntly in his now famous assertion: "The prophecies of what the courts will do in fact, and nothing more pretentious, are what I mean by the law" (1897: p. 461). At this early date he advocated a more scientific and less dogmatic, philosophical, or speculative investigation of law by pointing out that "The life of the law has not been logic; it has been experience" (1881: p. 1). According to him, law should not have been isolated from other social phenomena. It should have been studied as an integral part of the rest of the culture, not as an autonomous system of petrified abstract rules set in the old codices. To Justice Holmes, anthropology especially was the most appropriate discipline to deal effectively with this conceptual problem (1886: p. 741). The Holmesian position opened up the third path toward investigation of law and became a foundation upon which a school of legal realism developed.

In his work Llewellyn went far beyond Holmes' work, becoming the most prominent representative of the realistic legal thought. His criticisms of legalism were devastating, and he not only accepted Holmes' philosophical and theoretical position, but actually implemented what Holmes only suggested. He joined forces with an anthropologist, E. Adamson Hoebel, and with him produced an outstanding contribution to the study of law, which nowadays is regarded as a classic: *The Cheyenne Way* (1941). In addition to an unusual richness of theoretical observations and constructs, the book demonstrates most effectively the value of the "case-study approach" to law. Among the Cheyenne Indians of the Great Plains, law was exceedingly rarely "clothed in rules" (Llewllyn and Hoebel, 1941: p. 313). Yet the book contains a great wealth of theoretical as well as substantive legal principles of the Cheyenne, most derived from case material supplied by Hoebel. The two authors properly claim that this material can justifiably be compared with Roman law. If their investigation had used a concept of law based on abstract rules, this wealth of knowledge would have been missed and the authors would have been empty-handed. The value of the case-study approach could hardly be better demonstrated than by this work on Cheyenne law. It is with full justification that the authors conclude their theoretical discussion of the various approaches to the study of law by writing: "The trouble-cases, sought out and examined with care, are thus the safest main road into the discovery of law. Their data are most certain. Their yield is richest. They are the most revealing" (1941: p. 29). The book itself includes 53 cases, of which five constitute the introductory chapter. The rest are distributed throughout the book wherever a theoretical point is to be documented. Thus the cases support and illustrate the more abstract discussion and conclusions and provide a vivid matrix from which the various principles are skillfully abstracted with what I would call anatomical legal precision. However, they are not used as a consistent matrix which, as a whole, would be subject to a rigorous formal analysis.

Cases of conflict have been utilized in the anthropological literature by several other authors for illustration and documentation. However, in their writings the cases do not appear for extrapolating principles of broad theoretical validity; they serve merely as documentation for statements concerning the substantive law of the society under discussion. This type of casuistic approach is rather old, dating back to anthropologists like Barton (law of the Ifugao of Luzon: 1919) and including such authors as Lips (Naskapi law: 1947), Holleman (Shona law: 1952), and Berndt (law of the Kamano, Usurufa, Jate, and Fore of New Guinea: 1962). Of the many authors working with the case-study approach to abstract and elucidate the substantive law, Howell and his work on Nuer law deserve special mention (1954). On the basis of an extensive study of several thousand decisions of the Nuer tribunals (founded by the British Administration, but deciding cases under the heavy influence of the old Nuer customary law), Howell presents the main principles of the native law by systematically abstracting them from the case material. Although the actual presentation limits itself only to summarized cases illustrating the various legal observations, there is no doubt that the generalizations are solidly based and "induced from" an impressive number of decisions. Thus the decisions are not used for illustrations and vivid presentation only, but form the actual raw material from which most of the general statements were derived.

In his book, *The Judicial Process Among the Barotse of Northern Rhodesia,* Max Gluckman employs a modified casuistic approach. Unlike the authors cited above, Gluckman defines law in terms of abstract rules: "First, it is a body of rules which theoretically are certain and have socially permeated 'intrinsic' meanings. Secondly, the law also exists in court decisions in which concepts are specified for extrinsic referents in a particular dispute" (1967: p. 354). In his dualistic conception of law, Gluckman regards the form of the abstract rules that Lozi courts "ought to apply" as basic (1967: p. 164), and the decisions are regarded as application of these general rules to concrete cases, thus forming "the law for the cases" (1967: p. 227). Although one may suspect a European legalistic influence in this definition, Gluckman was obviously more influenced by the Barotse "folk concept" of law whose essence is abstract rules (1967: esp. pp. 256–257). Unlike the European legalists, Gluckman does not limit himself to the emphasis on abstract rules. The second part of his legal definition, which emphasizes legal decisions, induced the author to present a series of legal cases which nonsystematically but quite effectively document his generalizations. One may criticize this modified casuistic approach and dualistic definition of law on the basis of logical inconsistency. Since rules that ought to be enforced often deviate in a remarkable way from the principles that are actually enforced in legal decisions, one can hardly call both sets of principles, which sometimes differ to the point of contradiction, by the same term, "law."

Systematic analysis of matrices of legal cases did not remain limited to the investigation of substantive law only. Recent anthropological research employs systematic casuistic analysis for theoretical purposes, thus transcending the boundaries of the field of substantive law. In their work entitled *Zuni Law* (1954), Smith and Roberts subject to their casuistic analysis 97 legal cases adjudicated by the Zuñi Bow Priest Society and the Tribal and Great Councils. Unlike Howell's work, all the cases are fully described and organized under topical headings. Influenced by Kluckhohn's writings, the purpose of the analysis is to abstract from the case material cultural values that are upheld by the bodies mentioned. The abstracted, legally relevant values are then related to some aspects of the Zuñi culture, especially to the dichotomy of the secular and religious. Since this study omits consideration of abstract rules, I would call it a purely casuistic approach.

Working systematically with extensive case material, Laura Nader used the casuistic approach for an effective inquiry into the relationship of law and some aspects of the sociopolitical structure of the Zapotecan society. Accordingly, her case analysis elucidated the relationship between the distribution of conflict resolutions and patterns of authority (Nader and Metzger 1963), and between types of conflict and their outcome (Nader 1964). The case analysis also shows the kinds of individuals who bring their grievances to the attention of courts, the range of grievances, and the age of delinquency. These comparative and relational efforts constitute an important contribution not only to the study of law itself but also to general ethnography, demonstrating to the anthropologists, who in general have shown remarkable disinterest in legal matters, how investigation of court decisions may contribute in a significant way to a fuller understanding of social organization.

Whereas Smith, Roberts, Nader, and Metzger used the case-study approach for investigating relationships between law and extra-legal aspects of culture, my own casuistic efforts have so far been directed toward clarification of the concept of law itself, at empirically scrutinizing the effectiveness and importance of the various criteria of law, and at distinguishing between two types of law on the basis of the degree of their internalization (or support by the members of the particular group in which they are enforced) (see Chapter Five). The work with the case material allowed me to investigate the nature of legal change, and, by relating the various legal cases to the locus of their adjudication within the "societal structure" (segmentation of the society), led me to the conception of "legal levels" and to the recognition of the multiplicity of legal systems within a given society (1956, 1958a, 1958c, 1965b). Thus my use of case material was directed primarily toward the investigation of the legal field itself. In this endeavor I have abandoned the purely casuistic approach and, with my legal cases, I have also analyzed the pertinent abstract rules. The analysis of the comparisons between the abstract rules and the pertinent decisions clarified the relationships between the two sets of phenomena and their role in the field of social control in general, thus providing me with an empirical basis for a general theory of law (1956, 1958a).

The fruitful and manifold use of the case-study method gives ample testimony to the heuristic value of viewing the form of law as principles abstracted from legal decisions. To this evidence, which supports the third, casuistic pathway to the study of law as the correct one, I can add other arguments that may further demonstrate its significance. First, by accepting the casuistic solution to the problem of the form of law, the concept of law becomes universal, leaving nowhere in the world a residuum of "lawless societies," which gives the concept a value for cross-cultural comparisons. Second, unlike the abstract rules concept, legal decisions are widely publicized, thus becoming a form of effective social control known to all—not the property of a few. Third, legal decisions incorporate no dead rules that obviously do not play a role in the field of social control. Fourth, legal decisions are positive statements in intelligible and definitive language; unlike abstract rules, they do not incorporate a vagueness that allows different interpretations. In other words, decisions clearly delimit and make specific the broad and ambiguous concepts stated in the rules, such as "due care," "reasonable doubt," and the like. Fifth, unlike abstract rules, legal decisions are not "outdated," or "obsolete"; reflecting minute changes in law, the adjudication process itself may be seen as a continuum of change in the institutionalized social control of a society. Sixth, legal decisions reflect the contemporary culture and "life" of the society and are actually part of it. Llewellyn and Hoebel expressed this argument very well: "Not only the making of new law and the effect of old, but the hold and the thrust of all other vital aspects of the culture, shine clear in the crucible of conflict" (1941: p. 29). Seventh, through the idea of legal precedent, principles contained in the legal decisions become ideals not only for the public, but also for the authorities themselves, thus providing for public awareness and for continuity and certainty of the law.

Some ethnocentric Western lawyers may object that this conception of form of law, which differs so much from the traditional legalistic one of abstract rule, is misleading by being labeled "law." But according to Webster, the casuistic conception of law does no violence to the semantics of modern English, and the definition in Webster does not actually exclude it (Neilson *et al.* 1940: p. 1401). Critics holding to a traditional orientation may further argue that even if the dictionary's meaning of the term "law" is not violated, then certainly the common legal usage is. To be specific, they may argue that one refers to an abstract rule passed by the Congress as a "law." This is of course true. However, in this case we face a problem peculiar to the English language (see Chapter One). In European languages one distinguishes between an abstract rule (for example, *lex* in Latin, *Gesetz* in German, *zákon* in Czech, *loi* in French) and "law proper" (*ius* in Latin, *Recht* in German, *právo* in Czech, *droit* in French). The English language makes no such distinction, applying to the abstract rules of the law books (*leges*) as well as to the other kind of law (*ius*) the same term. What anthropologists are obviously arguing about is the more basic concept of *ius,* not the obvious and clear concept of an abstract rule designated in Latin by *lex.*

There is one more problem to be clarified. The Western folk tradition views as proper legal decision a formalistic act by a formally instituted authority pronouncing a formal verdict, which is then physically enforced. In most of the nonliterate, and in some literate but non-European societies, legal decisions may assume forms undreamt by Western jurists, of such informality that an anthropologist with even a slight Western folk bias would disregard them as of no legal consequence. As an illustration I shall describe a decision-making process among two Papuan tribes of New Guinea—the Kapauku of the Kamu Valley and the Manga of the Jimi River Area.

The Kapauku "process of law" starts usually as a quarrel. The "plaintiff" accuses the "defendant" of having performed an act which causes harm to the plaintiff's interests. The defendant denies this or brings forward justification for his action. The arguments are usually accompanied by loud shouting which attracts other people, who gather around. The close relatives and friends of the parties to the dispute take sides and present their opinions and testimony by emotional speeches or by shouting. If this sort of arguing, called *mana koto* by natives goes on unchecked, it usually results in a stick fight (cases 40, 55, 57, 59, 118: Pospisil 1958a) or in war (case 16). However, in most instances, the important men from the sublineage and from allied sublineages or lineages appear on the scene. First, they squat among the onlookers and listen to the arguments. As soon as the exchange of opinions reaches a point too close to an outbreak of violence, the rich headman steps in and starts his argumentation. He admonishes both parties to have patience and begins questioning the defendant and the witnesses. He looks for evidence that would incriminate the defendant, at the scene of the crime or in the defendant's house (cases 62, 74). This activity of the authority is called *boko petai,* which can be loosely translated as "finding the evidence." Having secured the evidence and made up his mind about the factual background of the dispute, the authority starts the activity called by the natives *boko duwai,* the process of making a decision and inducing the parties to the dispute to follow it. The native authority makes a long speech in which he sums up the evidence, appeals to a rule, and then tells the parties what should be done to terminate the dispute. If the principals are not willing to comply, the authority becomes emotional and starts to shout reproaches; he makes long speeches in which evidence, rules, decisions, and threats form inducements. Indeed, the authority may go so far as to start *wainai* (the mad dance) or change his tactics suddenly and weep bitterly over the misconduct of the defendant and the fact that he refuses to obey. Some native authorities are so skilled in the art of persuasion that they can produce genuine tears which almost always break the resistance of the unwilling party. An inexperienced Western observer confronted with such a situation may very likely regard the weeping headman as a culprit on trial. Thus, from the formalistic point of view, there is little resemblance between the Western court's sentence and the *boko duwai* activity of the headman. However, the effect of the headman's persuasion is the same as that of a verdict passed in our courts. There were only five cases in my material wherein the parties openly resisted and disobeyed the authority's decision (cases 54, 94, 105, 119, 168; 1958a: pp. 254–255).

The Manga of the Jimi River area afford an instance of an authoritarian "decision" in which, fantastically enough, not a single word was spoken. Only a research worker with a discernment and knowledge of the native language and the subtleties of informal social control equal to that of Cook would notice it, recognize its significance, and report it in the proper perspective. Briefly, a subclan leader named Wando of the village Kwiop, trying to stop a quarrel over a girl's marriage and punish the "guilty party" for being a public nuisance, shot and killed a man with an arrow in 1956. Six years later, during Cook's research among the Manga, a similar quarrel resulted over an elopement. As he had done six years before, Wando decided there had been enough quarreling by the girl's agnatic relatives. Not uttering a word, he went to his house, picked up a bow and arrow, came back to the scene of the dispute, and silently began to sharpen the arrow. In this wordless way, his decision that the girl's agnates should stop arguing was made public. By linking it to the "precedent," the parties to the dispute were made aware of the decision as well as of their potential danger. As a result the quarreling stopped, and the threat of an open conflict subsided (Cook: 1965).

CONCLUSION

On the basis of the arguments presented in this chapter I conclude that law (*ius*) manifests itself in the form of a decision passed by a legal authority (council, chief, headman, judge, and the like), by which a dispute is solved, or a party is advised before any legally relevant behavior takes place, or by which approval is given to a previous solution of a dispute made by the participants before the dispute was brought to the attention of the authority. This form of law has two important aspects: A decision serves not only to resolve a specific dispute, which represents the behavioral part played by the authority while passing the sentence, but it also represents a precedent and an ideal for those who were not party to the specific controversy. They regard the content of the decision as a revelation of the ideally correct behavior. Consequently, a legal decision may be considered a culturally important behavior insofar as the authority's act of passing his verdict (opinion) is concerned and as an ideal in its effect upon the "followers of the authority." Whereas the abstract rules lack the behavioral aspect, the actual behavior, or "living law" lacks the ideal. This is another reason why legal decisions should be preferred over the two other possibilities as manifestations of law. Thus the field of law consists of principles abstracted from the decisions of authorities. These may be identical in content with corresponding abstract rules (*leges*) in which case we may regard the rules as being actually enforced. Those rules that are not enforced—the dead rules—are, by their lack of exercise of social control, omitted from the legal field; they have no corresponding principles abstracted from decisions. Thus the legal nature and importance of enforced abstract rules is here neither denied nor diminished. I object solely to the inclusion of dead rules in the legal field, to the exclusion of legal decisions from it, and to the denial of the latter's paramount importance for the study of law, if by law is meant a form of institutionalized social control.

CHAPTER THREE
ATTRIBUTES OF LAW

"Those of us who have learned humility have given over the attempts to define law." This very well-known statement of Radin is often used by writers who have tried to find a justification for shunning the "formidable" prospect of conceptualizing the category of social phenomena called law (Radin 1938: p. 1145). Those legal scholars who, although certainly not lacking in humility, have realized the necessity of undertaking this onerous task, have to reject Radin's humble conclusion. Hoebel bluntly states, "Yet it cannot be that law is incapable of definition, for a definition is merely an expression of the acknowledged attributes of a phenomenon or concept" (1954: p. 18).

As I see it, Radin's statement stems from the false assumption that concepts are objective, as are phenomena—that something exists that may be regarded as the proper and absolute definition of law, which legal theorists have tried in vain to discover (see also Barkun 1968: p. 150). The only objective entities in the field of science are the phenomena, which for heuristic reasons (and therefore subjectively) are lumped into categories whose contrastive cognitive attributes form dimensions of a concept which is then, for communication purposes, provided with a name. Thus one may try to determine semantically the meaning of the English word "law." But this is hardly a task for a student of jurisprudence; actually it has been satisfactorily accomplished by the compilers of dictionaries. Rather than delve into semantics, my problem in this chapter will be to identify the attributes of an analytical concept of law, though not necessarily an English one, which may prove to be a useful tool for a legal scientist who is not limiting his comparative analysis to Western phenomena only. Thus my endeavor, like that of many of my colleagues, will be to arrive at an analytical concept of law that can be applied cross-culturally. This concept, defined by its several attributes, will deserve the appellation of "law" because it will, in general, conform with the definition of law as "rules or modes of conduct made obligatory by some sanction which is imposed and enforced for their violation by a controlling authority" (Neilson *et al.* 1940: p. 1401). That fact, however, does not mean that the concept would not be in many respects different from the English folk concept. I will not commit the error, deservedly criticized by Bohannan (1957: pp. 5–6) and Barkun (1968: p. 165), of promulgating the English legal folk conceptual scheme as a cross-cultural analytical device.

Although my concept will include the phenomena that English-speaking people designate as law, it will also include phenomena of institutionalized social control from non-European societies. In other words it will be more precise and relevant, by singling out those attributes that are cross-culturally and therefore analytically relevant, attributes which a semantic analysis of the English folk concept of law fails to reveal. Thus, basing my statements and analysis on a cultural comparative research, I reject explicitly the extremist position of the modern, but patently nonscientific cultural solipsists, who insist that a legal system be interpreted only in terms of its own folk concepts. The folk-concept analysis, as stated in Chapter Two, is very basic and should always precede the analytic conceptual presentation. But it is not the end product for an *ethnologist* because it would not contribute to the science of law, which is composed of cross-culturally derived generalizations (sociological laws), but only to a disjointed, noncomparable series of *ethnographic* reports (see also Gluckman 1965: p. 183).

Consequently, having discussed the form of law, I shall now analyze the legal phenomena derived from a sample of cultures (studied during my field or bibliographical research) and abstract the attributes they have in common. These attributes, in turn, will also serve as criteria for a more exact delimitation of the law's boundaries and for separating legal phenomena from other, nonlegal social categories. In the preceding chapter I have argued that the form of law should be seen as principles abstracted from decisions of a group's authority (leader, chief, judge, etc.). These decisions vary greatly, and they embrace many principles that cannot be called law. An authority of a group, either an informal leader or formal chief, makes not only legal decisions, but also those that are of purely political, religious, educational, or nonsanctioned customary nature. In other words, we have to define law by discovering characteristics that identify some of the authority's decisions as legal, thus differentiating them from his statements and decisions that do not deal with law. Scholars dealing with this problem have presented various definitions of law that may be divided into two broad categories.

The first category, which need not concern us much here because of its basically philosophic and nonscientific nature, often employs vague criteria and speculative sociological statements not substantiated by a solid empirical inquiry. For example, Michael Barkun's definition reads: "Law is that system of manipulable symbols that functions as a representation, as a model, of social structure" (1968: p. 92). This may sound pleasing to the ears of some "modern" political scientists, but it is one of the most confusing statements I have read about law. As a matter of fact, what it basically does is to equate social structure—the structure of social relations expressed symbolically—with law. Thus law, according to Barkun, would incorporate symbolic analysis of kinship behavior, kinship terminology, actual residence patterns, and voluntary associational patterns of individuals in a society—in other words the whole social structure as presented by ethnographers (because they always employ symbolism in their analyses). Since law then would actually be equal to social structure (because, of necessity, this can be presented only through manipulable symbols), the term "law" would be redundant. Fortunately, this is not the only way to define law. Barkun's basic fallacy is a semantic one: He does not seem to recognize the difference between sociological and jural law, though it has been often discussed in the literature. While the former is a scientific generalization pertaining to abstractions for what "is" in the society, the latter is a set of principles that has the quality of what generally "ought" to be and, therefore, what specifically the courts of law and other types of legal authorities try to enforce. Barkun's "legal universals," consequently, are nonlegal in nature. Thus a statement that law is a set of interrelated symbols may be used equally well as a "definition" of economic structure, religious structure, and so on. A claim that these symbols have "empirical referents" is a tautology because a symbol in science must always refer to an empirical fact. That such a set of symbols functions as a means of conceptualizing and managing the social environment is equally true for a religious system or for the *Weltanschauung* of a people as it is for law. Barkun's final universal that claims that a legal process involves transformation of dyadic interactions into triadic interactions is, although true for substantial part of the law, false for its totality, because many disputes originating from offenses against a chief or another type of authority retain, even during the process of adjudication, dyadic form (1968: p. 151).

The second category of definitions consists of those that utilize precise language and try to abstract attributes that do pertain to and are essential for the concept of law per se. This category may be further divided into two subsections. To the first belong definitions by those social scientists who have been searching for a single criterion of law that would constitute its essence. The most important early contributions to this approach were made by Radcliffe-Brown and Malinowski. Radcliffe-Brown (1952: p. 212) emphasized the physical sanction administered by a politically organized society as the basic criterion of law. The emphasis upon the "politically organized society'' led him to admit that there was an absence of law in some more "primitive cultures," and thus to limit the concept of law to cultures with a more formal political organization. Although I do agree with the importance of sanction as a criterion of law, I reject the idea that it is the only and most significant legal characteristic. Physical sanction is often applied in a "politically organized society" outside the field of law. Also, the requirement that law can exist only in a society that has to be overall politically organized will be shown to be erroneous in Chapter Four.

As a contrast to Radcliffe-Brown, Malinowski (1934: pp. 30–42) selected as his main attribute of law the principle of obligation—that is, the ties between two parties—which defines a phenomenon as law, punishment not being essential because conformity is achieved through mutual service based on expectance of future reciprocal favors. This theory is even less workable than the one discussed in the previous paragraph, although it allows for the universality of law. Timasheff criticizes it correctly by pointing out that although duels were obligatory in Europe, they were also illegal (1938: p. 871). I object to Malinowski's view because he defines law so broadly as to include most of the customs of a society. For this reason the theory is not a workable tool for the ethnographer. Moreover, there are many kinds of obligations, like moral or religious ones, that have to be differentiated from the legal. Consequently, a "legal obligation" must be defined more exactly, and additional attributes are needed to set it aside from the other nonlegal cases.

I do not object to the above theories on the basis of their invalidity. Indeed, each of them elaborates a particular attribute that is important for this inquiry. My objection is that these attributes are insufficient to characterize the essence of law. It is my contention, based upon the results of comparative research and my findings among the Kapauku Papuans, Nunamiut Eskimo, Hopi Indians, and Tirolean peasants, that not one but a whole pattern of attributes which coexist in time forms the core of the social phenomena that we call law. In this respect, then, I agree with the authors whose definitions are based upon a multiplicity of legal attributes, and thus form the second subsection of the category of rigorous and workable definitions of law. Probably the earliest of these authors, and those who influenced my thinking in this respect, were the Commentators, whose definition of Roman customary law included two attributes: *longa consuetudo* and *opinio necessitatis* (Sommer 1933: p. 10; for full discussion see Chapter Six).

Among other authors seeking a multiplicity of attributes of law should be mentioned here only two most outstanding scholars whose work preceded my early definition (Pospisil 1952): Karl Llewellyn and E. Adamson Hoebel. In their joint work, *Cheyenne Way,* they identified four "elements" essential to legal phenomenon: the "element of enforceability of an imperative," which ordains that a member of a given society *must* behave in a certain way; the "element of supremacy," which identifies the legal phenomenon by the fact that "if appealed to, it *prevails*"; the "system element," which points out that "the legal is *part of the going order*"; and the "element of officialdom," which provides the legal with an official, publicly recognized quality (1961: pp. 283–284). The authors claim that these four elements of law "cluster together to make up the phenomenon which is summed up as Authority in the group or culture" (1961: p. 284). From a subsequent discussion it seems that authority is then a summary of legal characteristics. It may attach itself to decisions passed by a person, but

> *in many groups and cultures it has happened that authority has become attached less to persons than to patterns of action ("procedures") or to norms for action. There can be known "ancient law" (e.g., tabu) with no standing officials to enforce it. There can be recognized procedures for settling grievance, say, by treaty and composition, or by oath, or by ritual combat, with no official even to mediate or preside. (1961: p. 286)*

As will be seen, this concept of "authority" is radically different from the one I am using in my repertory of legal attributes. While here it is an abstract quality of the legal, composed of several attributes, in my usage authority signifies a concrete person or group of persons passing a legal judgment, or decision. It will be seen also that, as a consequence of this concept of authority, I have to object to the statement that taboos not enforced by officials (leaders, chiefs, etc.) or procedures not involving them would be law. In his later work (1954: p. 28) Hoebel changed to a belief that privileged force (i.e., physical sanction) is the main criterion of law, aided by two others —regularity and "official authority" (meaning an individual or group possessing a socially recognized privilege of so acting). This position brings Hoebel much closer to my earlier (Pospisil 1952: pp. 35–73) and present conceptions of legal attributes.

On the basis of my legal studies in Czechoslovakia, my subsequent bibliographic studies in the United States, and my research among the Nunamiut, the Kapauku, the Hopi, and the Tiroleans, I have found four attributes of law that have proved to be of importance: authority, intention of universal application, *obligatio* (not to be confused with obligation), and sanction. In addition to these criteria a "law" has to be incorporated into a legal decision which constitutes its manifestation—its empirical form. This pattern of attributes, I contend, constitutes the essence of a viable concept of law and provides the ethnographer with a useful tool (see esp. Frake 1955, 1969; Pospisil, 1958a, 1964). Accordingly, law is here defined by a whole pattern of attributes, all of which must coexist in a social phenomenon in order to identify it as law. In this chapter I propose to identify the four attributes, to present theories of other authors that pertain to these attributes, and to document their existence as well as their heuristic value for an ethnographer by bibliographical material and particularly by legal material gathered during my research among two very primitive Stone Age societies in which it has been claimed that law is absent.

THE ATTRIBUTE OF AUTHORITY

A decision, to be legally relevant, or in other words, to effect social control, must either be accepted as a solution by the parties to a dispute or, if they resist, be forced upon them. Such a decision, of necessity, is passed by an individual, or group of individuals, who can either persuade the litigants to comply or who possess power over enforcement agents or the group membership in general to compel them to execute the verdict, judgment, or informal decision even over protests and resistance of either or both parties to the dispute. Individuals who possess the power to induce or force the majority of the members of their social group to conform to their decisions I shall call the legal authority. Whereas this authority is formalized and specialized on the state level in our own and in other civilizations, in tribal societies and in some of the state's subgroups it often coincides with the leadership of various groups that exercises several functions besides the legal one.

Argument for the Absence of Authority

It can be asked whether I do not run the risk of making my legal concept nonuniversal by employing the attribute of authority. Many ethnographers have declared that there is a genuine absence of authority in certain cultures. Some of them use expressions like "lateral social control" or "group as a whole" (Yang 1945: p. 134) when referring to the agency of social control. Such expressions are virtually identical with a statement claiming an absence of authority, if by this term we mean a specific individual or a group of individuals effecting social control. Let us investigate several such cases derived from the ethnographic literature. Two additional claims of absence of authority and leadership will be presented at the conclusion of this section, where they will be challenged with detailed material derived from my own fieldwork.

Martin Gusinde says of the customary laws of the Yaghan Indians of Tierra del Fuego "that they are faithfully followed is looked after by the group as a whole"[1] (1937, Vol. 2: p. 628). Not being satisfied with the face value of the phrase "group as a whole" (*Allgemeinheit*), we may ask: Who usually represents or speaks for this mysterious *Allgemeinheit?* The answer is found

---

[1]Translated by Pospisil. ". . . dass sie treu befolgt werden, darüber wacht die Allgemeinheit."

in the same monograph: "There is never a shortage of men who because of their old age, spotless character, long experience and mental superiority, gain such an extent of moral influence that it is equal to a peculiar domination"[2] (1937, vol. 2, p. 803). These strong men are called *tiamuna* by the people, and they are active in the local groups (*Lokalgruppe*) that form the important units in the Yaghan social structure. Their power does not derive from an office or from a formal act of investiture such as election, appointment by a superior, or succession to a title. The *tiamuna* may be regarded as an informal headman who achieved his position because of his personal endeavors and qualities. He holds his dominant position only as long as he is able to convince his followers of his superiority and thus influence their behavior (1937, vol. 2: p. 779; see also Koppers 1924: p. 43).

The Navaho Indians are a second society for which an absence of authority and leadership has been claimed by ethnographers. As in the preceding example, the literature exhibits a peculiar schizophrenia with respect to the question of authority. On one hand the authors categorically deny an existence of meaningful authority and leadership; on the other, and interestingly enough in specific instances, they show that authority and leadership indeed existed among these southwestern Indians. Accordingly Kluckhohn and Leighton speak of lateral social control in this tribe and claim that "the People themselves are the real authority" and that important decisions were reached at local meetings through the consensus of those present (1947: p. 69). In other words, here we have again the mysterious *Allgemeinheit,* "the group as a whole" or "the People," who make decisions and effect social control without requiring a leading personality or group of leaders. Here we have again a logically and empirically impossible statement which implies that somehow all members of a Navaho local band were equal in reaching decisions concerning their disputes and their political and economic life, that their voices—irrespective of their individual age, sex, experience, intelligence, prestige, aggressiveness, and mastery of rhetoric— were of equal importance.

That this cannot be is documented not only by the social-psychological material presented later in this chapter but also by the ethnographic material on the Navaho published by the same authors and by others. Sasaki and Adair state that "the collection of extended families usually recognized some older man as ultimate authority in the case of disputes and as a spokesman for the whole group" (1952: p. 102). Similar and more forceful is Lipps' statement that the Navaho

[2]Translated by Pospisil. "Niemals aber fehlt es an solchen Männern, die infolge ihres hohen Alters und tadellosen Charakters, ihrer langen Erfahrung und geistigen Überlegenheit sich einen moralischen Einfluss von solcher Stärke erwerben, dass er einer gewissen Beherrschung gleichkommt."

> have a number of "head-men" whom they recognize as leaders,
> generally because of their superior qualities, character and
> integrity. While their offices are often either elective or
> hereditary, still they are not always so. The office of "head-man"
> usually gravitates to the man who can hold it—a natural born
> leader of men. (1956: p. 35)

This means, then, that the various local groups of Navaho had leaders, who had usually achieved their position informally, and therefore deserve indeed to be called headmen. In several other local bands the status of leadership was conferred by a rather formal succession or by election (Hill 1940: p. 25; Collier 1966: pp. 62–163; Shepardson 1963: p. 47). The "election" in the old days was obviously a final unanimous decision which was reached either through persuasion or by long harangues "until those in opposition felt it was useless or impolitic to express further disagreement" (Kluckhohn and Leighton 1947: p. 71). This election was, according to some authors, often confirmed by a ceremony called "Chief Blessing Way" which officially marked the individual's assumption of the leader's office. The headmen of the local groups tried to resolve internal disputes by inducing the parties to accept their decisions or opinions, and were also involved in marriage arrangements and disputes between the spouses (Hill 1940: esp. pp. 26–27). Most explicit about the role of a Navaho headman is Dyk, who although allowing for group discussions to reach a consensus, shows in an impressive series of instances how decisions were handed down by important headmen and how these decisions were agreed to and obeyed by their followers (Dyk 1938: esp. pp. 107, 160, 185 ff., 201, 347, 357). Thus the idea that the Navaho were a leaderless functioning group in an egalitarian utopia is exploded.

An alleged absence of authority in other cases is usually quite similar to the two examples discussed above. When we go deeper into an investigation of the literary sources, the *Allgemeinheit*—the claim of an absence of leadership—changes, in specifically described incidents of the decision-making process into more definite factors of social control that invariably include an influential individual (or group of these): a leader. We find particular individuals initiating action in the group, resolving problems, and occupying positions of more or less importance. The difficulty with the authors who subscribe to the idea of leaderless groups and societies lies in the problem of what each author actually means by "authority." The concept is usually not clarified and its meaning is taken for granted. Most of the statements about the absence of an authority imply a definition that identifies the concept with a person of absolute power, whose acts, especially handing down decisions, are very formal. We may ask whether absoluteness and formality are the universal and most important characteristics of leadership and authority. I assert here that the essence of a meaningful and workable concept of authority does not rest with these characteristics, which are peculiar to some cultures only.[3] On the contrary, I believe the fact that the decisions and advice of an authority are followed by the rest of the members of the group constitutes the only important criterion of "authority." As will be shown more firmly later, an authority, therefore, is considered in this book not as a descriptive but as a functional concept. Absoluteness and formality are only its specialized, nonuniversal attributes.

A claim for an absence of leadership and authority in a tribal society may also stem from another serious mistake which has little to do with that concept per se. It arises from the old bias of ethnographers which treats a linguistic unit of people, usually called a tribe, as a "society" or a "social group" in a sociological sense, disregarding the fact that such a group does not form a unified society at all and therefore lacks an overall political structure. This position may be comparable to insisting that the "German tribe of Europe" has no political organization, no authority, and therefore no law because of the fact it lives in several rather than one unified state, its society being in a sense segmented into at least seven sovereign, completely independent units. Such an error with regard to a tribal "society" is equally ridiculous. Unfortunately, this is not yet fully realized by some anthropologists, who still adhere to outdated Durkheimean, Marxian, or evolutionary dogmas. They do not accept the simple truth that segmented societies such as the Kapauku or Nuer are not politically unified and therefore do not form a group—"a society"—in a sociological sense.

Although we shall deal with this fallacy fully in Chapter Four, because it involves a claim for an absence of authority we have to consider it briefly here. The fallacy has been stated by LeVine as follows:

> *Most anthropological students of stateless societies have concentrated their attention on the total-society level, analyzing the structure of intergroup relations in the absence of a central authority. In my opinion, a concept such as "segmentary society," which is at the total-society level of analysis, is an inadequate tool for the investigation of political variation and adaptation in African societies. (1960: p. 51)*

[3]Here I am in agreement with Hoebel, who maintains that coercion is not a necessary prerequisite for leadership (Hoebel 1954: p. 294). However, I have to register an objection to his claim that "the simplest primitive societies are democratic to the point of near-anarchy" (1954: p. 294). First, to me the concept of democracy has little to do with anarchy—a democracy may have a very strong leader with excessive power (see Roman and present French Gaullist democracy, or that of the U.S.). Secondly, the claim of near anarchy in most primitive societies results from either inadequate, superficial research of the ethnographer, or from his statement which visualizes the society as a whole and neglects the fact of leadership and political organization in that society's subgroups or segments.

Barkun's work, based on the investigation of the overall society level, in its conclusions neglected the society's segments. His totalistic approach led him to conclude that a law in segmented tribal society, strangely enough, has neither authority nor sanction. His theorizing about segmented society is mostly based on erroneous assumptions derived from his readings. First, he correctly maintains that law is not a monopoly of the state (certainly to the chagrin of Morton Fried 1967: esp. pp. 236–237) when he claims: "The state has been denied its customary honored place as the guardian and sine qua non of the legal order" (Barkun 1968: p. 166). Unfortunately, by misinterpreting Max Weber he wrongly accused that author of claiming such a fallacy (Barkun 1968: p. 64). In my view Weber is one of the social thinkers who must be credited with looking for law beyond the facade of the state (see Chapter Four).

Second, Barkun asserts that members of a segmentary lineage define their society as a system of descent groups (1968: p. 19). Although this may be true in some instances, it is certainly not so universally. Kapauku do not define their "linguistic group" in this way; as a matter of fact, they define it linguistically and territorially. Third, Barkun claims that segments in a tribal society are "more or less equal in number of individuals they include" (1968: p. 23). This ignores the old process of social dynamics in these societies by which whole segments simply die out or become so large that fission takes place. Far from being equal in numbers, the individual subgroups of a segmented society often exhibit *marked quantitative differences* in their group membership. Fourth, Barkun assumes that in conflict the fighting sides composed of allied lineages are approximately equal in strength (1968: p. 53). This is not true for the Kapauku or Dani Papuans, where it is well known that a fighting unit of lineages has often been either chased from its own territory by a superior enemy or simply wiped out. Finally, he assumes a qualitative difference between tribal and state societies by using terms such as "primitive law" (1968: p. 10) and "primitive society" (p. 12).

Barkun's gravest error is his totalistic, or as he puts it, "expanded view" (1968: p. 17). Trying to analyze politically and legally the disunited, politically independent lineages of a linguistic grouping (tribe), he arrives at the ambiguous (but for modern social mystics and philosophers probably intriguing) concept of "jural community." He defines it as "an area in which all the actors recognize that a common method exists for resolving disputes between them" (1968: p. 71), a "widest grouping within which there are a moral obligation and a means ultimately to settle disputes peaceably" (1968: p. 67). It is obvious from the definition that the concept, by itself imprecise and too vague a tool for ethnographic investigation, rests upon two major fallacies. First, it is usually the ethnographer and not the "actors" who recognize the existence of a common method for dispute settlement. If Barkun's thesis were to be applied to New Guinea, probably all the Highland tribes as well as many from the Lowlands, who settle their disputes in a similar way, would have to be lumped into one "jural community." That this would be impractical, confusing, and ludicrous is only too obvious to an ethnographer. Second, since the area is defined by a "moral obligation" criterion, it hardly can be called jural. There is a significant difference between the two terms. Law, logically, heuristically, and empirically, always entails legal, not moral obligations.

With such a confusing concept for analysis there is little wonder that conclusions about the "law" of the jural community are equally astounding. We are told that the law is "horizontal" (Barkun 1968: p. 65), possesses no "deterrent sanctions" (p. 155), "manifestly lacks the infrastructure [whatever this means] that sanctioned law requires" (p. 155), that the system (society) is "multicentric" (probably meaning politically disunited, lacking an overall unified political structure) (p. 161), and has "no centralization of power" (p. 34), no chiefs and powerful authorities (pp. 8, 152) that would make possible a "direct and authoritative propagation of norms" (p. 152). If the "jural community" is not politically organized centrally, possesses no authority to speak of, enforces no norms, and applies no sanctions, the question is: What legal qualities does it possess? The answer logically appears to be: none. Thus the millennial movements can hardly "signal the collapse of a legal system through the disintegration of its jural community" (p. 161) because there has never existed either an overall legal system or a jural community. The problem of law and adjudication of disputes in segmented tribal societies constitutes part of the wider problem of multiplicity of legal systems in a society. This problem will be discussed in Chapter Four. I am satisfied at this point to conclude this argument by a most adequate quotation from LeVine:

> *All societies have authority structures and values concerning the allocation of authority. In stateless societies, the proper unit for the analysis of such phenomena is not the total society, where we are likely to mistake lack of a central political hierarchy for egalitarianism, but the maximal decision-making unit (or some cohesive subgrouping within it). (1960: p. 58)*

Leadership and Authority

The relationship of members of any functioning group exhibits a structural pattern determined by the size of the membership, the functional nature of the group, the cultural content and values that affect the members' behavior, the stated purpose of the group's existence, and the economic resources that are available. In addition to these determinants the pattern always exhibits a power structure—the potential influence that any group member has over another. Because of personal characteristics of the group's members (their sex, age, temperament, wisdom, experience, aggressiveness, skills, wealth, and ability to persuade), the opinions of all individuals do not carry equal weight. Since the activities of a group have to be coordinated, an opinion concerning an activity has to, and does, prevail in a given situation. The opinion is invariably that of the most influential member of the group, whom we call a leader. However, it need not be, and usually is not, exactly the same opinion, he might have advocated originally. In other words a leader is usually influenced, at least to some small degree, by the opinions of other members. Nevertheless, his decision is certainly not implemented by a group opinion (as some sociological jargon puts it) but by his own, although modified, idea. When such a leader passes decisions by which internal conflicts of the group are resolved, I propose to call him a "legal authority."

The leadership in functioning groups is certainly universal, contrary to the statements of social thinkers and of some evolutionists (according to whom most primitive people possess almost no social and cultural characteristics, everything, including leadership and law having evolved during the subsequent cultural history of man). Aside from ethnographic investigation of examples from the inventory of the world's cultures, this universality is suggested by two kinds of research: in the societies of the subhuman primates and in the behavior of groups of human beings which are, as far as possible, uninfluenced by the values and customs of a particular culture. Research of the first type has been conducted by the modern physical anthropologist; the second is the endeavor of social psychologists.

Leadership in a group is not a social phenomenon over which man has a monopoly; packs of wolves, monkeys, and apes have their leaders too. In an investigated group of rhesus monkeys, for example, the condominium of two males, one of which was slightly more dominant than the other, controlled the behavior of the rest of the members. The two individuals formed the core of the group, were usually closely associated, and only rarely quarreled. As a contrast, of 119 observed encounters with other animals of the group, only in three instances did the "leaders" fail to exhibit dominance (Southwick, Beg, and Siddigi 1965: pp. 144, 149).

Similarly, among a group of baboons "the key functions or behavior pattern most prominently associated with the largest male," the leader, can be summarized as follows: He drove away any male from his favorite females; submissive gestures were directed much more frequently to him by the others; he exhibited far greater aggressiveness than the rest of the animals; if the group was endangered by a charging eland or a strange baboon he went ahead of the group; and during the day the females with newborns clustered around him for protection. "His retaliation against attacks on the mothers was immediate" (Hall and De Vore 1965: p. 56). As in the case of the rhesus monkeys, a condominium of three males was observed in another baboon group (Hall and De Vore 1965: p. 60). Hall states in general that these coleaders exercised social control within their group: "Discipline within the group is usually very adequately maintained by threat, or by beating and biting of the subordinate on the nape of the neck which very rarely result in any visible injury to the victim" (Hall 1968: p. 154). Studies of Japanese macaque monkeys revealed even a sort of hegemony in the fact that new leaders of the group were often the offspring of females who were "closely associated with the already dominant males" (Hall 1968: p. 154).

Although not so numerous, groups of apes also exhibit leadership. "A chimpanzee can be termed the leader of a group when it initiates group movements and regulates its speed and direction" (Goodall 1965: p. 454). Such an animal usually walks in front; when he stops the others wait for him and follow only after he moves again. He also exhibits dominance by being allowed to walk alone on a branch and by the willingness of his followers to surrender food to him. When he is angry, most of the rest of the group run away from him screaming (Goodall 1965: p. 453). One such chimpanzee leader named David even issued his orders to the troupe vocally: "Thus once, when leaving a feeding area, David turned his head toward three other males, gave a low 'huh,' and the others at once got up and followed him" (Goodall 1965: p. 454). This ape-leadership persists even in captivity, where upon removal of a dominant male another animal takes over the leadership. At the reintroduction of the former leader, the latter usually defends his position successfully (Gartlan 1968: p. 115). The recorded evidence on subhuman primate leads one to doubt the theories of leaderless human society; one asks why early ("primitive") man's society should lack leadership and be more primitive than that of contemporary monkeys, apes, and even wolves and horses.

For many social psychologists any functioning human group requires leadership, a central person, or several people who form a "focus about which a number of individuals may cluster to form a group" (Gibb 1966a: p. 88; see also Redl 1966: p. 76; Carter 1953: p. 262). Without leadership, without its focus, a proper social group cannot exist. Krech, Crutchfield, and Ballachey express this position on universality of group leadership as follows:

> Wherever two or more people are gathered together, *there will we find a leader. With the very formation of a group, some members are almost certain to take a more active role than others, to be preferred to others, to be listened to with more respect than others, to be dominant over others. This is the beginning of the differentiation of group members into leaders and followers. (1962: p. 422; italics in original)*

To substantiate the claim of the universality of leadership, social psychologists investigated group situations in which the cultural factor emphasizing authority has been virtually eliminated. For example, J. L. Moreno experimented in a nursery with babies ranging from birth to three years of age, who were allowed to interact freely. By observing the babies' behavior Dr. Moreno was able to conceptualize three basic stages in the emergence of dominance and leadership. The first stage, lasting from birth to 28 weeks, he called the "isolation stage" because almost no interaction occurred. The second stage, between ages 28 and 42 weeks, was marked by slight interaction in which no dominance could be observed and was called the "horizontal stage." After 42 weeks a third stage was reached, when the group interacted intensively and paid more attention to certain individuals who played a very active role. This stage, marking the emergence of leadership, was labeled "vertical" (Krech and Crutchfield 1948: pp. 434–435).

A similar experiment with the emergence of leadership in an unstructured situation was conducted by Muzafer Sherif on adults. He investigated the autokinetic effect upon the development of a subjectively evolved frame of reference. An individual was brought into a room where no light could penetrate. A tiny lighted dot appeared to him in the darkness. Although this dot was fixed and motionless, the person observing it (having no external frame of reference) was under the purely subjective impression that the light was moving. The same experiment was repeated with other subjects who were later permitted to tell each other about their perceptions and experiences. Thereafter they were asked to look at the dot once again and were told that this was done so that they could correct their observations and be more accurate. An interesting result was reported. The individual perceptions in the second trial tended to cluster in a narrow range, which was called by Sherif the "group norm." For the purpose of this thesis it is important that the individuals within this "group-norm range," who had changed their original statements of observations very slightly or not at all, were functioning as leaders, as persons with authority. The rest of the group were merely their followers (Sherif 1947: pp. 77–89). This however, does not mean that the leaders were uninfluenced by the other members of the group or, in Sherif's words: "that the group's norm is simply the original leader's norm" (Sherif 1966: p. 467). The leader's opinion is influenced by the discussion with the rest of the members of the group, although certainly far less than the opinions of his followers, which gravitate toward that of the dominant person.

Definition of Leadership and Authority

Leadership, like law itself, has been defined and redefined in terms of so many criteria and approaches that Bentz was able to list about 130 different definitions of the concept (Bass 1960: p. 87). Most of these definitions prove to have been mental exercises of the writers, who appear to have one common characteristic: they have investigated leadership in Western societies only, having conducted no cross-cultural studies. Some of the definitions collide even with our own Western semantics and logic, as, for example, when actual leadership is mistaken for esteem ascribed to individuals by their peers (Bass 1960: p. 87). The defining of leadership has even had its own cultural history by exhibiting, according to Tannenbaum and coauthors, three main stages: definitions based on universal leadership traits, on a situational approach, and on satisfaction of the needs of the followers (Tannenbaum, Weschler, and Massarik 1961: p. 23). Let us briefly survey some of these definitions.

Probably the most ancient but not necessarily the most naïve and confusing definitions of leadership concentrate on universal leadership characteristics, without the authors trying to arrive at the latter empirically by cross-cultural research (Cowley 1928: p. 144). These characteristics were sometimes even considered unique to leaders (Hollander 1964: p. 4; Gibb 1966a: p. 88), or at least the excessive accumulation of these qualities in a person was thought essential to leadership. The characteristics regarded by various authors as leadership criteria included intelligence, adjustment, wisdom, introspection, extroversion, dominance, masculinity, assertiveness, interpersonal sensitivity, and others (Hollander and Julian 1968: p. 893; Bass 1960: p. 108). Of all these, the trait of "assertiveness" probably most closely approximates a universal characteristic of leadership (Hollander and Julian 1968: p. 893). To secure data on these characteristics case histories have been collected (see esp. Bass 1960: p. 108), and even projective tests have been employed (p. 111). The confused state of the trait approach to leadership has been amply revealed by Stogdill (1948) in his survey of the pertinent literature. The basic fallacy of this approach was well recognized by several writers on the subject whose objections are well summarized by the following quotation: "The traits of the leader which are necessary and effective in one group or situation may be quite different from those of another leader in a different setting" (Hollander 1964: p. 5; see also Hollander and Julian 1968: p. 892). The cause of this fallacy was, as stated above, a lack of cross-cultural orientation in the research.

To correct this situation several of the researchers embraced a "situational" approach. Cattell (1951: p. 161), by using a scientific-sounding term, "group syntality," defined a leader as "a person who has a demonstrable influence upon group syntality." The dimension of leadership, according to Cattell (1951: p. 175), was *"the magnitude of the syntality change (from the mean) produced by that person,* i.e., by the difference in syntality under his leadership and the syntality under the leadership of the average or model leader" (italics in original). Syntality of a group is defined in terms of the degree of its integration, cohesiveness, synergy, morale, sociability, permeability, and other vague and confusing concepts (Carter 1953: p. 263). Carter objects to this grandiose but bewildering definition because of its unworkability, and substitutes a "pragmatic" approach of his own which is clear and explicit, but even more indeterminate and subjective than the one he criticized. Accordingly, a leader is characterized by behavior that an experimenter "considers to be signs of leadership." In other words, "leadership behaviors are any behaviors the experimenter wishes to so designate" (Carter 1953: p. 264). But by this statement the problem of leadership is not solved; rather it is dissolved. What confusion in concrete situations it may create is apparent from examples Carter gives, among which the leader of a basketball team is identified as a player "who shot the largest number of baskets" (p. 264). In his semantic exercise Carter confuses the player *leading* in the number of baskets with the player who initiates attacks, determines strategies, and otherwise influences the team activity, and is therefore obviously the leader of his group.

Instead of considering the leader's personality itself, Bass tried another approach to leadership by attacking the structural implications and concentrating upon the status attained and the different roles played by the leader of a group (1960: p. 109). Because of the high cross-cultural variability of this approach and because of the vague definitions of the various leadership roles (e.g., "orienter-evaluator, energizer, encourager, elaborator," etc.), it did not prove much more successful than the approaches discussed so far.

Dissatisfied with these endeavors, other writers turned to the teleological avenue by trying to determine the leader of a group on the basis of his advancement and contribution to the achievement of group goals. Specifically, to these writers "the momentary group leader is that person who is able to contribute most to progress toward the common goal" (Gibb 1966a: p. 89). Or, as Hollander and Julian put it, "leader influence suggests a positive contribution toward the attainment of group goals" (1968: p. 891). The trouble here lies more with the definition of "group goals" than with the fact that often the goals are set by the leader himself and not by the group, his followers being persuaded into following rather than determining the direction of the action. Both this and the "syntality" approach have a Durkheimean flavor and recall the theoretical position of Radcliffe-Brown. Equally vague and encased in sociological jargon are definitions of leaders in terms of "task-relevant group activities" (Fiedler 1967: p. 8). Do we have "task-nonrelevant group activities?" And if so, what are they, and why should not a person, directing the action of a group in this direction, be called a leader?

The last of the categories of nonfunctional definitions of leadership I shall mention here is that in which leadership is left to be determined by the members of the group themselves through the technique of the sociometric choice (Bass 1960: pp. 108–109). Authors subscribing to this approach simply confuse the phenomenon of actual leadership with the opinion of the members of the group about it. There is always a difference between what the people actually do and what they think they do. This approach measures the latter and certainly not the former. It is erroneous, consequently, to think that the actual leader is always the one whom the members of a group consider the leader (Carter 1953: p. 263). Although this sociometric approach, measuring in effect positive emotional feelings of group members, may well identify actual leadership where the status is formally defined, in cases of informal leadership it is certainly unreliable and may often fail (despite the assurance to the contrary by Hollander, 1964: p. 90) because it measures opinions rather than reality.

One more problem needs comment before I adopt a definition of leadership and authority that has proved workable in a cross-cultural context. The problem involves a conceptual dichotomy which contrasts leadership with "headship." The criteria for distinguishing the two terms are usually couched either in absolute statements or in obscure, ambiguous social-science language, while the heuristic value of this dyadic conceptualization is never demonstrated. Basically, in this dichotomy leadership is said to be determined by a free choice of the group's members, by a "popular selection and acceptance" (Gibb 1966a: p. 94). Therefore, individuals who gain their leading positions by coercion, political intrigue, appointment, imposition, hereditary succession, or other nonpopular (or "undemocratic") means cannot be called leaders (Carter 1953: p. 261). As a consequence, "the attitudes, ideals, and aspirations of the followers play as important a determining role as do the individuality and personality of the leader" (Gibb 1966a: p. 93). "The nature of the leadership role is determined by the goal of the group," which supposedly unites the followers with the leader whose goals are claimed to be the same; since leadership is thought to exist to achieve these common goals "it flourishes only in a problem situation" (Gibb 1966a: pp. 92, 93); and "a particular set of social circumstances existing at the moment determines which attributes of personality will confer leadership status and consequently determines which members of a group will assume the leadership role" (p. 91). Such leaders, of necessity, have influence (which an official head may not have), and, since this influence is based on popularity, physical coercion is never a tool of a leader (Tannenbaum, Weschler, and Massarik 1961: p. 27).

From this exposition, which reads like a political creed of democratic sociologists, it is only too obvious that the term "leader" can be used only in the context of small groups as they exist in the United States. The concept is inapplicable even in Europe, not to speak of African, Asian, and Papuan nations and tribal societies. Thus it is not an analytic concept that an anthropologist can use in comparative empirical work. It also includes several claims that simply cannot be true. If, for example, the leader must always follow the goals of his followers, how does he actually lead and influence his group? How do the group goals arise? Is it not the leader who usually formulates the goals and then influences his followers to try to achieve them? It appears to me that the group goal argument and conceptualization belong to the orthodox school of sociology, and the democratic free-choice qualifications of leadership to a modern American political philosophy.

The complementary term "headship" suffers no less from vagueness and cross-cultural inapplicability. A head, as distinguished from a leader, is supposed to be a person "occupying a formally designated position of headship" (Carter 1953: p. 261) which is "determined by caste, class, or other factors than popular selection and acceptance" (Gibb 1966a: p. 94). One may ask: What if a man from a certain caste, class, or of certain wealth (as among the Kapauku, where wealth is instrumental to leadership) is popularly selected as a leader? How do we designate such a hybrid? The sociological philosophers claim that heads, unlike leaders, need not have much influence in the group (Krech, Crutchfield, and Ballachey 1962: p. 423). To separate formal from informal leadership into two qualitatively and diametrically opposed categories and to assign to them two different terms (reserving "leader" for a very narrow, often chimerical popular, democratic, and informal *primus inter pares*) is an arbitrary procedure, heuristically undesirable from the comparative point of view. It reflects, perhaps, a current popular democratic philosophy, but it is certainly not the result of a conceptualization based rigorously upon empirical evidence of meaningful cross-cultural applicability. Rather than separate ascribed and achieved leaderships qualitatively in this way, I prefer to keep a unified concept of leadership and, in accordance with Krech, Crutchfield, and Ballachey (1962: p. 426), to make a simple distinction between formal and informal leadership, the two categories differing quantitatively only in the degree of formality and not in any qualitative respect.

From the above discussion it is clear that leadership cannot be defined, with any cross-cultural significance, by the personal attributes of a leader, because these reflect a multitude of cultures with a great variety of values specified for leadership, and of goals, structures, and functions of the groups in question (see also Krech, Crutchfield and Ballachey 1962: p. 423; Tannenbaum, Weschler, and Massarik 1961: p. 26). Nor is it helpful to employ sociological jargon and such impractical concepts as "syntality," "task-oriented activities," "pragmatism," "group-goal-advancement approach," and the like. To sum up the situation we may say that the qualitative characteristics of leaders and their roles, the content of their actions, and the goals to be achieved are all culturally relative and are therefore inapplicable to a cross-cultural definition of leadership.

The criteria for leadership that can be meaningfully employed in a universal sense are necessarily quantitative rather than qualitative in nature. They also have to be empirically demonstrable and easily accessible to ethnographers to be of heuristic value. Such criteria as changes in attitudes and values of followers, although quantifiable, are not easily observable. Actually, a leader in a sociological sense (rather than a psychological or philosophical sense) is not a person who necessarily influences the inner motivation and value system of the membership of a group; he is a person whose decisions are followed. In other words, he has an observable effect upon the *actual behavior* of the members of the group, who for this reason and only this reason, may be called his followers. Thus, to me, the definitions of leadership proposed by Krech, Crutchfield, and Ballachey—as persons "who influence the activities of the group" (1962: p. 423)—and by Bass, with his five types of leadership behavior (1960: p. 90), are infinitely more acceptable than those discussed above. It must be emphasized that the influence of a true leader has to be reflected in the behavior of his followers and that influence alone, without causing a behavioral effect (e.g., Tannenbaum, Weschler, and Massarik 1961: p. 24), is not adequate to define leadership. It was the behavioral changes of followers (their changed responses) that Muzafer Sherif measured in his experiments and that J. L. Moreno observed in his investigation of the interaction of infants (Sherif 1947; Bass 1960: p. 118; Krech and Crutchfield 1948: pp. 434–435).

For these reasons I shall not define authority qualitatively by attributes, by actions, or by "situational" criteria. Authority and leadership to me are functional concepts and as such should be functionally defined, as an individual or a group of individuals who initiate actions in a social group or whose decisions are followed by the majority of the group's members. This definition comes quite close to that of Chapple and Coon (1942: p. 333–335) and those mentioned in the preceding paragraph. It is also in agreement with Hollander and Julian (1968: p. 894), and includes as authorities the first three of ten types of "groups' central persons" listed by Redl: "the patriarchal sovereign," "the leader," and "the tyrant" (1966: pp. 77–86).

It is obvious that formality, a specific amount of power, and permissiveness are irrelevant for my definition of authority and leadership, although, of course, they will be important as soon as we consider different types of authorities. Also, an authority is not defined as an "expectation" of somebody's performance (as does Bass 1960: p. 226), but *ex post facto* by his actual performance—influence upon the behavior of his followers. If there are any universal attributes of leadership, they are assertiveness and initiative, which is supported by Carter's findings in his small-group research in which there was always a marked quantitative difference in these respects between the leader and the followers (1953: p. 273).

In practice, to determine who is the leader of a group, or whose legal decisions are accepted by a group, entails study and recording of actual cases of problems and conflicts, their outcomes, and the roles the various group members play in relation to these outcomes. It is not enough to rely on—although admittedly one often can trust (but not necessarily always!) the "sociometry of leadership"—the opinions of the group members. The result, contrary to the opinion of Gibb (1966b: pp. 669–674), is not an identification of leadership; it is only an identification of the people's opinion of who the leader or leaders are. Thus, unfortunately, we cannot employ the easy shortcut of eliciting people's opinions—we have to undertake the tedious and onerous task of generalizing on the basis of a thorough casuistic approach.

One more aspect of the definition has to be clarified. So far, I have used the terms "leader" and "authority" as if they referred to precisely the same concept. True enough, as far as the definition and discussion above are concerned; there has not yet been a need to differentiate them. Also, if my theorizing were limited to tribal societies the two terms could stand for exactly the same concept. Unfortunately, in civilized society, with the refined division and subdivision of labor and functions, a legal authority (a judge) can hardly be called a leader. First, a judge has ceased to be a political leader and specializes in matters of law only; second, it is not his duty to participate in the execution of legal decisions (because civilized societies have specialized executive organs such as police, administrative clerks, jailers, executioners, etc.). His only function is to hand down legal decisions. Thus I distinguish here between a leader who, in addition to making decisions, also *actively directs and thus participates* in the execution of his decisions, most of which are political and therefore nonrepetitive—*ad hoc* in nature, and an authority whose primary function is to pass decisions. In some cultures (especially tribal), of course, passing decisions is combined with actual participation in the group's activities and thus an authority may be—and in the tribal societies usually is—also a leader.

Types of Leadership and Authority

Because cultural values vary from society to society, specific cultures require special attributes from their authorities, attributes that often differ fundamentally. In one culture an aggressive individual with excessive power may be favored, whereas in another the opposite may be true. The nonuniversal attributes allow the authorities to be classified into categories of different types. The social-scientific literature contains a great assortment of these types, usually arranged in dichotomies. I present here four such dichotomies, two of which I regard as ethnologically important and cross-culturally applicable.

I will start with a dichotomy I regard as spurious: namely the "effective" versus "ineffective" (sometimes called "attempted") leadership. For Tannenbaum, Weschler, and Massarik (1961: p. 26) an attempt to lead seems to be sufficient for regarding an individual as a leader (see also Bass 1960: p. 90). If the attempt succeeds the leadership is called effective; if not, it is termed "attempted" or "ineffective." To confuse the issue even further, an effective leader is regarded as an individual who, through his leadership and the conformity of this followers, attains the latters' goals (Bass 1960: p. 119). Or, as Fiedler puts it, leadership effectiveness can be evaluated "in terms of group performance on the group's primary assigned task" (1967: pp. 9, 31). To these statements I reply first (since I have defined authority and leadership functionally as manifested by an actual conformance of the followers to the authority's decisions) that an attempted but unsuccessful (or ineffective) leadership is in my opinion no leadership at all. Second, if effectiveness is defined in terms of achievement of the "group goals" or "primary tasks" of the followers, then a leader who induced his constituency to achieve goals that he himself has conceived (goals that can hardly be called "group goals") would have to be, as absurd as it may sound, classified as "ineffective." Such leadership is actually more effective than leadership based on an achievement of goals already espoused by the followers.

Another dichotomy of leadership types has been labeled as "coercive versus permissive" or "authoritarian versus democratic." A coercive leader is supposed to control his followers by "brute force." He relies on orders (Krech, Crutchfield, and Ballachey 1962: p. 434) rather than on persuasion;

thus his personal ability is irrelevant, and his followers comply with his commands only in public. His power rests on the fact that his followers are strongly motivated to gain what the leader can give, a motivation that is held to be essential to any type of social control or leadership. Control itself is viewed as ability to impose standards and enforce rules (Bass 1960: pp. 222–228). Thus a coercive or authoritarian leader is regarded as achieving only public compliance by wielding absolute power and employing direct control by discouraging interpersonal relations (Krech, Crutchfield, and Ballachey 1962: p. 435). He is supposed to be aloof, determining all policies without discussing with his followers the goals, standards, and methods that he employs (Lippitt and White 1966: p. 525).

Opposed to this type stands the permissive democratic leader, who uses persuasion rather than coercion, who even permits his followers to select their goals from within a permitted range, and who uses his power in such a way as not to create the conflicts produced by coercion, thus effecting public as well as private compliance (Bass 1960: pp. 236–238). Unlike his authoritarian, coercive counterpart he is supposed to encourage interpersonal relations among his followers and their participation in the determination of the group's objectives (Krech, Crutchfield, and Ballachey 1962: p. 435). Under such leadership the followers are well informed about goals and standards and are rewarded with praise and criticism by their leader, who even delegates some responsibility to the group (Lippitt and White 1966: p. 525). To this dichotomy Lippitt and White add a third type of "laissez-faire leadership" in which the "leader" plays a fully passive role, leaving to the group complete freedom as to decisions and activity. This third type, if it actually exists anywhere, I would hesitate to call leadership. To an ethnographer with cross-cultural experience it is obvious that this dichotomy reflects categorization derived from the political philosophy of Western societies rather than from worldwide leaderships. The conglomerate of attributes of either of the polar types would prevent an ethnographer from including most tribal authorities and leaders within its scope. Consequently, I propose to disregard it in the following discussion.

Of far greater significance than the above dyadic leadership configurations are two sets of leadership and authority dichotomies which, by employing just one criterion each, distinguish between types on the basis of quantitative rather than qualitative differences. Whereas the first uses extent of power as its criterion, the second categorizes authorities and leaders according to their degree of formality. So we obtain two mutually independent and qualitatively different ranges of authority types within which the individual authorities will be quantitatively differentiated according to the amount (extent) of their power in the first range, or degree of formality in the second range. The extreme position in the first range will be occupied at one end by an authority with narrowly limited power and, at the other by one with absolute power. In the second range pertaining to the degree of formality, there is a gradation from a totally informal to a strictly formal authority. The extremes should be considered ideals, approximated in only a few cases. In terms of these two sets of dichotomies any given authority can be defined by a combination of their two attributes—by the particular positions they occupy in the two ranges.

The Power Range of Authority Types. The authority types are defined here by the extent of power. In accordance with current sociological and social-psychological definitions, power is defined as a potential to influence. A leader (authority) may be said to possess this potential when his followers are motivated to comply with his decisions and wishes because of their desire to gain what the authority is able to give (Tannenbaum, Weschler, and Massarik 1961: p. 26; Bass 1960: p. 222). The desideratum may be a reward of any kind—material, immaterial, or psychological, it may also be negative—(an escape from punishment). The particular amount of power may be expressed by the effectiveness of an inventory of rewards and punishments available to the leader, or by the limits imposed by a superior authority, custom, law, or public opinion upon his use of these. Consequently, definitions of power in terms of political or democratic ideals of Western sociology, such as those of Kelman, who defines power "as the extent to which the influencing agent is perceived as instrumental to the achievement of the subject's goals" (1966: p. 142), have to be rejected here.

An authority may set goals which may be contrary to the interests of his followers. Yet if he can induce or coerce them into achieving these goals, he must be said to possess power over them, whether a Western idealist likes it or not. The ideal authority extremes on this range of power may be defined as follows. A "limited authority" assumes his position through a procedure which is controlled by the society. Approval by the majority of the members of the group is necessary, or nomination by another person with relatively greater authority (and power) takes place. An authority of this type has very little power. If he breaks the law, he is punished either by the members of his group or by his superior. His power is thus checked by factors such as custom, public opinion, constitutional law, and power of a superior authority. On the opposite end of our power range stands the "absolute authority." His power is not limited by someone else, nor is it checked to any marked degree by custom or public opinion, or any other institution. An excessive subordination of his followers is emphasized in personal contacts. One tends to view such authority as an end in itself and not as a means for achieving something. The power range itself may be further subdivided into as many segments as the ethnographer wishes, identifying them either by new analytical labels or (while maintaining the dualistic nomenclature division of "limited and absolute") by providing the categories with epithets added to the main dyad (e.g., "extremely limited," "moderately limited," "moderately absolute," "excessively absolute" authorities, etc.).

The Formality Range of Authority Types.   The formality range is defined by the degree of formality and may be divided into two main parts. Specific authorities placed within this range in accordance with the amount of formality they possess can then be classified as informal or formal (see also Hollander 1964: p. 6). If these authorities happen to belong to tribal societies we may, in accord with the common ethnological usage, call the informal tribal authorities "headmen," and the formal tribal authorities "chiefs." An extreme informal authority may be characterized by an absence of ceremony and publicity as far as his selection for and assumption of office and as far as execution of his powers are concerned. The acquisition and the holding of this position tend to depend upon the personality of the informal authority, on his skills and achievements, and on his conformity with the ideal pattern of authority and leadership set up by the particular society. His rights, duties, extent of power, and procedures that he follows are not defined in any precise way by either law or custom.

This is the type of authority that Tannenbaum calls a leader because he possesses the ability to cognitively structure the changing social situation and adapt his political moves to it skillfully (1961: pp. 39–41). The opposite ideal of an extremely formal authority is characterized by the fact that his role, rights, duties, and procedures are defined by law or custom, or both. The publicity given to the ceremonial aspects of his investiture, to his activities, and to the relinquishing of his position are emphasized. The formal aspect of the office of authority is often so important that irrespective of the incumbent's actual ability and power vis-à-vis other individuals of his group, his position is sufficient to induce the other members of his group to regard him as a leader (see esp. Kohlberg 1963: p. 309; Hovland, Harvey, and Sherif 1966: pp. 194 ff.). Accordingly Cardinal Richelieu, although the power behind the throne of Louis XIII and the chief royal adviser and actual mastermind of the internal and external politics of France, and decidedly its most forceful and able politician, cannot be regarded as an authority and leader of the French people. The weak king, who listened to the cardinal's proposals and almost slavishly implemented them was the real French leader because it was to him and not to the cardinal that the people looked for guidance and decisions. If the king had had the courage to disagree with his cardinal, the king's word would have prevailed.

By measuring the two variables above, we should be able to place each authority in a position that indicates his qualities within the two ranges. An authority then will be defined by combinations of the two measured attributes as follows: formal and absolute, informal and absolute, formal and limited, or informal and limited. The distance from the extremes of the two ranges can be expressed qualitatively by labels, as suggested above, or quantitatively by numbers on a scale into which the given range may be subdivided.

Concrete Examples of Authority Types. Without attempting to set up exact subdivisions of the four main classes of authority (leadership) types, in the following discussion I shall give some examples of authorities drawn from various cultures. Because of an absence of pertinent formal law or custom, informal authorities of the same type of groups (such as clans, confederacies, etc.) in a given tribe may be represented by headmen whose power and consequent influence vary according to their differing personal abilities to such an extent that some must be regarded as belonging to the informal absolute and others to the informal limited types. For example, the Kapauku Papuans of New Guinea have lineage and sublineage authorities who are called *tonowi.* Because of a lack of ceremony in passing decisions, because of the dependence upon personal skill and the achievements of the individual, and because the rights, duties, and procedures of adjudicating cases are not explicitly defined by law or custom, the Kapauku *tonowi* has to be classified as an extremely informal authority. The Kapauku headmen accumulate power and influence which differ remarkably from one individual to another. Pigome Pegabii, the leader of the Pigome Obaaj lineage of the Obajbegaa village, had very limited power because of his placid personality and lack of assertiveness. In contrast, the *tonowi* of the Botukebo village, Dimiidakebo, can be called an absolute headman (an absolute and informal authority). Being a very rich and extremely aggressive individual and a shaman reputed to possess magical powers, he terrorized his followers into what may be properly called excessive submission. The freedom-loving Kapauku retaliated by sorcery which, according to the opinion of all Botukebo residents, killed the "immoral" headman (probably because of its psychosomatic effects). Nevertheless, during his tenure he represented a cultural paradox—a Kapauku *tonowi* with absolute power (for further information see Pospisil 1958a: p. 109).

A similar variation in the degree of power of an informal authority can be found among the Eskimo. Peter Freuchen described an Iglulik Eskimo, headman of a local band, who was the worst kind of despot (1931). On the other hand Kakiña, a Nunamiut Eskimo *umealik* (headman) of the Anaktuvuk Pass band, was certainly limited as far as power was concerned. Although a very skilled hunter and wealthy man who also possessed shamanistic skills, he had to compete for leadership in the band with Paneak and Mapterak, who also possessed outstanding leadership qualities and influence (Pospisil 1964: esp. pp. 413–26). Consequently, the families of these men and Mapterak's stronger political faction could not be dominated and terrorized as was the case in the band described by Freuchen.

The informal headmen of the Yaghan Indians of Tierra del Fuego, the *tiamuna,* also differed, from individuals with limited power to headmen who literally dominated their local groups (Gusinde 1937, vol. 2: esp. pp. 779, 803, 829). The *kemal* headmen of the neighboring Ona Indians presented a similar combination of informality with varying degrees of personal power

(Gusinde 1937, vol. 1: esp. p. 422). Among the Jivaro, however, the *kuhaku,* the informal leader of a subtribal unit, as a rule had such limited power that he could scarcely be classified even as an authority with less extensive power (Tessman 1930: p. 360; Karsten 1935: p. 253).

In the formal authority categories we generally find less variation in the extent of power within a specific authority type. This is only logical because the amount of power a given authority wields often has formally and explicitly been determined by law or custom. The authorities of the Inca Empire, for example, were all formal, their investiture, term of office, amount of power, and jurisdiction being formally stated. The various types ranged from the Inca emperor (*Sapa Inca*), the formal and absolute ruler, through *capac* (viceroys), *hunu curaca* (commanding 10,000 men), *huaranka* (commanding 1,000 men), down to centurions and decurions, with progressively limited power and jurisdiction. Within these authority categories, however, the amount of power, competence, and jurisdiction was formally determined and therefore scarcely varied from individual to individual (Baudin 1928: pp. 120, 183; Murdock 1934: p. 432; Rowe 1946, vol. 2: pp. 263–271). The Mongol Empire exhibited a parallel (decimal) hierarchy of formal authorities; the power and jurisdiction were precisely determined for every class of authority from the absolute *Kha-khan* down to the decurion. Officially, no variation of power was allowed among the individual authorities of the same rank (Prawdin 1940: p. 77; Hudson 1938: pp. 96–97).

The logic of the rather rigorous relationship between formality and the prescribed power of individual authorities is unfortunately violated in some societies. Comparative investigation shows that although there are some societies in which the ideal is observed, in others it is corrupted by the behavior of individuals. Consequently, adherence to formally constituted powers ranges among societies from Austria, where the amount of power prescribed for the various ranks is meticulously observed without variation of any consequence (Pospisil 1962–1969), to Imperial China, where power, although determined in a formal way by edicts, law, and custom, varied considerably from one individual to another.

Functions of Leaders and Legal Authorities

As one may expect from the elusive nature of the concept, the function of leadership has been differently conceived by various authors. Again attempts to identify universal leadership functions have suffered from inadequate cross-cultural evidence, often being based only upon sociological research of groups from the Western civilization. We have already discussed some of these Western sociological biases which view the primary function of the leader as advancement of "group goals," or of the mystical group "syntality." Krech and coauthors view a leader as an executive who assigns tasks, formulates the policy of the group, is a source of information and skill, represents the group in the outside, and controls internal relations by purveying rewards and punishments (Krech, Crutchfield, and Ballachey 1962: p. 429). In the present context the claim that his functions include being a judge and conciliator (as punisher and rewarder) is of most importance (1962: pp. 429–430). To have his decisions and his proposals for action accepted, he (as an informal authority of the West with limited power) often has to function as a discussion leader in order to convince his followers of the desirability and correctness of his solutions (see also Bass 1960: pp. 104–105). Many social psychologists, preoccupied with their interest in inner motivations and attitude formation, have conceived the function of a leader to lie primarily in his ability to influence private acceptance of his decisions by his followers and, somehow only secondarily, to influence the behavior of the people (esp. Bass 1960: pp. 91–92; Tannenbaum, Weschler, and Massarik 1961: pp. 28 ff.).

The conscious preoccupation with changes in the followers' attitudes and inner acceptance can be securely linked to modern Western leadership. It is by and large not applicable to the leaders of many other societies who are mainly interested in their followers' conformance and are not bothered at all by whether their constituents like it. As long as they overtly follow, the leader is satisfied. This is true of the Kapauku, Eskimo, Hopi, and Tirolean leaders whom I have studied. Interestingly enough, the change in the inner motivation of followers became an obsession not only of Western psychologists and sociologists but also of the leaders of modern Western totalitarian regimes. For the dictators, conformance in overt behavior (a sufficient achievement for Eastern despots and for most tribal authorities) is not enough. They not only want to lead and direct the behavior of their subjects, but at the same time they want to be loved and have their decisions accepted as good and proper. A famous technique for achieving this goal in the Nazi and Communist dictatorships has been the famous mass brainwashing of people through propaganda, censorship, constant threat of severe punishment, and of concentration camps, and isolation from the outer world (by the Iron Curtain, etc.), and by individual brainwashing in solitary confinement. In our democratic, Western and especially in the American society, the insistence upon the change of inner motivation of an underling starts with the phrase "don't you think so?" when it is obvious that the individual, who meant to proceed in an entirely different way, obviously does not "think so" at all. Because this emphasis upon changes of inner motivation is nonuniversal, and even in the West is a recent folk idea, I insist that the main and universal function of leadership is a change in only the overt human behavior. Consequently, for my definition of legal authority only the function of passing legal decisions that are overtly accepted by the majority of the members of the authority's group would be important. This acceptance has to be external and need not include an internal conviction of the desirability of the decision.

One more point should be stressed as far as the functions of legal authority are concerned. Unlike our Western society, an authority in a tribal society does not usually limit himself to the legal field. In most cases the headmen or chiefs also hand down political decisions. In some societies tribal authorities may even pass important decisions in the fields of religion, education, and the economy. Only in some of the more advanced cultures and civilizations have exclusively legal functions been vested in specialized personnel.

Alleged Absence of Leadership and Legal Authority

My broad definition of leadership is applicable universally, and is attested in societies in which Western observers have denied the existence of leadership and law.

The Kapauku.   One such society is represented by the Kapauku Papuans of West New Guninea. A European who spent some time among them informed me upon my arrival in that country that there was a virtual absence of authority and leadership among these people. Another experienced man, a Dutch administrator, whose opinion I value very highly, substantiated the first statement but with an important qualification: "There is a man who seems to have some influence upon the others. He is referred to by the name *tonowi,* which means 'the rich one.' Nevertheless, I would hesitate to call him a chief or a leader at all; *primus inter pares* [the first among equals] would be a more proper designation for him. If you find out about his attributes and function, please let me know. He is a mystery to me."

Before dealing with the nature of Kapauku *tonowi* I must discuss briefly two basic values of these Papuans that directly bear upon this concept: the emphasis upon individualism and upon the physical freedom of an individual. These two values affect profoundly the manner of passing and the execution of the authority's decisions and the types of punishment at his disposal. There is no such thing in Kapauku society as imprisonment, bodily restraint, or enforcement of prescribed behavior by torture or physical harm or by threat of these. Moreover, there is no institution of war prisoners, slaves, or anything that would even approximate the old domination of the European peasantry by the landlords. A heinous criminal or a captured enemy would be killed but never tortured or deprived of his liberty. A culprit might be beaten or even wounded with an arrow, but he would always have a chance to run away or fight back. If he did not do so, it would indicate that he preferred to accept the punishment and resume a normal life with his people. The Kapauku believe that freedom of action is essential to life. When a body is physically forced to remain in one place such as prison, or forced to work, the soul, displeased with the state of affairs and especially with the impossibility of directing the body's activity, leaves the body, thus causing death. "As in disease, you cannot move and the soul leaves," was the opinion of Ijaaj Awiitigaaj of Botukebo.

Freedom of movement and of premeditated action is the basic condition for life. Consequently, in this society one cannot expect to find a formalistic "enforcement of laws and of an authority's decisions." Inducement would be a more suitable description of the agent of social control. A child, for example, may be slapped for not having done something properly but cannot be beaten into doing it better. Sanction works as an inducement for better behavior in the future but not as an enforcement of immediate behavior. Thus, one is independent in the sense that all actions follow one's own decisions rather than those of someone else, which would be regarded as giving up the vital cooperation of soul and body—an equivalent to death.

It is natural that the pattern of Kapauku freedom and independence is reflected in the sphere of economics. We can call this phenomenon "individualism," and in many respects it exceeds even the American concept.

"Two people cannot work together, because they have two different minds," was the answer given by informants to a question about why there is always only one owner of a thing. A house, boat, bow and arrows, field, crops, patches of second-growth forest, or even a meal shared by a family or household is always owned by one person. Individual ownership, contrary to the findings in the Paniai region (De Bruijn 1953), is so extensive in the Kamu Valley that we find the virgin forests divided into tracts which belong to single individuals. Relatives and husbands and wives do not own anything in common. Even an eleven-year-old boy can own his field and his money and play the role of debtor and creditor as well. There is no communal territory or corporations. This type of economy thus reflects the basic cultural value placed upon personal independence in thinking and action.

"I do not like to be told when to make a field," would be another reason given for individual ownership. "That is yours, and here is my property, and everyone knows what belongs to him," is a common statement in defense of the system of private ownership. "If we were both owners we would quarrel too much, we would steal from each other in order to obtain most from the field. My children and wives would probably go hungry—oh, it would be bad."

This individualism and independence, reflected in various aspects of the Kapauku culture, as well as in the absence of "enforcement" and of the sequence "order—execution of order," give an outsider the impression of a virtual absence of authority and lead him to the conclusion that all the people are equal (*pares*) in the importance—that there are no leaders and no followers. But how does one account for the individual called *tonowi* and the fact that the people, although equal and independent, seem to follow the "mysterious man" referred to by the Dutch administrator. The easiest way to resolve this dilemma is to assume that "all people" move in a certain direction. The *tonowi* happens to be the *primus inter pares,* first among equals, who does not actually lead but happens to be the first one moving toward the goal which would be achieved by the rest of the people even without his guidance. This simple explanation, no matter how pleasing to some social determinists, is based upon the Durkheimean myth that the individual can be separated from society but it bears no relationship to reality at all.

The Kapauku *tonowi* is usually a healthy man in the prime of life. *Tonowi* means literally "a wealthy man," an individual who has a great amount of cowrie-shell money, extensive credit, several wives, approximately twenty pigs, a reasonably large house, and many cultivated fields. His wealth carries with it the highest prestige and is the main measure of his status. With the accumulation of personal property, he has climbed the Papuan social ladder, acquiring more respect until he reached the status of a *tonowi*. This is the dream of every Kapauku youth, a position achieved, however, by very few. Since the amount of riches a person assembles depends primarily upon his own work and skill, it is directly related to his physical condition. There are no *tonowi* who are feeble or immature and inexperienced. Although many *tonowi* achieve this position by their own endeavors, a generous inheritance may accomplish the same result if it is received by a capable man. In summary, the status of a *tonowi* depends on wealth, the increase and decrease of which cause parallel changes in the social standing of the individual, which is a condition *sine qua non* for political and legal leadership.

Although economic success is the basis for becoming a Papuan authority, not all *tonowi* have followers and can pass decisions. Only some of them achieve this status. In other words, there are criteria other than sheer wealth which define a man as a leader. The way in which capital is acquired and how it is used make a great difference; the natives favor rich candidates who are generous and honest. These two attributes are greatly valued in the culture. A man who steals from others, borrows without repaying, and acquires money under false pretenses rather than through honest business deals, or a selfish individual who hoards money and does not lend it never sees the time when his word will be taken seriously and his advice and decisions followed, no matter how rich he may become. The people believe that the only justification for becoming rich is to allow the redistribution of property through loans to one's less fortunate fellows—a procedure which also gains supporters. Thus, the emphasis upon capital and the acquisition of money is balanced by the highest value of the culture, *ba epi*— "generosity." In the Kamu Valley, the rich men who fail to comply with this expectation are ostracized, reprimanded, and thereby induced to become generous. In the Paniai Lake region the people go so far as to kill a selfish rich man because of his "immorality." His own sons or brothers are induced by the rest of the members of the community to dispatch the first deadly arrow. *Aki to tonowi beu, inii idikima enadani kodo to niitou* ("you should not be the only rich man, we all should be the same, therefore you only stay equal with us") was the reason given by the Paniai people for killing Mote

Juwopija of Madi, a *tonowi* who was not generous enough. The people resented the fact that his son, who helped execute his father, was put into prison by the white police. It did not matter that he was sentenced for only three months.

Because the highest status in the culture is achievable through the well-known Kapauku practice of lending money and the hoarding of wealth for its own sake is considered unethical and is punishable by reprimands, ostracism, and gossip, the people, although very willing to discuss their borrowing, are rather secretive about their cash so that no one can ask them for a loan or charge them with selfishness. A rich man in Kapauku society wears the same clothes as others, eats only a little better, and when he kills a pig he distributes the meat often without tasting it himself. His house is large, but not because he would like to display his wealth. He needs it because of his many wives, children, "helping boys," and friends who live with him, in the *tonowi's* house. Thus, (contrary to Veblen's generalization), the rich Kapauku Papuan is conspicuous, not because of his consumption, but because of his "generosity" (in making loans).

The *tonowi* who is generous and "moral" in the above-mentioned sense is sometimes called a *maagodo tonowi*—a really rich man. Only such a man becomes an authority with followers, most of whom are his debtors. Thus the economic institution of credit plays a basic role here in the political as well as legal structure.

Eloquence and the art of rhetoric are the final criteria of a Kapauku *tonowi*. Ijaaj Timaajjokainaago of Botukebo, although a very rich, generous, and honest man, is not a leader of his community because he is afraid to talk at a gathering. Unfortunately, he is pushed aside by a man who is less rich and less moral, but is brave and an excellent public speaker.

In addition to the wealth, generosity, and eloquence that define an individual as an authority in the Kapauku society, there are some qualities which, although not indispensable, enhance the position of a headman. Bravery in war makes a man a *jape uu me* ("a war leader"). If the *maagodo tonowi* has this quality his prestige is multiplied and his position is more secure. Skilled shamanism is highly valued by the natives, and the practitioner occupies a status second only to the headman. If the *maagodo tonowi* happens to be also a shaman, his prestige reaches the highest peak achievable in the Kapauku culture. This individual's power tends to transcend the limits of his community and to elevate him to the leadership of his lineage or even of the political confederacy, as we shall see.

Followers stand in various relations to the leader, and their obedience to the headman's decisions is motivated by their particular relations to him. Thus *imee bagee* (the kinsmen) support and follow their rich relative because their kinship ties create an emotional bond as well as a network of duties, rights, and expectations of future favors. It is good for a Kapauku to have a close relative as headman because he can then depend upon his help in economic, political, and legal matters. The expectation of future favors and advantages is probably the most potent motivation for most of the headman's followers. Strangers who know about the generosity of a head-man try to please him, and people from his own political unit attend to his desires. Even individuals from neighboring confederations may yield to the wishes of a *tonowi* in case his help may be needed in the future. As has been pointed out, one is never forced into obedience and not one of my 160 informants admitted being afraid of physical punishment from the leader. Most of them, however, tried to avoid public reprimand administered by the leader as well as the consequent ostracism by other people and loss of face.

Debtors form one of the most dependable categories among the *tono-wi's* adherents. Their fear of being asked to repay loans, coupled with appreciation for the credit allowed, makes them stout supporters. They are always dependable in war or in a legal suit. One might wonder whether the death of a *tonowi* would not afford the debtor an easy release from his obligation, but no assumption could be more erroneous. Debts and credits are inherited. Since one always has personal and, as a rule, cordial relations with one's creditor (whereas one cannot depend on the "generosity" of the heir), the life and welfare of the *tonowi* are of vital concern to his debtors.

Ani jokaani, ("my boys") form a very special group of the *tonowi's* partisans. These adopted young men are not only very dependable and faithful, but they are always at hand and ready to help whenever the need arises. They come to live with the rich man to learn, especially how he transacts business, to secure his protection, to share his food, and, finally, to be granted a substantial loan for buying a wife. In return, they offer their labor in the fields and around the house, their support in legal and other disputes, and their lives in case of a war. The boys may be from different sibs and confederacies, or they may be relatives. The *tonowi's* house thus constitutes an educational and economic institution, as well as a unit impor-tant in politics, law, and war. The "students" form a bodyguard for their *tonowi* and thus, by their physical presence alone, induce other people to respect the wishes of their leader. However, this contractual association is quite loose. Both parties are free to terminate it at any time and the boy is never treated as an inferior by the rich man. He had the right to be fed, housed, and protected. Moreover, the *tonowi* is morally obligated to buy a wife for "his boy" if the latter has fulfilled his duties. That is, the headman cannot be compelled legally to fulfill the obligation, but a boy, cheated by his master, would become his enemy and spread damaging propaganda about him.

The followers of a *maagodo tonowi* may constitute a political faction in a sublineage whose members live in one or several villages, a whole sublineage, a lineage, or even a political confederacy sometimes numbering over a thousand individuals. As the confederacy leader, he is usually the one to make decisions about war and peace. He can persuade the unit to support a man in a dispute or to fight for his cause against other confederacies. He may prevent a war, on the other hand, if he admits the guilt of his followers and pledges to repair the damage. Authorities of lesser groups also have much to say in such matters and can influence the decision of a confederacy leader. For some "justified reasons" they may withdraw the support of their constituents and thus sometimes induce others to oppose the decision of the headman. Since there are disputes between lineages, sublineages, and political factions within the confederacy, the leaders with their units may, in an extreme situation, wage an intersublineage or interlineage stick battle against their fellow opponents.

All the *tonowi* function as authorities in disputes among their followers. In this field of social control especially, the native leader's role as an authority, negotiator, and arbiter is most important for the effective functioning of the group. His word also carries weight in economic and social matters: the pig feast, the communal dance expedition to other villages, the inducement of a man to become a feast's cosponsor, the digging of a large drainage ditch, or the building and repairing of a bridge demands the support of a *tonowi.*

From what has been said, one would assume that a given group would have a single authority. Although this is usual, it is by no means the only possibility. Some villages are led by two *tonowi* who share the power. In most cases their condominium is marked by full cooperation and respect for each other's decisions. In the Dou village of Bunauwobado within the Ijaaj-Pigome confederacy two brothers, both *tonowi,* peacefully manage the political and legal affairs of the community. Dou Akoonewiijaaj of Bunauwobado, the older of the two brothers, seems to have slightly more prestige than his younger sibling, Dou Onetaka. Nevertheless, he always upholds his brother's decisions. When one of the *tonowi* argues in a dispute, the other keeps out of it, and his comments and answers to questions about his own opinion always convey the notion "You heard my brother, he spoke well." The jurisdiction is simply determined by the first comment from an authority in a given case. There are other villages in the southern Kamu Valley where the cooperation of two authorities is as smooth as that mentioned above. However, not all personalities are compatible, and thus not all Kapauku coleaders tolerate each other or show mutual respect. Rivalry for leadership within the group may split it into two political factions exhibiting mutual suspicion, intolerance, and even hostility, thereby weakening the solidarity and consequently the power of the unit as a whole. This was the case in the Botukebo sublineage.

The Ijaaj-Pigome confederacy is composed of the Ijaaj Gepouja lineage (which occupies five villages), the Pigome Obaaj lineage of the Obaj-begaa community, the small Ijaaj lineage of Notiito, and the Dou Pugaikoto lineage of Bunauwobado (a less closely allied member). The lineages have single *tonowis* excepting the Dou lineage, which has two brothers as leaders. The Notiito Ijaaj, the Obajbegaa Pigome, and the Bunauwobado Dou each occupy only one village. There is no differentiation into sublineages in the last three groups. Since they have relatively small populations, it is apparent that the much stronger Ijaaj Gepouja lineage would be most likely to furnish a leader for the confederacy.

An athletic man of about forty years of age whose name is Ijaaj Ekajewaijokaipouga, and whose large house (an area of sixty square meters) stands in the swamp of Aigii, the most western village of the confederacy, is headman of the whole political federation, as well as that of the Ijaaj Gepouja lineage. In his person he combines several political functions, and thus his position is a very complex one. He is the leader of the following units: his household, Ijaaj Jamaina sublineage, Ijaaj Gepouja lineage, and Ijaaj-Pigome confederacy. This accumulation is nothing exceptional. Actually it is a rule in this society that a man cannot control a more inclusive grouping unless he leads one of its constituent subgroups. The five different roles which converge in this one individual manifest themselves in decisions which are necessarily different, corresponding to their pertinent levels in the four-tiered hierarchy. When he is deciding a dispute between the members of his household, no other *tonowi* can say anything. On the contrary, in dealing with a case involving members of different lineages, he has to listen to the arguments of the leaders of the other lineages and try to convince them of the correctness of his own decision. The leaders of the other four lineages function always as consultants in matters that concern the whole political unit. Ekajewaijokaipouga is the richest man in the southern Kamu Valley and one of the greatest *tonowi*.[4]

This headman is also an excellent speaker and one of the most power-

---

[4]His fortune amounts to five wives, cash amounting to 2,400 Kapauku cowries (representing a buying power of 120 medium pigs, each weighing 90 kilograms), 3,600 imported cowries (equivalent to 18 medium pigs), 3,300 beads (equivalent to 5.5. medium pigs), 10 *dedege* necklaces and 10 *pagadau* necklaces (equivalent to one medium pig), and 5 axes (equivalent to one medium pig). In addition to this currency, he owns 42 pigs. His credit is about as extensive as his cash. He bought wives for eleven people who have not yet returned the money. These loans total 1,040 Kapauku cowries (equivalent to 52 medium pigs), 365 imported cowries (equivalent to two pigs of 70 kilograms of weight each) and 420 beads (equivalent to a 45-kilogram pig). He has a credit with twenty other individuals amounting to 1,200 Kapauku cowries (equivalent to 60 medium pigs). His generosity is praised by all the people who know him. The large amount of cash mentioned above is not simply hoarded. 600 Kapauku cowrie shells and the same number of imported cowrie shells as well as 3,000 beads were set aside for the sons as their inheritance. Since this headman imposed a taboo upon this money, which prevents him from using it otherwise than for the inheritance mentioned, these savings are considered most generous and give the man additional prestige. The rest of the cash is hidden, and other people do not know of its existence. I, as the best friend of this man, have been told the exact amount of the headman's property.

Index of values: One 90-kilogram pig equals 20 Kapauku cowrie shells, equals 200 introduced cowrie shells, equals 600 beads, equals 20 *dedege* necklaces, equals 20 *pagadau* necklaces.

ful shamans in the region, as well as a brave warrior. He mocks the enemy in songs, never takes cover in the tall grass, and dashes as close as thirty meters to the enemy's battle line to attack, with no shield on his back. Several deep scars on his chest, back, and limbs tell the story of his war exploits. In 1955 he had five boys as apprentices who lived in his house. About fourteen others already have married and left him, but their emotional bonds with their master persist.

Ekajewaijokaipouga is a shrewd politician who lends money to important people outside the confederacy, thus establishing a network of relationships all over the Kamu Valley. Because of this economic influence, his word is important beyond the boundaries of the Ijaaj-Pigome political unit, and his wishes and decisions, given support by his various debtors, form the nucleus of a phenomenon which although certainly not legal in nature, nevertheless recalls in its function our international law. Since he is considered very moral, and since his decisions incorporate the ideals of the Kapauku culture, these verdicts and opinions are respected even by some traditional enemies of his confederacy. Thus his judgments resemble a decision of the international court in The Hague. In this function, Ekajewaijokaipouga utilizes his relations with his best friends as the pillars to hold up his whole network of interconfederational influence.

The informality of the Kapauku headmanship, as well as the nature of the social control which relies primarily upon inducement rather than enforcement led Dutch friends of mine (administrators as well as missionaries) to conclude that Kapauku society lacked leadership and, consequently, also law. The Western cultural bias upon which this conclusion rests is too obvious to necessitate any further elaboration of my argument.

The Eskimo.   In a similar way some ethnographers have deprived Eskimo society of their leaders and their law. Their research was often hampered not only by Western folk concepts of social control and political leadership, but also by the unreasonable brevity of their research, ignorance of the Eskimo language, and reliance upon interpreters and "secondary informants" such as Western missionaries, travelers, and administration officers. Because of its formal and rigid nature, ethnographers have seldom disputed the existence of leadership and authority in the Eskimo family. In the nuclear and polygynous families the father wielded power and punished offenses not only psychologically (reprimand, admonition, ostracism) but also physically (e.g., slapping the children, beating the wife). In the more inclusive extended family, the old man (*HuFa* or *WiFa*) was the formal leader. He planned the hunting activities, directed the moving of camp in pursuit of game, and kept law and order within his group by restoring basically to psychological sanctions. Physically he could punish only his own spouse or young children.

When we turn from the family types to more inclusive groups, we find that previous writers either hesitated to recognize leadership within these units or absolutely denied that any exists. Hoebel, for example, calls a band's *umealik* (leader and owner of the large *umiak* boat) ambiguously "first among equals" (1954: p. 82). This seems to be a compromise, reflecting his reluctance to accept the paradox of leaderless, lawless, but functioning groups, as ethnographers have insistently portrayed the Eskimo. Nevertheless, he is quite explicit about the presence of leaders in the Eskimo local groups and villages and describes them as shrewd, rich owners of large boats, deriving their powers from informal recognition of their followers (1954: pp. 81–82). In contrast, Spencer acknowledges the presence of leadership among the Tagemiut and Nunamiut *umiak* crews and hunting bands, but he hesitates to ascribe political functions to this leadership and considers it primarily "ceremonial" (1959: p. 446). My data on the Nunamiut do not accord with such an interpretation. Although an *umealik* did have ceremonial functions, these were secondary to his economic and political ones.

For the Netsilik Eskimo, similarly, Van den Steenhoven claims a "formal anarchy" and absence of leadership beyond the family level. The reason for this claim is clearly stated: Individuals of influence lacked "formal authority" and "recognized jurisdiction" (1959: p. 17).

If we insist on formal criterion of leadership, we have to agree on its absence in a Nunamiut band or faction. Indeed, an *umealik* was an individual whose "star rose and fell," in Van den Steenhoven's words (1959: p. 17), with his popularity and prestige, and whose recognition by his followers was primarily a matter of their free choice. We may ask why the terms "authority" and "leadership" must be divorced from any consideration of personal prestige and personal achievement or of voluntary recognition by followers, when these represent the customary qualifications for leadership and authority. Leadership based, as we have seen, solely on such qualifications has actually been recognized in the literature as a type to which the term "headman" is applied.

The position of a Nunamiut headman was determined by two things. One was his attributes as a person—his personal qualifications for leadership. The other was his position in the societal structure (e.g., segmentation of society; for concept see Chapter Four), the subgroups to which he happened to belong, and the extent of his personal kindred and other quasi-group (i.e., ego-centered grouping) connections.

For leadership, possession of wealth was the most obvious attribute of an *umealik.* Personal wealth consisted of crystal beads, a large number of dogs, a tent, caches full of wolverine and wolf pelts, several kayaks, an *umiak,* and more than adequate supplies of food. It suggested to the Nunamiut the material security which its owner momentarily enjoyed, and of which followers might partake if they joined him, and it was also a manifestation of other important personal qualities. Amassed personal wealth showed beyond doubt that a man was a good hunter and a clever trader and husbander and that he possibly possessed numerous kindred. Accumulated wealth was freely displayed to friends as well as to outsiders. An *umealik* invariably wore fine garments, precious headbands, labrets, and neck laces, and drove a well-fed and well-trained dog team.

A candidate for Eskimo leadership created wealth by his hunting skill and shrewd trading with outsiders. However, his personal achievements alone were usually insufficient for leadership. His personal possessions had to be frequently augmented by generous gifts and loans extended by members of his kindred and by his friends. Thus these quasi-groups of consanguineal relatives and friends gathered and invested property for the benefit of an individual, often literally elevating him to the status of an *umealik*. It goes without saying that a Nunamiut who made such an investment selected from his kindred a man who was a good risk (energetic, or a good hunter, etc.). Consequently, other attributes were as important as the ownership of large property.

Spencer claims that hunting skill was not essential to the assumption of the position of an *umealik* (1959: pp. 445–446). It is true that a clever leader could find substitutes who would direct the hunt for him, although this was admittedly most unusual. But how would a poor hunter achieve a position of wealth and leadership? It is certainly unusual that a calculating Nunamiut would invest his riches in a man who was a poor economic risk. Moreover, wealth signified material security to the Eskimo, not because of itself (a band would consume an *umealik*'s property in a relatively short time), but because it suggested that its owner was a good provider—a security not so much for the present as for the future. Accordingly, an *umealik* had to be a good hunter, not only one who could shoot well and design the construction of a hunting corral, but especially one who could place the corral in an advantageous position and who could predict the movement of the caribou herds.

Also, an *umealik* was expected to be generous, especially with food and used clothing. Among the Nunamiut the simple hoarding of wealth did not attract followers; rather it created envy and hostility. Consequently, a headman was expected to distribute gifts at feasts following a successful hunting season, to care for widows and orphans of his group, to extend loans in the form of valuables, and particularly to save the families of his constituency for hunger in times of need. Especially he carried the continual burden of supporting the families of hunters who, through ignorance, physical handicaps, or age, were poor providers.

An *umealik* often augmented his fortune through successful trade deals in which he had to show unusual entrepreneurial skill and persuasive art. Also very important for holding his status was his mastery of Nunamiut lore, customary law, and ceremonial observance. Especially during ceremonies connected with hunting he had to impress his followers with his knowledge of ritual. A calm, unaggressive attitude was interpreted as a sign of the required high personal integrity and wisdom.

Calmness, however, should not be interpreted as weakness. An *umealik* was expected to pacify quarreling parties and to make important judgments, some of which might meet with public criticism. For these reasons he had to be assertive and decisive, and to have the courage to withstand public displeasure when his insight dictated unpopular decisions. Only such behavior, coupled with the other attributes, commanded the respect of his followers.

The power and influence of an *umealik* over his followers was often very pronounced, approaching at times that of an autocrat. This characteristic of the Eskimo headman was well recognized by Spencer: "In his own circle of relationship, the *umealik* could be a bully, and apparently often was, badgering his kin to be more cooperative and productive" (1959: p. 154). That such an individual was a political leader in his band can hardly be questioned. Only a persuasive and assertive *umealik* could keep effective control and hold the band together.

The foregoing personal attributes defined a Nunamiut *umealik* as a rich man who functioned in groups more inclusive than families as a political, economic, and legal authority. This status was achieved through his own initiative, as well as through the support he received from the members of his quasi-groups, such as his kindred, friends, trade partners. Consequently, acquisition and tenure of the status and title of *umealik* were functions of the social structure. On the other hand, the rank of a particular *umealik* within the Nunamiut leadership hierarchy was a function of the societal structure. Personal wealth and prestige alone could not disclose whether a particular *umealik* was a headman of a faction or of a whole band. In order to determine the headman's rank, the size and importance of his kin group, the number of close ties (through marriage or descent) with other kin groups, and the strength of these as against those groups affiliated with competing *umealit*[5] of the same band had to be taken into account.

A large Nunamiut band was not just a loose conglomeration of extended and nuclear (independent) families. Invariably, narrower alliances existed between these segments along political lines. These were often cemented by frequent intermarriages between families within these alliances which we may call "band factions." Each of these factions had a leader. If this individual was wealthy and possessed the other special criteria of Eskimo leadership, he held the social status of an *umealik*. His societal status, however, depended upon the relationship of his faction to the rest of the societal segments of the band. Accordingly, if his followers (not necessarily

---

[5] *Umealit* is the plural of *umealik,* the owner of an *umiak,* generally a wealthy man and an outstanding hunter and leader.

supporters from quasi-groups) were less numerous and of less prestige than those of his competitors, his authority was limited to his faction, and his societal status may be termed *"umealik* of a band faction."

If an ambitious, wealthy man aspired to the leadership of a whole band, he had first to command solid support from a large extended family. Consequently he was eager to have as many children as possible. Often he augmented the size of his nuclear or polygynous family by adopting orphans or children from poor homes. Thus the Eskimo "love for children" was founded on an important political consideration as well as on sentiment. To accentuate his influence even more, an ambitious man might try to extend his family by keeping as many of his married offspring as possible coresident with him. These efforts would draw criticism, especially if he attempted to dissuade his married sons from joining the families of their fathers-in-law. To avoid such criticism, a rich man would try to attract his sons' wives' relatives as well. This helps explain the web of intermarriages within band factions as they still occur in the Anaktuvuk band. Thus marriage ties served important political functions in the career of a Nunamiut headman. A band's *umealik* held two offices simultaneously; he was leader of his faction and also headman of the whole band. *Umealit* from the other factions supported him, remaining with their followers as segments of the band primarily for economic and defensive reasons. Also, an *umealik* of a band faction kept his group within the band in the hope that eventually he himself would succeed to the larger group's leadership.

Sometimes a faction had two wealthy men rather than one. Invariably the two were close relatives such as brothers, father and son, or more often father and daughter's husband. In the Anaktuvuk band, Kakiña and Paneak present an example of the last possibility.

We have demonstrated that an *umealik* wielded economic and ceremonial, as well as political, powers. Now it remains to show that an *umealik* was also an authority in the legal sphere, a leader who decided trouble cases and kept peace and order in his band.

Bands were united, as Spencer observes, through the presence of men of wealth (1959: p. 153). Need for leadership in the band was also stressed by my informant Iñualurak: "In the old days people tried to have a leader. A man who had a good position, who was wise, was taken as a head in the old days." As to his judiciary role, Iñualurak commented, "Anybody who was wrong was told [by the *umealik*] in the right way what he did wrong." The old hunter Ahgook corroborated these statements: "He [the *umealik*] tried to keep his people in line. If husband beat up wife, *umealik* would go after him and talk to him." Out of my 35 recorded disputes, 18 intraband trouble cases were settled by decisions passed by the *umealik*, supported by the old and wise men of the group. Only two were unadjudicated, probably because of their unimportance (both involved embezzlement of goods of little value). Six additional family cases were solved by pertinent

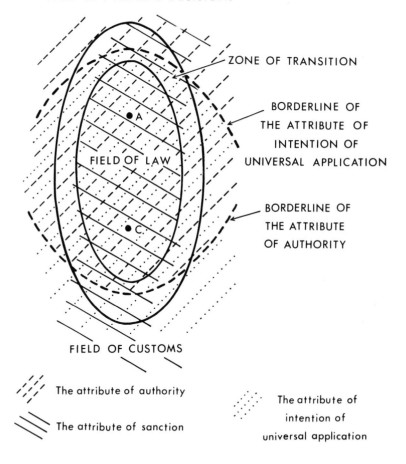

FIGURE 2. Attributes of Law

family authorities. By contrast, the remaining nine *interband* trouble cases did not involve any decisions but were settled through negotiations (four cases), were pacified by an *umealik* (one case), or resulted in feud and further killings (four cases).

An *umealik* derived his power over the litigants from his influence and economic importance in the community. Older men, who often formed a sort of advisory council for the *umealik,* supported his decisions, and, in the words of Iñualurak, "They threatened the guilty men to obey *umealik*'s decisions, otherwise they would not help him [the guilty man] in the future, [and] also they would not talk to him." The threat of ostracism was much feared and was a potent inducement to conformity. Ahgook characterized it as follows: "[The band members] make you feel like a lone wolf, it is probably everywhere the same." Most often, however, an *umealik* did not have to rely on support from other band members. His own threats of economic, political, or physical nature were enough to make people obey and accept his "verdicts." Ahgook gave me an example of such threats: "If you don't obey me you will get into trouble in the future. You will quarrel more in the future and I will not help you [then]." Threat of withdrawal of political protection used to be a very serious matter; it amounted to becoming a "legal outcast."

The decisions of an *umealik* were usually rendered informally, but formal "courts" were also held in the *karigi,* the men's house. A "native court" trying to solve a marital affair was actually witnessed and described by Ingstad (1954: pp. 114–118).

Ethnographers like Freuchen (1931), who meticulously described particulars of the Eskimo social life and were not satisfied with gross generalizations and superficial observations and accounts, could not miss, of course, the Eskimo leadership phenomenon. Nelson Graburn (another example), while describing the Taqagmiut Eskimo, refers constantly to local leaders (1968: pp. 2, 3, 7, 12, 15, 16) and specifically describes and emphasizes their making legal decisions and the compliance of their followers (1968: pp. 4, 5, 12). The execution of these decisions could hardly evoke the criticism of even our legal formalists (1968: pp. 5, 12).

THE ATTRIBUTE OF INTENTION
OF UNIVERSAL APPLICATION

While analyzing the library data on attributes of law as a preparation for my M.A. thesis on "The Nature of Law" (1952), I conceived of the field of law as an ellipse surrounded by a zone of transition which separated it from the rest of the culture (Figure 2). Social phenomena placed within the peripheral zone combined the overlapping criteria of the neighboring cultural categories to such an extent that it was difficult to determine which ones dominated the field. The attribute of authority, discussed in the previous section, constitutes the criterion that defines the lower boundary of the ellipse by separating law from the neighboring field of custom. Repetitive behavior, based upon the decisions and choices of followers, which is not the subject of the authority's decision is simply custom. At the upper end of the ellipse we find that the attribute of authority, covering the whole field of law, extends beyond the field's upper boundaries and penetrates the adjacent field of purely political decisions, which is situated in Figure 2 above the former.

In such tribal societies as the Nunamiut Eskimo, Kapauku Papuans, Cheyenne Indians, and Australian Aborigines, both political decisions and legal judgments are made by the same authority—the headman, the chief, or a council, as the case may be. Therefore there is evidently need for an additional criterion that would separate the legal and the political fields. The need is met by the second attribute of legal decisions, which I have called "the intention of universal application." This attribute, which I have found in various forms in the decisions of authorities of the societies I have studied or read about, demands that the authority, in making a decision, *intend* it to be applied to all similar or "identical" situations in the future.

The reader should note here that we are dealing with an intent and not necessarily with a regular, customary application of a rule or principle. Consequently, I recognize as legal a single unprecedented decision when this decision incorporates a principle that the adjudicating (deciding) authority intends to apply to similar cases in the future. This intention can take any of the actual forms that I describe below. The single decision that pronounces a new legal principle, whether by judge, chief, headman, or committee, we may regard as an act of legislation. In Chapter Six ("Change of Laws") I present a detailed and well-documented case of purposeful legislation by a Kapauku authority. That such a case is not unique in the tribal cultures is well documented by Llewellyn and Hoebel who cite a similar single legislative decision passed by tribal chiefs of the Cheyenne Indians:

> *Now we shall make a new rule: there shall be no more borrowing of horses without asking. If any man takes another's goods without asking, we will go over and get them back for him. More than that, if the taker tries to keep them, we will give him a whipping. (1961: p. 128)*

The explicit manifestation of the attribute of intention of universal application assumes different forms in the various cultures. In civilizations such as that of the Tirol or other countries of Continental Europe that have legal codes, the intention of universal application is expressed by a reference to a statute (abstract rule) made by the judge when he hands down a decision. It would be a mistake, however, to assume that such references to rules are the monopoly of civilizations. In some tribal societies, such as that of the Kapauku Papuans, a mental codification of abstract legal rules may exist. In decisions that resolve disputes among their constituents the Kapauku headmen refer to the rules that pertain to the legal problems at hand. In those civilized as well as tribal societies that have no such codification the discussed attribute manifests itself in the form of a citation of or a reference to a precedent (a particular decision of a case rather than a rule). In this sense a legal decision is, in Llewellyn and Hoebel's words, part of a "going order." In other tribal societies this attribute is manifested by an explicit statement of the authority that the decision being passed is in conformance with a well-established custom or current practice.

However, in many tribal societies such an explicit reference may not be made; it may be implied in grammatical form of the verb or in the syntax. Although in the decisions of the Kapauku *tonowi* the intention of universal application is usually made explicit by a reference to a particular rule or preceding judgment, the headman often satisfies himself with the use of the obligatory-repetitive tense aspect while referring to the nature of guilt and punishment. Accordingly, in the phrase *kou dani te tija* ("one does not act like that"), the verbal suffix *-ja* not only expresses the ideal, the moral obligation "ought," but it also stands for the customary, repetitive action which may be translated as "used to." In the anthropological literature, a statement which claims that the chief's decisions "preserved the old tradition, custom, or customary law" is nothing but the author's reference to the discussed attribute.

The presence of grammatical phrases or references to customs, precedents, or rules, used in all the decisions I have heard in societies that I have investigated, confirms my statement with respect to the ideal component of law discussed in the preceding chapter. As I stated there, not only does a legal decision solve a specific case, but it also formulates an ideal—a solution *intended* to be utilized in all similar situations in the future. The ideal component binds all other members of the group who did not participate in the case under consideration. The authority himself turns to his previous decisions for consistency. In a way, they also bind him. Lawyers speak in such a case about the binding force of the precedent, which is a form of legal justice. However, that does not mean that tribal or civilized authorities are always bound by the principles they have used in the past. By a change of law (new "legislation") or for personal gain they may introduce a new principle in an unprecedented decision. For example, Ijaaj Awiitijaaj of Botukebo certainly failed to emphasize an ideal when, for personal advantage and upheld by the strength of his following, he rejected his creditors' request for payment (1958a: pp. 232–233, cases 139–142). Nevertheless, he did not apply "unjust" decisions in cases where his own interests were not at stake (pp. 212, 220–221, 223; cases 105, 118, 119, 124). Because of the absence of the attribute of intention of universal application, several Kapauku cases recorded during my first research in New Guinea cannot be considered legal according to my theory (pp. 207, 232–233, 242; cases 97, 139, 140–142, 165). Kapauku informants agree, calling the decisions "bad" and "not binding," by which they actually mean "illegal."

The reader, however, should be cautioned against an assumption that inconsistency with the precedent alone excludes a decision as illegal. The decision in the legal case discussed later in Chapter Six (Pospisil 1958a: pp. 165–166; case 33; see also Pospisil 1958b) illustrates a radical inconsistency in the adjudication of the law of incest which, intended to be perpetuated and thus having the intention of universal application (a declaration that a formerly incestuous type of marriage was henceforth acceptable), does constitute law. It is the absence of this *intention,* rather than a lack of consistency, that excludes a decision passed by an authority from legality. Consequently, "regularity," or "system element," as Llewellyn and Hoebel called it (1961: pp. 284, 287), is, contrary to their opinion, not a true criterion of law, although it may be present in most of the cases adjudicated in a society. As these authors correctly and effectively observed,

> *the fact that the result in a trouble-case drives so strongly toward becoming precedent gives the imperative or standard repeatedly a chance to leap ahead of the actual behavior pattern—not to flow from a behavior pattern, but perhaps to create a pattern* on the model of even a single instance. *(1961: p. 287; italics mine)*

Indeed, if this is true, then certainly my criterion of "the intent" suffices to promote a single unprecedented decision to a law, without necessarily requiring a "regularity" or a "system element" that would also require the decision to be part of an already established "going order" (Llewellyn and Hoebel 1961: p. 284).

THE ATTRIBUTE OF *OBLIGATIO*

My cross-cultural comparative analysis of legal phenomena (decisions) brought out a third characteristic of law, an attribute which I call *obligatio.* It refers to that part of a decision which states the rights of one party to a dispute and the duties of the other. It defines the social-legal relations between the two litigants as they supposedly existed at the time of the defendant's violation of the law. It also describes the delict, showing how the relations became unbalanced by the act of the defendant. Thus the concept is a statement about a social relationship and as such it is two-directional. One direction originates in the person of the defendant, a person who by his (her, their) illegal act violated an approved relationship, thus creating on his (her, their) part a duty to correct the situation; the other direction emanates from the person who suffered a loss because of the act of the defendant, and who thus possesses the right to have the situation redressed, the right to expect an action or a sufferance on the part of the other party. As a consequence it is obvious that this criterion cannot be called obligation (as I originally did erroneously; Pospisil 1952: p. 70) because this English term refers only to the one-directional concept of the "duty" of the defendant. The old Latin term *obligatio* is more apt here because it refers to *iuris vinculum,* a legal tie between two parties, a tie that manifests itself in the form of a duty on the part of one and a right on the part of the other to a contract or litigation (Pospisil, 1956: p. 749; 1958a: p. 264).

In accordance with what I stated above, a pronouncement of an authority which gives one party a right while not stating the duty of the other one is not law even though the attributes of authority and of the intention of universal application are present. Such a statement becomes law only when a duty on the part of someone is implied or included in the decision. In my 1958 monograph on Kapauku law I described (1958a: p. 218; case 115) the mistreatment of a domesticated pig by its contractual breeder. The man neglected to feed the pig daily and the animal disappeared into the bush. The owner severely reprimanded the culprit and sought support from the local authority, but failed to receive a verdict imposing damages upon the man, who had obviously broken his contract. The culprit's liability for the loss of the pig was clearly recognized in the decision. The authority, however, probably for political reasons, did not affirm the right of the pig's owner for compensation. He only admonished both parties to the dispute to avoid violence. This case, then, does not represent the application of law because of the lack of the attribute of *obligatio.* Recognition of the defendant's liability reminds us of the fact that we are not confronted here with a verdict of not guilty.

Four additional trouble cases which I collected among the Kapauku (Pospisil 1958a: pp. 232–233; cases 139–142) demonstrate "verdicts" in which the pertinent authority acknowledges the rights of his creditors either explicitly or tacitly but, by using force and his influence as headman, avoided his duty to pay (these cases, in addition to the *obligatio* also lack the attribute of universal application). Thus absence of the attribute of *obligatio* results in an inconclusive settlement of a dispute and prevents the decision from becoming legal.

From what has been said above it should be clear that *obligatio* is not an obligation, in the English sense of the word. In his working paper MacCallum, while commenting on my book on the Kapauku law (1958a), made precisely this mistake. He identified *obligatio* with obligation, which led him to conclude that sanction is identical with *obligatio,* thus making sanction redundant as a legal attribute and allowing him to entitle his paper "Law without Sanction" (MacCallum 1964: esp. pp. 4, 5, 7). He viewed *obligatio* as the specific sanction (obligation) which the judge (legal authority) imposes upon the defendant in order to achieve a settlement of the trouble. Accordingly he views as *obligatio* such obvious sanctions as payment of indemnity or blood money, contractual payments, restitution, etc. (1965: p. 3). He failed to understand that what I meant by *obligatio* was a social relation which forms the basis for the authority's decision, a relation that involves the respective right and duty of the two parties to a dispute created by the illegal act of the defendant. Sanction is an additional and often separate part of the verdict, the judge's statement about how the *obligatio* should be resolved, and how the situation should be rectified. Although the duty, which forms part of the *obligatio*, is a general and categorical finding by the judge that the defendant is guilty of a breach of law (of violating the rights of the plaintiff), sanction is always specific—the judge's (authority's) decision about how the conflict should be resolved, how the *obligatio* should be balanced and the situation corrected. Even in our courts the verdict of guilty is often separated (sometimes by many days) from the "sentencing," or imposition of a particular sanction by the judge.

MacCallum further fails to make a distinction between the imposition of a sanction by the judge and "sanctioning"—the execution of a sanction imposed by a judge but performed by duly appointed executioners, jailers, police, and the like (1964: pp. 8, 9, 11). He speaks about "performance of *obligatio*" not realizing that *obligatio* cannot be "performed" (MacCallum 1964: p. 18), and he excludes sanction from the legal concept because the *sanctioning* is performed by individuals other than the authority (1964: pp. 11, 14). MacCallum also contends that *obligatio* is a sort of "consensus," a voluntary agreement of the two parties (1964: pp. 4, 12, 14). This is undoubtedly the case, but only when we deal with contracts whose violation made it part of an *obligatio*. However, in criminal cases such as murder, rape, and so on, we can hardly speak of any voluntary consensus between the parties, or about the "fact" that *obligatio* arises out of consensus (1964: p. 14). The obsession with consensus and absence of sanction and force from law leads MacCallum to a belief in the state's and legislator's legislative impotence (they discover law, they do not create it: 1964: p. 14), and that the authority is always an impartial third party (1964: p. 15). However, by far his most serious error is the failure to distinguish between jural and sociological (scientific) laws. Although we have to agree fully with MacCallum that "law is regularity discerned in the social data," nevertheless such regularity forms a sociological (scientific) law rather than a jural law. We are, of course, dealing here with a jural rather than a sociological concept. It is unfortunate that the two concepts bear the same term, which is indeed confusing. The 4,000-year-old error, by which the two types of social concepts—"laws"—were equated in Mesopotamia (because of the religious contention that God gave nature and man laws according to which they ought to behave) persists even nowadays, alas even among some anthropologists!

Another important characteristic should be noted while dealing with the *obligatio*. This attribute of law which forms part of the authority's decision is necessarily a new phenomenon created by the authority. It should not be mistaken for the actual, objective social relation or obligation existing or incurred previous to the decision, an infringement of which brought about the suit and the legal decision. This is because the legal authority, no matter how objective and just he may be, is in most cases unable to learn all the facts about the preexisting social relations or rights, obligations, and the violation. What counts in a legal decision is not what objectively existed but what is said in the decision to have existed, because this leads directly to the solution of the problem being adjudicated. The question of how far the actual facts differ from those included in the *obligatio,* and of whether the decision is therefore proper (just), belongs to the factual part of the problem of justice which is not our concern here. For example, in my collection of Kapauku Papuan legal cases (Pospisil 1958a: p. 195; case 81) the Ijaaj-Pigome confederacy headman decided that Akoonewiijaaj, accused of stealing one of his pigs, was not guilty of the crime. This outcome was due to a lack of conventional evidence about the crime, and it had little to do with the true state of affairs. My informants were thoroughly convinced that Akoonewiijaaj committed the crime. Although, according to the rules, if he stole the pig he was obligated to restore the stolen property, the *obligatio* of the decision failed to incorporate his guilt, and the verdict absolved the defendant from any responsibility. Thus the actual facts about the crime and the defendant's involvement were opposite to the *obligatio*—the statement of the rights and duties of the parties to the dispute in the verdict.

One more quality of *obligatio* is important for the ethnologist as well as the legal scholar. *Obligatio* is a relation between two parties who are both represented by living individuals. Hence all obligations toward the dead and toward the supernatural are excluded from legal consideration unless the interests of the dead or of the supernatural are represented by living people. On this point, then, I differ from Llewellyn and Hoebel (1961: p. 286) and maintain that a religious taboo "with no officials to enforce it" is not law, no matter how firmly such a taboo is established and believed in as a procedure for social control, but is a strictly religious phenomenon. If we were to include such taboos (where the privileged party is not represented by living people) in the legal field, this field would cease to exist because any kind of religious custom could creep in and break down its boundaries.

Because of these considerations I have excluded from the scope of law taboos imposed by Kapauku shamans upon specific individuals (Pospisil 1958a: p. 156; cases 17, 18). While in these cases the form of a decision and the criterion of an authority in the form of a shaman were present, the attributes of intention of universal application and of the *obligatio* were not part of the decision. First, the shaman did not intend to impose the same taboos upon other individuals in similar (in the Kapauku view "identical") cases. Any one of these specific taboos was regarded as a special remedy for a given case, with a particular consideration for the individual subjected to it, not to be repeated in the future. Second, the "entitled party," the supernatural, was not represented by the shaman who would act on his behalf as a plaintiff. On the contrary, if anything at all, the authority—the shaman—was more on the side of the subject of his cure (the defendant) whom he tried to help by the imposition of the taboo.

Another type of Kapauku religious taboo is represented by the prohibition of consuming (by mouth or by fire) a totemic animal or plant. This taboo, unlike those discussed above, does imply the intention of universal application which is reflected in the Kapauku rule (no. 12, Pospisil 1958a: p. 157) which states categorically: "An individual is tabooed to burn or eat totemic plants and animals of his own sib, his mother's sib, and also of the sib of his wife. The violator will become deaf." Although it comes closer in this respect to law, it lacks the attribute of authority and that of *obligatio,* and must consequently be regarded as a purely religious taboo.

In contrast to these nonlegal taboos are those which can be classified as laws because they possess the *obligatio.* Into this category fall the following two Kapauku trouble cases (Pospisil 1958a: pp. 157–158, no. 19, 21). In 1940 Dou Maga of Jotapuga village violated a taboo imposed upon all Kapauku women and ate fruits of the native plant called *apuu.* As a consequence, as it was believed, her husband Ijaaj Kagajtawii of Aigii died within a few days. Ijaaj Tideemanbii of Kojogeepa, the son of the victim, and one of the victim's other wives heard about the delict and reported it to Ijaaj Ekajewaijokaipouga of Aigii, the headman of the local confederacy. The latter, after having heard the witnesses and the defense of the defendant, was convinced that the charge was correct and decided on capital punishment. The victim's son, acting as executioner, shot the woman with an arrow while she worked in her garden. Other people of the Aigii village erected a platform in the community and left the corpse exposed on it with the executioner's arrow in the wound, as local custom prescribed. Thus, as a punishment, the defendant lost her husband to the "justice of the supernatural," and her own life to the justice of her society.

The other case involved violation of a Kapauku rule which states that a nightmare experienced by a woman during her first two menstruations, should be reported to her husband; not reporting it would cause her husband to die. A violator was to be beaten by her husband; in case of his death, she was to be executed by her husband's closest relative. Ijaaj Jokagaibo of Itoda, a sublineage headman at that time (June 1955), became sick. Ijaaj Umamuuma of Botukebo, a skilled shaman, diagnosed that three of Jokagaibo's five young wives had not reported nightmares during their menstrual periods. Since the shaman was not sure which of the wives were involved,

Jokagaibo refrained from ordering punishment and satisfied himself with only a few general threats and public complaints because sufficient proof for legal action was not produced.

As can be seen, in both these cases (of the second, legal category) there was, in addition to the violator of the taboos, a plaintiff who possessed the right to have the culprit punished. In the first (religious) category the punishment would be left to the discretion of the supernatural, and therefore be "more or less uncertain." In the second (legal) type of taboo the plaintiff himself, or a representative of his interests, would see to it that a "proper trial" took place and that the punishment was carried out.

Interestingly enough, Kapauku Papuans themselves have different attitudes toward the two sets of taboos which I have separated into two contrasting categories by the attribute of *obligatio*. They talk freely about violations of the purely religious taboos. Indeed, some individuals even boast about their disregard of supernatural prohibitions in order to demonstrate their bravery and courage. The violation of what we may call "legal taboos," on the contrary, is kept secret, since one does not boast in public about one's crimes punishable by the society.

The attribute of *obligatio* separates religious customs, exemplified by the purely religious taboos of the first category discussed above, from religious law. The latter, in addition to the legal taboos, includes all legal cases in which the supernatural is represented by a living individual, who acts as plaintiff, and in which, consequently, secular punishments either are added to the supernatural ones or take their place completely. For example, a Kapauku legal case concerned embezzlement by the headman of a political faction (formerly a sublineage headman) named Ijaaj Dimiidakebo of Botukebo village. This influential and rich man borrowed in 1953 a considerable amount of goods and shell money from Ijaaj Idakebo of Botukebo, who had received them as part of *dabe uwo,* the reward for killing an enemy. A failure to repay such a debt is believed to be punishable supernaturally, by death. After two years the creditor asked for repayment of the debt, but the rich man stated that he had no money on hand. This was an obvious lie. The dispute which followed resulted in a stick fight in which many people participated. There were many injuries on both sides, and the creditor suffered a broken forearm. Awiitigaaj, the sublineage authority, helped by Ekajewaijokaipouga, the headman of the confederacy, stopped the fight. The latter in his decision held the debtor liable for payment. After long argument with this headman, Dimiidakebo paid back only a small part of the loan, promising to pay the remainder in the future. As an additional penalty Ekajewaijokaipouga publicly reprimanded the culprit and put a "supernatural" curse on him. A few months later Dimiidakebo became sick and died. Thus, the people believed, he was punished for his frauds by the headman's reprimands and black magic, and by the headman's ancestor-ghost's "execution" (see also Pospisil 1958a: pp. 220–221, no. 119). This case, by presenting a decision, which possesses all the attributes of law and the headman's sanction of restitution, public reprimand, and sorcery, must be classified as religious law.

In another case a religious taboo prohibiting the payment of bride price on the day of the bride's first menstruation was violated by Ijaaj Ekajewaijokaipouga, the Ijaaj-Pigome confederacy headman himself. As a result of this delict, he became violently sick. The shaman Ijaaj Iibii of the Aigii village was called in and diagnosed "correctly" the cause of the disease. In order to save the man's life, he added a secular punishment to that imposed by the supernatural: The man was ordered to divorce his new wife. The heartbroken husband complied with the shaman's order, thus escaping the supernatural's ultimate punishment—death. Since there were no children of the marriage, the bride price was repaid in full to the husband (see also Pospisil 1958a: p. 175, case 46). Here the religious authority, the shaman, also acted as legal authority.

In conclusion let me restate that the attribute of *obligatio* functions as a criterion which not only segregates true law from instances in which the right of one party is not linked in a jural *nexus* with the legally recognized duty of the other, but it is also a measure that dissociates religious customs from religious law. We are confronted with the latter only when the interests of the supernatural are represented by a living individual such as a priest or shaman. Religious law will never be left to the decision and punishment of the supernatural only, as may be true in a violation of a purely religious custom. A religious taboo is law only if all four of the legal attributes are present (an authority's decision, intention of universal application, *obligatio,* and sanction); otherwise it should be classified as a religious custom.

THE ATTRIBUTE OF SANCTION

The last, but not necessarily the least important, attribute of law is sanction. Sanction as a criterion of law has played a paramount role in various legal theories; in some of them law has been almost equated with it. Without attempting to underestimate its importance, I would question that this attribute is an exclusive criterion of the concept of law and that it takes precedence over the other legal factors, the coexistence of which form the actual essence of law. Sanction alone cannot define a social phenomenon as law for the simple reason that many political decisions which are made *ad hoc,* without the leader's intention to apply them to future "same" or similar situations, certainly are not laws, because they lack one of the most essential legal attributes which I have identified broadly as the "intention of universal application."

To define law even more narrowly, legal sanction has often been conceived of as physical in nature. In his early work Hoebel defined a social norm as legal "if its neglect or infraction is met by the application, in threat or in fact, of the absolute coercive force by a social unit possessing the socially recognized privilege of so acting" (1940: p. 47). That by this absolute coercive force Hoebel meant a physical one is clear from another statement in which he maintained that

> the exercise of physical force to control or prevent action is the absolute form of compulsion . . . the characteristic feature of law, as distinct from mere force, is the recognized privilege of a person or social group to apply the absolute form of coercion to a transgressor when conduct deemed improper may occur. (1940: p. 47)

In his later work Hoebel still maintained that the *sine qua non* condition of the existence of law is "the legitimate use of physical coercion" and defined a social norm as legal only "if its neglect or infraction is regularly met, in threat or in fact, by the application of physical force by an individual or group possessing the socially recognized privilege of so acting" (1954: pp. 261, 228). In his work with Llewellyn the reference to the physical nature of sanctions is not made so explicit, although one may still view it in the statement that "law has teeth for the case of breach or trouble" (Llewellyn and Hoebel 1961: p. 287). As I shall demonstrate by examples from various cultures, this statement may be regarded, strictly speaking, as correct, but only if by the "teeth" is not meant exclusively physical violence but also punishment of a social or psychological nature which is often more effective than physical force.

Although Hoebel did not carry his stress on the physical nature of sanction to an objectionable extent in specific ethnographic analyses, other scholars have done so. Spencer, in dealing with the law of the Tagemiut and Nunamiut Eskimo, relied so heavily on physical punishment in defining law that he seems to have regarded virtually any type of physical violence as legal sanction. As a consequence he neglected economic and verbal delicts and selected as legal only those cases in which physical violence played the main role. He claims "offenses of any kind related to the inter-family disputes . . . relate almost exclusively to murder" (1959: p. 97). Of the twelve legal cases he described, eight were killings, and two were physical violence against women (abduction of a wife and attempted rape). In contrast, of my 35 randomly collected trouble cases of the Nunamiut Eskimo, only eight dealt with killing, one with attempted killing, and one with rape. A great majority of the rest of my cases (25) involve economic delicts (fourteen cases of violation of hunting laws, embezzlement, and theft) and slander or verbal quarrels (eleven cases). I deliberately did not include intrafamily legal cases, many of which involved children as parties to the disputes, so as to make the sample comparable to Spencer's. This already limited sample of legal cases is further distorted by the fact that informants remembered the infrequent but spectacular murder cases rather than the numerous but unexciting minor offenses. It is most surprising that economic and verbal delicts (with one exception, his eleventh case), which do occur in most societies in great abundance, were almost completely omitted from Spencer's list of "legal cases."

If I had accepted the notion that a legal sanction is necessarily physical in nature, many of my Kapauku, Nunamiut, and Tirolean cases would not be "legal" and, moreover, law would not be a universal phenomenon, for there are peoples and cultures among which physical sanctions are almost lacking.

The Incas represent an interesting blend of the two punishment traditions, physical and nonphysical. They designed two different legal codes, one for their commoners and one for their nobles. While punishing the former physically by flogging, scourging, forced labor, and death (Murdock 1934; p. 432), the Inca "held that public ridicule and loss of office hurt a noble as much as exile or torture would a poor man, and that the prestige of the nobles as a class must be upheld." Only for grave crimes were the nobles punished physically—usually by death (Rowe 1946, vol. 2: p. 271). Since the Inca, in their punishments of nobles relied almost entirely upon nonphysical sanctions, law in their empire would have been limited to dealing with the offenses of the commoners only, who were physically punished. The behavior of the nobles would have been considered to be outside the law. Aside from such an absurdity, we may ask whether the *form* of sanction is so important as to make the existence of law dependent upon it. Is not the effect (social control, conformity) of a sanction more important than its form? In this case, as identifying the concept of authority, I prefer the functional approach. I suggest that the effectiveness of social control is the only important qualification of a legal sanction, not the form it assumes.

In my rejection of physical coercion as the exclusive form of legal sanction I do not go, of course, as far as Barkun who, neglecting the relationship of the societal structure to the multiplicity of legal systems in a society, rejected altogether the necessity of a sanction in a legal decision (1968: pp. 64–65; for an explanation of his position and my criticism thereof see Chapter Four). Sanction is certainly an essential criterion of legal decisions, although it may take a nonphysical form. Some psychological sanctions are very potent; ostracism, ridicule, avoidance, or a denial of favors—sanctions that are sometimes very subtle and informal—nevertheless may be more effective than the corporal punishment to which we tend to attach an undue importance even in our own society.

Kapauku consider being shamed in public much worse than anything except capital punishment. I once witnessed a Kapauku trial lasting several days in which psychological sanction was used exclusively. A notorious criminal and embezzler was reprimanded continuously for seven days while the authorities debated whether to continue this kind of nonphysical sanction or to execute him (see Pospisil 1958a: pp. 223–224, case 124; see also my film on the Kapauku—Pospisil 1955). The defendant sold most of his possessions in order to pay his debts and rectify his embezzlements, satisfy his creditors, and put an end to the punishment. Nevertheless, he endured seven days of public rebuke, while he squatted in front of his house and looked at the ground, before his ordeal was over. Even so, the social consequences of the shaming were harder on him than the lengthy verbal punishment. The villagers ostracized him and avoided meeting or even looking at him, and Gipemeide, the culprit's maternal relative who shared his house, moved away. "If they would beat me and take all my belongings it would be better than this," complained the unhappy delinquent. In my sample of 176 Kapauku trouble cases there are 24 which have public reprimands as their sanction. Because in all of these the other attributes of law are present, they certainly belong in the field of law, in spite of the absence of physical punishment.

In his interesting article, "The Internalization of Political Values in Stateless Societies," LeVine contrasts the Nuer and the Gusii of Africa on the basis of different value systems, the kind of childhood training and the resulting psychological features of the society, and the use of different types of punishment. The Nuer have egalitarian values, grow up with warm, demonstrative fathers who only scold but do not beat their children; the Gusii are authoritarian adults, and as fathers their authority is remote, frightening, and severely physically punitive (LeVine 1960: esp. p. 55).

Like the Nuer fathers the Yakan of Mindanao use fines as sanctions, "listening to admonition," and "performing a prayer of reconciliation" (Frake 1969: pp. 161–162). Although the emphasis upon physical punishment is absent in these cases, Frake correctly does not hesitate to talk about litigation and law while referring to this type of social control among the Yakan. The Yaghan Indians of Tierra del Fuego consider the most effective punishment of the children, as reported by Gusinde, to be sent away by their parents or to be banished from the hut (Gusinde 1937, vol. 2: p. 747). The *tiamuna,* the local leader of these Indians, availed himself almost exclusively of nonphysical sanctions, such as shaming and scolding the culprits, while administering law and maintaining order in his group (1937: vol. 2, p. 1005). Among their neighbors the *kemal,* the leader of the kin group of the Ona Indians, also used quite frequently as his main sanction public shaming, which ultimately punished the culprit by ostracism and public contempt (*Allgemeine Verachtung;* Gusinde 1937, vol. 1: p. 422). As a contrast, the militant Jivaro Indians of eastern Ecuador, when meting out justice, rely mostly upon such physical punishment as pouring infusions of tabacco into the eyes and nose of a culprit, or piercing of legs and breasts of a female with a lance or knife.

In contrast to the insistence upon physical sanction as a criterion of law and the exaggerated emphasis put upon it, there are theories that would do away with sanctions altogether and define law without employing this important legal criterion. I have discussed earlier in this chapter the paper of MacCallum entitled "Law without Sanction" (1964). As I explained, the writer arrived at his erroneous conclusion because he misinterpreted my concept of *obligatio* (including within it several types of sanctions) and because he did not distinguish between sanction as a legal provision and "sanctioning" as the execution of a legal decision (1965: esp. pp. 3, 8, 9, 11). In a book with the same title, Barkun argues from a similar position. However, his mistake is that he fails to recognize that law exists only in a politically organized group that possesses a political leadership and legal authority. His so-called "horizontal legal systems" are not legal systems in any sense; they are conglomerates of "vertical legal systems" (if we want to use the author's nomenclature) belonging to independent groups that have no common political superstructure that would unite them—that have no common legal system. It is no surprise to find, therefore, his further conclusion that these horizontal systems are entirely consensus based. Of course they have to be, in the same way that all nonviolent conflict resolutions between sovereign states are achieved through international agreements— through treaties that we certainly do not call law! The Kapauku Papuan tribe, because it is not politically united, does not possess any law of its own. Law exists only on the level of the Kapauku political confederacies whose legal systems vary quite profoundly. Barkun would be delighted to find no coercive deterrent sanctions (Barkun 1968: p. 155) on the Kapauku tribal level, just as one does not find them on the European or Western civilization level. I shall deal more fully with the problem of the multiplicity of legal systems in the Chapter Four.

In the popular literature as well as in some sociology books it is nowadays quite fashionable to criticize sanctions not only on the philosophic basis of cruelty and inhumanity but also on some pseudoscientific proofs of their ineffectiveness. Very often the authors set out to determine the effectiveness of sanctions, especially those of a physical nature, with a preconceived idea of their impotence. Of course, with selected statistics, as is well known, one can prove almost anything. The evidence from the United States that should clearly show the ineffectiveness of the death penalty (which "evidence" Barkun uses for his antisanction argument—1968: p. 63) is biased by several miscomprehensions. One stems from the failure to realize that any sanction to be effective must be immediate. Because of delays, appeals, and technicalities which may not only delay an execution of the verdict almost indefinitely but also sometimes set free a known murderer, the effectiveness of the physical sanction of execution in the United States is indeed destroyed. If, however, one looks at the horrible and tragic effectiveness of executions in Nazi Germany and the modern Communist states, where the great majority of subjects are forced effectively by the state's legalized terror into conformance, one may easily comprehend the importance of sanctions, especially those of a physical nature, for the achievement of social control. All that is required here is to look at other cultures than our own—to employ social and comparative anthropology rather than provincial pseudosociology. To a comparative scholar it is not surprising to find as correct conclusions of social psychologists and psychologists which state, for example, that "the data suggest that the realistic punishment [of children] in the *immediate* [italics mine] situation is the most important variable in eliciting cheating or honesty" (Kohlberg 1963: p. 284), or, "habits that have been disrupted by punishment are much less subject to recovery than habits that have been disrupted by extinction" (Dollard and Miller 1950: p. 51). The individualistic and precise psychological tests are certainly preferable to the pseudosociological United States or Western-biased statistics. In my research experience, whether with the hunting Eskimo, Stone Age horticulturist Kapauku Papuans, farming Hopi Pueblo Indians, or civilized Tirolean peasants, immediate sanction most definitely played the most important role in the social control· in all these societies.

From the above discussion and from comparative cross-cultural research it follows that sanction, on one hand, is a necessary criterion of law and, on the other, that it need not consist of corporal punishment or a deprivation of property (physical sanctions). The form of legal sanctions is certainly relative to the particular society or to the particular subgroup in which it is used; it may be physical or social-psychological. I may, then, define legal sanction either as a negative device in withdrawing rewards or favors that otherwise (if the law had not been violated) would have been granted, or as a positive measure in inflicting some painful experience, physical or psychological. It should be stressed again that *sanction as a legal criterion* appears as a statement in the decision of the legal authority; it is certainly not the execution of it which is often assigned to the executive branch of a state government (rather than the judicial) or even to private parties, as is often the case in a tribal society.

To conclude this theoretical discussion I will give a more extensive survey of the sanctions employed in two tribal societies I have investigated. In deciding 132 legal cases among the Kapauku (Pospisil 1958a: p. 272), tribal authorities availed themselves of the following types of sanctions. Under "corporal punishment" they used execution in eight cases for the delicts of murder, sorcery, taboo violation, incest, stinginess, and instigation of war. Usually the punishment was carried out by a close patrilineal relative of the culprit or by the plaintiff or the plaintiff's close patrilineal relative. The individual was usually shot from ambush with a bamboo-tipped arrow. Employment of patrilineal relatives to participate in the killing was a clever cultural device to prevent internal strain and feuds within the political confederacies. This sanction was used on the sublineage, lineage, and confederacy levels of their societal organization. Another type of corporal punishment was beating the head and shoulders of the culprit with a stick, applied in 34 cases for delicts ranging from murder and treason to refusal to pay a debt. This punishment was used in all types of Kapauku subgroups (on all levels of their societal structure). The culprits submitted without trying to defend themselves, since the beatings were at a headman's order. Slapping the defendant was used in one case, when a wife failed to provide her husband with food. Slapping is used as punishment for wives and children. Banishment is always an alternative to physical sanctions. The culprit leaves his community in order not to be subject to these punishments. In my sample this happened in two cases.

Economic sanctions are by far the most preferred ones among the Kapauku. Payment of blood money for killing a man in order to avoid capital punishment was ordered in four cases (usually 120 old cowries, a sum which would buy 600 pounds of pork). Indemnity is another economic sanction which often works as a substitute for a corporal one. A rich defendant is often asked to pay more than a poor man. This sanction was used in thirteen cases of my sample. Payment of a sum stipulated in a contract is another economic sanction which the Kapauku used in nine cases of failure to repay a monetary loan, or to pay for goods, labor, or a bride. Restitution of a commodity or shell money acquired by the defendant in a contract or through a delict was a sanction used in fourteen cases. Destruction of the property of a culprit who committed adultery, theft, or an act of insubordination to an authority followed the defendant's escape from the community to avoid corporal punishment, or his refusal to pay what he owed. The plaintiff was granted the privilege of executing the verdict in all three decisions of this kind. Confiscation of all property was invariably the sentence for deserters who went to the enemy's side in a war. The Kapauku employ a legal fiction here of the death of the deserter, allowing his property to be inherited by his heirs. This sanction was used in two cases. To ask a defendant to return a loan made to him by the authority works as a very effective punishment in cases of insubordination. The Kapauku used it in three instances in my sample of legal cases. A cessation of offending behavior (usually of making claims to other people's property) was ordered in two cases.

The most dreaded and feared of the psychological and social sanctions of the Kapauku is the *public reprimand.* It may be used against any of the delicts that a Kapauku may commit and, according to the delict, it may be of varied severity and duration. It consists of intermittent public scolding, shouting of reproaches, and dancing of a "mad dance" in front of the squatting defendant. The Kapauku regard this psychological punishment as the most effective in their entire inventory of sanctions. They used it in 24 cases of my sample.

Warning as a sanction is used in private by the authority in minor violations of a taboo, lying, or insubordination. The defendant suffers a loss of face once it becomes known that he was punished in such a way. Defendants in two of my cases were subject to this type of punishment. Divorce is used as a sanction against a spouse who has violated his or her marital duties; three cases in my sample carried this punishment. Passive resistance and refusal of the followers to support him is often the result of a decision passed by his superior against an unjust and stingy headman. In my sample it was used once against a tight-fisted Kapauku *tonowi*. Punishment by direct sorcery or through the shaman's helping spirits brought doom upon four culprits in my case inventory. Although these psychological sanctions are infrequent, they are used when the culprit is strong enough to resist the headman's decision or if he has violated taboos specifically imposed upon him by the shaman. Disease and death are the ultimate (psychosomatic) effect of this "supernatural" punishment.

A special type of punishment, which turned out to be of physical nature in most cases, is legalized self-redress of the plaintiff. Regaining his property or punishing the offender without prior authorization constitutes the self-redress. When later approved by the authority's decision it becomes *ex post facto* a legal sanction. Of ten cases in which it was used in my sample, the plaintiff destroyed the defendant's property in four, beat the culprit with a stick in two, seized the offender's property in three, and killed one offender *in flagrante delicto.* In conclusion I should say that sometimes several sanctions were used in the same case (therefore 139 sanctions were used in 132 legal disputes). Psychological sanctions were utilized in 34 cases, a little over one-fourth of my sample.

Although the Kapauku use a substantial inventory of nonphysical sanctions, their reliance on physical punishment is still considerable. As a contrast, the Nunamiut Eskimo legal authorities—the father, the head of the household, or the *umealik* (political faction or local band leader) used nonphysical, often psychological, means of social control almost exclusively. Fathers and household heads exercised jurisdiction over the members of their families and residential groups by relying almost entirely on verbal castigation, admonition, or stern "advice." In extreme cases they used a milder form of the dreaded psychological sanction of ostracism or resorted to eviction. The Nunamiut band leaders and, in bands that were politically segmented, the political faction leaders, all called *umealit,* also relied almost exclusively on nonphysical, that is, verbal and psychological punishment. Public reprimand, admonition, giving the culprit a derogatory name by which he could be called for the rest of his life, or, in the most serious cases, ostracism and eviction from the band were their most frequently used sanctions. Ostracism and eviction were utilized especially in convictions for murder. In such a case, if the culprit refused to leave the band, the band literally left him. Silently the people packed their tents while the offender was sleeping, and took off, taking care to leave no tracks and to change the direction of their march several times. Only in cases of criminal recidivism did an *umealik* invoke the penalty of execution. Thus the Nunamiut Eskimo represent a society in which legal sanctions (decisions about *intragroup* punishment meted out by an authority) were almost entirely of nonphysical nature, while physical violence, in form of feuds and wars, was almost exclusively reserved for intergroup conflicts.

Law has to have teeth, as Llewellyn and Hoebel have pointed out. These teeth have been labeled sanctions. They are one of the universal attributes of law, although certainly not always of physical nature. The importance of nonphysical sanctions has been grossly underestimated in our society, due to our formal emphasis on physical punishment. That psychological sanction can be very effective becomes quite obvious from such an example as giving a derogatory name. A Nunamiut who steals a kayak is renamed Kayak and called by that name by everyone so that in a few years his real name is forgotten. Every time the name is used the offender is reminded, in a public and shaming way, of his crime. To me such a punishment is more severe and more effective (and certainly more feared and dreaded by my Eskimo informants) than even a severe beating, the pain of which will be ultimately forgotten. It is strange to me that such a severe punishment would be ruled out as a legal sanction by some legal scholars.

The heuristic value of the recognition of sanction as a criterion of law, aside from its inducement to conformity, is its function of separating the so-called neutral customs from law. An authority may well express his opinion (or "decision") about a custom which carries no provision of punishment for its breach. "If in truth nothing is done about it," as Llewellyn and Hoebel put it (1961: p. 25), if not even gossip, ridicule, or taunting affects its violator, then such an observance has to be regarded as a neutral, nonlegal custom, although it may possess all the other three legal attributes.

CONCLUSION

To summarize my position on the definition and attributes of law, I conceive of law as principles of institutionalized social control, abstracted from decisions passed by a legal authority (judge, headman, father, tribunal, or council of elders), principles that are intended to be applied universally (to all "same" problems in the future), that involve two parties locked in an *obligatio* relationship, and that are provided with a sanction of physical or nonphysical nature. Since this concept, defined by its "form" and the four attributes, is applicable to the Western concept called law, I am adopting this term for my cross-culturally derived category of phenomena of authoritative (but not necessarily authoritarian) social control, rather than coining another term. Adoption of this analytical concept of law enables me to make cross-cultural analysis of law for comparative purposes (see Frake 1969: esp, pp. 154, 158–160; Pospisil 1958a; 1964).

This conceptualization of law has some revolutionizing aspects. One is that law is to be found not only in every human society but also in every functioning subgroup of society, as will be shown in Chapter Four. This unorthodox definition may cause some alarm in the more conservative members of the anthropological and legal disciplines, who stagnated on nineteenth-century legal theories that are often elevated to infallible dogmas. For example, Fried introduces a "strong" argument against my conceptualization of law by pointing out how Austin would have dealt with some of my Kapauku cases: "He would probably have rejected them for their spontaneity and formlessness" (Fried 1967: p. 152). To this argument I reply that I care little for the opinion of those who condemn contemporary theories as heresies committed against outdated dogmas of the past.[6]

---

[6]This argument based on 3 carefully selected legal cases of my repertory of 132, to which Fried, due more probably to superficial reading than intent, adds one case which I disqualified as nonlegal, explicitly stating that no authority's decision was present (see Fried 1967: p. 151; Pospisil 1958a: pp. 227, 272), leads me to comment further. Austin's opinion of my theory of law or my Kapauku legal cases would seem to be as relevant as Isaac Newton's opinion of modern physicists and their theories of relativity physics.

CHAPTER
FOUR
LEGAL
LEVELS
AND
MULTIPLICITY
OF
LEGAL
SYSTEMS

"Where there are subgroups that are discrete entities within the social entirety," Hoebel has observed, "there is political organization—a system of regulation of relations between groups, or members of different groups within the society at large" (1949a: p. 376). Since all human societies

This chapter is reprinted with minor changes from Leopold Pospisil, "Legal Levels and Multiplicity of Legal Systems in Human Societies," *The Journal of Conflict Resolution,* vol. 9, no. 1 (March 1967), pp. 2–26, with the kind permission of the publisher.

contain some sort of subgroups (e.g., families, clans, bands, communities, etc.), Hoebel's statement implies universality of political organization—a virtual absence of human societies without pertinent political structures. Moreover, this concept is of paramount importance for a proper presentation and analysis of any political and, consequently, any legal system because it emphasizes the relationship that necessarily exists between such a system and the conglomeration of a society's subgroups. Since the regulation of the network of interrelations that gives this conglomeration its particular structure is the essence of the society's political organization, no significant analysis of the politics or law can be made without a proper and consistent reference to the particular system of subgroups to which it pertains.

Yet there are numerous anthropological studies that fail to relate accounts of political and legal organizations to the segmentation systems of the pertinent societies. Although one invariably finds an exposition of the membership characteristics and functions of the subgroups, the individual natives are usually not portrayed as taking part in the various activities primarily as members of such groups. Presentations are so focused upon the role and status of the individual that he appears to participate directly in the life of the society as a whole. As a consequence, a misleading impression of a "monolithic society" consisting of interacting individuals, rather than a complex society composed of subgroups of different membership inclusiveness, is likely to be created. It is one of the basic premises of this chapter that social relations (relations of individuals to ego) as well as societal relations (relations among the segments of a society) are equally important for a meaningful analysis of a political and legal system.

In purely legal matters the anthropology of law has also neglected societal structure (segmentation of the society into its constituent subgroups; for elaboration of this concept see Pospisil 1963a: pp. 32–41; 1963b: pp. 32, 37–46; 1964: pp. 398–399, 409–417). Law of a primitive people has been almost invariably described as an expression of a well-integrated single legal system with few, if any, inconsistencies and discrepancies in its content and application. If any of the most obvious deviations from the abstract "prevailing rule" is described, its existence is explained as a variation or aberration, or it is flatly denied legality and labeled "illegal." Had the importance of subgroups for analysis of political organization, so well expressed in the above quotation from Hoebel, always been borne in mind by the anthropologist, his analysis of the power structure and social control of a society could not have been presented as a politically integrated system with a single, smoothed out, all-embracing legal system. Instead, careful analysis would have revealed marked differences in the judiciary activity and informal social control exercised by the authorities of the various subgroups. Any human society, I postulate, does not possess a single consistent legal system, but as many such systems as there are functioning subgroups. Conversely, every functioning subgroup of a society regulates the relations of its members by its own legal system, which is of necessity different, at least in some respects, from those of the other subgroups. The multiplicity of legal systems within any given society will form the major theme of this chapter. I propose to explore its historical development and application to different societies, to introduce some additional relevant concepts, and to debate some of the arguments for and against it.

HISTORY OF THE IDEA OF THE MULTIPLICITY OF LEGAL SYSTEMS WITHIN A SOCIETY

Traditionally, law has been conceived as the property of a society as a whole. As a logical consequence, a given society was thought to have only one legal system that controlled the behavior of all its members. Without any investigation of the social controls that operate on the subsociety levels, subgroups (such as associations and residential and kinship groups) have been *a priori* excluded from the possibility of regulating their members' behavior by systems of rules applied in specific decisions by leaders of these groups—systems that in their essential characteristics very closely parallel the all-embracing law of the society. This attitude was undoubtedly caused by the tremendous influence the well-elaborated and unified law of the Roman Empire exerted upon the outlook of the European lawyer. Had classical Greece exercised such influence over the legal minds of our civilization, our traditional concept of law might have been much more flexible and, cross-culturally speaking, "realistic." Most of the early ethnographers did not escape the traditionalist influence. Their insistence upon seeing law exclusively on the society level resulted either in a description of a simple, pervasive legal system in the investigated society (Barton 1919, 1949; Hogbin 1934; Lips 1947), or, if the society under scrutiny did not have a comprehensive political organization and the ethnographer was not sophisticated enough to look for law elsewhere, in a denial of the existence of law among that people (Radcliffe-Brown 1952: pp. 216–217). This denial of law in a society that lacks an overall political organization has been maintained, for example, even by authors who have entitled their works *Nuer Law,* or *Leadership and Law among the Eskimos of the Keewatin District Northwest Territories* (Howell 1954: p. 225; van den Steenhoven 1962: p. 112).

The tendency to dissociate law from the structure of the society and its subgroups (society's segments) has unfortunately persisted until the present time and led Spencer (1959) to treat the laws of the Tagemiut and Nunamiut Eskimos as if they belonged to a single system. An extreme of this traditionalist tendency has possibly been reached by Berndt. In his book *Excess and Restraint* (1962), he treated law and social control as though they were unrelated to the societal structure in which they occurred and represented some sort of a supracultural material. He discussed the law of four linguistically and culturally different Papuan societies (Jate, Usurufa, Fore, and Kamano) as if it constituted a single consistent legal system. Accordingly, his cases of conflict and dispute were taken from wherever they occurred, lacking identification with the groups within which the controversies arose. As a result, the reader is often not even sure of the ethnic provenience of the litigants. Even if one is quite ethnocentric and biased by the tradition of the West, one can hardly argue that the legal systems of four different Papuan peoples are identical.

Even when the close relationship between law and societal structure has been suggested by an ethnographer, a subsequent report of the same society by another author may neglect the suggestion and follow the old traditional path. For example, in spite of Evans-Pritchard's outstanding account of the Nuer social organization, Howell's analysis of law of this Nilotic tribe became so heavily influenced by the traditionalist view that it disregarded confirmations of the relationship between the social control and the subgroups that Evans-Pritchard had made quite explicit. The latter contended, for instance, that "the structural interrelations of tribal segments are seen in the relativity of law, for Nuer law is relative like the structure itself" (1940: p. 169); but this went apparently unnoticed by Howell, who concluded his study of Nuer law with the following summary:

> *It is less confusing to adopt the hypothesis that the extent of the law is limited to social control which is maintained by organized legal sanctions and applied by some form of organized political mechanism. By this definition, the Nuer had no law, for, as we have already seen, there was in the past nothing in the nature of politically organized society. (1954: p. 225)*

True enough, the Nuer had no law on the levels of the society or tribe. This had been recognized by Evans-Pritchard, who stated:

> *In a strict sense Nuer have no law. . . . In Nuerland legislative, judicial, and executive functions are not vested in any persons or councils. Between members of different tribes there is no question of redress; and even within a tribe, in my experience, wrongs are not brought forward in what we would call a legal form, though compensation for damage (ruok) is sometimes paid. (1940: p. 162)*

However, this is not the full story of the Nuer law for Evans-Pritchard, who acknowledges its existence in a significantly qualified way: "The first point to note about Nuer law is that it has not everywhere the same force within a tribe, but is relative to the position of persons in social structure, to the distance between them in the kinship, lineage, age set, and, above all, in the political systems" (1940: p. 169). Indeed, when one turns to the Nuer tribal subgroups, for example to the individual settlements, one finds that "within a village differences between persons are discussed by the elders of the village and agreement is generally and easily reached and compensation paid, or promised, for all are related by kinship and common interests" (1940: p. 169). In other words, while the Nuer society as a whole, or its individual tribes, are not legally organized, law does exist on a lower level in the Nuer villages, where the elders use it in their settlement of disputes. Thus, contrary to Howell's conclusion, the Nuer did not represent a society without law.

In her article on "Conflict Resolution in Two Mexican Communities" Laura Nader gives credit to Mauss (1906) and Malinowski (1959) for the idea that within a single society several legal systems may be operating, "complementing, supplementing, or conflicting with each other" (Nader 1963: p. 584). Unfortunately, although the implication of the existence of a multiplicity of legal systems within a society may be drawn from the work of both of these scholars, neither of them stated this idea clearly. Actually, each in his own way maintained the existence of a single system of law in the Eskimo and Trobriand societies. Mauss described two legal systems that operated in Eskimo nuclear and extended families. However, instead of showing the coexistence of these two systems, Mauss claimed that one followed the other in a rhythm dictated by the seasons: the legal system of the nuclear family controlled the behavior of the Eskimo during the summer; in the wintertime, when nuclear families established common residence and became an extended family, a legal system for the larger group was instituted (Mauss 1906: esp. pp. 103–124). One may justifiably wonder what happened to the nuclear family in the wintertime? Did it dissolve in the extended family group which somehow redefined the relationships between the nuclear family members for the duration of the arctic winter? From my research among the Nunamiut Eskimo I know quite well that the contrary is the case: both legal systems coexisted, functioning side by side, mainly by virtue of differentiated jurisdiction. Actually, among the Nunamiut Eskimo two additional legal systems functioned simultaneously with those of the nuclear and the extended family: that of the band and that of the band faction (Pospisil 1964: esp. pp. 424–426). Mauss, although describing two legal systems within an Eskimo society, failed to break away from the traditionalist doctrine: although there were two systems, only one, according to Mauss, was operational at a given time.

In contrast to Mauss, Malinowski did describe two conflicting systems of social control in the Trobriand society, both of which functioned at the same time. However, although his book provided a chapter with the heading "Systems of Law in Conflict" (1959: p. 100), the content did not correspond to the title. He defined law as duties and rights based upon the matrilineal principle, but the relations deriving from the conflicting patrilineal principle he called merely "usage." Actually, thus, it was martrilineal law and "patrilineal usage" that were in conflict rather than two legal systems: "So that here the usage, established but non-legal, not only takes great liberties with the law, but adds insult to injury by granting the usurper considerable advantages over the rightful owner" (1959: p. 110). Consequently, Malinowski also failed to conceptualize multiple legal systems within the same society and link them to the pertinent societal structure.

Although the traditionalist view that law is monopolized by the state, or the "society as a whole," has made a profound impact upon sociology and anthropology and, as we have seen, still persists in many of the recent works on law in these two fields, its simplicity failed to satisfy some noteworthy legal scholars. In contrast to what one might expect, it is interesting to learn that credit for the nontraditionalist trend of thought which did not limit its inquiry to the level of state or society must be given to jurisprudence rather than to the social sciences.

In 1868 the legal scholar Otto von Gierke had already directed attention to the inner ordering of the *Genossenschaften* (associations), and he recognized in them the essential features of law. Eugen Ehrlich, one of his followers, writes:

> As a result of his labors, we may consider it established that, within the scope of the concept of the association, the law is an organization, that is to say, a rule which assigns to each and every member of the association his position in the community, whether it be of domination or of subjection (Überordnung, Unterordnung), and his duties; and that it is now quite impossible to assume that law exists within these associations chiefly for the purpose of deciding controversies that arise out of the communal relation. (1936: p. 24)[1]

So great was the enthusiasm of von Gierke for the more or less autonomous entities of the society's subgroups that he tended to an extreme view, diametrically opposed to the traditionalists' individualist legal thought of the nineteenth century. He promoted the associations to entities that somehow became distinct from the sum total of the members and of their interests. He went so far as to advance the idea of existence of a mystical "group-will" that was distinct from the wills of the members of such a group. Although this extremism obscured social reality by neglecting the role of the individual and by making a group of people into almost a living beast (thus giving rise

[1]"Nach den Ergebnissen seiner Arbeiten darf es wohl als feststehend betrachtet werden: soweit der Genossenschaftsbegriff reicht, ist das Recht eine Organisation, das ist eine Regel, die jedem Angehörigen der Genossenschaft seine Stellung, seine Über- und Unterordnung in der Gemeinschaft und seine Aufgaben anweist; und ganz unmöglich ist es jetzt anzunehmen, das Recht sei in diesen Gemeinschaften hauptsächlich dazu da, damit danach etwa Streitigkeiten aus dem Gemeinschaftsverhältnisse entschieden werden." (Ehrlich 1913: p. 18)

to the unfortunate "Durkheimean trend" in sociology and anthropology), his emphasis upon the legal importance of the society's subgroups (associations) proved most significant in the subsequent development of legal thought, represented especially by Ehrlich, a lawyer.

Following in the footsteps of von Gierke, Eugen Ehrlich refused to accept legal orthodoxy and to recognize the state's (or society's) monopoly on law. Indeed, he explicitly stated that "It is not an essential element of the concept of law that it be created by the state, nor that it constitute the basis for the decisions of the courts or other tribunals, nor that it be the basis of a legal compulsion consequent upon such a decision" (1936: p. 24).[2] To Ehrlich, law was "an ordering" of human behavior, in any group of interacting people, no matter how small or how complex (1936: esp. pp. 24, 36–37). To Ehrlich human society was not composed of individuals who acted independently, but of people who of necessity acted always as members of some of the society's subgroups. Thus the people's behavior is not necessarily ordered by the all-comprising state law, but primarily by the "inner ordering of the associations"—Ehrlich's "living law." "The inner order of the associations of human beings," writes Ehrlich, "is not only the original, but also, down to the present time, the basic form of law" (1936: p. 37).[3] Excellently and prophetically, Ehrlich points out in his own words the basic interrelationship of law and societal structure: "All attempts that have been made until now to comprehend the nature of law have failed because the investigation was not based on the order of the associations but on the legal propositions" (1936: pp. 37–38).[4] Thus Ehrlich actually laid the foundations for the modern anthropology of law, allowing law to be in existence also within those societies which were not legally unified or politically organized.

Ehrlich's genius unfortunately failed when he inquired into the nature of the inner ordering of the society's subgroups. Being influenced by Gierke's philosophy of "group-will," he conceived of law as of the principles contained in the actual behavior of the members of the associations (1936: esp. pp. 493, 497, 502). To him, people conformed to these principles because of some amorphous social pressure of the association as a whole. He reacted so thoroughly against the traditionalist conception of the monopolistic state law (created by the order and will of the legislator) that he failed to uncover

[2] "Es ist dem Rechte weder begriffswesentlich, dass es vom Staate ausgehe, noch auch, dass es die Grundlage für die Entscheidungen der Gerichte oder anderer Behörden, oder für den darauffolgenden Rechtszwang abgebe." (Ehrlich 1913: p. 17)

[3] "Die innere Ordnung der menschlichen Verbände ist nicht nur die ursprüngliche, sondern auch bis in die Gegenwart die grundlegende Form des Rechts." (Ehrlich 1913: p. 29)

[4] "Alle bisherigen Versuche, sich über das Recht klar zu werden, sind daran gescheitert, dass nicht von der Ordnung in den Verbänden, sondern von den Rechtssätzen ausgegangen worden ist." (Ehrlich 1913: p. 29)

within the associations formal or informal leaders who actually influenced and molded what he called "living law." His unfortunate assumption that the source of law was the actual behavior of the people themselves rather than principles contained in the decisions of the leaders of the various associations led him to generalize about the living law as if the behavior of people in all the associations within the same society were identical. Thus he actually telescoped the various legal systems and subsystems of the associations into a more or less generalized whole called "living law," which he contrasted with the statutory law of the state "the legal propositions" (1936: esp. p. 38). However, no matter what our criticisms of Ehrlich may be today, it goes without saying that he revolutionized thought in the field that may be quite properly called the science of law, showing the way to the social scientists who, as he was writing, were still blinded by the European state-law tradition.

In his work *Wirtschaft und Gesellschaft* (1922) Max Weber, without trying to generalize for the laws of the various associations on the society's level and without attempting to force these into a nonrealistic "living law" that would contrast with the legal systems of the state, expressed quite explicitly the idea of the existence of several legal systems within a given society. First, he defined law so broadly as to be applicable to the ordering systems within the various social subgroups; then,

> for the sake of terminological consistency, we categorically deny that "law" exists only where legal coercion is guaranteed by the political authority. There is no practical reason for such a terminology. A "legal order" shall rather be said to exist wherever coercive means, of a physical or psychological kind, are available; i.e., wherever they are at the disposal of one or more persons who hold themselves ready to use them for this purpose in the case of certain events; in other words, whenever we find a consociation specifically dedicated to the purpose of "legal coercion." (Weber 1967: p. 17)[5]

Second, to Weber the nature of the coercion mechanism of the various consociations was not some sort of a mystical group will or group opinion but an authority, in many ways comparable to that of the state: "It goes

[5]". . . aus der hier festgehaltenen Terminologie heraus, wird von uns selbstredend abgelehnt, wenn man von 'Recht' nur da spricht, wo kraft Garantie der politischen Gewalt Rechtszwang in Aussicht steht. Dazu besteht für uns kein praktischer Anlass. Wir wollen vielmehr überall da von 'Rechtsordnung' sprechen, wo die Anwendung irgendwelcher, physischer oder psychischer, Zwangsmittel in Aussicht steht, die von einem Zwangsapparat, d.h. von einer oder mehreren Personen ausgeübt wird, welche sich zu diesem Behuf für den Fall des Eintritts des betreffenden Tatbestandes bereithalten, wo also eine spezifische Art der Vergesellschaftung zum Zweck des 'Rechtszwanges' existiert." (Weber 1922: p. 372)

without saying that this kind of coercion may be extended to claims which the state does not guarantee at all; such claims are nevertheless based on *rights* even though they are guaranteed by authorities other than the state" (1967: p. 18).[6] Thus Weber saw no basic qualitative difference between the state legal system and those systems created and upheld by the various subgroups of the society. He maintained no basic dichotomy comparable to Ehrlich's state law versus living law. Consequently, there is little doubt that Weber's sober approach to his inquiry into the nature of legal phenomena, by rejecting the mysticism and unnecessary philosophizing of his predecessors in favor of an empirical disclosure of social reality, marks a very significant advance in the field of the sociological jurisprudence.

However, it was not until the joint effort of a lawyer and an anthropologist produced *The Cheyenne Way* (Llewellyn and Hoebel: 1941), that the idea of multiplicity of legal systems within a society was formulated, and the relationship of the society's law to the legal systems of the subgroups (associations) was explicitly stated. According to the two authors, investigation of the all-embracing legal system of a society as a whole (the traditionalist law) does not offer a complete and workable conception of the legal order within that society. "What is loosely lumped as 'custom' [on the society's level] can become very suddenly a meaningful thing—one with edges—if the practices in question can be related to a particular grouping" (1941: p. 53). In other words, if one changes one's point of reference from that of the society as a whole and focuses upon the individual subgroups,

> there may then be found utterly and radically different bodies of
> "law" prevailing among these small units, and generalization
> concerning what happens in "the" family or in "this type of
> association" made on the society's level *will have its dangers.
> The total picture of law-stuff in any society includes, along with
> the Great Law-stuff of the Whole, the sublaw-stuff or bylaw-stuff
> of the lesser working units. (1941: p. 28)

Although the authors did not systematically explore and contrast the differences between the various legal systems of the Cheyenne society's subunits, the book clearly laid the theoretical groundwork of a field of inquiry for the anthropologists of the future. Hoebel's subsequent departure from the well-expressed relativity of law and custom is to be regretted. In his more recent work he seems to hold a position that is not consonant with the views expressed above, and the orthodox emphasis upon the whole society's monopoly of the law appears to be resurrected when he states: "There are, of course, as many forms of coercion as there are forms of power. Of these,

[6]"Und natürlich kann sich dieser Zwang auch auf staatlich gar nicht garantierte Ansprüche erstrecken: dann sind diese trotzdem subjektive Rechte, nur mit anderen Gewalten." (Weber 1922: p. 372)

only certain methods and forms are legal. Coercion by gangsters is not legal. Even physical coercion by a parent is not legal if it is too extreme" (1954: p. 27). But, of course, this is true only if we take the society as a whole as the point of reference. According to the society's legal system, some regulatory means of its subgroups may indeed be "illegal."

LEGAL SYSTEMS AND LEGAL LEVELS

In one of my early articles I defined the political structure of a society as "a configuration of analytically derived relationships of those purposive activities of individuals and groups of individuals which establish or maintain authority and determine its legislative, executive and judicial functions" (Pospisil 1959: p. 1). While anthropologists may agree in principle with this definition in discussing political structure, in their actual work they have often tended to concentrate so much on the relationships between individuals (describing fully their various roles and statuses) that they have deemphasized or even neglected the relationships of a society's subgroups. Thus a smooth, relatively static and simple picture of legal structure has been presented. Were the emphasis on subgroups always borne in mind by the ethnographers they could hardly have proposed such a simplified view of the social reality. Instead, they would have described a configuration of semiautonomous or autonomous groups possessing leaders with different personalities, abilities, education, and experience. If the judgments or decisions of these subgroup leaders engaged the author's attention, he would have to consider that they were based upon the application of different legal systems administered by these various leaders.

In my quantitative investigation of the disputes among the Kapauku Papuans, Nunamiut Eskimo, and Tirolean peasants I found that the decisions of the leaders of the various subgroups bore all the necessary criteria of law (in the same way that modern state law does): the decisions were made by leaders who were regarded as jural authorities by their followers (that means that the leaders' decisions were actually complied with—criterion of authority); these decisions were meant to be applied to all "identical" (similar) cases decided in the future (criterion of the intention of universal application); they were provided with physical or psychological sanctions (criterion of sanction), and they settled disputes between parties represented by living people, the decision being based upon the right of one party to a certain behavior from the other party and, conversely, obligating the other party to such a behavior (criterion of *obligatio;* see Chapter Three and see Pospisil 1956: pp. 748–751 and 1958a: pp. 257–272). Consequently, the judgments and decisions of the authorities of the various subgroups were legal in the subgroups in which they were issued, being based upon their particular legal systems.

Because of these findings I reject the traditional presentation of law on the level of the society only and follow the unorthodox path of legal thought characterized by von Gierke, Ehrlich, Weber, Llewellyn, and Hoebel. Indeed, I go a step farther and claim categorically that "every functioning subgroup of a society has its own legal system which is necessarily different in some respects from those of the other subgroups" (Pospisil 1958a: p. 272). Also, I am more radical than Llewellyn and Hoebel in proposing to delete the words "bylaw stuff" and "sublaw stuff" from the vocabulary of my discussion and refer to the matter that forms the content of the systems of social control of the subgroups as what it really is—the law (*ius*). Consequently, the totality of the principles incorporated in the legal decisions of an authority of a society's subgroup constitutes that subgroup's legal system. Since the legal systems form a hierarchy reflecting the degrees of inclusiveness of the corresponding subgroups, the total of the legal systems of subgroups of the same type and inclusiveness (for example, family, lineage, community, political confederacy) I propose to call *legal level*. As there are inevitable differences between the laws of different legal levels, and because an individual, whether a member of an advanced or a primitive society, is simultaneously a member of several subgroups of different inclusiveness (for example, a Kapauku is a member of his household, sublineage, lineage, and political confederacy, all the groups being politically and legally organized), he is subject to all the different legal systems of the subgroups of which he is a member. Consequently, law in a given society differs among groups of the same inclusiveness (within the same legal level); thus different laws are applied to different individuals. Law also exhibits discrepancies between legal systems of subgroups of different inclusiveness (between different legal levels), with the consequence that the same individuals may be subject to several legal systems different in the content of their law to the point of contradiction.

In order to demonstrate these theoretical points, I shall give a rather detailed example from the Kapauku Papuan material that I gathered in the years 1954–1955. I take my first example from this primitive culture because it is in such simple societies that complexity or even the existence of any kind of law has so often been disputed. The Kapauku Papuans, a linguistic group of approximately 45,000 individuals, live by means of horticulture in the western part of the central highlands of West New Guinea (West Irian) in the area of the large Wissel Lakes. Patrilineal descent, patrilocal residence, and, ideally speaking, patriarchal polygnous family are the main characteristics of their social structure. About fifteen households, each of whose members live in one main house (and sometimes have several additional small houses for women), form a village. The male villagers and their children (except for an occasional outsider) belong to the same patrilineage.

For defense and for other political purposes members of two or more patrilineages, which may belong to the same or different sibs, unite themselves into political confederacies. These unions are reasonably stable and vary as to numbers of lineages and members, and they are the most inclusive politically organized groups within the Kapauku tribe. In the southern half of the Kamu Valley (the place of my fieldwork) a typical confederacy consists of two, three, or four lineages of different sibs, whose members (usually about 600 people) inhabit three to nine villages. This union is a confederacy in the sense that any of its constituent lineages is politically and legally semi-independent, and need not participate (although this is rare) in wars of the rest of the confederated lineages if its headman regards the war as unjustified. Aside from its political role, the confederacy has no economic, educational, religious, or ceremonial functions. Whereas the headman administers law and order within this group, the confederacy's relations beyond its territorial boundaries are confined to political negotiations and wars.

The confederacy's headman, who must possess the four Kapauku qualifications for leadership (health, wealth, generosity, and eloquence), is usually a middle-aged individual, brave in war and skilled in magic. Invariably, he is also a leader (*tonowi;* see Chapter Three) of the most numerous lineage, within which, if it is further subdivided, he is the *tonowi* of the most powerful sublineage. Furthermore, within the sublineage he is the head of its largest constituent household. Thus the statuses of a headman are cumulative: achievement of a higher status in a more inclusive group depends on his being headman of the strongest constituent subgroup. In settling internal disputes the headman of the confederacy functions as a sort of a "chief justice" for the whole political unit. His word is also most decisive in interconfederational affairs, including disputes of his constituents with outsiders, and problems of war and peace. Every subgroup of the confederacy (lineage, sublineage, household) has a leader of its own with the same personal qualifications required of the confederacy headman, whose scope of jurisdiction and political activity is limited by the inclusiveness of his subgroup.

Of the political unions of the southern part of the Kamu Valley the Ijaaj-Pigome Confederacy provides an outstanding example of a multiplicity of legal systems whose laws, even as basic and important as those of incest, differ in their content from one system to another, to the point of contradiction. As Figure 3 shows, the confederacy consists of four lineages whose members belong to three different sibs; two lineages are segments of the Ijaaj sib, the third is a subgroup of the Pigome sib, and the fourth belongs to the Dou sib. Because all the Kapauku sibs are subdivided into named subsibs, the two Ijaaj lineages of the confederacy belong to the Buna-Ijaaj, the Dou lineage to the Dou Pugaikoto, and the Pigome lineage to the Pigome Umaagopa subsibs. The core of the confederacy is formed by the Ijaaj-Gepouja and the Pigome-Obaaj lineages. Their members reside in five of the seven confederacy's villages—the Ijaaj-Gepouja people live in Botukebo, Aigii, Jagawaugii, Kojogeepa, and in half of the Obajbegaa village; the less

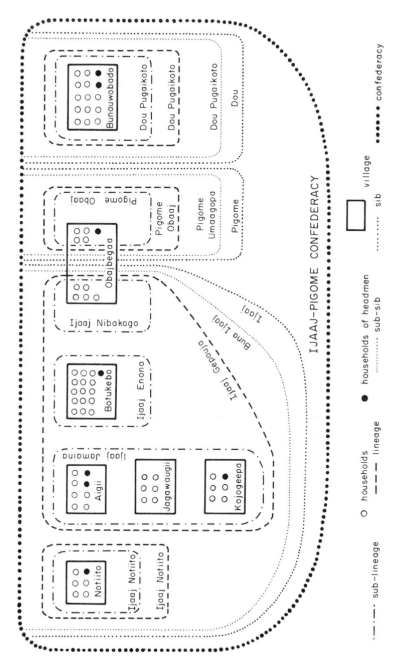

FIGURE 3. Structure of the Kapauku Ijaaj-Pigome Confederacy

numerous Pigome-Obaaj Kapauku reside only in the other half of the Obaj-begaa community. The Ijaaj-Notiito and Dou Pugaikoto lineages, whose members make their homes in the villages of Notiito and Bunauwobado respectively, are more peripheral members of the political union, participating only in some of the wars of the confederacy. Because the Ijaaj-Gepouja grew very numerous they separated into three sublineages: the Ijaaj-Jamaina sublineage whose houses are located in the villages of Aigii, Jagawaugii, and Kojogeepa; the Ijaaj-Enona sublineage, all of whose members live in one village of Botukebo; and the smallest sublineage of Ijaaj-Nibakago whose population satisfies itself with only one-half of the Obajbegaa village. Following the Kapauku rules of political leadership (described above), the power within the confederacy was delegated to Ijaaj Ekajewaijokaipouga, the wealthiest man of the Ijaaj-Jamaina sublineage. In this group he is the head of the most numerous household, located in the village of Aigii. Since this sublineage is the most numerous subgroup of the Ijaaj-Gepouja lineage, Ekajewaijokaipouga is also the headman in that more inclusive grouping. Finally, because this lineage is the strongest of all the five confederated lineages, it is he who functions as the head of the whole confederacy.

In order to understand the plurality of law that exists within the Ijaaj-Pigome Confederacy we have to project it and view it constantly against the societal structure—the diagrammed pattern of the confederacy's subgroups. A rather detailed account of the history of a multiple system of laws of incest within the political union is given in Chapter Six. Here I may just state that the multiplicity of laws of incest was caused by an incestuous love affair, and subsequent successful "legislation" of Awiitigaaj, the headman of the Ijaaj-Enona sublineage of the village of Botukebo. He succeeded in changing an old rule of sib exogamy into a new law that permitted intrasib marriages as close as between second cousins. As time went on more and more young men followed the example of the innovator. The new law did not remain confined to the Ijaaj-Enona sublineage. Two other sublineage headmen, six additional men from allied villages, and even the head of the confederacy himself, Ekajewaijokaipouga, chose their wives from their own sibs. Finally the whole Ijaaj-Gepouja lineage accepted, with some modifications, the new incest regulations. The law of incest in the Ijaaj-Pigome Confederacy became complicated and to a casual observer bewildering. While marriages of second paternal parallel cousins who even resided in the same village became permissible in the Ijaaj-Enona sublineage, in the rest of the related Ijaaj sublineages only a marriage with a girl from the same sib but of a different sublineage was legal. These regulations contrasted with the law of the Pigome lineage in which intrasib marriages remained prohibited under punishment of severe beating. The Dou lineage proved to be the most resistant to the innovation and continued, in accordance with the tradition, to punish by execution offenders of the taboo on intrasib marriages.

It would be only logical to assume that these striking differences between the laws of incest of the various subgroups within a single political confederacy would pose serious problems as far as jurisdiction is concerned. After all, the confederacy headman, who, being of the Ijaaj-Gepouja lineage, himself publicly rejected and actually violated the old rule of sib exogamy, ruled over lineages whose authorities punished such violations by beating or execution. The solution to this problem may be found in the societal structure and rules of jurisdiction. As there is only one lineage in the Pigome or Dou sibs, a couple could commit incest only if both the male and the female were members of the same lineage of either of the two sibs. Because the Kapauku have a rule according to which an individual may be tried only by an authority of the group to which he belongs, a dispute is referred to the authority of the least inclusive group that includes both litigants as its members. Consequently, in the case of Pigome and Dou people, it is the lineage headman rather than the leader of the whole confederacy who exercises the jurisdiction. As there is no appeal from a verdict among the Kapauku, the decision is final and never subject to revision by the confederacy headman. The same jurisdictional principles are, of course, applied within the Ijaaj-Gepouja lineage; thus the law of incest has different content in the three sublineages of that kinship group (Pospisil 1963a: pp. 49–50).

The differences between the various legal levels of the Ijaaj-Pigome Confederacy are not, of course, limited only to the content of the law that is adjudicated. The types of adjudicated offenses and the use of particular sanctions in the decisions passed by the various headmen also mark important differences between the legal systems of the different types of the Kapauku social groups. For example, disputes arising from refusal of economic cooperation are adjudicated only on the family and household levels. The legal authorities of sublineages, lineages, and the confederacy do not recognize such disputes; only if additional delicts are committed, such as physical violence, do these cases become legally pertinent at those levels, but even then only as cases of physical assault, murder, and so on. Similarly, breaches of etiquette and verbal quarreling are punishable only on the family level. Outside the family such instances are not subject to the authoritarian decisions or advice of the various leaders. War crimes and disloyalty during interconfederational hostilities are brought exclusively to the attention of the headman of the entire confederacy and adjudicated by him and his counsels. As far as specific types of legal sanctions (that form one of the four essential attributes of the legal decisions) are concerned, their use is in some instances also restricted to specific legal levels. Accordingly, slapping as punishment for delicts is confined to the family and household levels; a death sentence cannot be legally pronounced by the head of a household (although it is used on all other legal levels ranging from the family to the confederacy). Also, payment of blood money and confiscation of all property are punishments which only authorities of more inclusive groups than a household can mete out.

The multiplicity of legal systems in cvilized societies has long been realized and mentioned in the legal literature by such authors as von Gierke, Ehrlich, Weber, and Llewellyn; its validity need not be demonstrated. It suffices here merely to point out, in a very sketchy way, examples of multiplicity of legal systems in three civilizations—the West, the Chinese, the Inca—that are not related to each other by legal tradition.

In a Western society that is composed of autonomous or semiautonomous administrative units, such as the United States, there exist, besides the federal or national legal system that is applied to the whole society (nation), the legal systems of its component states, many provisions of which actually contradict and conflict with federal law and the constitution. Many of these flagrant contradictions have been maintained until the present, when some of them are being ruled out by the US Supreme Court as unconstitutional (e.g. state laws pertaining to segregation and racial discrimination), while others are being carried on into the future. However, the multiplicity of legal systems does not end, according to von Gierke, Ehrlich, Weber *et al.,* at the level of the states. These authors clearly recognize that the various associations within the states have also formal bodies of regulations which, in essence, belong in the field of law, especially when they are recognized as valid by the superimposed state law.

I would like to go even farther and acknowledge the existence of legal systems in any organized group and their subgroups within the state. Consequently and ultimately, even a small grouping such as the American family has a legal system administered by the husband, or wife, or both, as the case may be. Even there, in individual cases, the decisions and rules enforced by the family authorities may be contrary to the law of the state and might be deemed illegal. Indeed, there are ruthlessly enforced legal systems of groups whose existence and *raison d'être* are regarded by the state not only as illegal but even criminal. That criminal gangs such as Cosa Nostra have their rules, judicial bodies, and sanctions that are more severe than those of the state, is common knowledge. What is not realized is that their rules and judicial decisions embody the same types of criteria as does the state law (authority's decision, *obligatio,* intention of universal application, sanction). Therefore the principles contained in the gang leaders' decisions qualify to be regarded as parts of legal systems, although these would be illegal, criminal, and invalid according to the legal systems of the states. To disregard such systems, as is often done in the writings of legal scholars, reflects not a cool scientific introspect but a moral value judgment that has its place in philosophy but not in the sociology or anthropology of law.

The multiplicity of legal systems in the West is, however, not a unique phenomenon that may be attributed to the industrial revolution. China, during the Imperial and Republican eras, had several legal levels, of which those of the state, province, village, clan, and family were the most universal. A traditional juristic view of law would assume that behavior within the

Chinese family would be controlled by the law of the state, at least in such important aspects as physical punishment, marriage, and inheritance. But this is not borne out by the facts. To adhere dogmatically to the traditionalist view, which means insisting upon the existence of an all-regulating, consistent, and unified single legal system within the Chinese society, and to gloss over the obvious impossibility of applying this dogma by making such biased statements as "China still applies its laws in the old 'more or less' way," certainly does not help matters, and it impedes an analytical and accurate introspect into the nature of the complex Chinese system of social controls (Lang 1946: p. 220).

The recognition of multiple legal systems and levels, on the other hand, makes the pre-Communist Chinese legal situation understandable and meaningful. What appeared to a traditionalist as a corrupt, confusing, and unpredictable system, characterized by an almost absolute disregard of law, becomes a meaningful configuration of legal systems pertaining to specific groups, arranged into several levels according to the degree of inclusiveness of the types of social groups. Their study becomes a fascinating inquiry into the jural relationship of the structural units of the Chinese society rather than a frustrating exposition of confusing, illegal behavior of the Chinese people.

The statements above, referring to corrupt and illegal behavior, suggest that law differed profoundly on the various levels of Chinese society and was often contradictory. Thus, although the power of the father over the rest of the members of the group was curbed by the law of the state, in actuality in individual families "There was no *de facto* limitation on punishment by the father, whatever the *de jure* ones may have been" (Levy 1949: p. 76). The extreme punishment applied by the Chinese father, which certainly was "illegal" from the point of state law, was "severe flagellation with a bamboo rod from which a boy does not recover for a month" (Lang 1946: p. 240); the sons "sometimes were even beaten to death" (Levy 1949: p. 242). Similarly, although Article 985 of the Civil Code of the Republic of China stated explicitly that "A person who has a spouse may not contract another marriage" (Ching, Chow, and Chang 1931: p. 9), the law within the family ignored the state provision to such an extent that literally "thousands of businessmen, officials, landlords and others" who violated this provision and took several wives were "open to prosecution" (Lang 1946: p. 220) but were not prosecuted. The difference of familial law in this respect, and its disregard for state law, are best characterized by the following statement of Olga Lang: "The chief of police in a Shantung town in which the author stayed in 1936 introduced both his wives to his guests and proudly showed pictures of both weddings. And he was supposed to enforce the new law!" (Lang 1946: p. 220).

On the family legal level the state laws regulating inheritance fared no better. Although Article 1144 of the Civil Code stipulates that there should be no discrimination as to the sex of the spouse, and either should inherit equally from the other (Ching, Chow, and Chang 1931: p. 50), in actuality the family or clan law preferred males (and sons over wives) and ignored the provision. Similarly, "the difference between the status of boys adopted as legal heirs and adopted 'out of charity' was abolished by the legal code but was still observed generally: the legal heir had to be a member of one's clan" (Lang 1946: p. 179).

Legal systems that markedly differed in content from the all-embracing law of Imperial China were also those of the Chinese gilds. "In China the gilds have never been within the law. They grew up outside it, and, as associations, have never recognized the civil law nor claimed protection from it" (Morse 1909: p. 27). Law within a Chinese gild was administered by an elected committee of twelve individuals, one of whom acted as chairman. The effectiveness and power of the gild's legal decisions was so great that it sometimes forced a member to commit a murder (according to state law) by executing an offender against gild law. For example, in Soochow a member of the local Goldbeaters' Gild, being within the state law and enjoying the protection of the magistrate, violated the rules by acquiring more apprentices than the gild's law allowed. For this offense he was sentenced to be bitten to death: "Gild members to the number of 120 each took a bite, no one being allowed to leave the place whose lips and teeth were not bloody, and the rebel against the gild was soon no more" (Morse 1909: p. 30).

The Inca Empire presents an interesting case of multiplicity of legal systems. Although unbelievably centralized, regimented, and controlled, the Inca allowed and actually supported a multitude of differing legal systems. The overall one dealt mainly with matters pertaining to the economic problems of the empire and to serious crimes, leaving other delicts and civil disputes to be adjudicated according to the local law of the pertinent *ayllu* community (Murdock 1934: p. 432). This situation came about by conquest. When new tribes and localities were conquered by the Inca, the tribal customs and laws were not abolished; neither were their chiefs removed if they surrendered. "The Imperial policy never favored complete submission; the Incas necessarily evolved methods for preserving local institutions" (Gibson 1948: p. 11). Accordingly, "the former clan chief, instead of being deposed, was allowed to remain in office; he was absorbed into the official hierarchy as a 'centurion' " (Murdock 1934: p. 416). This official, then, enforced in his local court the imperial code and the common (customary) law of the local *ayllu*. His legal procedure had a dual character. Whereas it was characterized by a legalistic and very rigid enforcement of the imperial code, in the sphere of the common law it consisted of a rather creative interpretation of the customary law of the local *ayllu*. In the adjudication of the common law the official enjoyed relative freedom, unrestricted by the Inca statutes:

"When the law of the Incas was violated the judge had to apply the sanction without any modification; on the contrary, he enjoyed a certain leeway when he dealt with the local customary rules" (Baudin 1928: p. 183, tr. Leopold Pospisil).[7] Thus "the Incas altered but slightly the customary laws prevalent in the various parts of the empire, merely superimposing upon them a body of regularized rules designed to guarantee the stability of the state and its fiscal and social system" (Murdock 1934: p. 431). This multiplicity of legal systems, however, was not limited only to the *ayllu* community level. In the law of the Empire there were, in a sense, also two legal systems in existence. However, unlike the *ayllu* level, where the jurisdiction of the various systems followed the principle of territoriality (e.g., being applied to subjects according to the place of the crime and domicile of the defendant), the two imperial systems followed the principle of personality of law: there were different rules and punishments for delicts of the commoners and those of the nobles. One of the striking differences lay in the sanctions—physical punishment was the rule for the common people, but it was believed that the nobility could be more effectively punished by various psychological sanctions (Means 1931: p. 348).

CENTER OF LEGAL POWER

In our Western civilization we are accustomed to regard the law of the state as the primary, almost omnipotent standard to which the individual looks for protection and with which he tries to conform in his behavior. Only within the framework of this basic conformity, we tend to think, may there exist additional controls of the family, clique, association, and so on. In other words, in the West it is assumed that the center of power controlling most of the behavior of the citizens of a modern nation lies on the level of the society as a whole. If we identify the center of power in a given society with that legal level whose authorities pass decisions that prevail in situations of conflict with similar judgments of authorities of groups from other legal levels, then there seems (at least on the surface) to be some justification for that assumption. Nevertheless, even in this respect Max Weber found exceptions.

> *The law of the state often tries to obstruct the coercive means of other consociations; the English Libel Act thus tries to preclude blacklisting by excluding the defense of truth. But the state is not*

[7]"Lorsqu'il s'agissait d'une violation de la loi de l'Inca, le juge devait appliquer la peine sans pouvoir la modifier; il jouissaît au contraire d'une certaine latitude lorsqu'il avait à s'inspirer des règles coutumières locales qui importaient peu aux pouvoirs publics." (Baudin 1928: p. 183)

always successful. There are groups stronger than the state in this respect, for instance, those groups and associations, usually based on social class, which rely on the "honor code" of the duel as the means of resolving conflicts. With courts of honor and boycott as the coercive means at their disposal, they usually succeed in compelling, with particular emphasis, the fulfillment of obligations as "debts of honor," for instance, gambling debts or the duty to engage in a duel; such debts are intrinsically connected with the specific purposes of the group in question, but, as far as the state is concerned, they are not recognized, or are even proscribed. (Weber 1967: p. 18)[8]

Weber goes beyond his examples and generalizes: "This conflict between the means of coercion of the various corporate groups is as old as the law itself. In the past it has not always ended with the triumph of the coercive means of the political body, and even today this has not always been the outcome" (Weber 1967: p. 19).[9] Indeed, even in the United States nowadays, several decades later, the center of power does not always lie with the state or federal law. The law of the criminal gang is usually provided with sanctions much harsher and infinitely more effective and immediate in application than sanctions of the official law of the country; therefore members of such organizations conform primarily with the legal system of their illicit organization. Thus, as far as the gangsters are concerned, the legal center of power is located in the gang rather than on the level of the society as a whole. Consequently, the dogma regarding the law of the state as the most powerful source of social control proves to be a myth in some instances in our Western civilization. How badly this dogma must fare in cultures where it is not only not held, but is never even thought of!

In China, for example, the imperial law was regarded only as a

model according to which other cases might be solved. Therefore the rule Nullum crimen sine praevia lege poenali *could*

---

[8]"Das Recht der Staatsanstalt stellt sich Zwangsmitteln anderer Verbände nicht selten in den Weg: so macht die englische 'libel act' schwarze Listen durch Ausschluss des Wahrheitsbeweises unmöglich. Aber nicht immer mit Erfolg. Die auf dem 'Ehren-kodex' des Duells als Mittel des Streitaustrages beruhenden, dem Wesen nach meist ständischen Verbände und Gruppen mit ihren Zwangsmitteln: im wesentlichen Ehren-gerichte und Boykott, sind im allgemeinen die stärkeren und erzwingen meist mit spezifischem Nachdruck (als 'Ehrenschulden') gerade staatsanstaltlich nicht geschütze oder perhorreszierte, aber für ihre Gemeinschaftszwecke unentbehrliche Verbindlich-keiten (Spielschulden, Duellpflicht)." (Weber 1922: p. 372)

[9]"Dieser Kampf zwischen den Zwangsmitteln verschiedener Verbände ist so alt wie das Recht. Er hat in der Vergangenheit sehr oft nicht mit dem Siege der Zwangsmittel des politischen Verbandes geendet und auch heute ist dies nicht immer der Fall." (Weber 1922: p. 373)

*not exist. This idea moreover involved that the written law was
not necessarily always implied. It was only a model to be
followed under certain circumstances and had no binding force
as such. (van der Valk 1939: p. 13)*

Matters were not helped when a Western lawyer labeled the Chinese system
as corrupt because the law of the Emperor, or later of the Republic, was
simply disregarded and the magistrates of the various provinces followed
different principles. These, in spite of the Western legalistic objections, have
to be regarded as legal. However, it would be a mistake to think that the
center of power in China lay on the level of the province, or that it was the
law created and maintained by the magistrate to which the individual tried
primarily to conform. In the old China the center of power most definitely
was located in the family. It was because of this that the "magistrates have
held the entire family responsible for the conduct of its members" and
authorities of old China were applying sanctions to whole families rather
than to the individual criminal (Latourette 1934, vol. 2: p. 183). The powerful
and influential position of the Chinese family is best reflected in the following
statement by Latourette: "The family has been looked upon as a model for
the government, and the state has been thought of as a large family" (1934,
vol. 2: p. 183). Even within the Chinese clan (*tsu*) the decisions of the
chia-chang, the family head, was for a Chinese the primary standard to
conform to. Consequently, "A *chia-chang* might follow a *tsu* ruling concerning his family but his family members would not obey a *tsu* ruling as
opposed to one of the *chia-chang*" (Levy 1949: p. 165).

If we turn from civilized to tribal societies, the fallacy of the dogma
that the true and most powerful type of law exists only on the society level
becomes even more obvious. There are many ethnic groups whose society
lacks an overall political organization. There are no tribal chiefs, headmen,
or councils of elders to adjudicate intratribal disputes. For the Western-
biased anthropologist the solution to the problem was often simple indeed:
He invented a society without law, or with a "law" that was manifested in
such flagrantly antilegal phenomena as feuds, *lex talionis,* and war. Rather
than to indulge in such intellectual gymnastics for the sake of saving an
ethnocentric bias from annihilation, I propose to relinquish not only the
discussed dogma, but also the Durkheimean generalizations and, in our
quest for law, to turn to specific functioning of politically organized subgroups of these societies.

The "lawless," politically unorganized tribe of the Kapauku Papuans
may provide an example. The Kapauku do not have an overall tribal organization with chiefs who would solve internal problems and keep peace by
application of a tribal law. In other words, there is, strictly speaking, no
"Kapauku law." Indeed, an overwhelming majority of wars and feuds in
which these Papuans engage takes place within the tribe. However, this does

not mean that we have to declare this society to be devoid of law, and settle for this very easy and comfortable solution. Law implies regularity and order and its existence requires an organized group of people who uphold the order and take care that it is enforced in situations involving individuals who are unwilling to conform. Consequently, it is at the politically organized confederacy level, and those of its subgroups, that we have to look for the law that is responsible for social control in this native society.

Members of these functioning subgroups cannot allow offenses to go unpunished and disputes within the groups to continue indefinitely without a solution, for the simple reason that these disorders challenge the very existence of these groups. Thus, unlike the Kapauku tribe, which does not represent a group in a social sense, the tribe's functioning subgroups cannot exist without law and order. Adjudication of disputes and determination of the rights and duties of the parties (including punishment for offenses) are entrusted to their headmen. It is interesting to note that even within this hierarchy of subgroups the center of power does not lie on the most inclusive level of the political confederacy. Because of the amount of power manifested in the severity of sanctions (including even execution), and the degree of control over dependable followers, the center of power in the Kapauku society lies on the level of the sublineage or nonsubdivided lineage. Thus I may conclude that, although there is no law on the level of the Kapauku society as a whole, and despite the fact that the center of legal power lies below the level of the most inclusive political unit—the confederacy—the Kapauku people do possess law, in the same way as do the German-speaking peoples of Europe, who are not politically unified (thus lacking an overall unifying legal system), and who live in the states of West Germany, East Germany, Switzerland, Austria, Liechtenstein, Luxembourg, and Italy.

In the long perspective the center of power, of course, is not a static phenomenon. The relative amount of power at the various levels within a society (in the different types of groups of varying inclusiveness) may diminish or increase, with the result that the center of power (defined by the relative amount of control power of the various societal segments) may shift its position to another level. Among the Kapauku of the Kamu Valley, for example, in the years 1955 and 1956 the power center started to shift from the sublineage to the confederacy, and from there, before it became firmly entrenched, to move again to the village, formerly a completely unimportant societal segment. These shifts were the result of the emerging Dutch control in the area, and reflected the attitude of that administration. The Dutch regarded as politically relevant those groups whose membership was defined on the basis of political affiliation or residence. They did not understand and consequently, did not pay too much attention to, the lineages and sublineages, whose organizational principle was kinship—a principle that appeared to the Dutch officials to have no place in the field of politics and law.

Similarly, in recent years we have witnessed in China a shift of the center of power from the family to the newly centralized Communist state. In Peru, among the Quechua, the power center traditionally was divided between the state and the local community (*ayllu*). However, in the contemporary Peruvian situation the administrator of the community has often been deprived of all power and responsibility, with the result that "the Governor of the district intervenes in all the affairs of the community" (Mishkin 1946: p. 446). As a consequence the Quechua, who distrust and dislike the Spanish-speaking administrators, have ceased to look to the community official as a representative of a law that should prevail locally, with the effect that "the authority exercised by the head of the family extends beyond the economic sphere into the political and religious life of the *Quechua*" (Mishkin 1946: p. 450). Nowadays, "according to the native theory, family interests determine the community interests." Since the interests of the various families often diverge, "the interests of the community appear contradictory and confused. . . . Unified community action consequently becomes relatively rare," with the result that "as the community loses its force and significance, the institution of the family gains in stature. . . . In the end, after a prolonged interfamily feud, the community is torn with internal strife, while the family is all the more strengthened" (Mishkin 1946: p. 450).

Among the Araucanian Indians of Chile contact with Western civilization produced a similar "downward shift" of the center of power. In the aboriginal days "the unilocal household seems to have been the central element in the system" (Titiev 1951: p. 54). Its head, *loñko,* administered the land held in common by the household. However, with the Chilean introduction of individual land ownership the *loñko*'s position lost importance: "As long as men hold individual titles to their land and its usufruct, they do not need to rely on a *loñko* to tell them when or where to farm" (Titiev 1951: p. 146). Thus the center of power among the Araucanians moved to the level of the family.

DYNAMICS OF LEGAL LEVELS

The number and types of legal levels in a given society is, of course, not constant. Some types of political groupings within a society may disappear (for example, a collapse of a centralized government with a subsequent shift of sovereignty to the formerly unified provinces), and new types may be created. From the logical point of view new levels may be created by subdividing existing groups of a given level or by unifying them into more inclusive groups, thus superimposing in the existing hierarchy a new level upon the old one. In the recent history of Western civilization we find plenty of examples of segmentation of political groups into new types of units of a lower level. For example, by introducing the administrative and legislative dualism of Austria and Hungary, the once monolithic Habsburg Empire interposed a new political and legal level between that of the Empire and its individual "lands."

Among the primitives, segmentation usually occurs in a gradual and informal way, as a response to some demographic, economic, or political pressure, rather than through an authoritative and formal act of a political nature. In the old days, among the Kapauku societal segments with political functions the village was conspicuously absent. If one understands the nature of an old Kapauku village and that of the sublineage, the reason for this absence becomes obvious. The territory of the old Kapauku sublineage constituted a true home of the natives. There they could and did own garden land in any part and they were free also to build their houses in any part of this territory. Clusters of their homes formed villages of a semipermanent nature. When the cultivated area around such a settlement had been exhausted, the people, often individually, moved their homes to new localities. New villages sprang up in former forests or marshes, and old residential localities reverted to bush. Thus on the sublineage or nonsubdivided lineage territory there were often several communities, their location and number changing with time. The enduring grouping was the sublineage, not the village. To this kinship-oriented group the political and judicial functions were attached. A village was invested only with purely economic roles of a temporary nature, and was politically integrated into the more inclusive sublineage. A sublineage whose members reside in several villages was likely to have several headmen. If these happen to live in different villages they tended to be identified with the place of residence, and superficially resembled village headmen.

To sum up the situation, prior to the pacification of the area by the Dutch authorities the villages, although they were in existence, did not constitute politically organized groups. The sublineage headman who administered justice in them actually had jurisdiction over all the villages of the sublineage territory, irrespective of his own residence (which often shifted because he might own houses in several villages). With the coming of the Dutch administration, the officials, often ignorant of the native political structure and influenced by their past experience in Indonesia, regarded the local strongmen as *kapala kampoeng* (village chiefs) and attributed to them jurisdiction within the local villages. Indeed, for convenience and efficiency's sake they often gave them the official title of *kapala* (although this was not authorized by the Dutch government), which in turn conveyed the idea of village chieftainship. Because they preferred to deal with *kapala*s rather than with the more elusive informal headmen of poorly understood kin units, a new legal level of village authority was created. As the administration gained importance through economic influence and police enforcement of the administration's law, the formal village leaders gained strength and prestige, thus securing the political position of the village in the Kapauku hierarchy of legal levels.

Creation of a new legal level through unification of politically organized groups that formerly were legally and politically independent may
occur in three ways: through a formal agreement to form a political union,
through conquest of one group by another and a simultaneous retention of
the former groupings as segments of the new overall political structure, or
through a slow evolutionary process—a gradual emergence of a new legal
stratum recognized as binding by the groups which, through the practices
of their members (informal procedures as well as various formal agreements), have slowly developed it.

International law administered through the court at The Hague, the
law governing the Coal and Steel Community, and the legal system dealing
with the economic problems of the West European Common Market may
serve as examples of creation of a more inclusive legal system through the
mechanism of formal agreements. To show that such a formalistic agreement
is not necessarily limited to civilized peoples I may turn again to the Kapauku
Papuans, in particular to the history of the Ijaaj-Pigome Confederacy of the
southern Kamu Valley. The valley used to be a lake. As the Edege River cut
its bed deeper through the southern outlet from the old Kamu Valley, it
drained the waters of the huge lake and exposed a flat and fertile alluvial
plain. Approximately 120 years ago Ijaaj Gepouja with his relatives arrived
in the region from the neighboring Mapia Valley and claimed part of the
fertile but still periodically inundated territory. From the north (Paniai Lake
region) came a lineage of the Pigome sib. Originally they settled in the Debei
Valley, but after an agreement they became political allies of the Ijaaj lineage, receiving from them part of their land and settling in one of the five
villages on the Ijaaj-Gepouja lineage territory, thus laying the foundations for
a new political confederacy. Through additional agreements the Notiito
lineage of the Ijaaj sib and the Bunauwobado lineage of the Dou sib joined
the union to protect themselves against the raids of the surrounding hostile
neighbors. Throughout the hundred years of its history the confederacy
recognized as its leader the richest and most influential man, who invariably
came from the strongest Ijaaj lineage of Ijaaj-Gepouja and, after it segmented, from its most numerous subdivision—the Ijaaj-Jamaina sublineage.
Through adjudication of disputes between the members of the constituent
lineages the succession of confederacy headmen created a new legal system
for the confederacy, which was superimposed upon the legal systems of the
four constituent lineages.

The conquest of a politically organized group by another may lead to
creation of a new legal level if the organization of the old group is maintained
and a new, unifying, overall system, represented and created by the leadership of the conquerors, is imposed upon it. Conquest "kingdoms" of
Polynesia may serve as examples of this process. In some cases, however,
the superimposition of a new legal level may not be so simple and may,
structurally speaking, produce significant changes in the nature and compo-

sition of the conquered groups. These changes may occur without any intent or effort exercised by the conquerors.

An interesting example of such a development is presented by the changes that occurred in the Kapauku Papuan political alliances of lineages in the Kamu Valley after the Dutch "pacification" of the territory in 1956. Prior to this time, there existed about a dozen of the traditional political confederacies as described above. Later, when a Dutch resident administrator arrived in the Kamu Valley, he decided to make his home at Moanemani village in the western part of his new domain, which was the area most suitable for construction of an airstrip. He began to hold courts in his residence, settling disputes among the people, especially those that involved individuals from formerly hostile confederacies. Thus a new legal system (and level) was substituted for the former diplomatic negotiations and wars. In the nearby village of Mauwa an enterprising local headman called Jupikaapaibo, of the Goo sib, seized upon the new opportunities and befriended the Dutch administrator to such a degree that the latter made him some sort of a contact man between himself and the Kapauku. After this appointment the old system of Kamu Valley confederacies started to disintegrate, and the constituent lineages began to group themselves into two large conglomerations. One was led by Jupikaapaibo, the friend of the Dutch administrator, the other by Jokagaibo of the Ijaaj sib, who was already a very wealthy man and, since 1960, the leader of the Ijaaj-Pigome Confederacy. Jokagaibo derived additional prestige from friendship with myself, the only other "secular white man" in the valley. In its final stage in 1962 the valley was neatly divided politically. The supporters of Jupikaapaibo occupied the northern and western part; Jokagaibo's followers belonged to the lineages residing in the eastern, central, and southern portions of the Kamu Valley. Thus Jokagaibo wielded legal and political authority in a new group, much larger than his former Ijaaj-Pigome Confederacy (in which, in 1954–1955, he was only a sublineage leader), which united his old constituency with the confederacies of his former traditional enemies. As he explained to me, the situation had changed and with it the political issues and alliances. The power of Jupikaapaibo, backed unwittingly by the Dutch administrator, became overwhelming and required an adequate and concentrated opposition which the old type of smaller and numerous confederacies could not provide. Therefore a new alliance system, resembling a sort of "superconfederacy," had to be formed. In his new role Jokagaibo not only adjudicated disputes among his followers but also defended their interests at the court of Moanemani, especially when the opponent in the dispute belonged to Jupikaapaibo's camp.

Formation of a new, superimposed legal level through the process of unification of formerly independent politically organized groups may be also achieved through an evolutionary process. A gradual emergence of a new level is often accomplished by small, gradual steps, of which establishment of agents for diplomatic contact and avoidance of warfare is usually the first and fundamental one. It is often preceded by a development of trade relations between the involved groups, which usually requires travel and protection through the well-known institution of trade partnership. Such was the origin of the incipient territorial organization among the Kalinga of Northern Luzon. At the time of the advent of the Americans, this territorial organization was already in existence and its pertinent legal level was superimposed upon the older legal levels of groups of lesser inclusiveness: the family, the kin group, and the community (village or town). Any scholar interested in the emergence of the state organization has an opportunity to study it in its initial stage (Barton 1949: pp. 137–217).

The Kalinga family, with its head (either of the spouses) who controlled some of the behavior of his family's members, was tightly knit into the structure of the more inclusive unit—the Kalinga kin group. Through informal arbitration and more formal decisions, the kin group leader, called *kadangyan,* kept peace and order within this group. There he wielded such power that the loss of his support to a kinsman amounted to an excommunication from the village, a hopeless individual existence among hostile kin groups (Barton 1949: pp. 32–83).

The Kalinga community, composed of several such kin groups, stands under the leadership of several *pangats.* These are powerful and wealthy individuals who, by their past exploits in headhunting, knowledge of ethics and law, wisdom, and skill in settling interfamily and interkin group disputes, command the respect of their coresidents (Barton 1949: pp. 147–149). In settling local disputes within a village or town by inducing the natives to follow their opinions, the *pangats* informally create and uphold a community legal system which is superimposed upon the legal systems of the kin groups, thus functioning not on the basis of the principle of personality of law (in which jurisdiction is determined by the kinship status of the parties to the dispute), but on the principle of territoriality (in which jurisdiction is determined by the place of residence of the disputants). Should they need detective and police work for the success of their decision-making and moderating activity, they rely upon their close kin and unrelated henchmen (Barton 1949: pp. 147–163). Whereas in internal disputes they function individually and their roles resemble those of counselors of the parties, arbiters, or judges in Western society (Barton 1949: p. 160), in intervillage disputes they meet in public gatherings, together with the rest of the citizens, in order to decide upon the policy that their community should follow (Barton 1949: p. 159). Thus they function as legal counsels and authorities in internal disputes, while in external cases of trouble they play the role of politicians, representing the interests of their own community rather than acting as a third party in a role of arbiter, moderator, or judge. Consequently, *pangat* law does not transcend the boundaries of the local community.

To curb incessant killings and prolonged feuds, and to provide an avenue for peaceful coexistence of communities, the Kalinga have invented pact holders. The individual who assumes this status is already a *pangat* who has concluded, through long and complex ceremonies involving feasts, visiting, and gift exchange, a "peace treaty" with a *pangat* of another community. As a prerequisite of his officialdom a pact holder in a town or village is also approved by the members of the formerly hostile community of his pact holder partner, and subsequently confirmed by *pangats* of his own village or town. Thus the formally instituted pact holder functions in his home as a sort of ambassador representing the interests of the coresidents of his partner, the pact holder of the other community. The purpose of this envoy-like institution is primarily to ensure peace between the two settlements. This is accomplished by bringing to an end the existing feuds through payment of blood money, by protection of the foreigners in the pact holder's village against injustice or criminal acts of the latter's covillagers, by aiding the foreigners in their pursuit of trade, and by offering them shelter and food during their stay in the community.

The pact contains additional agreements concerning the eventuality of sickness or death of the foreigners in the pact holder's village. Should a man break the treaty by killing an individual whose community is represented by the pact holder, the latter has the right as well as duty to investigate the case and, if the killing is found unjustified, either to kill the offender or to collect blood money for the relatives of the slain man. A Kalinga pact holder thus actually adjudicates the cases of trouble and in some of them avails himself of the supreme penalty—capital punishment—which he inflicts upon his coresident. Principles that permeate individual decisions of the pact holders, whether they emanate from the formal wording of the treaty or from customary usages not made explicit, may be regarded quite justifiably as legal, belonging to a system that in its application transcends the boundaries of a community, linking two of these into a new incipient territorial unit (Barton 1949: pp. 194–199). The resulting network of dyadic Kalinga pacts Barton calls a "budding state" (1949: p. 199), and its legal systems may be assigned, according to my conceptualization and Barton's terminology, to the "legal level of the Kalinga budding state." Like Barton, I am inclined to believe that a future development, if undisturbed from outside, would eventually solidify the Kalinga territorial unit into what may be justifiably called a state, provided with leadership derived from the institution of the pact holders, and governed by a unified legal system whose roots rest in the principles incorporated in the original individual pacts.

CONCLUSION

The essential feature of law is its existence in concrete legal decisions. Rules for behavior that are not applied in legal decisions and consequently not enforced, although appearing in codifications in the form of dead laws, do not belong in the realm of law proper for the simple reason that they do not exercise social control. The essential feature of legal decision, in turn, is that a third party (authority) possesses the privilege to pass it. Furthermore, in order to pass a legally relevant decision whose provisions can actually be enforced, the adjudicating authority has to have power over both parties to the dispute—he must have jurisdiction over both litigants. In anthropological or sociological language this means that all three, the two litigants as well as the authority, have to belong to the same social group in which the latter wields judicial power (has jurisdiction). Law thus pertains to specific groups with well-defined membership; it does not just "float around" in a human society at large.

Because of this fact we should not expect to find law pertaining to a society as a whole if the society is not politically organized (unified). That, of course, does not mean that law would be absent in such a society. Society, be it a tribe or a "modern" nation, is not an undifferentiated amalgam of people. It is rather a patterned mosaic of subgroups that belong to certain, usually well-defined (or definable) types with different memberships, composition, and degree of inclusiveness. Every such subgroup owes its existence in a large degree to a legal system that is its own and that regulates the behavior of its members. Offenses within such a group cannot go unpunished and disputes cannot be allowed to continue indefinitely lest they disrupt and destroy the social group. Thus the existence of social control, which we usually call law, is of vital necessity to any functioning social group or subgroup. As a consequence, in a given society there will be as many legal systems as there are functioning social units.

This multiplicity of legal systems, whose legal provisions necessarily differ from one to another, sometimes even to the point of contradiction, reflects precisely the pattern of the subgroups of the society—what I have termed "societal structure" (structure of a society). Thus, according to the inclusiveness and types of the pertinent groups, legal systems can be viewed as belonging to different legal levels that are superimposed one upon the other, the system of a more inclusive group being applied to members of all its constituent subgroups. As a consequence, an individual is usually exposed to several legal systems simultaneously—to be exact, to as many systems as there are subgroups of which he is a member. This conception of a society as a patterned mosaic structure of subgroups with their specific legal systems and with a dynamic center of power brings together phenomena and processes of a basically legal nature that otherwise would be put into nonlegal categories and treated as being qualitatively different. It helps us to understand why a man in one society is primarily a member of his kin group or village and only secondarily of the tribe or state, whereas in another society the most inclusive, politically organized unit (a tribe or a state) controls him most. A gangster's behavior is not "absolutely illegal"; while it is definitely so on the state or national legal level, it has to be, at the same time, regarded as legal from the viewpoint of the gang. The field of law, it is obvious, does not escape the spreading notion of relativity.

Reflecting upon the above data and their interpretation, I have arrived at this conclusion: the examples and discussion have made it abundantly clear that any penetrating analysis of law of a primitive or civilized society can be attained only by relating it to the pertinent societal structure and legal levels, and by a full recognition of the plurality of legal systems within a society. After all, law as a category of social phenomena cannot be considered (as it traditionally has been) unrelated to the rest of the organizing principles of a society.

CHAPTER
FIVE
CHANGE
OF
LEGAL
SYSTEMS

As an integral part of culture, social phenomena that we classify as law are not static entities. Of necessity they have to change as the culture, of which they form a constituent part, changes. In the past, legal dynamics caught the fancy of many lawyers, philosophers, sociologists, and an-thropologists of law who concentrated their legal-theoretical efforts in this field. Soon it was recognized that the various inquiries into the history and principles of legal change were not of the same kind. Authors differed, one from another, not only in the methods they used and in theoretical conclu-sions they reached but also, and most importantly so, in the subject matter they chose to investigate. Vinogradoff categorized their efforts into two disciplines: legal history and historical jurisprudence. Accordingly he writes:

> In describing the way in which legal systems arise in the course
> of European development, our aim ought to be to strike averages
> and to discover the balance of forces, not to trace the
> innumerable fluctuations of the growth and decay of actual laws.
> The latter task belongs to legal history, while historical
> jurisprudence has to deal with the relation between the legal
> rules and the institutions of an epoch in their doctrinal
> connexion. (Vinogradoff 1922: p. 10)

Although he correctly distinguished the two categories of inquiries, I disagree with his conclusion that the nature of the two is such that they necessarily belong to two different disciplines. The difference, it seems to me, lies in the subject matter that is investigated. In the first instance it is the individual laws and their changes that are subjected to study; in the other it is the whole legal system as such, and its changing nature, which forms the focus of scholarly inquiry. In both cases we deal with social facts, and in both instances we are after abstract principles that govern the two types of changes. Therefore it is my opinion that both types of inquiry—investigation of social facts by empirical methods in order to arrive at generalizations (sociological laws)—constitute legitimate grounds for anthropological research. The first type of inquiry I shall call study of "the change of laws" (Vinogradoff's "legal history"); the second a study of the "change of legal systems" (Vinogradoff's "historical jurisprudence"). The second type became a favorite field of theorizing for lawyers, anthropologists, sociologists, and philosophers of the past and present. In contrast, the study of the change of laws has generally been neglected.

Because of the twofold division of the field of legal dynamics and because of the great amount of theoretical material that belongs to it, I propose to deal with its description and analysis in two subsequent chapters, in correspondence with the dichotomy discussed above. In the following chapter on change of laws I make my own theoretical contribution to the field; in this chapter I present a historical sequence of theories that not only contributed to the development of the science of law but also to the development of social science in general.

MONTESQUIEU (1689–1755)

Traditionally, law has been regarded by Europeans as an absolute and autonomous entity, independent of space and time, not related in any particular way to the nature of the society in which it existed. The doctrine of "Natural Law" constitutes philosophically the most elaborated form of this legal conception. Having its origin in ancient Greece, it assumed that human nature, and therefore also the human mind, was the same all over the world. Human nature was regarded as highly rational, just, moral, and social. The meaning of the concepts of justice, rationality, morality, and sociability were, of course, those that the Greeks and other later European societies derived from their own philosophies and value systems. Ultimately, Natural Law was thought to consist of a body of principles inherent in the nature of objects and living organisms, which, if allowed full and complete development, would create a universal harmony. Natural Law, as far as it referred to principles governing man's conduct and his relations with his fellow man, yielded principles that judges were supposed to employ in their adjudication

of conflicts, irrespective of time and space. This philosophy, which dominated European legal thought well into the nineteenth century, of course, left
little room for conceiving of law as a dynamic phenomenon and prevented
legal scholars from theorizing about legal change.

Apart from the trend of thought of his times, and anticipating a development that occurred more than a century later, Charles Louis Joseph de
Secondat, Baron de la Brède et de Montesquieu challenged the basic tenets
of Natural Law philosophy and dominating traditionalist legal theories by
presenting a radically different conceptualization of law and society. By his
revolutionary theorizing, which brought an avalanche of criticism from his
learned contemporaries, he earned the admiration and recognition of many
leading scholars of the two succeeding centuries. His impact on Western
jurisprudence and social philosophy was so great that it prompted Durkheim
(1960: p. 61) to the following evaluation: "It is Montesquieu who first laid
down the fundamental principles of social science" and "instituted a new
field of study, which we now call *comparative law*" (1960: p. 51).[1] "He
did not always interpret history correctly, and it is easy to prove him wrong.
But no one before him had gone so far along the way that led his successors
to true social science" (1960: p. 2).[2] Similarly, Stone (1950: p. 401) claims
that "Montesquieu's work laid the basis simultaneously of sociology in general and of sociological jurisprudence in particular" (1950: p. 401). Montesquieu's accomplishment was basically a radical change in the approach to
the study of law. With him it was no more a preconceived and purely
philosophical speculation achieved in the depth of an armchair. To him law
was composed of specific phenomena that one had to investigate. Of his
main work, *De l'Esprit des Lois,* Stark (1960: p. 9) says, "It is remarkable
for its insistence on the concrete, the tangible and the individual." Although
he still argues basically deductively, and uses data only to illustrate his
conclusions, Durkheim argues that he nevertheless introduces induction
(Durkheim 1960: p. 53).

Through his more exact outlook Montesquieu realized that law in a
given society was not a reflection of a universally valid set of legal principles
but rather an integral part of a particular people's culture. It was closely
related to the people's constitution, to the type of government, the political
and military fields, and to the other institutions existing in a particular society.
In other words, social orders, of which law is a part, were to Montesquieu
almost organically coherent wholes, so that "when the principles of government are once corrupt, the best laws become bad, and turn against the state;

---

[1]". . . a inauguré un nouveau genre d'études que nous appelons aujourd'hui
le droit comparé." (Durkheim 1953: p. 97)

[2]"Il n'a pas toujours correctement interprété l'histoire, et il est facile de le
convaincre d'erreur; mais personne auparavant ne s'était avancé aussi loin dans la
voie qui a conduit ses successeurs à la vraie science sociale." (Durkheim 1953, p. 28)

when its principles are healthy, the bad laws have the effect of good ones; the force of the principle pervades all" (Stark 1960: p. 170).[3] About the relationship of a legal system to a principle on which a particular government is founded Montesquieu had the following to say: "This connection of the laws with the appropriate principle controls all the links of the governmental system; and the principle itself receives in its turn a new force from it" (Stark 1960: p. 173).[4] The relationship of the type of political ("constitution") and of the pertinent legal system in force is not one-sided. It is not always the "constitution" that exercises influence and molds the legal system of a society; rather, it is an interdependence of law and constitution. Law itself may start a change and affect its superordinated constitution: "A small change in the civil laws often produces a change in the constitution. It appears small and has immense consequences" (Stark 1960: pp. 173–174).[5]

In view of the recognition of the law's dependence upon the rest of the culture in which it exists, it amounts almost to folly to think that a legal system of one nation can be easily transplanted into another culture and applied to another society. The laws "should be so proper to people for which they are made that it is a very great accident if those of one nation may suit another" (Stark 1960: p. 207).[6] Only in rare cases does Montesquieu admit a possibility of transplantation of law—when the institutions of the donor and those of the recipient society are "the same." "As the civil laws depend upon the political laws, because it is always for one society that they are made, it would be good, if it is desired to carry a civil law of one nation to another, to examine at the outset if they have both the same institutions and the same political law" (Stark 1960: p. 189).[7]

Thus Montesquieu, by conceiving of law as a relative phenomenon,

[3]"Lorsque les principes du gouvernement sont une fois corrompus, les meilleures lois deviennent mauvaises, et se tournent contre l'État; lorsque les principes en sont sains, les mauvaises ont l'effet des bonnes; la force du principe entraîne tout." (Montesquieu 1750, vol. 1: p. 168)

[4]"Ce rapport des loix avec ce principe tend tous les ressorts du gouvernement; et ce principe en reçoit à son tour une nouvelle force." (Montesquieu 1750, vol. 1: p. 57)

[5]"Un petit changement dans les lois civiles produit souvent un changement dans la constitution. Il paroît petit et a des suites immenses." (Montesquieu 1951: p. 1112)

[6]". . . doivent être tellement propres au peuple pour lequel elles sont faites, que c'est un très grand hazard si celles d'une nation peuvent convenir à une autre." (Montesquieu 1750, vol. 1: p. 9)

[7]"Comme les loix civiles dépendent des loix politiques, parce que c'est toujours pour une société qu'elles sont faites; il seroit bon que quand on veut porter une loi civile, d'une nation chez une autre, on examinât auparavant si elles ont toutes les deux les mêmes institutions, et le même droit politique." (Montesquieu 1750, vol. 2: p. 343)

broke with the traditionalist doctrine of natural law that depicted legal principles as absolute and universal. Accordingly, "the relation between law and
the manners (*moeurs*) of the particular people, at the particular time" was
the actual and crucial criterion of legal justice (Stone 1950: p. 272). Thus his
theory of law "challenged the current natural law assumption that ideal rules
of law were constant from age to age and from people to people, and could
be discovered by contemplation of man's ideal nature" (Stone 1950: p.
401).

Already in 1721 this theme of relativity of law formed a theoretical
backbone of Montesquieu's famous *Lettres Persanes,* a series of commen-
taries expressed by an imaginary, rational visitor from Persia, upon the
cruelties and abuse of criminal justice in Western civilization (Montesquieu
1929). In his *L'Essais sur le goût* of 1756, Montesquieu expressed his theory
of legal relativity in the following succint metaphor: "To judge the beauties
of Homer, it is necessary to place oneself in the camp of the Greeks, and
not in a French army" (Stark 1960: p. 39).[8] Without the necessary identification of the society from which a law came Montesquieu doubts that one can
grasp the proper meaning of the written rule. He asks: "How can one apply
a law if one does not know the country for which it has been made, and
the circumstances in which it has been made?" (Stark 1960: p. 76).[9] Even
if the provenience is identified, it is still necessary, for full appreciation of a
precept of a legislator, to specify the time in which the particular law originated: "We shall never judge men well if we do not allow them the prejudices of their time" (Stark 1960: p. 39).[10] Although in his realization of the
law's relative nature Montesquieu might have been influenced, as Stark and
others suggest (1960: p. 36), by some works of his contemporaries (such as
Gravina's *Origines Juris Civilis,* 1713), his work remains truly a revolutionary
accomplishment that influenced many later jurists and contributed to Bentham's conversion to philosophy and to his formulation of utilitarianism
(Stone 1965: p. 112).

This relativism pertains, of course, only to the law used for settlements
of disputes and punishment of offenders. This type of jural law, created by
legislators, Montesquieu distinguished from social-scientific laws. The latter,
to the contrary, are absolute (Montesquieu 1949, vol. 1: p. 1537); they are
of psychological nature (Durkheim 1960: p. 19), and hide behind the relative
laws which we find positively established in individual societies (Stark 1960:

[8]"Mais pour juger des beautés d'Homère, il faut se mettre dans le camp des
Grecs, non pas dans une armée française." (Montesquieu 1949, vol. 1: p. 1023)
[9]"Comment peut-on appliquer une loi si l'on ne sait pas le pays pour lequel
elle a été faite, et les circonstances dans lesquelles elle a été faite?" (Montesquieu
1949, vol. 1: p. 1076)
[10]". . . on ne jugera jamais bien des hommes si on ne leur passe les préjugés
de leur temps." (Montesquieu 1949, vol. 1: p. 1340)

p. 203). Durkheim explains Montesquieu's legal dichotomy by pointing out that to Montesquieu's mind the jural laws (as contrasted with scientific laws) "are based on reality, but not in the same way as the natural laws, since they result from the nature not of man, but of societies" (Durkheim 1960: pp. 19–20).[11]

Although it is the legislator, and ultimately the society, that creates and determines the particular legal system that he or it employs in controlling the people, in their relativity the jural laws, according to Montesquieu, are not and should not be limited to the society only. Instead:

> They should be relative to the physical nature of the country; to the climate, ice-bound, burning or temperate; to the quality of the territory, its situation, its size; to the way of life of the peoples [whether] tillers of the soil, hunters or herdsmen; they should accommodate themselves to the measure of liberty which the constitution may admit; to the religion of the inhabitants, their inclinations, their wealth, their number, their trade, their mores, their manners . . . It is in all these aspects that they must be considered. (Stark 1960: p. 208)[12]

Although this quotation suggests that Montesquieu might have been at least to some degree an "environmental determinist," in other places in his writings this suspicion is effectively dispelled. He shows that the real determining factors are those of the demography and nature of the particular society—in other words social factors. Geographical factors enumerated above work only as "dispositions," as a sort of inducement that may or may not affect the people and their legislators. In his defense and explanation of De l'Esprit des Lois ("Réponses et Explications Données à la Faculté de Théologie" and "Défense de l'Esprit des Lois") he clearly presents this position: "It can be said that the book of the Spirit of Laws presents a perpetual triumph of morality over climate, or rather over the physical causes in general" (Stark 1960: p. 152).[13] And, "In one word, the physique

---

[11]"S'il ne donne pas le nom de naturelles à ces diverses formes du droit, il ne les estime pas cependant étrangères à la nature, mais fondées dans la réalité d'une autre façon que les premières: elles résultent en effet, selon lui, non de la nature de l'homme, mais de celle des sociétés." (Durkheim 1953: p. 50)

[12]"Elles doivent être relatives au physique du païs, au climat glacé, brûlant, ou tempéré; à la qualité du terrain, à sa situation, à sa grandeur, au genre de vie des peuples, laboureurs, chasseurs, ou pasteurs; elles doivent se rapporter au degré de liberté que la constitution peut souffrir; à la religion des habitans, à leurs inclinations, à leurs richesses, à leur nombre, à leur commerce, à leurs moeurs, à leurs manières . . . c'est dans toutes ces vues qu'il faut les considérer." (Montesquieu 1750, vol. 1: p. 9)

[13]"L'on peut dire que le livre de l'Esprit des Lois forme un triomphe perpétuel de la morale sur le climat, ou plutôt, en général, sur les causes physiques." (Montesquieu 1951, vol. 2: p. 1173)

of the climate may produce various dispositions in minds [of man]; these dispositions are apt to influence the human actions" (Stark 1960: p. 152).[14] The dispositions, of course, are not considered as determinants—they merely present themselves to the legislator who, as Montesquieu thinks, takes them into account while shaping the law of his society. In the same way, biological factors and heredity have nothing to do directly with the shaping of the laws of the country (Montesquieu 1750, vol. 2: esp. p. 200).

This explanation of the role of the nonsocial factors and that of the volitional creative action of the legislator were expectedly attacked by Durkheim, who refused to explain social facts by influences and causes that lie beyond the realm of sociology, that are nonsocially natured. As a consequence, he unjustly attacks Montesquieu and states that "anyone who limits his inquiry to the final causes of social phenomena, loses sight of their origins and its nature to science. This is what would happen to sociology if we followed Montesquieu's method" (Durkheim 1960: p. 44).[15]

From the total work of Montesquieu, and especially from his defense of De l'Esprit des Lois, it is clear that law is regarded by him as a part of the culture of a particular society. The organizing principle that penetrates the culture's political structure and the people's "constitution" penetrates also the people's legal system, and as its formative backbone shapes it into a special type (Montesquieu 1750, vol. 1: esp. pp. 166 ff.). Therefore, reasons Montesquieu, specific types of political structures have to be, and actually are, related to specific legal systems. According to him there are five basic types of societies with corresponding legal systems, two of which, the savage and the barbaric, possess political structure without clearly defined sovereign power (Durkheim 1960: p. 35). As a contrast, the remaining three types, monarchic, republic (aristocratic or democratic), and despotic have a clearly defined sovereign power. "Severity suits despotic government, whose principle is terror, better than monarchy and republic which have for their basis honour and virtue" (Stark 1960: pp. 125–126).[16]

Thus in a society whose political system may be called despotism, characterized by absolute, often whimsical power of the ruler, a society "in which only the head is alive, having absorbed all the energies of the organism,"[17] the legal system is weakened and typified in the people's submis-

[14]"En un mot, ce physique du climat peut produire diverses dispositions dans les esprits; ces dispositions peuvent influer sur les actions humaines." (Montesquieu 1951, vol. 2: p. 1145)
[15]". . . celui qui borne ses investigations aux causes finales des choses sociales, laisse échapper leurs origines et mutile ainsi l'image de la science. Or telle sera la science sociale si nous suivons la méthode de Montesquieu." (Durkheim 1953: p. 86)
[16]". . . la sévérité des peines convient mieux au gouvernement despotique dont le principe est la terreur, qu'à la monarchie et à la république qui ont pour ressort l'honneur et la vertu." (Montesquieu 1750, vol. 1: p. 116)
[17]". . . dans lequel la tête seule serait vivante, parce qu'elle aurait tiré à elle toutes les forces de l'organisme." (Durkheim 1953: pp. 67–68)

sion to the ruler's will by a sole reliance on fear (Durkheim 1960: pp. 31–32). Because in this type of society all the people have, from the legal point of view, the same status, they do not seek honor that would elevate them socially and legally and provide them with privileges. Neither do they strive for virtue, because they are prevented from actively participating in the society. As a contrast, people in a monarchy are not constantly exposed to the overwhelming whimsical nature of a despot's rule. Law establishes different statuses characterized by certain types of privileges of legal nature that may be achieved by following an honor code. Thus, according to Montesquieu, honor binds people as well as the monarch, and compliance with its precepts rewards the subjects by ascribing to them the various statuses (Montesquieu 1750, vol. 1: pp. 38–40). Finally, in a republic, in which people have equal status, law relies on moral virtue, the same for all the people as well as for their law giver: "In the Republic he who puts the laws into execution feels that he will himself be subject to them and will feel their weight" (Stark 1960: p. 160).[18] Thus the equality of the citizens vis-à-vis the law of the country is the major legal attribute of those legal systems that pertain to a republic.

The generating force of law according to Montesquieu, is the legislator. He not only promulgates laws that the society somehow induces him to formulate, he also creates laws that are expected to improve the well-being of the society. In both of these roles his law embodies principles for the particular structure of the society and for the particular content of its culture. Montesquieu does not assume that the creative role of the law giver is detached and uninfluenced by the social experience to which he is subject throughout his life and of which he himself is a product. Indeed, his whole conceptualization of the reality of law in terms of time and place is derived from the realization that the legislator creates law out of a mental inventory that is particular to the given culture, and not on the basis of some aloof and supreme contemplation of man's ideal nature guided by logic common to all men, as the doctrine of Natural Law presupposed.

This position—this brilliant achievement of Montesquieu—was, astonishingly enough, misunderstood by Durkheim. In his view, Montesquieu committed a serious mistake by not making the law giver simply a mouthpiece for some unformulated social pressures that forced him into promulgating what was in some fashion already socially destined to appear as law. "As everybody knows," writes Durkheim, "customs are not created deliberately but are engendered by causes that produce their effects quite unbeknownst to men. The same applies to the origin of most laws" (Durkheim

---

[18]". . . dans la République, celui qui fait exécuter les lois sent qu'il y sera soumis lui-même, et qu'il en sentira le poids." (Montesquieu 1951, vol. 2: p. 1181)

1960: p. 43).[19] According to him law has little creative or causal power. Certain rather mysterious social forces are responsible for shaping the culture and social relations of people as well as their laws. "The equality and frugality, which according to Montesquieu were imposed by the laws, were not created by these laws. They resulted from a way of life and were merely consolidated by the laws" (Durkheim 1960: p. 43).[20] As far as the legislator was concerned, he "produces nothing—or next to nothing—that is new. Even if he did not exist, there would have to be laws, though they would be less sharply defined. However, he alone can frame them. Granted. But he is only the instrument of their promulgation, not their generating cause" (Durkheim 1960: p. 42).[21] Thus Durkheim proves to be a social determinist, a man who failed to recognize what Montesquieu's genius clearly saw 150 years before: that there are some laws (which I call authoritarian) that are imposed upon the society by the legislator, even sometimes against the will of the society's members; that the legislator is not simply a pawn who is moved on a chessboard of the life of the society by some mysterious and superorganic social forces, but that he assumes his creativity in shaping the culture and law by new recombinations of ideas which his culture provides. The recognition that these new recombinations are novelties, not necessarily present already in the "social forces," was one of the great achievements of Montesquieu. How much better was Montesquieu understood and appreciated by Stark, who writes:

> The legislator is for Montesquieu the organiser of the polity in the specific sense that he introduces and institutes what will allow the society concerned to lead an organically integrated and harmonious life . . . for Montesquieu, the lawgiver is he who, in and for life, unfolds the basic principle of a state and society—he who realizes the vital possibilities inherent in it, he who draws the fruit from the seed. (Stark 1960: p. 164)

Thus according to my opinion and to Stark's, Montesquieu's concept of the legislator was neither of the two extremes that Durkheim mentions;

[19]". . . personne n'ignore que les moeurs ne sont pas d'institution volontaire, mais qu'elles sont engendrées par des causes qui produisent leurs effets à l'insu des hommes eux-mêmes. Aussi bien l'origine de la plupart des lois n'est-elle pas différente." (Durkheim 1953: pp. 85–86)

[20]". . . l'égalité et la frugalité que Montesquieu nous dit imposées par les lois, ce n'étaient pas celles-ci qui les avaient créées; issues de ce genre de vie, les lois ne firent que le consolider." (Durkheim 1953: p. 85)

[21]". . . il n'invente rien ou presque rien de nouveau; même s'il n'existait pas, rien n'empêcherait qu'il y eût des lois: elles seraient seulement moins bien définies. Elles ne peuvent être rédigées que par lui, soit! Mais il est l'instrument qui permet de les établir plutôt que leur cause génératrice." (Durkheim 1953: p. 84)

he was not a mental and creative nonentity pushed by social forces, as proposed by Durkheim, nor an individual who spontaneously formulated law unrelated to the social reality that surrounded him, a chimera that Durkheim criticized. Fortunately, Montesquieu was not a man whose sub-conscious mind was embedded in the dialectics of dichotomies as was the case with many later sociologists, lawyers, and anthropologists, especially those of the twentieth century. Also, through his emphasis upon the law of the "law-giver" he analytically separated the legislative, judicial, and executive powers, a separation that later proved to be important from the social scientific as well as practical point of view (Montesquieu 1750, vol. 1: pp. 215–230).

Amazingly like a modern anthropologist, Montesquieu, writing in the eighteenth century, views law as only one of several types of social control that operate in a society and effect conformity of people's behavior with the prevailing values. These controls, although analytically and formally distinguishable, are mutually dependent. The brilliance of his discussion of the interrelatedness of cultural material is so impressive that, while reading the following (in Stark 1960: p. 174) and other of Montesquieu's passages, I felt that I could have been reading Kluckhohn's elucidation of the concept of configuration of culture:

> *The States are governed by five different things: by religion, by the general maxims of government, by the particular laws, by the mores and by the manners. These things all have a mutual connection with each other. If you change one of them, the others follow but slowly; and this spreads everywhere a sort of discord. (Stark 1960: p. 174)*[22]

Montesquieu indeed conceived of a society and its culture as of an interrelated and integrated whole in which a change in one part produces chain reactions and readjustments in other parts. If this integration went as far as it had done in China where "the manners, mores, laws, religion were the same thing,"[23] then social control and society had achieved such stability and coherence that even outside conquerors could not destroy the culture; on the contrary, this unified social control affected the foreigners and they became Chinese in their culture (Montesquieu 1750, vol. 1: p. 437). Consequently, one cannot distinguish between the different types of social

[22]"Les États sont gouvernés par cinq choses différentes: par la Religion, par les maximes générales du Gouvernement, par les lois particulières, par les moeurs et par les manières. Ces choses ont toutes un rapport mutuel les unes aux autres. Si vous en changez une, les autres ne suivent que lentement; ce qui met partout une espèce de dissonance." (Montesquieu 1949, vol. 1: pp. 1156–1157)

[23]". . . les manières, les moeurs, les loix, la religion y étant la même chose." (Montesquieu 1750, vol. 1: p. 437)

control on the basis of the intensity because "the mores rule as imperatively as the laws" (Stark 1960: p. 60).[24] Indeed, if one of the mentioned types of controls weakens, another has to compensate, to become stronger and take over the burden of making people conform (Montesquieu 1750, vol. 2: pp. 160–162). The distinction between the various types of social controls lies rather in the form the particular control assumes, and in its objectives. Thus, for example, religion has as its goal, according to Montesquieu, to "create good" and addresses itself primarily to the individual, while law tries to punish offenses and prevent crimes and is more concerned with "men in general" than with the individual (Montesquieu 1750, vol. 2: pp. 156, 159–168, 204–205).

Law, consequently, being an integral part of a culture, has been subject to changes either by broad cultural trends or by the thinking of the legislator. This inevitable conclusion of Montesquieu, which revolted against the dogmas of Natural Law and its static and universal legal conception, made him, so to speak, the father of theories on change of legal systems. With him law changes not only in space but also in time. In some of his statements Montesquieu conceived of a society as going through something that resembles a life cycle. Law, being part of the society's culture, was thought to undergo similar changes: "There are principal laws and accessory laws, and there arises, in each country, a kind of generation of laws. The nations, like each individual, have a succession of ideas, and their total way of thinking, like that of each private person, has a beginning, a middle, and an end" (Stark 1960: p. 74).[25]

Although Montesquieu talked about change of legal systems in human societies he refrained from designing a grandiose scheme of evolution for them, as other authors of the nineteenth century. Thus Durkheim states rightly that Montesquieu, when he "attempts to interpret the history of a society, he does not situate it in a series of societies, but concerns himself only with the nature of its topography, the number of its citizens, etc." (Durkheim 1960: pp. 59–60).[26] On the other hand Durkheim did injustice to Montesquieu when he claimed that Montesquieu "fails to recognize the process whereby a society, while remaining faithful to its nature, is con-

[24]". . . les moeurs, qui règnent aussi impérieusement que les loix." (Montesquieu 1951, vol 2: p. 193)
[25]"Il y a des lois principales et des lois accessoires, et il se forme, dans chaque pays, une espèce de génération de lois. Les peuples, comme chaque individu, ont une suite d'idées, et leur manière de penser totale, comme celle de chaque particulier, a un commencement, un milieu et une fin." (Montesquieu 1951, vol. 2: p. 1102)
[26]"Quand il entreprend d'interpréter l'histoire d'une société, il ne recherche pas quelle place elle occupe dans la série des sociétés, mais seulement quelle est la nature du sol, quel est le nombre des citoyens, etc." (Durkheim 1953: pp. 108–109)

stantly becoming something new" (Durkheim 1960: p. 59):[27] Montesquieu did recognize this process, and his importance lies exactly in his tenet that society and its law do change in time, as can be seen from the quotations above.

Another criticism of Durkheim focuses on Montesquieu's "unawareness of the idea of progress." Indeed, Durkheim is correct when he claims that Montesquieu did not recognize this idea. However, I regard this "neglect" of Montesquieu, and his failure to see "that societies issue from other societies and that the later are superior to the earlier" (Durkheim 1960: p. 58),[28] as a remarkable achievement rather than a matter for criticism. Montesquieu, when "he did not suspect that these different kinds of societies grow successively from the same root" (Durkheim 1960: p. 58),[29] did recognize the significance of the societies' long histories, and he refused to speculate about their common origin and apply to them a value judgment by evaluating them as "superior" or "inferior," an activity which is usually regarded as highly unscientific. Nevertheless, his failure to view types of societies arranged "genetically" in a sequence that implies an ever-increasing degree of "superiority" does not mean that to Montesquieu a given society remained static and was not "constantly becoming something new," as Durkheim charges (Durkheim 1960: p. 59). He not only emphasized changes of law, but his outline of the various types of societies, with their corresponding legal systems, also suggests the idea of an evolution whereby a society radically changes from one type to another, reflecting its change in the mode of subsistence (Montesquieu 1750, vol. 1: esp. pp. 397–403).

In conclusion, it was Montesquieu who first effectively challenged the entrenched Western theory of Natural Law, with its absolute conceptualization of legal phenomena that were regarded as static and constant through the ages and throughout the world, and whose principles one could detect through purely philosophical speculation about, and contemplation of, what was regarded as "human nature." With his ideas of the relativity of law in space as well as in time, and with his emphasis on specificity and empiricism, he can be regarded as the founder of the modern sociology of law in general and of the field of legal dynamics in particular.

[27]"Il méconnaît ce processus continuel par lequel la société, tout en demeurant toujours fidèle à sa nature, devient sans cesse quelque chose de nouveau." (Durkheim 1953: pp. 107–108)

[28]". . . les sociétés sont issues les unes des autres et que les plus récentes l'emportent sur les sociétés antérieures." (Durkheim 1953: p. 106)

[29]". . . il ne soupçonne pas que ces différentes espèces de sociétés descendent de la même souche et qu'elles se succèdent les unes aux autres. . . ." (Durkheim 1953: pp. 106–107)

FRIEDRICH KARL VON SAVIGNY (1779–1861)

The legal thinking of the second part of the eighteenth century and the first half of the nineteenth century was still dominated by the doctrine of Natural Law, and Montesquieu's early achievement of relating legal systems to the particular societies in which they originated was forgotten or extinguished in the morass of popular conformism with the established doctrine of legal thought. Dissatisfaction with the shortcomings of the doctrine, together with the influence of developing European nationalist thought and an emphasis upon national histories, resulted in an emergence of the school of "historical jurisprudence," of which Friedrich Karl von Savigny, a German jurist of French Protestant descent, became the founder and uncontested master. Orphaned at an early age, he was exposed to the ideas of Natural Law by his guardian Neurath, a lawyer and state official who laid down the dominant legal theory in an authoritarian and dogmatic manner. Reacting to this intellectual rigidity, Savigny became receptive to ideas opposed to the established legal doctrine, ideas with which he became acquainted during his teaching at the universities of Marburg and, later, Berlin. His newly developed interest in historical inquiry led him to the path of legal theory opened by Montesquieu more than a half century ago.

Following the direction pointed out by his great predecessor, Savigny rejected the doctrine of Natural Law and its belief in a universally valid law that was independent of space and time and derived its existence from "pure reasoning," whose canons were the birthright of all mankind. He saw a special relationship that linked a given legal system to a specific functioning society and its history. To him, such a legal system was a part of a particular people's culture of a given time, and its growth depended on a rather impersonal unfolding of the thought of the people and their group conviction of their legal system's indispensability. This process of historical unfolding of spiritual activity of a particular people Savigny regarded as one of the manifestations of the people's *Volksgeist* (national spirit), defined by Stone as a "unique, ultimate, and often mystical reality" that not only formed a dominant configuration of the people's culture but also was believed to be linked, at least to some extent, to their biological heritage (Stone 1966: p. 102; Savigny 1831a: esp. pp. 8–15). Law then, in Stone's words, was to Savigny and emanation of this mystical reality, "to be watched for and discovered rather than made or tampered with" by a legislator (Stone 1966: p. 102). It was not a content category of a culture (such as economy or religion). Rather, it was a manner in which the cultural phenomena were ordered and had to operate, "a totality of life seen from a specific viewpoint" (Stone 1966: p. 30). The formulation of true law did not occur through an arbitrary act of a legislator; it developed as a response to a silent operation of impersonal powers that may be regarded as a sort of essence of vitality of the nation's *Volksgeist.*

Savigny and the budding German nationalists successfully used this theory of the uniqueness of *Volksgeist* and of its specific legal system to reject the French code. Even after this rejection, German law of the nineteenth century, as taught at the universities and also practiced in most of the German states as their common law (*Gemeinrecht*) still remained foreign in essence. It consisted mostly of the Justinian codification of Roman law, adapted to German conditions by injections of local legal ideas. Having historical consistency in mind, one would expect that Savigny would turn against this type of law and foster a resurrection of the old Germanic law, for example, by abstracting pure German legal ideas from the locally diverse laws of the various states (*Landrecht*) and bringing them into a codified and logically consistent system. On the contrary, he became convinced that the very fact that Roman law had been adopted was proof of the inadequacy of the old Germanic law to express properly the German *Volksgeist.* He maintained that through the centuries since its adoption, Roman law not only proved to be successful where Germanic law failed, but also actually became part of the German society and its culture and *Volksgeist* to such an extent that to separate these would prove an almost impossible task and would only do harm to the German nation (Savigny 1840: esp. pp. 38–40, 43).

Unlike his great predecessor Montesquieu, Savigny did not limit himself to theorizing. Whereas his *Vom Beruf unsrer Zeit für Gesetzgebung und Rechtswissenschaft* (Of the Vocation of Our Age for Legislation and Jurisprudence, 1814) expressed his theoretical position and served as a program of his future work and as its guide and justification, he turned subsequently to an exploration of the substantive basis and development of the *Gemeinrecht* (common law) of Germany. At the outset he proposed to view and explain Roman law, the basis of the *Gemeinrecht,* not *in abstracto* (as was then the usual practice) but as an integral part of the Old Roman civilization, and to interpret the meaning of its precepts through the institutions of that civilization. One of his main works, *Geschichte des römischen Rechts während des Mittelalters* (History of Roman Law during the Middle Ages, 1831), traces in six volumes changes undergone in Old Roman law, viewed in the abovementioned perspective, through the centuries after Justininan's rule but before the reception of it in Germany. His subsequent seven volumes, *System des heutigen römischen Rechts* (System of Modern Roman Law, 1849) represent a thorough analysis and exposition of the received Roman law (already modified to fit German conditions) as it was used by jurists at that time. Savigny's voluminous life work thus represents not only a theoretical formulation of a historical approach to a study of law but also its masterful application.

Savigny's historical exposition of the development of Roman law from the times of Justinian to its reception in Germany and his analysis of its final form adjusted to German conditions of the nineteenth century rested on a theory of legal dynamics already formulated in the author's pragmatic work, *Of the Vocation of Our Age for Legislation and Jurisprudence* (1831a). All law, according to Savigny's hypothesis, originated as customary law through slow growth and long usage, supported by a popular faith in its indispensability. Only much later did law begin to be created by juristic activity (Savigny 1840: pp. 13–14). However, being a rigorous historian, this putative explanation of the origin of the earliest law Savigny holds only as an empirically unproven hypothesis when he explains that "in the earliest time to which authentic history extends, the law will be found to have already attained a fixed character, peculiar to the people, like their language, manners, and constitution" (1831a: p. 24).[30]

True to his doctrine of *Volksgeist* and historicism, Savigny limited himself to theorizing about legal change as it pertained to particular societies (nations) and refrained from designing a grandiose worldwide scheme of legal evolution into whose stages or types legal systems of individual cultures could be fitted. Consequently, to call his theory a "pre-Darwinian concept of evolution in the juristic field" (Allen 1927: p. 47) is rather misleading. In his conceptualization and terminology he viewed a nation and its state as an organism which is born, matures, declines (ages), and dies. The well-being of the state's or nation's organism he called *Gesundheit* (health). Law is an inseparable part of this national organism. In Savigny's words: "Law grows with the growth, and strengthens with the strength of the people, and finally dies away as the nation loses its nationality" (1831a: p. 27).[31] This cyclical, lifelike process of the growth and decay of society and its law was regarded as automatic, divorced from the actions and influence of individuals, and resulted, in Stone's words, in "a fatalistic assumption that tendencies of the past must inexorably work themselves out; that men could observe the progress and perhaps even foresee, but never check it or divert it" (1950: p. 439). Thus in many respects Savigny's theory reminds us of Oswald Spengler's philosophy of the history of cultures and civilizations, especially that of the West, with its "life cycle" of youth, maturation, and decline, published about 100 years later (*Der Untergang des Abendlandes,* 1921–1922).

In accordance with his main thesis, Savigny divides the life cycle of an ethnic entity and its law into three developmental stages. All nations

[30]"Wo wir zuerst urkundliche Geschichte finden, hat das bürgerliche Recht schon einen bestimmten Character, dem Volk eigenthümlich, so wie seine Sprache, Sitte, Verfassung." (Savigny 1840: p. 8)

[31]"Das Recht wächst also mit dem Volke fort, bildet sich aus mit diesem, und stirbt endlich ab, so wie das Volk seine Eigenthümlichkeit verliehrt." (Savigny 1840: p. 11)

presumably can be fitted into these and therefore are supposed to exhibit also their major characteristics. Accordingly, "young nations" that sprang up through acquisition of their "national identity" that distinguishes them from their neighbors are supposed to possess a political element of law: a respect for and a clear awareness (*klares Bewustsein*) of their legal system. These principles of their law are also part of their "national convictions" (*Volksglauben*), although they are not incorporated into explicitly stated abstract legal rules—statutes (Savigny, 1840: pp. 9, 11). On the contrary, the legal principles are only implicitly present in formal symbolic transactions (*förmlichen Handlungen*) which command the high respect of the population, form a grammar of the legal system of a young nation, and constitute one of the system's major characteristics, as is attested by the form and nature of Old Roman Law (Savigny 1840: p. 10). In its "young period," however, the legal system lacks the "technical element" of law, namely a precise juristic conceptualization, linguistic expression, and a well-defined logical method (*fehlt es an Sprache und logischer Kunst*), so that any attempt at a meaningful codification of law during this period is unrealistic (1840: pp. 12, 25). Savigny's contention became so influential that it delayed for almost a century the codification of German law.

The only feasible period for codification of law, according to Savigny, is the middle period of development (*mittlere Zeit;* 1840: p. 26) when law, while retaining the "political element" of the people's awareness of and their emotional attachment to and support for its legal system, also acquires the "technical element" of the juristic skill, elaborate conceptualization, and administration of a group of legal specialists (1840: p. 26). Thus this period marks not only the peak of a general cultural achievement of a nation but also a culmination of the nation's juristic excellence. To codify law at such a time is feasible, although unnecessary as far as the society is concerned. The only reason to codify law at this time is to preserve its excellence for posterity—for the era of decline (Savigny 1840: p. 26).

In this period of ascent and culmination, law acquires another important characteristic. Due to its methodological, linguistic, and substantive elaboration law achieves such complexity that its administration is, of necessity, entrusted to specialists, a class of jurists who practice law in a scientific way. Thus law, according to Savigny, starts to "live two lives": as a social and cultural heritage of the life of the whole nation of which it continues to be a part as *natürliches Recht,* and as a special body of knowledge (*Wissenschaft, gelehrtes Recht)* in the hands of the jurists (Savigny 1840: pp. 12, 13).

In the declining period of a nation, which he believes ends in the ultimate loss of national identity, law loses its former popular support and becomes the property of a few experts. However, even the "technical element" decays to the extent that "almost everything is wanting—knowledge of the matter, as well as language" (*es fehlt meist an allem, an Kennt-*

niss des Stoffs wie an Sprache; Savigny 1840: p. 26). Certainly this is not the time for a codification.

Although Savigny's work constitutes a very significant historical step toward the development of modern sociology and anthropology of law, from an anthropological point of view his theory has many shortcomings. These originate mainly from the fact that next to nothing was known in his day about anthropology in general, about law of tribal societies, or about legal systems of the non-Western civilizations in particular. No wonder then that he underestimated creativeness and the role of the individual in shaping the law of a tribe, that he created a mystical *Volksgeist* as a blend of cultural and physiological factors acquired not only through learning but also through biological heredity and that, as a consequence, he and his followers arrived at a fatalistic view of law. The contention that "men could observe progress and perhaps even foresee it, but never check it or divert it" (Stone 1966: p. 101), actually means subscribing to an idea of legislative impotence. In the following chapter we shall return to this kind of fallacy when discussing the difference between customary and authoritarian law. Some of Savigny's mistakes had an unexpected influence on the political history of Germany; they not only delayed codification of German law by almost a century, but the idea of the mystical *Volksgeist* became one of the most important ingredients of the Nazi conception of "nation" and "race," thus providing a pseudoscientific justification for one of the doctrines of twentieth-century extremism.

SIR HENRY MAINE (1822–1888)

The most outstanding follower and, at the same time, critic of Savigny's historical approach was an English jurist, Sir Henry Maine, Regius Professor of Civil Law at Cambridge, a reader in Roman Law at the Inns of Court, a legal member of the Council in India, Professor of Jurisprudence at Oxford, and, finally, Professor of International Law at Cambridge. His famous work *Ancient Law,* published in 1861, made an impact on English and on world jurisprudence that is comparable to the effect of Einstein on physics, Freud on psychology, or Durkheim on sociology. Perhaps unconsciously, he contributed to the foundations of what we may regard as the science of law. While retaining Savigny's rejection of the *a priori* philosophy of Natural Law, his insistence on an empirical recognition of differences in legal systems of the various peoples, and his stress on historical method, he moved away from Savigny's purely historical approach by rejecting the idea of the uniqueness of the mystical *Volksgeist* of the various nations. By this he removed the artificial barrier to scientific investigation and allowed for a comparative approach that was directed at abstracting principles governing historical changes, principles that equated the evolution of law with that of other institutions and cultures. His work, although nowadays open to criticism of its theoretical aspects, definitely manifests the three basic ingredients of scientific inquiry: investigation of phenomenal (objective) data, studied through empirical method, to arrive at universally valid generalizations.

At the time of Maine's writing, the impact of biological evolutionary theory upon sciences and upon philosophical thinking in general was so intense that it was only logical to extend it to the field of social relations. Maine did not escape this influence, and, as a consequence, his work on legal change was set within an evolutionary framework which in some respects resembles the unilinear evolutionist doctrine of early anthropologists. Although in several later statements he refuted the idea that culture history of the various people had everywhere been the same (e. g., "So far as I am aware, there is nothing in the recorded history of society to justify the belief that, during the vast chapter of its growth which is wholly unwritten, the same transformations of social constitution succeeded one another everywhere, uniformly if not simultaneously" Maine 1883: pp. 218–219), in the phrasing of his comparative historical findings of 1861 he did cast his theory into an evolutionist form, postulating and even documenting existence of stages of social development common to the various human societies he studied. To these evolutionary stages he attached, often in a very loose way, a scheme of development of law and legal ideas that he abstracted from the study of a few societies. In striving to uncover generalizations that would be applicable to the development of law everywhere, he seized upon evolutionary theory, that in *Ancient Law* appears to have some unilineal characteristics (e.g., a single set of evolutionary stages), and tried to justify it in terms of "stability of human nature," which concept reminds us of the basic unilineal evolutionist postulate of the "psychic unity of mankind." Using this concept he castigated Montesquieu for his lack of generalizing about human legal history:

> *Montesquieu seems, in fact, to have looked on the nature of man as entirely plastic, as passively reproducing the impressions, and submitting implicitly to the impulses, which it receives from without. . . . He greatly underrates the stability of human nature. He pays little or no regard to the inherited qualities of the race, those qualities which each generation receives from its predecessors, and transmits but slightly altered to the generation which follows it. (1963: p. 112)*

Maine's own scheme of evolution starts with the "archaic society," a group that may be characterized in modern anthropological jargon as an "extended family": "The family then is the type of an archaic society in all the modifications which it was capable of assuming" (1963: p. 128). Influenced by his research on Old Roman, Hebrew, and Hindu civilizations, and on Brehon (Irish) law, he assumed that during this stage of development the society was patrilineal and patriarchal:

> *The Agnatic Union of the kindred in ancient Roman law, and a multitude of similar indications, point to a period at which all the ramifying branches of the family tree held together in one organic whole; and it is no presumptuous conjecture, that, when the corporation thus formed by the kindred was in itself an independent society, it was governed by the eldest male of the oldest line. (1963: p. 227; also see p. 178)*

Although this male pronounced judgments and meted out punishments to misbehaving members of his family, he did not, according to Maine, enforce any unwritten law. His judgments were rather disconnected and, like the *themistes* (the pronouncements of judges of Old Greece), did not reflect a binding legal principle (Maine 1963: p. 4). Moreover, Maine claimed that the true ancient law that developed in a later stage "knows next to nothing of Individuals. It is concerned not with Individuals, but with Families, not with single human beings, but groups" (Maine 1963: p. 250). Since, in Maine's opinion, the earliest law adjusted only relationships between families, and because the human society in its first developmental stage consisted of only a single family, such society could not logically have had law.

Law, according to Maine, was not present even in the early part of the second evolutionary stage of the human society—the tribal state. Tribal societies arose through a merger of the family groups that in the resulting society remained autonomous as far as social control was concerned. The head of the family still wielded power over his kin. As in the first stage, "the Family, in fact, was a Corporation; and he was its representative or, we may almost say, its Public officer" (1963: p. 178). The uniting principle of the tribe, Maine believed, was a fiction of patrilineal relationship, a belief in a common descent from a male founder of the tribe: "The characteristic of all these races, when in the tribal state," wrote Maine, "is that the tribes themselves, and all subdivisions of them, are conceived by the men who compose them as descended from a single male ancestor" (Maine 1875: pp. 65–66).

Although no true law characterized social control in this early period of social evolution, the fundamental prerequisites for the rise of law had already been laid down in the family and the early stages of tribal society. As far as the content of law is concerned, Maine contended "it may be shown, I think, that the Family, as held together by the Patria Potestas, is the nidus out of which the entire Law of Persons has germinated" (Maine 1963: p. 147). As far as the essential characteristic of law is concerned, namely its nature as a system of abstract principles, the chiefs of the late tribal societies as well as the authorities of the incipient territorial states, by pronouncing the same judgments in similar situations, were unwittingly creating a set of abstract principles. "Here we have the germ or rudiment of a custom, a conception posterior to that of Themistes or judgments" (1963: p. 5); that is, in the evolution of human society, custom became the source and content of the earliest law.

As evolution progressed and the tribal societies began their transition into the next stage, the common territory emerged as a unifying societal principle, additional to that of kin relationship (actual and fictive). This territoriality principle did not assume its dominant unifying role until Maine's next stage—the territorial society. Equipped with abstract customary principles manifested in judgments passed in similar situations, mankind moved into this next evolutionary epoch. Its origin, according to Maine, has to be ascribed either to a natural growth of the number of tribesmen, or to the merger of several tribal groups either by incorporation of one into another on the basis of adoption or by absolute subjugation of one by the other.

> The earliest and most extensively employed of legal fictions was that which permitted family relations to be created artificially, and there is none to which I conceive mankind to be more deeply indebted. If it had never existed, I do not see how any one of the primitive groups, whatever their nature, could have absorbed another, or on what terms any two of them could have combined, except those of absolute superiority on one side and absolute subjection on the other. (1963: pp. 125–126)

As time went on, the need to keep the fiction of common descent slowly gave way to the new unifying social principle—the idea of coherence that went with occupation of a common territory.

Emergence of true law, that is, of abstract principles that were applied in adjudication of the various disputes by patriarchal authorities, seems, according to Maine, to fall into the concluding phase of the tribal society stage and into the period of its transition into a territorially organized society. In that period law began to be differentiated from ethics and religion, and a truly political authority began to exercise jurisdiction over its subjects. At first the law was administered, as before, through the personal judgments and judicial decisions of the patriarchs. However, because various "states" slowly deemphasized their kinship bond in favor of the principles of territorial unity, administration of law, which already took the form of abstract customary principles, became the object of study and a tool in the hands of a segment of society—its "elite" (1963: p. 12). Maine expressed this transition as follows:

> At some point of time—probably as soon as they felt themselves strong enough to resist extrinsic pressure—all these states ceased to recruit themselves by factitious extensions of consanguinity. They necessarily, therefore, became Aristocracies, in all cases where a fresh population from any cause collected around them

which could put in no claim to community of origin. (1963:
p. 127)

In the legal sphere a segment of the established aristocracy usurped jurisdiction from the patriarch and "what the juristical oligarchy now claims is to monopolize the *knowledge* of the laws, to have the exclusive possession of the principles by which quarrels are decided. We have in fact arrived at the epoch of Customary Law" (1963: p. 11). As to the nature of this judicial oligarchy, Maine, basing his argument on books on Hindu law, says the following: "They enable us to see how law was first regarded, as a definite subject of thought, by a special learned class; and this class consisted of lawyers who were first of all priests" (1883: p. 26). However, he contends, the priestly legal monopoly was slowly broken and secular authority took its place. Weak as it was, it had to rely upon the established custom. With individual abuse of the norms of the established custom, and especially because of the invention of writing, it became necessary for the sake of social stability and elimination of distrust to put the enforced customary law into writing (1963: p. 14). Thus originated the early legal codes which had little in common with modern legislation. They were repositories of the age-old enforced custom, repositories regarded superior to those of memories of the specialized judicial oligarchy: "Everywhere, in the countries I have named, laws engraven on tablets and published to the people take the place of usages deposited with the recollection of a privileged oligarchy" (1963: pp. 13–14; see also p. 17).

Yet society and its law do not stand still. Changes in population composition, patterns of residence, technology, and values necessitate alterations in the existing law. Thus arose a dilemma for the judicial oligarchy: how to adjust their law to the ever-changing social conditions and still maintain the illusion of sacrosanct old and "unchangeable" custom. Once law was deposited in legal codes the unconscious change, characteristic of the previous era, ceased. Law had been fixed in the form of written language and to change it conscious effort had to be exercised and special devices had to be designed. At this time of evolution, Maine finds human societies divided into two major types: those that retarded progress and became more or less stationary, and the few others that moved on and became "progressive"; in Maine's words: "after the epoch of codes the distinction between stationary and progressive societies begins to make itself felt" (1963: p. 21).

In order to change the existing law and to adjust it to the changing social conditions, the juridical elite of the progressive societies resorted successively to three media, of which the first two were as old as law itself or even antedated its historical beginning: fiction, equity, and legislation (1883: p. 121). The first, fiction, which maintained the pretense of the unchangeability of the law, made the necessary adjustments to the ever-changing society through "interpreting and reinterpreting" the meaning of the legal rules. In Maine's words, legal fiction signifies "any assumption which conceals, or affects to conceal, the fact that a rule of law has under-gone alteration, its letter remaining unchanged, its operation being modified" (1963: p. 25). The second medium of change, equity, had its origin in Rome "in a modified ancestor-worship and a change in the religious constitution and religious duties of the family" (1883: p. 121). Essentially, equity meant a "body of rules existing by the side of the original civil law, founded on distinct principles and claiming incidentally to supersede the civil law in virtue of a superior sanctity inherent in those principles" (1963: p. 27). Application of these principles of morality and justice differ from legal fiction in that it openly interferes with the existing law and assumes that the princi-ples supersede it. The third and most advanced type of medium of legal change, legislation, is a purposive creation of new law based upon the authority vested into an autocrat or an elected or appointed body of "legisla-tors." Unlike equity, the law created through a legislative process is not dependent upon the special and superior nature of principles (ethical, logi-cal, or religious) to which the existing law ought to conform.

To be sure, the progressive societies themselves did not change at a constant rate; some became "retarded" while others moved at considerable speed. Although the rate of change varied, "the movement of the progres-sive societies has been uniform in one respect. Through all its course it has been distinguished by the gradual dissolution of family dependency and the growth of individual obligation in its place" (Maine 1963: p. 163).

As a contrast to this growing emphasis upon the individual, the law of the stationary societies, that is, the early law, "takes notice of Families only" (1963: p. 147). While the early law admitted to litigation only persons exercising *patria potestas* (e.g., heads of the families), in the progressive societies "the individual is steadily substituted for the Family, as the unit of which civil laws take account" (1963: p. 163). This legal emancipation of members of the families from the power and domination of the family heads is marked by a profound change in the nature of their relations vis-à-vis other members of the society. Their rights, duties, powers, and liabilities are no longer determined by an ascribed status. With emancipation, and the result-ing egalitarian tendency, their relations can be determined by their will through the medium of contract. Maine presented his most famous thesis as follows:

> Starting, as from one terminus of history, from a condition of society in which all the relations of Persons are summed up in the relations of Family, we seem to have steadily moved towards a phase of social order in which all these relations arise from the free agreement of Individuals. . . . All the forms of Status taken notice of in the Law of Persons were derived from, and to some extent are still coloured by, the powers and privileges anciently residing in the Family. If then we employ Status, agreeably with the usage of the best writers, to signify these personal conditions

only, and avoid applying the term to such conditions as are the
immediate or remote result of agreement, we may say that the
movement of the progressive societies has hitherto been a
movement from Status to Contract. *(1963: pp. 163, 164–165)*

The contractual agreement itself, according to Maine, underwent changes that can be summarized into four evolutionary stages marked by four types of contracts. (1) The verbal contract, the most formalistic and ancient of all, viewed the parties as bound together by *nexum,* a bond that originated through precise uttering of a legally determined formula and concluded by conveyance of the promised services or goods (1963: pp. 316 ff.). (2) The second stage of the contractual evolution was reached when agreements assumed the form of a literal contract in which the obligations and rights emanating from it depended upon the written evidence of an entry of the sum due on the debit side of a ledger (1963: pp. 320–321). (3) Next came the "Real Contract." In this type of formalistic stipulation was no longer necessary to validate the agreement. On the contrary, "performance on one side is allowed to impose a legal duty on the other—evidently on ethical grounds" (1963: p. 321). (4) The final point of this development was reached when law began to recognize "consensual contracts" in which all formalities were held irrelevant and the validity of the agreements depended entirely upon the proof of mutual *consensus* of the parties (1963: pp. 321 ff.).

As in the case of contract, Maine developed an evolutionary sequence of criminal law, the infringement of which was no longer a private matter but was conceived as an "injury to the State or collective community" (1963: p. 372). In his evolutionary scheme, which he seems to have re-garded as universally valid, "the primitive history of criminal law divides itself therefore into four stages" (1963: p. 372). Crime, according to Maine, began to distinguish itself from tort (or a civil delict that lacks the involvement of the community and that usually carries only a monetary compensation paid to the individual plaintiff) after written codes came into existence (1963: p. 358). The first stage of the development was reached when the public authority "itself interposed directly, and by isolated acts, to avenge itself on the author of the evil which it had suffered" (1963: p. 372). The second stage was reached when crime was not dealt with by isolated actions of the public authority itself, but when powers to adjudicate and to mete out punishment for a particular criminal offense were delegated to a special commission. The next step involved periodic appointment of commissions that dealt with many crimes of a special type instead of being created to deal with one particular offense. The last stage of the evolution of criminal law, and its complete emancipation from civil law, took place when a permanent com-mission to deal with crimes was established.

Maine's evolutionary scheme of society and law can be attacked, *ex post facto,* on many accounts. Data about primitive societies, which were not available to Maine at the time he wrote, disclose that his patriarchal conception of a primitive society, his idea of a complete lack of territorial bond among the tribal people, and his assumption that in the primitive societies "the individual creates for himself few or no rights, and few or no duties" and that "the rules which he obeys are derived first from the station into which he is born, and next from the imperative commands addressed to him by the chief of the household" (1963: p. 302) are not universally applicable. Consequently, even the famous dichotomy between the static, status-oriented primitive societies on one hand, and the progressive, contract-oriented societies on the other is not borne out by exact research. First, there are tribal societies, such as the Kapauku of New Guinea, in which *patria potestas* is nonexistent in the form as Old Rome and Maine knew it, in which the individual is relatively free and is able to create for himself rights and duties through quite an impressive inventory of different types of contracts (see Pospisil 1963a: pp. 313–356). Second, in the civilized "territorial and progressive" society of North Tirol the rights of individuals in their relations depend *de facto* mostly on the status into which they are born or which they acquire through their occupation, although theoretically and *de iure,* there is available to them a host of contract-types by which they can regulate their roles (Pospisil, unpublished results of research of the years 1962–1969). Of course, in some places Maine explicitly denied universal validity of his scheme, in spite of the quoted statements that suggest the opposite. I am convinced that he would have corrected or even abandoned his evolutionary scheme had he lived long enough to have at his disposal the results of ethnological research of the twentieth century. It is my firm belief that if Maine wrote today he would, unlike some of his contemporary followers, disregard his own dichotomies and those of many other authors, enumerated by Gluckman (1965: p. 213).

Maine's everlasting contribution to the field of jurisprudence and anthropology of law lies not so much in his specific conclusions as in the empirical, systematic, and historical methods he employed to arrive at his conclusions, and in his striving for generalizations firmly based on the empirical evidence at his disposal. In this meticulous and exact effort he blazed a scientific trail into the field of law, a field hitherto dominated by philosophizing and speculative thought. His evolutionary scheme is inapplicable today only because of the lack of comparative ethnographic data on non-European societies at the time he wrote his famous *Ancient Law.*

HERBERT SPENCER (1820–1903)

Influenced by Darwin's theory of biological evolution and by the social evolutionary ideas of the nineteenth century Herbert Spencer, unlike Sir Henry Maine, advanced an explicitly rigid theory of evolution of law postulating several developmental stages, arrived at nonempirically on the basis of speculation and "logic." In his armchair sociological approach Spencer, a former engineer for a railway company and a subsequent subeditor of several periodicals, conceived of the origin of law as religious in nature. Accordingly, society's law was supposed to have been regarded by early man as decrees of gods or as commands of deceased deified chiefs. Both forms of this divine law were, in Spencer's words, nothing but "dictates of the dead to the living" (Spencer 1899: p. 518). Since both forms were thought to be of divine nature and provided with supernatural sanctions, and because in both instances the society, being guided by a feeble authority, resorted to self-help and revenge in punishing criminals in a secular way (Spencer 1899: pp. 524–525), "no distinction is made between sacred law and secular law" at that early stage of development (Spencer 1899: p. 518). The divine nature of early law, the violation of which was conceived as a sin against the Gods (Spencer 1899: p. 531), and the "supposed supernatural sanction" with which it was provided made it rigid and stable (Spencer 1899: p. 519). Although conceptualized by the natives as "divine commands or dictates," the early law's provisions were, in Spencer's view, actually nothing but "injunctions of the undistinguished dead," that were "qualified by the public opinion of the living" (Spencer 1899: p. 535); they were a "government by custom," that persisted "through long stages of progress" (Spencer 1899: p. 513). This custom was ultimately an expression of mutual adjustment of interests of the members of the early and most primitive society, and therefore such a "law initiated by the *consensus* of individual interests, precedes the kind of law initiated by political authority" (1899: p. 528).

As society progressed and its institutions became more complex, reasoned Spencer, divine law and sanctions did not change and became, therefore, inapplicable and obsolete.

> *The instance is one showing us that primitive sacred commands, originating as they do in a comparatively undeveloped state of society, fail to cover the cases which arise as institutions become involved. In respect of these there consequently grow up rules having a known human authority only. By accumulation of such rules, is produced a body of human laws distinct from the divine laws; and the offense of disobeying the one becomes unlike the offense of disobeying the other. (Spencer 1899: p. 527)*

Thus the second evolutionary stage through which law developed is marked by the rise of secular law that becomes "progressive," flexible and changing, and clearly differentiated from the rigid sacred legal system. The necessity of the emergence of secular law, holds Spencer, manifests itself in spite of the fact that prior to its onset "divine law" had already tried to cope with the changing social situation by using legal fictions (for meaning of the term see above under Maine) which "have been the means of modifying statutes which were transmitted as immutable" (1899: p. 520). Nevertheless, the progress of the society later became so swift that even this device proved insufficient.

Deprived of sacred sanction, the new secular law no longer regarded delicts as sins or sacrilege, but as transgressions against the interests of the human community (Spencer 1899: p. 532). Like the preceding divine law, in its early stage this secular law, because of the weak political authority that originated it, was regarded as a product of the *"consensus* of individual interests" rather than provisions that explicitly "derive their obligation from the will of the governing agency" (Spencer 1899: p. 527). However, as soon as the ruler acquired more power and his authority strengthened and expanded, allegiance to his leadership and obedience to his decrees became the primary duty of his followers and subjects (Spencer 1899: p. 523). With respect to the gravity of its offense treason began to replace sacrilege. To be sure, transgressions against the laws of the various rulers who started to claim divine origin began to be conceived of as a combination of treason and sacrilege, thus commanding prestige and obedience on secular as well as religious grounds. In this way human law arrived at a "predatory stage of progress" in which law, made by the rulers, was imposed upon the society as a whole. The consensus and will of the population as reflected in the law was, however, not completely eradicated: it "survives, if obscured" (Spencer 1899: p. 528). According to Spencer this predatory stage of law continues to exist in the "predominantly militant societies" in which it is upheld as "the will of a divine ruler, or the will of a human ruler, or, occasionally, the will of an irresponsible oligarchy" (1899: p. 536).

In the modern industrialized society with its "free population," Spencer contends, "the humanly-derived law begins to sub-divide; again some law originates in the *consensus* of individual interests. Slowly it begins to dominate over the part which originates in the authority of the ruler" (1899: p. 536). Thus modern society somehow returns to the legal conditions that dominated the origin of law in its distant primitive past: "As industrialism fosters an increasingly free population . . . there again grows predominant this primitive source of law—the *consensus* of individual interests" (Spencer 1899: p. 528). The dominance of authority becomes less and less necessary because, as Spencer views it, through the sociobiological process of the survival of those individuals that are socially the fittest and most capable of interrelating their own interests with those of their cocitizens, a consensus law becomes dominant, a law that is the expression and the realization of the ultimate principle of human justice as it evolved through history. He expresses its simple formula as follows: "Every man is free to do that which he wills, provided he infringes not the equal freedom of any other man" (Spencer 1893: p. 46). Consensus of individual interests as expressed in a sort of ethical rather than enforced legal code will ultimately fully dominate the human society of the future. The necessity of compulsory law as we know it will become obsolete. The "best individuals" that will survive the selection test of history will leave little social function for law. This course of events, dictated by the expediency of social fitness, is inevitable because "it is impossible for artificial molding to do that which natural molding does . . . the molding has to be spontaneously achieved by self-adjustment to the life of voluntary co-operation." Spencer summarizes his legal prophecy as follows:

> The impersonally-derived law which revives as personally-derived law declines, and which gives expression to the consensus of individual interests, becomes, in its final form, simply an applied system of ethics—or rather, of that part of ethics which concerns men's just relations with one another and with the community. (Spencer 1899: p. 534)

Looking at historical events that followed the Industrial Revolution and at law as it exists about seventy years after Spencer's writing I have to agree fully with Stone's statement that "The events, as we have seen, belied the prophecy" (Stone 1950: p. 654).

KARL MARX (1818–1883)
AND FRIEDRICH ENGELS (1820–1895)

Karl Marx and Friedrich Engels designed a kind of social philosophy which, by explaining the past world's cultural history, was supposed to be capable of not only solving contemporary problems but also, by being projected into the future, of unveiling the inevitable cultural destiny of man. They were influenced by the eighteenth- and nineteenth-century historical school which maintained that law reflected historical changes and was not an immutable set of rational principles of the doctrine of Natural Law. They employed the dialectic method of Hegel that caused social history to be viewed as a struggle of contradictions and relied heavily upon the unilinear evolutionist theory of Morgan for an interpretation of evolution of human cultures as following a single path of predetermined developmental stages, and used a philosophy of materialism and economic determinism as an explanation for culture change. The two writers viewed culture as composed of two structural segments. The basis of any human culture was supposed to be its material system of production and the corresponding economic relations. This base supports the rest of the culture, a superstructure ultimately determined by its materialistic foundation. Consequently, any changes in the economic basis of a culture must sooner or later be reflected in changes in its superstructure. In this way the Marxist doctrine became firmly based in materialism and in economic determinism. The economy of a society (esp. its means of production) became, in the view of these philosophers, the culture's prime mover, the true initiator and determinator of culture change. In Marx's words:

> *In the social production which men carry on they enter into definite relations that are indispensable and independent of their will; these relations of production correspond to a definite stage of development of their material powers of production. The sum total of these relations of production constitutes the economic structure of society—the real foundation, on which rise legal and political superstructures and to which correspond definite forms of social consciousness. (Marx 1959: p. 43)*[32]

The nature of change in the two structural segments of culture was conceived of as qualitatively different, so that "distinction should always be made between the material transformation of the economic conditions of production, which can be determined with the precision of natural science, and the legal, political, religious, aesthetic, or philosophic—in short, ideological—forms in which men become conscious of this conflict and fight it out" (Marx 1959: p. 44).[33] In other words, while modes of production and economic relations change and are ultimately determined by the material conditions, the superstructure adjusts itself to these economic changes only afterward, thus creating a "cultural lag" (see also Engels 1959: p. 66).

Law, as a part of the cultural superstructure, was also believed to change in such a way that it reflects alterations in the economic life. Thus there are no legal principles that can be applied universally and arbitrarily to all human societies at all times. Consequently, the followers of the doctrine of Natural Law who attempted such a universal application were regarded by Marx and Engels as biased and ethnocentric (compare Marx and Engels 1959: p. 24). Legal relations, according to Marx, cannot be "understood by themselves nor explained by the so-called general progress of

[32]"In der gesellschaftlichen Produktion ihres Lebens gehen die Menschen bestimmte, notwendige, von ihrem Willen unabhängige Verhältnisse ein, Produktionsverhältnisse, die einer bestimmten Entwicklungsstufe ihrer materiellen Produktivkräfte entsprechen. Die Gesamtheit dieser Produktionsverhältnisse bildet die ökonomische Struktur der Gesellschaft, die reale Basis, worauf sich ein juristischer und politischer Überbau erhebt, und welcher bestimmte gesellschaftliche Bewustseinsformen entsprechen." (Marx 1964b: p. 8)

[33]" . . . muss man stets unterscheiden zwischen der materiellen, naturwissenschaftlich treu zu konstatierenden Umwälzung in den ökonomischen Produktionsbedingungen und den juristischen, politischen, religiösen, künstlerischen oder philosophischen, kurz, ideologischen Formen, worin sich die Menschen dieses Konflikts bewusst werden und ihn ausfechten." (Marx 1964b: p. 9)

human mind" (Marx 1959: p. 43)[34]; they are rather "historically-given by-products of socio-economic life," subject to change whenever the situation in the material means of production demands it (Stone 1966: p. 492).

Since in the more advanced societies with social classes the means of production are owned and controlled by the ruling class it is this class that formulates the precepts of the legal system in power (Engels 1964: pp. 156 ff.; Marx 1946: pp. 141–142; Marx 1964a: p. 801). Statutory law (*zakon*) to a Marxist is nothing but "the expression of the will of the classes which have emerged victorious and hold political power" (Lenin 1935–1938: p. 237).[35] Addressing himself to the bourgeois, Marx lectures:

> *Your very ideas are but the outgrowth of the conditions of your bourgeois production and bourgeois property, just as your jurisprudence is but the will of your class made into a law for all, a will whose essential character and direction are determined by the economic conditions of existence of your class. (Marx 1959: p. 24; also pp. 18, 19)[36]*

To summarize, to Marx and Engels law in a civilized society was an expression of the will of the ruling class; it reflected its basic values which ultimately were derived from the economy and material means of production.

Of course, an expression of the will of the rulers, no matter how brilliantly presented, is not enough to induce the population to behave in accord with its precepts and to assure the smooth functioning of a society. Such an assurance can come only from an apparatus that is effective in execution of such a will—the public authority. To Marx and Engels there are different types of public authorities which, because of their superordination over the rest of the population and their use of armed bodies, have the power to enforce the will of the ruling class (Moore 1960: p. 657). If this public authority does not represent an entire community but only a segment of it (the ruling class), and if its armed bodies are separated from the population assuming the form of a police force or an army, then such a public authority is regarded by the two authors and their contemporary followers as a "state" (see esp. Moore 1960: pp. 643, 657–658; Stone 1966: p. 491; Lenin 1943: p. 11). This specialized form of the public authority, the state, is regarded by the Marxists not only as a nonuniversal and strictly historical

[34]" . . . weder aus sich selbst zu begreifen sind noch aus der sogenannten allgemeinen Entwicklung des menschlichen Geistes." (Marx 1964b: p. 8)

[35]"vyrazhenie voli klassov, kotorye oderzhali pobedu i derzhat v svoikh rukakh gosudarstvennuyu vlast." (Lenin 1961: p. 306)

[36]"Eure Ideen selbst sind Erzeugnisse der bürgerlichen Produktions- und Eigentumsverhältnisse, wie euer Recht nur der zum Gesetz erhobene Wille eurer Klasse ist, ein Wille, dessen Inhalt gegeben ist in den materiellen Lebensbedingungen eurer Klasse." (Marx and Engels 1959b: p. 477)

phenomenon, but also as a characteristic of a developmental stage, dependent upon the existence of a class structure in a society (Engels 1964: p. 155). It did not exist prior to, and will disappear after, the period marked by the existence of social classes. In the words of Engels:

> *The state, therefore, has not existed from all eternity. There have been societies which have managed without it, which had no notion of the state or state power. At a definite stage of economic development, which necessarily involved the cleavage of society into classes, the state became a necessity because of this cleavage. We are now rapidly approaching a stage in the development of production at which the existence of these classes has not only ceased to be a necessity, but becomes a positive hindrance to production. They will fall as inevitably as they once arose. The state inevitably falls with them. The society which organizes production anew on the basis of free and equal association of the producers will put the whole state machinery where it will then belong—into the museum of antiquities, next to the spinning wheel and the bronze ax. (Engels 1964: p. 158)[37]*

According to Marx and Engels the existence of law (*ius*) was made dependent upon the presence of a public authority. While to Lenin the concept of public authority meant only the state, without which statutory law (*zakon, lex*) could not exist (Moore 1960: p. 651), Marx and Engels applied the term broadly and recognized as types of public authority also those political formations that did not possess all the attributes of a state. As a consequence, in their opinion law (*ius*) had existed in the primitive (gentile) society prior to the emergence of a state (Moore 1960: p. 653; Engels 1964: pp. 89, 90). Engels identified these nonstate types of public authorities as follows:

> *In each such community there were from the beginning certain common interests the safeguarding of which had to be handed over to individuals, even though under the control of the*

[37]"Der Staat ist also nicht von Ewigkeit her. Es hat Gesellschaften gegeben, die ohne ihn fertig wurden, die von Staat und Staatsgewalt keine Ahnung hatten. Auf einer bestimmten Stufe der ökonomischen Entwicklung, die mit Spaltung der Gesellschaft in Klassen notwendig verbunden war, wurde, durch diese Spaltung der Staat eine Notwendigkeit. Wir nähern uns jetzt mit raschen Schritten einer Entwicklungsstufe der Produktion, auf der das Dasein dieser Klassen nicht nur aufgehört hat eine Notwendigkeit zu sein, sondern ein positives Hindernis der Produktion wird. Sie werden fallen, ebenso unvermeidlich, wie sie früher entstanden sind. Mit ihnen fällt unvermeidlich der Staat. Die Gesellschaft, die Produktion auf Grundlage freier und gleicher Assoziation der Produzenten neu organisiert, versetzt die ganze Staatsmaschine dahin, wohin sie dann gehören wird: ins Museum der Altertümer, neben das Spinnrad und die bronzene Axt." (Engels 1962a: p. 168)

community as a whole: such were the adjudication of disputes; repression of encroachments by individuals on the rights of others; control of water supplies, especially in hot countries; and finally, when conditions were still absolutely primitive, religious functions. Such offices are found in primitive communities of every period—in the oldest German Mark-communities and even today in India. They are naturally endowed with a certain measure of authority and are the beginnings of state power. (Engels 1935: p. 204)[38]

Since law in the Marxian theory appears to be defined as "rules of conduct sanctioned by public authority" (Moore 1960: p. 642), it would seem that Engels meant the law to be almost universal. Since in many primitive societies there are no well-formulated abstract rules of conduct that could be incorporated into judicial decisions directly or through the media of *Gesetze* (legal rules), such a conclusion could be regarded as false. Nevertheless Engels, and Marx as well, did postulate existence of law in primitive society (Moore 1960: pp. 649–651), but not necessarily in the form of explicit rules. There most of it was in the form of customary law; only some of it originated through purposeful legislation. This law in a nonstate society was supposed not to have been enforced formally through executive power but informally, mostly through public opinion (see esp. Engels 1964: p. 154).

The emergence of law and its successive historical changes were linked by Marx and Engels to the history of human culture in general. Being heavily influenced by the unilinear evolutionism especially of Morgan, McLennan, and Bachofen (see esp. Engels 1964: pp. 7–18), they conceived of the world's culture history as an evolutionary sequence of developmental stages through which the various societies had to pass. The existing culture differences among these societies were attributed basically to two causes: the differential speed with which some societies progressed along the evolutionary line (Marx 1966a: p. 144) and ecological factors. The natural resources of a country influenced its system of production, which in turn determined a special type of economy with its dependent cultural superstructure (see esp. Engels 1964: pp. 21–22).

[38]"In jedem sochen Gemeinwesen bestehen von Anfang an gewisse gemeinsame Interessen, deren Wahrung einzelnen, wenn auch unter Aufsicht der Gesamtheit, übertragen werden muss: Entscheidung von Streitigkeiten; Repression von Übergriffen einzelner über ihre Berechtigung hinaus; Aufsicht über Gewässer, besonders in heissen Ländern; endlich, bei der Waldursprünglichkeit der Zustände, religiöse Funktionen. Dergleichen Beamtungen finden sich in den urwüchsigen Gemeinwesen zu jeder Zeit, so in den ältesten deutschen Markgenossenschaften und noch heute in Indien. Sie sind selbstredend mit einer gewissen Machtvollkommenheit ausgerüstet und die Anfänge der Staatsgewalt." (Engels 1962b: p. 166)

The Marxian analysis in terms of evolutionary stages relied heavily on the conceptualization of Morgan and of his less outstanding anthropological contemporaries. Marx and Engels made "no attempt," observes Hobsbawm (1966: p. 57) "to apply the analysis outside Western and Central Europe," with two possible exceptions—when they made a few remarks concerning eastern Europe and Russia. Whereas "the stages of prehistoric cultures" were a direct republica of Morgan's evolutionary scheme (Engels 1964: pp. 19–24), and all of them were lumped together under the first "gentile" superstage of development (Marx and Engels 1962: p. 22; Stone 1966: p. 581; Hobsbawm 1966: p. 27), the remaining stages of protohistorical and historical societies that eventually possessed cities and states are results of Marx and Engels' analysis freed from a complete reliance on Morgan (Marx and Engels 1962: pp. 22–27; Hobsbawm 1966: pp. 27–38). In abstracting the following evolutionary outline from Marx and Engels' writings I was often hampered by their vagueness, lack of precise expression, and implicit contradictions. It is no wonder that writers on Marxism often contradict each other in their interpretation of the work of the founders of the Communist movement.

The first six stages of cultural evolution, devised by Morgan and accepted by Engels, that are often referred to by a single generic term, "gentile society" or "primitive society," are: the Lower, Middle, and Upper Stages of Savagery; and the Lower, Middle, and Upper Stages of Barbarism (Engels 1964: pp. 19–24). Their major characteristics are lumped together and summarized by Marx and Engels as follows: "The first form of property is the tribal property. It corresponds to the underdeveloped stage of production, which provides a people with food secured through hunting and fishing, animal husbandry, or at the most through agriculture" (Marx and Engels 1962: p. 22, tr. L. Pospisil).[39] In this stage the division of labor is still little developed and the social structure is dominated by kinship, the major societal segments being based on the extension of the family. Toward the end of this stage there appear three main social divisions of the members of a tribe: chiefs, tribesmen, and slaves. Slavery originated as a result of an increase of population and of its needs, and as a consequence of the outward extension of tribal contacts through war and barter. During this first long epoch of human cultural development, law was mostly absent (Engels 1964: p. 36). It is only in the lower stage of barbarism that law makes its first crude appearance in some tribes (e.g., Iroqouis; Engels 1964: p. 87). It fully emerges only in its last stage, the Upper Stage of Barbarism (Engels 1964: pp. 78, 82, 85, 87, 89; also Marx's view—Moore 1960: p. 650). This stage

---

[39]Translated by Pospisil. "Die erste Form des Eigentums ist das Stammeigentum. Es entspricht der unentwickelten Stufe der Produktion, auf der ein Volk von Jagd und Fischfang, von Viehzucht oder höchstens vom Ackerbau sich nährt." (Marx and Engels 1962: p. 22)

is represented by societies such as "the Greeks of the heroic age, the tribes of Italy shortly before the foundation of Rome, the Germans of Tacitus and the Norsemen of the Viking Age" (Engels 1964: p. 23).[40] Although these societies had law and authority, the public authority determining the law was supposed to have been so weak that "the lowest police officer of the civilized state has more 'authority' than all the organs of gentile society put together" (Engels 1964: p. 156).[41] There was "no public power separate from the people which could have been used against the people" (Engels 1964: p. 94),[42] so that the gentile society "possessed no means of coercion except public opinion" (Engels 1964: p. 154; also on Marx—Moore 1960: p. 651).[43] Thus enforcement of the authority's decision was supposed to have been informal, dependent upon the group as a whole.

From this primitive or gentile stage some societies passed into a second stage which Marx and Engels thought had at least three, possibly four, variants (types). Although they are often vague in their description, one may generalize and say that all three variants of the second stage were characterized by some development of class structure with institutionalized slavery (with a possible exception of the Oriental despotic type), by dissociation of *Gemeindeeigentum* (community ownership) from *Privateigentum* (private property), and by a more developed division of labor. This stage of society was reached when, as Marx thought, several tribes united themselves politically through a treaty or conquest and founded a political union or association (Germanic type) often marked by presence of a city (*Stadt*) and always by a well-defined territory, thus forming in at least two of the variants (Oriental and Ancient) a state. Within such a state contradictions became imminent. A contrast developed between the city (*Stadt*) and hinterland (*Land*), between public and private property (Ancient type especially), between citizens and slaves, and within the city, between industry and commerce, especially maritime trade (Ancient type). Although the development of private property in the Ancient and Germanic types marked an important innovation, communal property still played, at least in the Oriental and Ancient types, the leading role (Marx and Engels 1962: pp. 22–23). Of the three variants or types of this stage, two (the Ancient and the Germanic types) became more progressive by being amenable to change (Hobsbawm 1966: pp. 32–35).

[40]". . . die Griechen zur Heroenzeit, die italischen Stämme kurz vor der Gründung Roms, die Deutschen des Tacitus, die Normannen der Wikingerzeit." (Engels 1962a: p. 34)

[41]"Der lumpigste Polizeidiener des zivilisierten Staats hat mehr 'Autorität' als alle Organe der Gentilgesellschaft zusammengenommen." (Engels 1962a: p. 166)

[42]". . . noch keine vom Volk getrennte öffentliche Gewalt, die ihm hätte entgegengesetzt werden können." (Engels 1962a; p. 103)

[43]". . . hatte kein Zwangsmittel ausser der öffentlichen Meinung." (Engels 1962a: p. 164)

The first type, Oriental despotism, is described as resistant to alterations and therefore to progress and is the most stable variant of this stage of societal development. Its economic foundation "is tribal or common property, in most cases created through a combination of manufacture and agriculture within the small community which thus becomes entirely self-sustaining and contains within itself all conditions of production and surplus production" (Marx 1966a: p. 70).[44] This economic self-sustenance is regarded by Marx as the main reason for this type's nonprogressive nature and resistance to change. Its foundation rests upon communal property with a virtual absence of individual ownership (Marx 1966a: p. 79). The surplus of the production of the local communities is delivered in the form of labor or tribute to the satraps or princes who personify the unity of the state. They live in governmental centers, cities created in locations favorable to either external trade or exchange of collected tribute for the labor of the subjects (expended especially on irrigation, roads, palaces, and defense). The head of the state, the Oriental despot, is not only a political representative of the union of the communities but also the owner of the land and of all other property. His subjects are legally propertyless, their work being done on land or raw material with tools granted to them by the despot. Thus the individual is never independent of his community, which prevents him from initiating change and progress. Degree of centralization and amount of the ruler's power may vary, so that in some instances actual "Oriental-type" societies may appear to be more despotic and in others more democratic. Class structure is still very rudimentary and law is the expression of the will of the despot (Marx 1966a: pp. 69–71, 83). In addition to the Asian examples Marx includes certain Celtic societies and the Peruvian and Mexican societies (Marx 1966a: p. 70; Hobsbawm 1966: p. 34).

The Ancient type of society, the most dynamic variant of the three, produces the true city which becomes its center of development and its actual politicoeconomic basis. It is surrounded by a territory (*Land*) first cultivated by the city dwellers and later dotted with villages in which food is produced that is exchanged for manufactured goods and services provided by the artisans of the city. Thus the important economic unity and, at the same time, contradiction between city and countryside is developed. The fast developing division of labor and specialization in the city marks another fundamental contrast—that of trade and industry. In these conditions the class structure assumes a well-defined form—the distinction between citizens and slaves becomes especially prominent. Communal property (or public property), still dominant, is separated from private property,

[44]". . . Stamm oder Gemeindeeigentum, erzeugt meist durch eine Kombination von Manufaktur und Agrikultur innerhalb der kleinen Gemeinde, die so durchaus self-sustaining wird und alle Bedingungen der Reproduktion und Mehrproduktion in sich selbst enthält." (Marx 1953: p. 377)

which, as time passes, assumes greater and greater importance (Marx: 1966a: esp. pp. 71–74, 79, 83–84; Marx and Engels 1962: pp. 22–23). Law and courts are present and well developed, formalized, and elaborate (Engels 1964: pp. 115–116).

The third variant of this developmental stage is called by Marx and Engels the "Germanic type." It starts as a conglomeration of individual, independent farming households, scattered throughout a territory. A typical Germanic individual household "contains an entire economy, forming as it does an independent center of production" (Marx 1966a: p. 79).[45] Neighboring autonomous households form an "association" for the purposes of defense, internal peace, and exchange. Because of a lack of a political "union" among these households one cannot call their conglomerate a state. Unlike the ancient type, the property of the individual household owners forms the basis for the economy, and in its early development there is no unifying city with its official figuring as head of the state (Marx 1966a: pp. 78–80). Thus the Germanic period of development "starts with the country-side as the locus of history, whose further development then proceeds through the opposition of town and country" (Marx 1966a: p. 78).[46] Class structure is slowly formed and law is administered from the onset of this period by the occasional assembly representing the association of the Germanic households (Marx 1966a: p. 80; Hobsbawm 1966: p. 37).

The foregoing résumé presents the Oriental, Ancient, and Germanic types as variants of the same stage, as alternatives rather than successive stages through which a given society had to move. However, this interpretation of Marx and Engels' writings is not the only one that can be construed on the basis of the available written evidence. Nevertheless, Hobsbawm (1966: p. 36) defends the above presentation and objects to the idea that three types are successive unilinear evolutionary stages because "in the literal sense this is plainly untrue, for not only did the Asiatic mode of production co-exist with all the rest, but there is no suggestion in the argument of the *Formen,* or anywhere else, that the ancient mode evolved out of it." This indeed may be true, but it is equally true that in his preface to *Critique of Political Economy* Marx presented the three types as successive stages rather than as variants (alternatives) of the same stage (Marx 1964a: p. 9).[47] Also in *Formen* Marx does suggest that the Germanic form followed (evolved) from the Ancient form rather than coexisted as an alternative of

[45]"Das ökonomische Ganze ist au fond in jedem einzelnen Hause enthalten, das für sich ein selbständiges Zentrum der Produktion bildet." (Marx 1953: p. 383)
[46]". . . geht vom Land als Sitz der Geschichte aus, deren Fortentwicklung dann im Gegensatz von Stadt und Land vor sich geht." (Marx 1953: p. 382)
[47]"In grossen Umrissen können asiatische, antike, feudale und modern bürgerliche Produktionsweisen als progressive Epochen der ökonomischen Gesellschaftsformation bezeichnet werden." (Marx 1964b: p. 9)

it (Marx 1966a: p. 78). Be that as it may, I followed Hobsbawm's exposition and found it more logical to present the types as alternatives. However, having in mind the strong unilinear evolutionist influence manifested in the work of the two authors, I still think it possible that the types were meant as evolutionary stages rather than as variants of the same stage—but who knows what Marx and Engels actually thought?

The collapse of Old Rome and of the Ancient society was marked by large-scale destruction of city life and industry. Agriculture suffered also, but it was actually the rural area, with its thinly spread population located in villages, which gave rise to the new epoch—that of feudalism. By this time the less productive class of slaves had been replaced by the small farmers. The land was divided into segments belonging to hierarchically arranged noble classes which exploited the productive class of small farmers by transforming them into serfs with limited freedom. The former communal property was transformed into collective property of the feudal lords as a group. Their power was backed by the Germanic military organization which derived its recruits from the serf stratum of the society.

In opposition to this rural development of the power of the nobility emerged a parallel development in the city. There the artisans became not only producers of goods but also merchants. Their apprentices provided the necessary labor which, toward the close of the period, was supplemented by unskilled workers paid for the amount of time spent on work (*Taglöhner-pöbel*). The artisans imitated the historical segmentation of the rural nobility and organized themselves into guilds. The landed property of the rural nobility and the skills and workshops of the urban master craftsmen became the most important form of property in the feudal system of production. Marx regarded the division of labor in the feudal stage of social evolution as still largely underdeveloped and associated with rather sharp divisions of rank (king's family and princes, noblemen, clergy, serfs, master craftsmen, apprentices, day laborers). The dual hierarchy in countryside and city was united under feudal kings who reigned over the whole state. The law administered by the courts was created by and reflected the values of the dominant class, that of the king and the feudal lords (Marx and Engels 1962: pp. 24–25; Hobsbawm 1966: pp. 28–29, 37).

The rise of the capitalist stage of social evolution is attributed by Marx to the cities. There the division of labor was greatly intensified as a result of an expansion of trade that eventually engulfed the whole world. The burghers of the city emancipated themselves from the rule of the guilds and feudal lords by concentrating on foreign trade and by giving rise to manufactures exempt from the rule of the guilds. Individual towns and cities developed their own specializations in production. This new division of labor made cities and even countries interdependent, slowly creating the world market. Thus through a linking stage of mercantilism, that emphasized economic competition on a national scale, society slowly changed into a capitalistic type that was founded on world market, dual class division of capitalist (the owners of the means of production and formulators of the dominating legal system) and proletariat (who supplied the necessary labor and were paid by time wages). Unlike feudalism, capitalism did not appropriate the people but only their labor (Marx 1966a: pp. 84–86, 118, 130; Hobsbawm 1966: pp. 29–32).

With the lapse of time, says Marx, the material basis of production has slowly changed, thus coming into conflict with the old capitalist economic and property relations, which have failed to make corresponding adjustments. As a consequence, the sociopolitical superstructure also becomes outdated and lags severely behind the ever-changing forces of production, thus creating a mutual alienation—an ever-increasing social gap between the two major segments of population of the capitalist state: the bourgeois and the proletariat (Marx 1959: pp. 43–44). Of necessity this situation leads to an ultimate confrontation of the two forces, to an "unusually violent class struggle"—a revolution (Lenin 1943: p. 31). In this struggle the aim must be, according to Marxists such as Lenin, to destroy the bourgeois state (1943: pp. 33–35). However, the destruction of the capitalist state does not mean abolition of the state organization altogether. Lenin writes,

> We are not Utopians, we do not indulge in "dreams" of how best to do away immediately with all administration, with all subordination; these Anarchist dreams, based upon a lack of understanding of the task of proletarian dictatorship, are basically foreign to Marxism. . . . No, we want the Socialist revolution with human nature as it is now, with human nature that cannot do without subordination, control, and "managers." (Lenin 1943: pp. 42–43)[48]

Thus a new state is actually created—a dictatorship of the proletariat (Lenin 1917: p. 13; Stalin, in Stone 1966: p. 501). It should incorporate democratic ideals as far as the proletariat class is concerned, and principles of a dictatorship with regard to the overthrown capitalist class (Lenin 1943: pp. 30–31). The task of the "*new type* of state" is not to exploit any class of laborers, but it has "the task of completely emancipating them from all oppression and exploitation, the task facing the dictatorship of the proletariat" (Stalin 1965: pp. 245–246).[49] Stone feels that by 1890 Engels certainly

[48]"My nye utopisty. My nye 'mechtayem' o tom, kak by srazu oboitis' bez vsyakogo upravlyeniya, bez vsyakogo podchineniya; eti anarkhistskie mechty, osnovannye na neponimanii zadach diktatury proletariata, v kornye chuzhdy marksizmu. . . . Nyet, my khotim sotsialisticheskoi revolyutsii s takimi lyudmi, kak tyeper', kotorye bez podchineniya, bez kontrolya, bez 'nadsmotrshchikov i bukhgaltyerov' nye oboidutsya." (Lenin 1962: p. 49)

[49]". . . a k zadacham polnogo ikh osvobozhdeniya ot vsyakogo gnyeta i ekspluatatsii, k zadacham diktatury proletariata." (Stalin 1947: p. 120)

"would not have been outraged by Stalin's claim that the transitional state and law could be used as a main instrument for preparing for the advent of communist society" (Stone 1966: p. 503). Thus in this stage of evolution law is still regarded by Marxists as an indispensable tool of social control in the hands of proletarian judges and legislation—indeed Vyshinsky went as far as to declare that "socialism and not capitalism, brought law to its highest stage" (Stone 1966: p. 502).

Unlike the preceding dictatorship of proletariat, the final stage in the evolution of the human society, communism, is supposed to be reached gradually, through a slow process of the withering away of the socialist state. In Lenin's words:

> *The state is withering away in so far as there are no longer any capitalists, any classes, and, consequently, no class can be suppressed. But the state has not yet altogether withered away, since there still remains the protection of "bourgeois right," which sanctifies actual inequality. For the complete extinction of the state, complete communism is necessary. (Lenin 1943: p. 78)*[50]

There will be no revolution, no abrupt change necessary for the advent of the communist society; certainly the socialist state will not have to be abolished, it will slowly dissolve by itself (Engels 1935: pp. 315 ff.; Engels 1907: p. 77). In this communist stateless society law and law-enforcing agencies will disappear altogether. This is supposed to happen because the people will become accustomed to observe the rules of social intercourse "without force, without compulsion, without subordination, without the *special apparatus* for compulsion which is called the state" (Lenin 1943: p. 74).[51] This statement applies, according to Lenin, to the people in general. He does not rule out a possibility of individual criminality when he states:

> *We are not Utopians and we do not in the least deny the possibility and inevitability of excesses on the part of individual persons, nor the need to suppress such excesses. But, in the first place, no special machinery, no special apparatus of repression is needed for this: this will be done by the armed people itself, as simply and as readily as any crowd of civilized people, even in*

[50]"Gosudarstvo otmirayet, poskol'ku kapitalistov uzhe nyet, klassov uzhe nyet, podavlyat' poetomu kakoi by to ni bylo klass nelzya. No gosudarstvo yeshche nye otmerlo sovsyem, ibo ostayetsya okhrana 'burzhuaznogo prava' osvyashchayush-chego fakticheskoe neravenstvo. Dlya polnogo otmiraniya gosudarstva nuzhen polnyi kommunizm." (Lenin 1962: p. 95)

[51]". . . bez nasiliya, bez prinuzhdeniya, bez podchineniya, bez osobogo apparata dlya prinuzhdeniya, kotoryi nazyvayetsya gosudarstvom." (Lenin 1962: p. 89)

modern society, parts a pair of combatants or does not allow a
woman to be outraged. (Lenin 1943: p. 75)[52]

Thus, somehow, people will revert to social conditions that also apply, in the opinion of the Marxists, to primitive man. There will be no need for law in the future of mankind, in a future that will be marked by the last stage of human evolution, the stage of stateless and lawless communism that is supposed to persist forever.

So much for the philosophy, dreams, and prophecies of Marxism. It is amazing how much of Marx and Engels' philosophy relied on Morgan and on the first putative evolutionary stage of a lawless communal society, a stage empirically not documented. It is even more astonishing when one realizes that at the time of Marx and Engels' writing next to nothing was known about primitive peoples, and the work of the two writers "was not based on any serious knowledge of tribal societies" (Hobsbawm 1966: p. 25). Even if one admitted that this scheme of evolution pertains only to Europe and Western society and is not universally applicable in the unilinear evolutionist way, one finds overwhelming empirical evidence that the evolutionary sequence, especially the conceptualization of the last two stages, is incorrect. First of all, the dictatorship of the proletariat, that was surprisingly enough established in rural Russia and not in industrialized western Europe, was actually a dictatorship not of the proletariat but of one man only—Stalin, and later Khrushchev—and now, temporarily, of an oligarchy. Second, the Soviet socialist state and its law, after half a century, show no signs of withering away. Rather, they display unusual vitality. It is true that up to 1930 the "withering away of law and state" doctrine prevailed in the Soviet Union and was actually preached there. However, as Rostow writes, "Since 1936 the teaching and practice of law have been rehabilitated, new codes have been promulgated, and a tone of positive legalism has suffused Soviet Society" (Rostow 1952: p. 103). While doing this, the leaders of the Soviet socialist state "satisfy their consciences by pushing its [communist society's] achievements so far into the future that it is not an active consideration in their planning" (Hazard 1957: p. 5). Thus the dogmatic politicians of communism of the twentieth century are caught in another "dialectic" contradiction: their dogma of a transition to a lawless communist society and the actual practice—the Soviet state that somehow refuses to fade away.

[52]"My nye utopisty i niskol'ko nye otritsayem vozmozhnosti i neizbezhnosti ekstsessov otdel'nykh lyits, a ravno neobkhodimosti podavlyat' takiye ekstsessy. No, vo-pervykh, dlya etogo nye nuzhna osobaya mashina, osobyi apparat podavleniya, eto budyet dyelat' sam vooruzhennyi narod s takoi zhe prostotoi i lyegkostyu, s kotoroi lyubaya tolpa tsivilizovannykh lyudei dazhe v sovremennom obshchestve raznimaet derushchikhsya ili nye dopuskaet nasiliya nad zhenshchinoi." (Lenin 1962: p. 91)

Stone has probably a good explanation of the contradiction between the Soviet leaders' dogmatic pronouncements of the arrival of the communist society and their pragmatic actions supporting the existing Soviet state and its legal order:

> *In some degree, both as to Khrushchev and his predecessors, we suspect that pronouncements which seem to manifest schizophrenia are often but verbal comforters extended to those who dream of a law-free, self-governing communist society, by those whose political sophistication makes them more aware of how difficult of attainment the dream is. (Stone 1966: p. 508)*

The thousand-times repeated Marxist dogmas, unfortunately, trapped not only some unsophisticated Marxists but also some "Western scholars" (even some anthropologists!) who "are surprised by the fact that state and law are growing in Russia rather than withering away" (Stone 1966: p. 505). These scholars somehow did not realize the fact that the communist doctrine which assumes a period of culmination of law and strength of the state to be followed by a period of their total absence flies, in the words of Stone, "in the face of elementary truths about the phenomenon of power in human society" (Stone 1966: p. 512) and, I may add, in the face of anthropological knowledge of culture change. They did not realize the absurdity of the claim that with the achievement of the communist evolutionary stage the evolution and social change could somehow abdicate and communism would persist into eternity. I may conclude with Stone's words that the communist prognostications will not materialize "nor is the world likely to see in the future any generation of Soviet leaders who voluntarily leave the stage of history, fervently proclaiming: *'L'État c'est Nous! L'État est Mort! Vive la Société sans Nous!'*" (1966: p. 512).

ÉMILE DURKHEIM (1858–1917)

Spencer's attempt to link law with the rest of the society's culture by viewing it as an institution that secures the gratification of individuals' desires and their pursuit of self-interests (especially so in contracts), and by regarding "its evolutionary stages" as an expression of a *consensus* of such interests (esp. 1899: pp. 527, 536) was effectively challenged by Émile Durkheim, who with Max Weber was one of the two founders of modern sociology. Durkheim not only rejected Spencer's utilitarian conceptualization as a false "cement" for the social fabric of human society, he also refused to include the role and activity of the individual in the inventory of data that explain the existence and change of social phenomena: "The determining cause of a social fact should be sought among the social facts preceding it and not among the states of the individual consciousness" (Durkheim 1966: p.

110).[53] It would be false, however, to assume that Durkheim eliminated consideration of the individual altogether. As far as the existence of a social phenomenon such as solidarity is concerned he admitted that "it must be contained in our physical and psychic constitution" (1964: p. 67).[54] However, to explain social and cultural history and the structure of a society through an exploration of consciousnesses of individual minds, even those of great national heroes or innovators of any type, was to Durkheim a basic fallacy. The consciousness of people was only the medium through which social phenomena manifested themselves. The nature of the social phenomena could be understood only as resulting "from special cultivation which individual consciousnesses undergo in their association with each other, an association from which a new form of existence is evolved" (1966: p. 124).[55] Thus social facts are somehow *sui generis;* they exist in a world of their own, and a sociologist investigating their causes, nature, and social effects (function) "must endeavor to consider them from an aspect that is independent of their individual manifestations" (p. 45).[56]

Most of Durkheim's theories concerning sociology appear in his four major works: *The Division of Labor in Society* (1893), *The Rules of Sociological Method* (1895), *Suicide* (1897), and *The Elementary Forms of the Religious Life* (1912). Of these, the first two will be of particular importance here. In both these works the normative aspect of social facts is stressed, and law assumes an almost paramount role as far as Durkheim's sociological methodology is concerned. Accordingly, a social fact itself exhibits two major criteria: it possesses "the power of external coercion," exercised upon individuals and manifested by the presence of either a sanction or a nonexplicit "resistance offered against every individual effort that tends to violate it," and it is widely "diffused" (or general) in the group in which it occurs (1966: p. 10). For us the first criterion is of special interest. Accordingly, a social fact is defined as *"every way of acting, fixed or not, capable of exercising on the individual an external constraint"* (1966: p. 13).[57] The form in which this constraint (sanction) is manifested becomes for Durkheim a major working tool—it indicates presence of a corresponding type of social

[53]"La cause déterminante d'un fait social doit être cherchée parmi les faits sociaux antécédents, et non parmi les états de la conscience individuelle." (Durkheim 1895: p. 135)

[54]". . . il faut que notre constitution physique et psychique la comporte." (Durkheim 1893: p. 70)

[55]". . . résulte de cette élaboration spéciale à laquelle sont soumises les consciences particulières par le fait de leur association et d'où se dégage une nouvelle forme d'existence." (Durkheim 1895: p. 151)

[56]". . . il doit s'efforcer de les considérer par un côté où ils se présentent isolés de leurs manifestations individuelles." (Durkheim 1895: p. 57)

[57]". . . toute manière de faire, fixée ou non, susceptible d'exercer sur l'individu une contrainte extérieure. . . ." (Durkheim 1895: p. 19)

solidarity (a cement that holds the social fabric together), and the extent of its occurrence measures the amount of the type of solidarity that operates in a given society.

Social solidarity—a cohesion among the society's members—"is a completely moral phenomenon which, taken by itself, does not lend itself to exact observation nor indeed to measurement." It is an "intangible phenomenon" whose "visible symbol is law" (1964: p. 64).[58] Law, being not only a symbol but actually springing from, and producing in turn, the social solidarity, is a social phenomenon and should be studied as such. Social solidarity produces and permeates social relations. The more there is of solidarity the more there are of social relations. Their number "is necessarily proportional to that of the juridical rules which determine them" (1964: p. 64).[59] Law, then, is the regulating principle of social life—it is its very organization. "The general life of society cannot extend its sway without juridical life extending its sway at the same time and in direct relation. We can thus be certain of finding reflected in law all the essential varieties of social solidarity" (1964: p. 65).[60] Law not only reflects and expresses its corresponding social solidarity but it is, heuristically speaking, solidarity's most easily measurable effect. Moreover, it reflects only those types of social solidarity "which are essential and they are the only ones we need to know" (1964: p. 66).[61] Since, then, argues Durkheim, "law reproduces the principle forms of social solidarity, we have only to classify the different types of law to find therefrom the different types of social solidarity which correspond to it" (1964: p. 68).[62] The criteria for classification of "the different types of law" that pertain to the types of social solidarity are to be found, he says, in the types of legal sanctions with which the jural rules are provided. In this respect Durkheim recognizes two different kinds of sanctions that group corresponding laws into two major categories: repressive sanctions that pertain mainly to penal law and restitutive sanctions that are used mainly in civil, commercial, procedural, administrative, and constitutional law (1964: p. 69).

[58]". . . est un phénomène tout moral qui par lui-même ne se prête pas à l'observation exacte ni surtout à la mesure." (Durkheim 1893: p. 66)

[59]". . . est nécessairement proportionnel à celui des règles juridiques qui les déterminent." (Durkheim 1893: p. 67)

[60]"La vie générale de la société ne peut pas s'étendre sur un point sans que la vie juridique s'y étende en même temps et dans le même rapport. Nous pouvons donc être certains de trouver reflétées dans le droit toutes les variétés essentielles de la solidarité sociale." (Durkheim 1893: p. 67)

[61]". . . qui sont essentiels et ce sont les seuls que nous ayons besoin de connaître." (Durkheim 1893: p. 68)

[62]". . . le droit reproduit les formes principales de la solidarité sociale, nous n'avons qu'à classer les différentes espèces de droit pour chercher ensuite quelles sont les différentes espèces de solidarité sociale qui y correspondent." (Durkheim 1893: p. 71)

In a similar way, of course, one may measure any other social phenomena and relations, not only the intangible social solidarity. For example, to measure the extent of the division of labor that bears upon the social solidarity it would be sufficient "to compare the number of juridical rules which express it with the total volume of law" (1964: p. 68).[63] Of course, to pronounce law as almost the only, and decidedly the best, measure of social life presents some difficulties even for Durkheim in this oversimplification. It is commonly known that law (especially codified law) often lags behind actual social development, but Durkheim simply brushes it aside by the pronouncement: "Normally, custom [actual activity and social relations] is not opposed to law, but is, on the contrary, its basis" (1964: p. 65).[64] However, what about "abnormal" situations? There Durkheim owes us an answer.

The first type of social solidarity, which Durkheim attributes to "early societies," primitive societies, and Western civilization until the rise of capitalism, is called "mechanical." It develops in a social organization characterized by a lack of, or simplicity in specialization of, the society's members in particular types of production, and by their uniformity of behavior, values, attitudes, desires, and beliefs. Although some specialization may develop in these societies, it is not significant enough to break up the cultural homogeneity postulated by Durkheim. In the legal field this homogeneity causes each breach of established custom to affect equally the whole society; its members feel that they are directly threatened by any kind of delict. Thus in the societies with mechanical solidarity a "crime shocks sentiments which, for a given social system, are found in all healthy consciences" (1964: p. 73).[65] The offended sentiment is therefore social, because the sentiments are found in the minds of all members of the society. Furthermore, these injured sentiments arouse a psychological reaction, "there emerges a unique temper, more or less determinate according to the circumstances, which is everybody's without being anybody's in particular. That is the public temper" (1964: p. 102).[66] Furthermore, the collective sentiment which is aroused by crime is not only widespread and even universal to a society's membership, it has also an intensity (1964: p. 77) and it is precise —which means it is defined in people's consciences as well as in penal rules (1964: pp. xiv, 79). Because of the individual's identity and the collective's

[63]". . . comparer le nombre des règles juridiques qui l'expriment au volume total du droit." (Durkheim 1893: p. 71)

[64]"Normalement, les moeurs ne s'opposent pas au droit, mais au contraire en sont la base." (Durkheim 1893: p. 68)

[65]". . . le crime froisse des sentiments qui, pour un même type social, se retrouvent dans toutes les consciences saines." (Durkheim 1893: p. 77)

[66]". . . se dégage une colère unique, plus ou moins déterminée suivant les cas, qui est celle de tout le monde sans être celle de personne en particulier. C'est la colère publique." (Durkheim 1893: p. 110)

conscience, the penal law attaches directly "and without mediation . . . the individual to society" (1964: p. 115).

In this trend of nonempirical thinking Durkheim went so far as to claim that in primitive society, where, according to him, "law is wholy penal, it is the assembly of the people which renders justice" (1964: p. 76).[67] This is because punishment is a passionate reaction to a crime that "emanates from society" (1964: p. xiv; see also p. 85), and thus "it is the society that metes out punishment" (1964: p. 93). "Everybody is attacked; consequently, everybody opposes the attack. Not only is the reaction general, but it is collective" (1964: p. 102).[68] Thus "we know that, in origin, the assembly of the people in their entirety functioned as the tribunal," and "in certain cases, indeed, the people themselves executed the sentence collectively as soon as it had been pronounced" (1964: p. 104).[69] In this execution of justice the primitive peoples punished for the sake of punishing, "without seeking any advantage for themselves from the suffering which they imposed" (1964: p. 86). As cultural evolution progressed and society became politically more complex, the collective reaction to crime that takes a form of condemnation and punishment was relegated to "a definite organ as an intermediary" (1964: p. 96), and the assembly of people itself became incarnated in the person of a chief, who "became, totally or in part, the organ of penal reaction" (1964: 104).

The nature of punishment, according to Durkheim, is a violent satisfaction of the society (and not of its individuals), a collective force directed against the culprit with an intensity that keeps it alive. Moderation, therefore, is out of place here (1964: pp. 99–101). This society's vengeance, the sanction, although a rude defensive weapon, is far from being only negative. It has its positive worth in that it is an expression of instinct of the society's will to self-preservation exacerbated by peril (1964: p. 87), "it serves to heal the wounds made upon collective sentiments," and thus "its true function is to maintain social cohesion intact" (1964: p. 108).[70] What society avenges and the criminal expiates "is the outrage to morality" (1964: p. 89). Punishment, then, consists essentially of "a passionate reaction of graduated intensity that society exercises through the medium of body acting upon

[67]". . . le droit est tout entier pénal, c'est l'assemblée du peuple qui rend la justice." (Durkheim 1893: p. 80)

[68]"Tout le monde est atteint, par conséquent tout le monde se raidit contre l'attaque. Non seulement la réaction est générale, mais elle est collective. . . ." (Durkheim 1893: p. 109)

[69]"On sait, en effet, qu'à l'origine, c'est l'assemblée du peuple toute entière qui faisait fonction de tribunal. . . . dans certains cas, le peuple lui-même qui exécutait collectivement la sentence aussitôt après qu'il l'avait prononcée." (Durkheim 1893: p. 111)

[70]"Sa vraie fonction est de maintenir intacte la cohésion. . . ." (Durkheim 1893: p. 115)

those of its members who have violated certain rules of conduct" (1964: p. 96).[71]

It has to be understood that this violent reaction is that of the society and not of its individuals avenging themselves for injustice suffered at the hands of other members of their group. A private retaliation, *vendetta,* may be recognized as legitimate only by the society, but in itself does not constitute social punishment, and the injustice so avenged "is not completely a delict" (1964: pp. 93, 94). "It is far from true that private vengeance is the prototype of punishment; it is, on the contrary, only an imperfect punishment" which is "only on the threshold of penal law" (1964: p. 94).[72] Durkheim states emphatically that "not a single society can be instanced where the *vendetta* has been the primitive form of punishment" (1964: p. 92).[73]

In its effect upon the malconduct of delinquents, punishment is of repressive nature. This type of sanction pertains to penal law and is invoked by an act which "offends strong and defined states of the collective conscience" (1964: p. 80).[74] Such an act constitutes a crime (1964: p. 70). The law of primitive societies, according to Durkheim, is composed almost entirely of penal provisions and thus appears "entirely repressive" (1964: pp. 93, 138). "Even in the fourth century in Rome, penal law still represented the greater part of juridical rules" (1964: p. 143).[75]

To conclude Durkheim's argument about mechanical solidarity, which exists in primitive societies and nonindustrialized civilizations and which is expressed in penal law and its repressive sanctions, we may underscore his firm belief that it is generated by common conscience, by an "organized totality of beliefs and sentiments common to all the members of the group," and that it "binds the individual directly to society without any intermediary" (1964: p. 129).[76] This solidarity he compares to a "cohesion of an inanimate body." In a society with such a solidarity the individual's personality vanishes and "at the moment when this solidarity exercises its

[71]". . . une réaction passionnelle, d'intensité graduée, que la société exerce par l'intermédiaire d'un corps constitué sur ceux de ses membres qui ont violé certaines règles de conduite." (Durkheim 1893: pp. 102–103)

[72]"Il s'en faut donc que la vengeance privée soit le prototype de la peine; ce n'est au contraire qu'une peine imparfaite . . . seulement sur le seuil du droit pénal." (Durkheim 1893: p. 100)

[73]"On ne peut pas citer une seule société où la *vendetta* ait été la forme primitive de la peine." (Durkheim 1893: p. 97)

[74]". . . il offense les états forts et définis de la conscience collective." (Durkheim 1893: p. 85)

[75]". . . même au IVe siècle de Rome, le droit pénal représentait encore la majeure partie des règles juridiques." (Durkheim 1893: p. 154)

[76]". . . organisé de croyances et de sentiments communs à tous les membres du groupe . . . relie directement l'individu à la société sans aucun intermédiaire." (Durkheim 1893: p. 138)

force . . . we are no longer ourselves, but the collective life" (1964: p. 130).[77]

As society grows and its "material density" of population is accompanied by a growth of "moral density" (a concomitant increase of commercial and other interactions of individuals), the struggle for existence is intensified so that it induces an occupational specialization, the division of labor (1964: pp. 257 ff). This specialization and differentiation of functions provides for the specialized segments of the population different skills, education, and values, thus differentiating also their interests and cultural orientation. However, in spite of and because of this differentiation, people become more mutually dependent. They are no longer self-sufficient and are unable to satisfy their needs by themselves—they depend on other specialists. The resulting cohesive force that holds the society together is no longer mechanical solidarity; the structure of the society no longer resembles the rings of an earthworm: its segments are no longer a repetition of the similar and homogeneous. On the contrary, Durkheim compares the specialized groupings or categories of individuals to organs in the body of a more advanced animal, each organ having its specific role to play. Hence this solidarity that he calls "organic" (1964: pp. 129, 131, 181).

The legal system that expresses this solidarity underwent radical changes from the type it assumed in societies with mechanical solidarity. It became, of necessity, very complex and specialized because it reflects the division of labor with its diversified occupations. As a result, it ceases to be property of the society as a whole. Rather, people are now aware only of those segments, of the legal system that pertain to their specialized occupation and interests with the result that the totality of legal rules is no longer an object of the common conscience and sentiment. These cannot possess the superior force that their counterparts in nonindustrialized societies exhibit, and their violation does not result in an outraged common moral conscience of the society which demands expiation through punishment. Since all that the society as a whole is interested in now is a smooth functioning of its complex organism, the former punishment is replaced by restitutive sanctions, and the law becomes cooperative (rather than repressive) in nature (Durkheim 1964: pp. 115, 127–128, 131). The law of contracts is its example par excellence (Durkheim 1964: p. 123). The authority of this type of law does not derive from the public opinion in general, "but from an opinion localized in restricted regions of society" (Durkheim 1964: p. 127). Although the violent and emotional reaction to the breach of law decreases as the cultural homogeneity of the people disappears, actually, "the objective need for legal regulation is greater with organic than with mechanical solidarity" (Stone 1950: p. 472). The question arises: Which type of law is

[77]". . . au moment où cette solidarité exerce son action . . . car nous ne sommes plus nous-même, mais l'être collectif." (Durkheim 1893: p. 139)

actually needed to reflect the division of labor and to express the organic solidarity? Certainly penal law, with its repressive sanctions—the punishments—is not pertinent here. It does not cease to exist, but it fails to increase proportionately with the growth of the body of the law in general. Of the remaining law, the regulations that pertain to the real rights (*ius in rem*)—regulations that unite things with persons and thus produce a "solidarity of things" rather than of persons—have to be excluded. This "restitutive law of real things" generates a "negative solidarity" because its function is "not to attach different parts of society to one another, but, on the contrary, to put them outside one another, to mark clearly the barriers which separate them" (Durkheim 1964: p. 119).[78] Thus if we subtract from law that is provided with restitutive sanctions the *ius in rem,* we obtain the law that expresses the "positive organic solidarity," namely "domestic law, contract-law, commercial law, procedural law, administrative law, and constitutional law" (Durkheim 1964: p. 122).

It has been said above that the law expressing the positive organic solidarity is a law that is provided with restitutive sactions. The society, says Durkheim, is interested only in the reestablishment of the status quo, of the equilibrium disturbed by the delict. Thus "it intervenes more or less concomitantly and more or less actively, through the intermediary of special organs charged with representing it" (Durkheim 1964: p. 115).[79] The restitutive sanction itself "consists only of the return of things as they were, in the reestablishment of troubled relations to their normal state" (Durkheim 1964: p. 69).[80] "The damage-interests have no penal character" (Durkheim 1964: p. 111). Since rules provided with restitutive sanctions express the organic solidarity derived from the division of labor (in the same way that a nervous system regulates the organs), they serve well as a measure of the volume of the two social phenomena (Durkheim 1964: p. 128). To determine the relative importance of the mechanical solidarity and organic solidarity in a given social type "it is enough to compare the respective extent of the two types of law which express them, since law always varies as the social relations which it governs" (Durkheim 1964: p. 132).[81] The proportion of the two types of law that is provided, respectively, with the repressive and

[78]". . . non de rattacher les unes aux autres les parties différentes de la société, mais au contraire de les mettre en dehors les unes des autres, de marquer nettement les barrières qui les séparent." (Durkheim 1893: p. 127)

[79]". . . elle intervient de plus ou moins près et plus ou moins activement, par l'intermédiaire d'organes spéciaux chargés de la représenter." (Durkheim 1893: p. 122)

[80]". . . consiste seulement dans *la remise des choses en état,* dans le rétablissement des rapports troublés sous leur forme normale." (Durkheim 1893: p. 72)

[81]". . . il suffit de comparer l'étendue respective des deux sortes de droit qui les expriment, puisque le droit varie toujours comme les relations sociales qu'il règle." (Durkheim 1893: p. 141)

restitutive sanctions serves well as an index of the relative importance of the two types of social solidarity, mechanical and organic, in a given society.

Although Durkheim's theory, philosophically speaking, appears to be very logical and ingenious, from the empirical (scientific) point of view it is highly questionable. First, a typical Western dichotomization forms the backbone of his doctrine. Like Maine, Wiese, Weber, Gluckman, and others, Durkheim divided human societies into two qualitatively different categories, with different types of legal systems, social structures, and solidarities. All this is based upon wholly unsatisfactory knowledge of the tribal societies. Although he tried to acquire extensive knowledge of the ethnography of primitive peoples (especially Australian Aborigines), the data in Durkheim's time were so inadequate that they led him to assume a uniformity of knowledge and behavior among primitive people of a given tribe (Durkheim 1912: pp. 7–9; 1964: p. 133). Because of this mystical unreal uniformity he concluded that in a primitive society "the assembly of people" rendered justice and punished the culprit for his delicts (Durkheim 1964: pp. 76, 104).

This belief in uniformity of desires, values, knowledge, skills, and behavior of primitive peoples also compelled him to succumb to the Marxian doctrine of primitive communism of people who, according to Durkheim, form a society because of their mechanical solidarity: "Communism, in effect, is the necessary product of this special cohesion which absorbs the individual in the group, the part in the whole. Property is definitive only of the extension of the person over things. Where the collective personality is the only one existent, property also must be collective" (Durkheim 1964: p. 179).[82] I think that at present, with massive ethnographic evidence denying the Durkheimian dogma, there is no need to repeat Firth and argue in this place against the existence of communism in primitive societies (Firth 1939: p. 352). It is far more important to point out that Durkheim did not treat society as a structured conglomerate of subgroups that have their own legal systems. He ignored the possibility that while on one legal level of the same society the juridical system may be primarily of a penal nature, on another it may restitutive. Among the Kapauku Papuans of New Guinea the household level has mostly a restitutive legal system, while the systems of the more inclusive groups are predominantly dominated by rules provided with punitive sanctions. As a contrast, among the peasants of the Tirol the household legal level is characterized by an overwhelming reliance on punitive sanctions, while the village, regional (*Land*), and state legal systems

[82]"Le communisme, en effet, est le produit nécessaire de cette cohésion spéciale qui absorbe l'individu dans le groupe, la partie dans le tout. La propriété n'est en définitive que l'extension de la personne sur les choses. Là donc où la personalité collective est la seule qui existe, la propriété elle-même ne peut manquer d'être collective." (Durkheim 1893: p. 195)

utilize mostly restitutive sanctions as their corrective measures (Pospisil 1962–1969).

Although Durkheim's contribution to the development of modern sociology is unquestionable, he made many errors. Most of them are excusable because little adequate research had been done in his day on tribal societies. However, "his devotion to sociology as an autonomous science becomes doctrinaire and misleading" (Lowie 1937: p. 206) and runs counter to the evidence from Western civilization, an evidence that was at his disposal. His arbitrary insistence on explaining all social facts by other social facts, to be almost straitjacketed within the scope of sociology, is certainly unscientific and contrary to modern endeavor which tends to link scientific researches and bridge rather than create arbitrary boundaries between scientific disciplines (e.g., biochemistry, biophysics, ethnolinguistics, etc.).

While Durkheim, like Marx, was certainly a genius, Durkheimists and Marxists of the second half of the twentieth century are certainly not. Being the worst conservatives and most egrerious reactionaries of modern times, they, in spite of overwhelming evidence to the contrary, promote Durkheimian and Marxian theories and hypotheses to absolute and unquestionable dogmas, and transform the sociologies and philosophies of the two men into religions. Certainly, in 1969 Durkheim would not write over again his division of labor, nor would Marx hold his outdated theories, now more than a century old, as dogmas. While the world progresses to new vistas, the worshipers of nineteenth-century philosophies are becoming the "revolutionaries of yesterday."

SIR PAUL VINOGRADOFF (1854–1925)

Maine's endeavor to correlate social with legal development in terms of successive, qualitatively different stages was carried on by Paul Vinogradoff, a scholar of Russian origin who taught jurisprudence at Oxford in the early part of this century. After having devoted an early volume to an analytical inquiry into the work of his famous predecessor, *The Teaching of Sir Henry Maine* (1904), he utilized Maine's comparative approach in his subsequent historical studies and enriched it by a meticulous insistence on detailed and accurate exposition of cases, rules, and institutions of particular societies, especially in his *The Growth of the Manor* (1905), *Roman Law in Medieval Europe* (1909), *Common-Sense in the Law* (1914), *Villainage in England* (1892), and *English Society in the Eleventh Century* (1908). The historical studies served as a basis on which he built his contribution to the theory of law, expressed especially in the Introduction to his *Outlines of Historical Jurisprudence* (1923). The last part of this Introduction is devoted to a scheme of evolutionary stages of legal systems which is of particular interest to us.

Being influenced by the current sociological and juristic emphasis on abstract rules, he defines law "as a *set of rules imposed and enforced by a society with regard to the attribution and exercise of power over persons and things*" (Vinogradoff 1914: p. 59). He claims that these legal rules emanate "from a certain limited number of authoritative sources, and that in the process of their elaboration they follow certain grooves according to the character of their origin" (1914: p. 117). Their source is legislation made in advance or the judicial decisions declared by the courts of justice. The legal rules that arise from judicial decision, the "judge-made law," are actually formulated by judges on the basis of three different types of considerations: they are based on established "customary law" as manifested in "traditional usage," or on precedent (one or a series of preceding judicial decisions), or, finally, on the idea of "equity," defined by Vinogradoff as "general considerations of justice and fairness" applied to the decision of legal conflicts (1914: pp. 117–118). The basic principles that are comprised in the traditional usage of the customary law, in the precedent, in the canons of equity, and in the legislative process are, according to Vinogradoff, ideas —ideas that evolve through history by a kind of unfolding of their implicit potentialities, ideas that "are mobile entities, passing through various stages —indistinct beginnings, gradual differentiation, struggles and compromises, growth and decay" (1923: p. 160). Thus, ideas of jurisprudence and law evolve somehow autonomously, almost in a Hegelian way (see Stone 1950: p. 465). However, they do not have their sole origin in the economy of the people, in their kind of production, as claimed by Marx (Vinogradoff 1923: pp. 81–83). The task of historical jurisprudence, then, is to trace this evolution of juridical ideas and their relation to "the institutions of an epoch in their doctrinal connexion" (1922: p. 10).

While reading these statements of Vinogradoff, it would be a mistake to assume that he subscribes to an extreme type of idealism. Although he calls his method ideological, he qualifies his emphasis upon ideas by first linking them to the type of society in which they exist and with which they change. Accordingly, one of the essential influences upon the change of law and its rules is "a central conception derived from the nature of the social tie—that of co-ordination of individual wills" (1923: p. 157). Second, the juristic ideas of law are also regarded by Vinogradoff as being influenced by historical conditions: "In a word, the chronological process of history cannot fail to affect the ideological deductions from a social type" (1923: p. 159). Thus material necessities of a society, external material forces, as well as the society's type of economy, be it pastoral, agricultural, or industrial, all have their influence upon the evolution of a legal order, along with the social forces mentioned above (1923: p. 159). The interplay of the social type of the society and its ideological law with historical conditions (viewed mainly as material necessities and forces) produce historical types of legal systems. "The essential point is to recognize the value of *historical types* as the foundation of a theory of law" (1923: p. 160). It is these historical types and their sequence that Vinogradoff tries to describe in his major work *Outlines of Historical Jurisprudence*. Still it has to be borne in mind that Vinogradoff, while not disregarding historical conditions and the dynamic nature of society, is primarily interested in the ideal component of the historical types and that he regards his treatment, therefore, as primarily "ideological and not chronological" (1923: p. 158).

Vinogradoff describes six stages of the evolution of juridical ideas. Whereas the last two (individualistic jurisprudence and socialistic jurisprudence) have as their diagnostic characteristics the nature of the prevailing legal ideas, the first two stages (totemistic society and tribal law) have as their primary criteria the types of the society to which they pertain. The two middle stages, civic law and medieval law, are not as clear-cut and seem to combine both types of criteria (1923: p. 158). A further incongruity appears in the fact that while the last four stages are restricted explicitly to Western civilization, the first two "take into account materials collected by anthropological inquiries from a wider range, in fact from all inhabited parts of the world" (1923: p. 158). This discrepancy Vinogradoff explains by pointing out the limited amount of material for the first two stages from the European area and by the assumption that the first two stages, found in primitive societies, existed in Europe prior to the onset of the historical era (1923: pp. 137–138).

The juridical evolution is supposed to start with the stage called totemistic society, in which "there is not much technical law" (1923: p. 158). Although Vinogradoff does not attempt to describe or even to point out major characteristics of this stage, satisfying himself with a casual remark in reference to Durkheim, he does present his opinion about the origin of law at this stage when he writes, "It is not conflicts that initiate rules of legal observance, but the practices of every-day directed by the give and take considerations of reasonable intercourse and social co-operation" (1920: p. 368).

As a contrast to the neglect of the first stage, Vinogradoff spends more than half the first volume of the *Outlines of Historical Jurisprudence* on a comparative presentation of tribal law, his second developmental stage of the juridical evolution (1920: pp. 163–369). Although the author declares that his generalizations of this stage are based on worldwide considerations and on data secured from anthropologists, the disappointed reader will find that Vinogradoff, like many of his juristic and sociological contemporaries, relies primarily on old accounts of early (tribal) European societies and of India. Influenced by these sources, that often deal with broad generalization and so-called rules, Vinogradoff views the position of a tribal legal authority as declaratory rather than legislative. The tribal leaders' juridical activity does not consist of issuing new laws in the form of commands or decisions: "The ancient lawgiver never considers himself as issuing an order to particular persons or the community in general: his primary function is to *find the law* and give expression to the sense of the community in regard to juridical acts" (1920: p. 361). While this search for law constitutes the main criterion of the procedure of the tribal law, Vinogradoff characterized the substantive aspect of this law by its extreme reliance on formalism and use of fiction (1920: pp. 364–366), and its punishments, meted out for the breach of the law, as "a violent reaction against harmful acts, a form of self-defense" that often took the shape of a feud (1923: p. 53).

The third stage of Vinogradoff's evolutionary scheme, civic law, is defined by its pertinence to social relations of city life. Its legal rules "depend on one dominant fact—the nature of the city commonwealth (*polis*)" (1922: p. 2), and their sanctions are carried out as "retribution in the name of the government" of the political community (1923: p. 53). Thus even in this stage the major factor of law characteristic of the "type of the legal system" is not inherent in the nature of the legal ideas or thought but in the type of society in which it exists. As an example of this stage Vinogradoff deals with Greek law. He prefers this legal system over that of Old Rome because so much has been written about the latter, whereas Greece has not captured the attention of legal writers, and because Roman law pertains also to the Imperium Romanum that evolved from the city-state, while Greek law pertained almost exclusively to the "city commonwealth."

The essence of the following evolutionary stage, that of medieval law, is a combination of two heterogeneous systems of legal thought that appear "to a great extent antagonistic" to each other: the feudal and the canon law. Whereas the first derives its theocratic conceptions from the social ties of divine guidance and is regarded as applicable to all of mankind, feudal law deals with social ties of "human fidelity" and has as its narrow basis "the economy of the manor"—it starts with the feudal estate. The main reason why Vinogradoff fuses these two systems, on the surface disparate, into the same ideological type is not a chronological consideration of their coexistence in time and space. True to his ideological orientation he argues that the two systems were actually complementary rather that disruptive to each other. While feudal law dealt mainly with the land and status of people, canon law claimed as its domain the theory of justice, of equity, and of crime. This mutual relationship and dependence induced Vinogradoff to regard the two systems as belonging to a single evolutionary juridical stage (1923: pp. 157, 159).

Medieval law was slowly replaced by the evolutionary stage of individualistic jurisprudence, characterized by "the tendency of the legal mind to co-ordinate and to harmonize its concepts into a coherent and reasonable whole on a given basis—the basis of individualism" (Vinogradoff 1923: p. 155). The main assumption of the legal thinkers of this stage was their emphasis upon the individual and their conceptions of the society "as a combination of reasonable beings" (1923: p. 108). They tended to disregard social forces and history, and their approach centered around the problem of assuring the individual of maximization of his happiness and minimization of his pain. This tendency reached its peak, according to Vinogradoff, in Bentham's philosophy (1923: p. 110). Thus this philosopher and his followers, especially Austin, are regarded by Vinogradoff as the main representatives of individualistic thought.

The last stage of evolution of juristic ideas was thought to be the stage of socialistic jurisprudence, which began to develop in Vinogradoff's time. This juristic trend of thought, marked by a decline of concern for the individual and by a primary attention to social forces and problems, was expected to reconsider "all the positions of jurisprudence" and redirect legal thought into a radically new theoretical path (1923: p. 157). For example, in the field of criminology, crimes came to be regarded as a "social anomaly" and the punishment as a treatment or as a measure of "social education" rather than retribution (1923: pp. 53, 57, 59). In this new juristic and philosophic development Vinogradoff deplored Marxism with its "materialistic fatalism" and, true to his orientation, promoted an idealistic version of socialism as the only practical solution for the future of the society and its law (1923: pp. 82–83).

Aside from the factual considerations and a lack of adequate empirical evidence, the evolutionary scheme of Vinogradoff may be criticized on the basis of logic by pointing out that it fails to possess a unifying matrix of social coordinates. Instead of characterizing his scheme of evolutionary stages by a homogeneous set of criteria, Vinogradoff, in the first half of his stage sequence, emphasized the type of society as a major characteristic, while in the second half he concentrated on the quality of the legal ideas as criteria for his juridical evolution. Thus we have to agree with Stone's critical remark about Vinogradoff that

> in short, his plan for "ideological" treatment of legal development straddles unhappily the theories, on the one hand, that the law is mainly a product of social conditions, and, on the other, that law is the unfolding of ideas in history which it is our task to identify and trace. (Stone 1966: p. 143)

Vinogradoff may have an excuse for neglecting types of legal ideas as criteria of the first two stages. However, in the third stage, for which abundant material was available, his categorical emphasis upon the type of society was hardly justifiable even on the grounds of "pragmatism."

L. T. HOBHOUSE (1864–1929)

Spencer's application of the Darwinian concepts of the struggle for existence and the survival of the fittest to the evolution of human societies provoked a profound negative reaction in Leonard Trelawny Hobhouse, a fellow of Norton College and of Corpus Christi and, later in his life, a staff member of *The Manchester Guardian* and *Tribune* in London. He not only rejected the extreme position of nineteenth-century laissez-faire liberalism but also avoided the pitfalls of the philosophical antithesis, the "official socialism" (Ginsberg 1968: p. 487). In order to explain the evolution of human societies and cultures he developed a sociological theory in which rationalism was combined with an unusual striving for adequate empiricism. Unlike so many of his predecessors and, unfortunately, some social scientific scholars of the present, he refused to rely primarily upon armchair philosophizing and speculation and attempted to base his theories upon cross-cultural evidence. The philosophic and theoretical basis of his social evolutionary theory, in his major works *The Theory of Knowledge* (1896), *Mind in Evolution* (1901), and, especially, in *Morals in Evolution* (1908, first edition 1906) and *Development and Purpose* (1913), consists of a firm conviction that the source of power that propels human societies along a path of evolution is to be found in the human mind—its effect upon social evolution being manifested by an orderly, well-structured growth. Thus mental development, as seen in the increase of scientific knowledge and in its application to the control of the natural and social environment, as well as in the more liberalizing tendency in ethical, aesthetic, and religious thought, Hobhouse regarded as broadly correlated with the general development of the societies and their economies, technologies, and social institutions.

In designing his theoretical framework he did not commit the errors of unilinial evolutionism and Marxian materialism: the mental advance and the correlated evolution of human societies did not follow a single line of automatic development. According to Hobhouse, individual societies develop in their own way and at different rates. The speed and kind of the development are not determined by either a speculative psychic unity of mankind or an environmental influence and an inevitable progress in change of means of production manifested in a dogmatic setup of politicoeconomic stages. Moreover, he does not regard the changes as determined by a free human will and mind, detached from social forces. Rather, the evolution of a given society is a historical phenomenon, produced by human minds whose mental processes have been shaped by the particular society's culture —affected by pertinent environmental, biological, psychological, and sociological conditions. This, however, does not mean that one would be unable to generalize and draw theoretical conclusions about the social evolution of man. Actually, this is the goal of Hobhouse's endeavor which he empirically tests and reshapes in his book written with G. C. Wheeler and M. Ginsberg, *The Material Culture and Social Institutions of the Simpler Peoples* (1930). This, for the date of its completion (1915) a gigantic comparative endeavor, constitutes one of the most significant and influential works in social science, a predecessor to the works of such contemporary scholars as Child, Hoebel,

Murdock, and Whiting, to name just a few. In the following paragraphs I shall try to abstract Hobhouse's theory of legal development from the works mentioned above and present it in a unified, more or less consistent picture.

In his approach to the fundamental notions underlying the process of the "evolution of law" in human societies, Hobhouse became a follower of the trend of thought represented by Montesquieu, Otto von Gierke, Eugen Ehrlich, and Max Weber. To him, as to his great predecessors, law was not the property monopolized in a society by the institution of the political state. The substate associations he regarded of equal importance in this respect, believing that the state had no absolute authority over the associations, that it was but one of many organizations of the human society (esp. Nicholson 1926: pp. 56–60). Consequently, the legal structure of a society was dependent upon a pattern of the particular types of associations in existence, which, like the state, were regulated by their own legal systems. Thus in a given society, "the group-formation dominates ethics and law" (Hobhouse 1927: p. 170). Law he defined as "a rule couched in universal terms and applied impartially, that is, with accurate equality, to all cases that fall within its definitions" (Hobhouse 1922: p. 103). Since he regarded deliberate innovations among simple people as exceptional (Hobhouse 1924: p. 260), law in his mind was a product of a slow process by which either the old local custom was codified or by which traditional custom was slowly transformed by the activity of local courts into "a consistent set of rules which becomes the common law of the land" (Hobhouse 1924: p. 260). After its "birth" law started to evolve, and its advance was made possible by the trend toward consolidation of the government and the extension of the area of organized society. This trend, in turn, was conditioned by "the advance in the economic scale" (Hobhouse, Wheeler, and Ginsberg 1930: pp. 52–53). With respect to progress on the economic scale Hobhouse, together with Wheeler and Ginsberg, grouped the existent human societies into the following developmental stages (1930: p. 83): Lower Hunters (e.g., Dieri), Higher Hunters (e.g., Yurok, Haida, Kwakiutl), and Dependent Hunters (e.g., Batak). These were followed by two alternative branches of pastoral peoples evolving through stages of Pastoral I (e.g., Dinka), Pastoral II (e.g., Kalmucks, Kirghiz), and agricultural peoples evolving through stages of Agricultural I (e.g., Iroquois), Agricultural II (e.g., Maori, Balinese, Azande), and Agricultural III (e.g., Pima, Pueblos, Benin). Law developed along with these advances in economy, but its changes were not so closely related that its sequence of stages did not coincide exactly with those of the economy. Thus Hobhouse did not construct a simplistic and unified picture of cultural evolution as designed by the unilineal evolutionists of the past and present.

In his *Social Theories of Hobhouse* Hugh Carter stated that Hobhouse believed that law developed along two different lines of evolution—either through reduction of self-redress to "a regular system" or through a regular settlement of disputes by chief men who, while acting on behalf of the community, slowly became "a regularly constituted organ to administer justice" (Carter 1927: p. 28). However, it is my impression that although Hobhouse, for analytical purposes, often treated the two approaches separately, he conceived of them as the same process, one approach dealing with it from the aspect of the dispute, the other from the point of view of the deciding authority. Accordingly, for example, he writes:

Public justice advances upon the whole though less regularly with the advance in material culture in the tribes that we have before us, and we therefore seem justified in regarding pure self-redress as the initial stage of development, and public control as superimposed by successive stages upon that method of maintaining order. (Hobhouse, Wheeler, and Ginsberg 1930: p. 78)

Hobhouse's first stage of the evolution of law present in the "primitive society" of "the most simple peoples" was one marked by an almost complete absence of public, objective justice (Hobhouse, Wheeler, and Ginsberg 1930: p. 82). In this type of society, characterized by small, self-dependent communities held together by ties of kinship that create an "inner group" which is fortified by magico-religious ideas of the totem, by the clan, or by the "matrimonial class," all persons enjoy equal rights while the outsiders of the community possess none (Hobhouse, Wheeler, and Ginsberg 1930: p. 47; Hobhouse 1927: p. 170). This same distinction between community and the outside world is also maintained in those communities of the simplest peoples that increased in size and became composed of several rather than a single inner group (Hobhouse 1927: p. 170). In this first evolutionary stage the leadership is assumed usually by the "eldest and most capable male, whose authority is in general limited by his personal capacity" (Hobhouse 1966: p. 135). Although he settles some of the disputes, there is lack of an "organized method of securing or enforcing order and justice" (Hobhouse 1966: p. 135), the existent private wrongs being revenged by private individuals (Hobhouse 1908: pp. 80, 84; also Hobhouse, Wheeler and Ginsberg 1930: p. 54). This is mainly so because, as Hobhouse wrongly reasons, "the group is normally a peaceable society of equals" in which quarrels are rare, indeed in some of them crime is almost nonexistent (Hobhouse 1966: p. 135). To these "gentle, quiet peoples" who live in their undifferentiated groups "custom appears to have acquired almost the force of instinct" (Hobhouse 1927: p. 165; also 1924: p. 260). Its change is not premeditated; neither is it conscious, reflecting simply the pressures of man's needs (Hobhouse 1927: p. 221). However, even in this most simple stage, reasons Hobhouse, the rudiments of public justice are already to be found on the occasions when a whole community, in order to protect itself against a habitual delinquent or against a curse invoked by violation of a basic custom, turns upon an offender and expels him or puts him to death (Hobhouse 1908: pp. 81–82; also Hobhouse, Wheeler, and Ginsberg 1930: p. 56). Hobhouse regards these instances of this sort of lynch law as "a kind of public hygiene" by which the society as a whole cleanses itself of the impurity left on it by a crime (Hobhouse 1908: p. 83). Thus, in some of these rare occurrences the primitive community is already some sort of public justice in cases of private offense (Hobhouse, Wheeler, and Ginsberg 1930: p. 56).

As the society evolves from its most primitive stage of isolated communities into a tribe (which at its first appearance assumes the form of an aggregate of communities united by their language, common name, centralized political authority, intermarriage, and religious ceremonies), and as the structure and solidarity of the family, clan, and community become consolidated, an offended person "no longer stands by himself or herself." In a search for justice and redress he or she is supported by the family and extended kin (Hobhouse 1908: p. 84; Hobhouse, Wheeler, and Ginsberg 1930: pp. 48, 82). This mutual support of members of a kin group in cases of disputes transforms the original and simple self-redress by a single injured person into a group affair, a feud, thus marking a next stage of the evolution of law, called by Hobhouse the Blood Feud Stage (1908: p. 84). Because of this consolidation of structure and solidarity of the members of the group, which results on one hand in the mutual help and dependence in the quest for revenge and, on the other, in a common responsibility for crimes, society in this stage of evolution uses the fear of the feud as its most effective means of intergroup control and an excommunication from the protection of the clan or family as the most feared and dreaded form of intragroup punishment (Hobhouse 1908: p. 89).

As time goes on and the system of blood feud becomes regulated by customary rules, *lex talionis* develops. While private delicts are being taken care of by this system of blood revenge, aided by some assistance from chief and arbiters who pass decisions but leave their execution to the entitled party, public justice limits itself to tribal offenses (e.g., incest, witchcraft, treason, cowardice, etc.) held to injure the community as a whole (Hobhouse, Wheeler, and Ginsberg 1930: pp. 54, 55, 79). This is apparently a continuation and a further development of the spontaneous "lynch law" practice of the preceding stage. In all these types of settlement of disputes and punishment of crimes the intent of the culprit is held irrelevant as far as the assignment of guilt and gravity of punishment are concerned. There is no distinction made between an accident and a design (Hobhouse 1908: p. 93).

In addition to the effect of creating collective responsibility and revenge (feud) the solidarity of the primary groups (clans, families, bands, etc.) also enhanced the power and political influence of the chiefs or council. They became entrusted with suppression of crimes deemed destructive, first to the primary and, later, to the more inclusive "secondary groups"—aggregates of the primary groups (Hobhouse, Wheeler, and Ginsberg 1930: p. 48). Most importantly, the chiefs and councils, although representing the secondary groups, began to interfere with the system of feuds. As time elapsed, further litigation of blood feuds was supposed to have occurred by the introduction of blood payment (of money or other chattel) as a substitute for revenge, thus introducing a new stage in the development of law—the Stage of Composition (Hobhouse 1908: p. 86). Slowly the payment, involving common pecuniary responsibility of the offender's group, became customary by being regularly enforced by the tribal chiefs. The amounts become regular, reflecting not only the gravity of crime but also the status of the persons offended. Thus a system of wergilds becomes established. This stage of legal development, according to Hobhouse, was achieved by some Higher Hunters and peoples of the economic stages of Agriculture I and Pastoral I (Hobhouse 1908: pp. 86–89). In negotiating peace among the conflicting primary groups and, later, by direct adjudication of intergroup disputes, the chiefs and councils not only succeeded in slowly controlling the feuds and in pacifying the tribal affairs, they also actually extended the scope of law beyond the primary group of kinsmen to a larger, usually territorial unit, thus bringing order to the society at large (Hobhouse 1927: p. 170). Moreover, observes Hobhouse, the chiefs' activity in settling intergroup disputes may be regarded as the start of true legal trials, and the institutions conducting these trials may be called courts. Although parties to the dispute might not yet have been interested in and afraid of the decisions backed by the slowly evolving power of the chief, they certainly were induced into following these decisions by the force of public opinion, which usually sided with the incipient judge (Hobhouse 1908: p. 98; Hobhouse, Wheeler, and Ginsberg 1930: p. 80). To be sure, at this early stage, reasons Hobhouse, the function of the emerging courts was not so much to hand down an impartial and objective justice as to "prevent the extension of wild and irregular blood feuds" (Hobhouse 1908: p. 101).

The next step in the legal development Hobhouse named the Stage of Kingly Power. Here a new central authority of a whole district has replaced the local chiefs (Hobhouse, Wheeler, and Ginsberg 1930: p. 48) and has become so consolidated in its power and procedure that it does not have to rely so much on the force of public opinion. He can summon the clans and parties to the bar, "decide their cause, and require them to keep the peace" (Hobhouse 1908: p. 99). "Custom at this stage becomes definite law in the sense that it is formulated and announced by authority and enforced by the executive power. It becomes 'the command of a Superior,' and at least in ideal it is impartially applied" (Hobhouse 1927: p. 168). The local varied customs are superseded by law that is often codified, a law that is backed by the pertinent authority and his use of force (Hobhouse 1927: p. 221).

In the more developed societies of this stage (the "earlier forms of state"), law begins to be created by deliberate legislation of the community (Hobhouse 1927: p. 221). It is first applied to particular times and places (markets, highways), but later it is extended to the whole territory and to all times, thus becoming regular and, for the group concerned, universal (Hobhouse 1908: p. 105). The law of this epoch, trying to be impartial, is no longer based upon vengeance that would give advantage to the strong. True enough, in specified cases private self-help is still permitted by law (especially in cases of *in flagrante delicto*), but this permission is made specific by the courts or in the codification, and usually it is limited to a short time period after a crime has been committed (Hobhouse 1908: p. 105; 1927: p. 168). Because crime and acts of violence and injustice now become a public matter, not only revenge but also private peace is abolished. It now takes the court's action to close a case of criminal procedure—not merely a simple agreement of private parties (Hobhouse 1908: p. 105). The courts are no longer a casual institution to which parties may or may not resort—the procedure becomes compulsory and the parties may be summoned to the court by force if need be (Hobhouse 1908: p. 101). Backed by authority and its power, the law, composed of rules applied to all people, is now grounded on a common moral sense "which recognizes in various men and women various rights, and enjoins on all a number of duties" (Hobhouse 1927: p. 168). Compliance with it is effected in part because of the fear of punishment, which at the beginning of this stage of development is very severe (death, mutilation, torture, burning, whipping, etc.), in part because of a conviction in the law's moral basis, and also because of beliefs in supernatural punishments which are expected to affect the culprit, irrespective of the court's action, before or after his or her death (Hobhouse 1908: p. 111; 1927: p. 168).

The system of private vengeance of the preceding stage dealt with two types of delicts: private injury suffered by an individual and offense against the society whose well-being was believed to be endangered by the criminal action. The law of the Stage of Kingly Power, Hobhouse believed, kept the two aspects separate, thus giving rise to two legal categories: civil justice deriving from the private injury type of offenses, and criminal justice deriving from the offense against the society (Hobhouse 1908: p. 108). Once public interest had been introduced, culpability and intent of the criminal became of paramount importance, especially so in criminal law where the amount of injury, also still important, played a secondary role (Hobhouse 1908: p. 107). To determine the objective facts concerning a delict as well as the culpability of the accused, the early law of this stage relied heavily upon brutality and the supernatural. It made use of torture in order to extract confessions (Hobhouse 1908: p. 110), and of curse and oath to frighten the culprit or witnesses by a threat of eventual supernatural punishment into a revelation of truth. Furthermore, the court, according to Hobhouse, not being in a position to try the merits of the case and secure the necessary evidence, made through the institution of ordeal an appeal to the judgment of God, thus testing the falsity or truth of the case by resort to a magico-religious process which not only unburdened the court of the pain of collecting the evidence but also, in some cases, provided for a swift and immediate punishment. In many cases, to be sure, ordeal might have administered justice by psychologically protecting the innocent and revealing the actual culprit, who through fear, for instance, might have choked on swallowed bread (Hobhouse 1908: pp. 102–104). As development continued, the reliance upon and appeal to the supernatural slowly gave way to a sole reliance upon true empirical evidence (the Lateran Council had already prohibited ordeals in 1215: Hobhouse 1908: p. 108).

Hobhouse sees the last phase of the legal evolution in the stage of the Modern State. There, except for such inequities as arise from racial differences and existence of differential inheritance that favors only some individuals, "the elementary rights of protection are secured to all" (Hobhouse 1927: p. 225). Furthermore, the severity of punishment of the previous stage subsided and became "proportioned to the imputed degree of moral guilt" (Hobhouse 1908: p. 119; 1927: p. 225). Its justification is no longer couched in terms of retribution and revenge, but reference is made to its effect on keeping order and accomplishing a reform of the criminal. The criminal has a right to be "so punished that he may be helped in the path of reform" (Hobhouse 1908: p. 119).

On the surface, Hobhouse's argument and his sequence of developmental legal stages seem plausible. However, upon closer scrutiny of his underlying assumptions and of the quality of the marshaled empirical evidence, one realizes that even this evolutionary theory of law suffers from serious shortcomings. First, and possibly the most serious mistake, is Hobhouse's overwhelming reliance upon the development of legal thought of the West, to the neglect of the development of legal theory in other such civilizations as the Chinese, Japanese, Indian, and Inca. If data from these cultures had been equally stressed, the last two stages certainly would have had to be conceptualized differently. Moreover, if better research and empirical data had been used for the first stages, it would have been inconceivable to portray the "primitive society" as a peaceable association of equals with almost no crime, no quarrels, and no judges. Indeed, while reading Hobhouse, I was again painfully reminded of the stubborn persistence of the myth of the lawless Golden Age, sung about by Ovid, embraced by Marx, and assumed by Hobhouse and others. One may continue to criticize by pointing out, for example, the scholar's disregard of the relativity of legal levels or his failure to allow for some legal initiative of chiefs and primitive headmen which could hardly be explained as symptoms or manifestations of an unfolding process of an almighty deterministic custom. These and other shortcomings are dwarfed by the two previous criticisms, which show Hobhouse's scheme of legal evolution as composite of Western legal myth (as

far as the primitive society is concerned) and Western history of legal thought
and practice (as far as one has the latest stages in mind). In this light Hobhouse's scheme appears to me, and probably to many non-Western legal
scholars, as a mixture of Western legal folk philosophy and a cherished
Western legend.

E. ADAMSON HOEBEL (1906–   )

Influenced apparently by the empirical and comparative approach of
Hobhouse as well as by the results of his work, E. Adamson Hoebel, professor of anthropology at the University of Minnesota and the leading American
scholar in the field of anthropology of law, presented his views on evolution
of the legal systems in an essay entitled "The Trend of the Law" which forms
the concluding chapter in his book *The Law of Primitive Man* (Hoebel 1954:
pp. 288–333). His approach is empirically based on an assumption that
rejects any unilineal and universal evolution of law in human societies. He
finds that there is "no straight line of development in the growth of law"
(Hoebel 1954: p. 288). Although a discernible sequence of very general
"levels" may be recognized, for example, in the sphere of economic evolution, even there, "in its own particular history *a* society does not have to
go through all successive steps of the technological sequence." This is especially so because of the phenomenon of borrowing (Hoebel 1954: p. 292).
Indeed, in the field of law, where "there is no automatic connection between any legal measures or machinery and level of cultural development,"
the variations, alternatives, and exceptions are so great and numerous that
Hoebel is even reluctant to use the term "evolution" when referring to the
developmental changes in legal systems. Instead, he speaks only about
"trends" (Hoebel 1954: pp. 289, 325). His conceptualization and description of these trends is based upon the assumption that the cultures of contemporary primitive peoples exhibit characteristics that are similar "to those
that presumably prevailed in the early cultures of the infancy of mankind"
(Hoebel 1954: p. 290). Furthermore, because of the homogeneity of values
and intimacy of the relations of these hunters and gatherers, their culture is
regarded as more primitive than that of the early agricultural and pastoral
people and, consequently, their need for adjudication of the infrequent
quarrels they have is relatively small. Generally speaking, argues Hoebel,
"the more civilized man becomes, the greater is man's need for law, and
the more law he creates. Law is but a response to social needs" (Hoebel
1954: p. 293). These needs, of course, differ from society to society and
differ among subgroups. Although not always explicit about the subject,
Hoebel does view a legal system as a property of a specific community or
subgroup of a society. For example, he states; "Without the sense of community there can be no law. Without law there cannot for long be a commu-

nity'' (Hoebel 1954: p. 332). Thus even in the simplest societies law has to exist to some extent (Hoebel 1954: p. 309). If we accept this important view, then we need not be preoccupied, as Hoebel sometimes seems to be, with what happens on a society's level that is often not integrated politically (Hoebel 1954: pp. 316, 318, 321). Absence of law there does not mean, as Hoebel certainly would agree, that law is nonexistent in a society's subgroups, whether or not these are organized on a kinship principle, as are the clans.

In such societies, not unified politically, feud is certainly not a substitute for or an expression of law, because it is basically an intergroup rather than an intragroup phenomenon. To Hoebel ''feud marks an absence of law'' and certainly not a primitive form of it (Hoebel 1954: p. 330). Therefore, there are no societies in which there would be no striving for the elimination of intergroup feuds (Hoebel 1954: pp. 329, 330). I may add, there are no tribal societies in which there is no law on the subgroup level, or no attempt to try to establish it, or at least to approximate its effects of pacification, on the level of the society as a whole. Although force is the ingredient of both international (or I may say intergroup) relations and intragroup law (Hoebel 1954: p. 331), these two concepts should not be equated.

Hoebel starts his description of the trend of law with a discussion of the ''lower primitive societies,'' the hunters and gatherers, such as the Andamanese Islanders, Shoshone Indians, Australian Aborigines, and Barama River Carib (Hoebel 1954: p. 293). In these most simple societies, generalizes Hoebel, the community, which is autonomous, consists of a few related families that constitute a kindred. The relationship is bilateral, and leadership rests with a local headman who is lacking ''in both the means to exploit and the means to judge'' (Hoebel 1954: p. 294). He declares that a patriarchal tyrant is a figment of the nineteenth century, the societies are ''democratic to the point of near-anarchy,'' and there is little need for any suprafamilial authority (Hoebel 1954: p. 294). This objectionable generalization is mitigated and corrected in subsequent paragraphs from which I assume that Hoebel's opening generalizations pertained to only some of the most primitive communities of these societies. While discussing particular ethnic groups he shows how the leader of a local group of the Andamanese Islanders can easily stop an outrage from being committed by a member of his group, how even intra- and intergroup offenses are ''punished physically'' among the Australian Aborigines (the punishment often suggested and supervised by headmen or councils of old men), and how local headman's opinions among the Barama River Carib are respected although he seems not to have ''special power to enforce his orders'' (Hoebel 1954: pp. 297, 298, 305). Although no single ''public'' offense seems yet to constitute a crime, a repetitive and ''excessive'' abuse of the customs and codes of social relations committed among the Carib or Eskimos does. In these cases, when the offender may be beaten or even killed by the men of the community, "we have law in the full connotation of the word—the application, in threat or in fact, of physical coercion by a party having the socially recognized privilege-right of so acting" (Hoebel 1954: p. 300).

The next category of peoples with a greater cultural complexity are "the more highly organized hunters," as exemplified by the Cheyenne, Comanche, Kiowa, and Indians of the Northwest Coast of North America (Hoebel 1954: pp. 309, 311). On this level of cultural development the size of the local group increased as a result of a richer food supply. Moreover, because of increased and continuous interaction these more numerous local groups became "consolidated into a higher unit of organization—the band (e.g., Comanches), and in some instances the bands might be welded into a yet higher political structure—the tribal state (e.g., the Cheyennes)" (Hoebel 1954: p. 309). Kinship continued to be important in the legal systems of these warlike peoples, who still on the local group level were led by headmen. However, Hoebel's emphasis on physical sanctions leads him to conclude that local kin groups of the Northwest Coast Indians handled their internal social control problems on other than a legal basis. Shaming an individual often proved to be an adequate means of making a man conform (Hoebel 1954: p. 316). As the reader remembers from my discussion of the attributes of law, shaming, if used by the local authority (kinsman or not) as a punishment for delicts does constitute a kind of psychological (nonphysical) legal sanction.

On the band and tribal levels a more formalized chieftainship develops, with a tendency toward hereditary succession (Hoebel 1954: pp. 309–310). Although among these peoples application of law still exhibits the major weakness of resting mostly upon the willingness of its acceptance by the contending parties, public opinion exercises a notable pressure for submission to a superior judicial authority. While homicide and adultery still represent major difficulties, the development of criminal law remains weak. Because of a lack of diversification of property interests and a consequent paucity of "clashing claims as to economic rights," Law of Persons is still by far the bulkiest part of the legal systems of these tribes (Hoebel 1954: pp. 310–311). As a progressive aspect of this developmental level Hoebel notes the possibility of an equation of goods with physical hurt, thus enabling compensation in cases of private delicts (Hoebel 1954: p. 310). Since Hoebel regards law on the next level of "the gardening people" as more advanced, an interesting consideration is implied. Because the Plains Indians were mostly agricultural peoples prior to the introduction of the horse, and therefore more advanced, it should follow that their law had to have retrogressed, becoming more primitive as they took up their nomadic life on the prairies.

"The real elaboration of law begins with the expansion of the gardening-based tribes," such as Samoans, Ashanti, Trobrianders, Iroquois, etc. (Hoebel 1954: p. 316). The gardening activity provides an economic basis that can support larger populations which, because of the size of their membership, can no longer maintain face-to-face relationships among all the tribesmen. Kinship, instead of diminishing in importance, expands along the lines of unilineal descent, thus forming large kin groups, usually called clans in the anthropological literature. Clans as parties to the disputes loom large in the law of these people, one of whose major efforts seems to be to maintain an equilibrium among these interacting unilineal groups. The leaders of these groups are either council members or already institutionalized chiefs, some of whom are elevated to royal status (Hoebel 1954: p. 322). Since land and the material equipment to till it become of primary interest to the people, "the law of things begins to rival the law of persons" (Hoebel 1954: p. 316). "Clear-cut crimes" are conceptualized in many of the legal systems of these societies, and action for damages becomes even more frequent than on the preceding level (Hoebel 1954: p. 318).

With the level of the gardening-based tribes Hoebel exhausts the scope of primitive societies. The next level of development is reached by societies who become urbanized and consequently ceased to be primitive. The development of urban centers dissolves the extended kinship ties and makes the individual independent of his relatives. Because of these effects the government apparatus becomes a necessity and law the primary means of making the people conform (Hoebel 1954: pp. 330, 332).

From these levels of development Hoebel draws the following conclusions with regard to the concept of "trend of law." First, the development of law is marked by an increase in complexity and heterogeneity (Hoebel 1954: p. 327). Second, the right of prosecution shifts from the individual and his kin group to "clearly defined public officials" (Hoebel 1954: pp. 327, 329). Third, the judicial and executive powers become extended beyond local groups. Finally, "damages have generally replaced death as penalties in civil suits" (Hoebel 1954: p. 329). In this way, according to Hoebel, law of the human society developed over the ages. However, the laws of particular societies have not followed a single line of development through fixed, predetermined, and universal stages. Their change is characterized by a trend that, only in general, exhibits the characteristics described above. With the exception of early writers such as Montesquieu and Maine, Hoebel's conceptualization of the trend of the development of law, by being broad enough and based on empiricism, is to me the most adequate and certainly more acceptable than the more speculative and often oversimplified theories described and analyzed in this chapter.

CONCLUSION

Nine theories concerned with the changes of legal systems have been presented in a more or less chronological order. Eleven legal theorists (Marxism accounts for three in this sample), ranging from the eighteenth-century philosopher Montesquieu to the contemporary anthropologist Hoebel, have been selected on the basis of their fame, their influence on Western thought and social science, and, in some cases, the role they played in Western culture and political life in general. All these individuals, no matter how diverse their theories, have a very significant characteristic in common: they showed at least some attempt to base their theories on empirical evidence as it was available at the time they wrote. This characteristic was the most significant one for my selection, because I regard anthropology as a scientific discipline and therefore empirical. Speculative theories with little support from the available ethnographic evidence that often flout empiricism by dogmatically constructing "stages of evolution" for which no shred of empirical evidence can be found, no matter how popular or "exciting" they may be, have been rigorously excluded from my selection (e.g., Morton Fried 1967: esp. pp. 185 ff.).

The eleven theorists may be roughly grouped into three categories. The first, which includes Montesquieu and Savigny, is not concerned with any universal evolution of law. Rather than take this approach the two writers compare the development of law in the various societies to "life cycles" through which the systems move. The great achievement of these writers lies in their originating scientific and historic inquiry into the nature of law and in their successful demolition of the nonscientific and dogmatic theory of Natural Law. With them law became part of culture, changing in time and space. The second category of writers is marked by an overwhelming influence of the unilineal evolutionist theory. It is first represented by Maine, who cast his scheme into a unilineal sequence, although later he showed marked unhappiness with the simplicity of the unilineal scheme. His most important contribution was an attempt at a comparative investigation of law from which universal generalizations were to be derived. Thus, next to Montesquieu, he may be regarded as a founder of the science of law. After these giants comes a sequence of authors whose theories are marked by a decline from the previous scientific standards in the sense that they were more dogmatic in their adherence to unilineal evolutionism—e.g., Marx, Engels, Lenin, and Spencer. This category of scholars ends with Vinogradoff and Durkheim in whose theorizing evolutionism becomes more flexible and generalized and less dogmatic. The third category of theories, represented by the works of Hobhouse and Hoebel, puts scientific method and precision above the elegance of simplistic conceptualization, so characteristic of the preceding category. While still attempting to discover generalizations pertaining to the growth of law, they turned to a large sample of world societies and analyzed it by comparative method. The outcome of this endeavor is best represented by Hoebel's "trend of law," which suggests that evolution of legal systems of different societies may take divergent paths and that in terms of worldwide generalizations only overall trends and tendencies can be delineated rather than clear-cut, definitive, evolutionary stages.

The great contribution of the scholars dealing with the change of legal systems lies, strangely enough, not in their theoretical conclusions, but rather in their approach and methodology which laid the foundations of the science of law in particular, and of the field of social science in general. As a contrast, the theories themselves, particularly those that have embraced evolutionist orientation, exhibit many weaknesses. Their shortcomings are often based upon similar mistakes. First, influenced by the myth of the lawless society of the Golden Age and having poor or no knowledge of primitive societies and their social control, many of the writers postulated a first "lawless" or pacifistic evolutionary stage, with few offenses and no leaders or judges. Their idea of the lawless primitive society parallels, in my thinking, a similar popular notion that primitive languages have no grammatical rules. The error was compounded by an obsession with speculation about the ultimate origin of law, a philosophic rather than a truly scientific endeavor. Furthermore, some writers, reacting to the nineteenth century's undue emphasis upon individualism and the conception of free will, became dogmatic "social determinists" (especially Savigny, Marx, Engels, Lenin, and Durkheim) who went to the other extreme of crediting all changes in human society and law to abstract social forces, making the individual's role negligible, and preaching, in Stone's words, "legislative impotence' (Stone 1950: esp. p. 444). Finally, the conceptual dichotomizing that belongs to the *Weltanschauung* of the Western scholars made such an impact on the various legal theorists that their method became rigid and insensitive to social reality (dialectics of the Marxists), or it resulted in an arbitrary dual categorization of the legal systems (Maine, Durkheim).

These shortcomings of the past evolutionary theorists, the often speculative and thus unscientific nature of the traditional inquiry into the changes of the legal systems, and, most importantly, the lack of abundant comparative legal material and the presence of unreliable data collected by individuals not sophisticated in anthropology and law compels me to abstain from adding one more theory of the evolution of law to those in existence.

CHAPTER
SIX
CHANGE
OF
LAWS

In contrast to the previous theoretical, speculative, and mostly philosophically oriented theories of changes of legal systems, this chapter will concentrate upon a theory of processes that govern, in Vinogradoff's words, "the innumerable fluctuations of the growth and decay of actual laws" (1922: p. 10). To trace these fluctuations indeed belongs to the field of "legal history," as Vinogradoff contends, but the study and analysis of the principles that determine the processes of these historic "fluctuations" constitute a legitimate field of inquiry of the social scientist. Accordingly, I shall inquire into the origin of laws (whether abstract rules *enforced* in legal decisions, or uncodified or even nonexplicit principles abstracted from legal decisions), their structural changes during their lifespan, and their decline and elimination from the field of law.

With this objective in mind, the theoretical framework of this chapter will have as its major feature an inquiry into the nature of two types of laws, accounted for in anthropological and legal literature, and of the process that may be responsible for the transformation of a law from one type into the other. These two types of laws have been called "customary" and "authoritarian" (Pospisil 1958a: pp. 278–280). The former has been described by ethnographers; the latter—mostly a form of decree by a legislator or an abrupt "legislative" action by a tribal authority—has been grossly neglected in anthropological literature. It is illusory to consider that legal systems of tribal societies are composed exclusively of customary laws. This traditional attitude is a survival of our Western dichotomization of law into civilized (often meaning only Western) and primitive (usually reserved for the law of the rest of the world). I shall try to demonstrate that authoritarian laws are universal phenomena, present to varying degrees in every society, no matter how "primitive" or "civilized." The process by which one type of law changes into another will be identified as "internalization," and the distinction between the two types will be shown to be actually quantitative rather than qualitative. This theoretical framework will be documented by empirical evidence derived from the existing literature and from my own research.

When discussing the province of law in Chapter Three I pictured it, for simplicity's sake, as an ellipse surrounded by a zone of transition (see Figure 2). At that time the focus of my interest was to *differentiate* law conceptually from such social phenomena as pure custom and political decision. We return to the same figure but now to inspect the field of law itself, and to find out in what way law is *related* to political decisions on one hand and to customs on the other. To accomplish this we are led to examine the problem of the dichotomy between customary and authoritarian law. Their purest forms may be depicted in the ellipse as two foci, C and A, respectively (see Figure 4). Laws of a transitional nature which do not fit completely the characteristics of the two ideal types (at the two foci) are placed between them, and laws whose legal characteristics are weakly differentiated from the neighboring nonlegal categories are near these categories, just inside the zone of transition.

The term "customary law" is used in modern anthropological literature in a very vague and often meaningless way, connoting any type of nonlegislated law in a tribal society. Since accounts of legislative innovations are usually utterly lacking, the term in practice stands for all tribal law. Its two clearest attributes seem to be that it is unwritten and that it has been used for a long time. Since tribal people have no writing, the first attribute is not arguable, and because tribal laws are assumed to have existed from time immemorial, and usually no legislation is recorded by the ethnographers, anthropologists accept the second. However, as soon as exact knowledge of the origin of the law becomes available, the second criterion gets into difficulty. The logical question then is, how long must a law exist in order to qualify as customary? Similarly, in the literature on societies in which customary law is codified, the first attribute loses its value because the written law of the codex continues to be regarded and referred to as "customary."

Commentators—students of Roman law of the thirteenth and fourteenth centuries—did not fare much better by defining customary law in terms of *longa consuetudo* (long use). More significant was their other criterion of customary law—*opinio necessitatis*—by which they meant the people's conviction of the binding power of a legal precept (Sommer 1933: p. 10). Indeed, here seems to lie the real social significance of the concept, which then differentiates those laws that are supported by a conviction of their indispensability and which I propose to call "customary" (irrespective

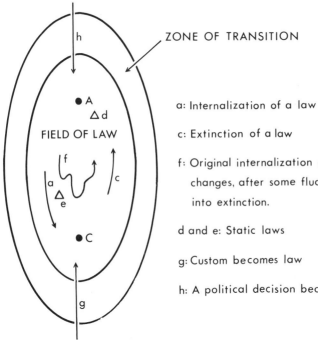

FIELD OF POLITICAL DECISIONS

ZONE OF TRANSITION

FIELD OF LAW

FIELD OF CUSTOMS

a: Internalization of a law

c: Extinction of a law

f: Original internalization of a law changes, after some fluctuation, into extinction.

d and e: Static laws

g: Custom becomes law

h: A political decision becomes law

FIGURE 4. Legal Dynamics

of their longevity) from the laws that enjoy no, or little, such support, which I shall label "authoritarian." The process by which a law becomes customary I shall refer to as "internalization."

By customary law, then, will be meant a law that is internalized by a social group. A law is internalized when the majority of the group considers it to be binding, as when it stands for the only proper behavior in a given situation. If such a law is broken, the culprit has a bad conscience or at least feels that he has done wrong—that he has behaved improperly. He would not condone such behavior in other members of the society. Conformity to such a law is not usually effected by external pressure—it is produced by an internal mechanism which we may call conscience in some cultures and fear of shame in others. This is the type of law the ethnographer has usually described and claimed to be the property of the group. He has not so readily recognized that even in well-internalized cases the individuality of the legal authority has played an important role in deciding, upholding, and changing, even if only slightly, the customary law. Without the authority's consent, customary law would cease to be law and would become just a custom.

Among the Kapauku Papuans of New Guinea I have recorded 176 trouble cases; 132 of these record legal decisions. The great majority of these, 114 to be precise, represent a compliance with customary law. In all these cases my informants agreed that the decisions were just. This agreement with the "verdicts of the authorities" is a manifestation of the internalization of those laws (Pospisil 1958a: p. 287).

Authoritarian law, on the other hand, is not internalized by a majority of the members of a group. A strong minority which supports the legal authority has elevated such a law as an "ideal" and may have simply forced the rest of the people to accept it. In some cases this kind of law is internalized only by the legal authority. An authority may even impose the law for reasons beneficial to himself, without believing in its propriety. In other cases the law owes its authoritarian quality to insufficient time for its internalization; opposing members of the group comply with it only under pressure of the authority and the strong minority who already have internalized it. The majority of the population considers the law unjust and feels no guilt in violating it; there is only fear of detection (viz., the U.S. prohibition law of the 1920s).

A principle of selfishness employed in a decision by a native called Amojepa may be regarded as an example of authoritarian law among the Kapauku. As head of the household and family, he decided that his sons and brothers could not take anything from his fields without his explicit permission. He punished his younger brother with a severe beating for violating this law. Most of the members of his household did not agree that his "law" and the consequent punishment were just; it differed from laws of other families where it was permissible for the members of the household to help themselves to fruit from gardens belonging to any household member, provided the food was taken for immediate consumption. Members of Amojepa's household were not the only ones who disagreed with the law; other people criticized his action and charged him with brutality. However, no matter how unjustified or even "criminal" his action appeared to the outsiders, in his own household it was perpetuated as "authoritarian law" (Pospisil 1958a: pp. 186–187).

In my sample of 132 Kapauku trouble cases involving legal decisions, there are 18 examples of authoritarian decisions. Among these, 11 differ from the rules. Thus there are 7 cases containing authoritarian laws, which, although conforming to the rules, are held by the people to be unjust. From this we can conclude that conformance to a given rule does not necessarily imply that it will be considered just by the majority—that the principle implied in it would constitute a customary law (Pospisil 1958a: p. 281).

The difference between the two types of law is not qualitative. Rather, it is the degree of internalization that distinguishes them. There is a gradual transition from authoritarian to customary law. The quantitative difference between the two foci is also emphasized by the fact that a given law can change from authoritarian to customary, a change which demonstrates the actual meaning of the word internalization. The process actually has two aspects. When the "internalizing individual" is regarded as its point of reference, the process is located in the individual's mind and is psychological in nature; it refers to a change in his value judgment and in his emotional attitude vis-à-vis the law that is being internalized. The effect of this psychological internalization is the individual's compliance with the law not mainly on the basis of external pressure but because of an internal mechanism that some authors may call morality, others superego, and still others conscience. Violation of such a law causes guilt feelings, remorse, or shame in the violator. When, however, the process of internalization is looked upon as a sociological phenomenon, when our interests are focused upon a group as a whole (community, family, clan, state, etc.), internalization refers to the increase in the number of members of the group in question who have psychologically internalized the law. Whereas psychological internalization refers to qualitative changes in the human mind, sociological internalization is quantitative in nature and pertains to a social group and its membership.

PSYCHOLOGICAL INTERNALIZATION

The process of psychological internalization starts at the time when an individual is confronted with a new response (behavior prescribed by a law) to a given situation. This initial part of the process is usually called learning. Miller and Dollard (1941: pp. 24–25) describe it as a change in the individual's opinion by which a new response becomes dominant over the previously accepted response. Essential to this learning process, the authors hold, is the reinforcement of the desired response through rewards and an extinction of the previous and now undesired response through the lack of reinforcement or through punishment. Thus only those responses are learned that are repetitively rewarded, and those that do not receive a reinforcement become slowly (or, with the application of punishment, more quickly and more permanently) extinct (Dollard and Miller 1950: pp. 48–51).

Piaget views the learning process not so much as a consequence of the strength of the superego and of a systematic application of rewards, as an active, conceptually organized role taking. While a child looks toward adult rules as sacred, absolute, and unchangeable phenomena that are sanctioned and imposed upon him, an adult complies with rules because of his sense of reciprocal justice. This grows out of the latter's participation in social relationships of a peer group in which rules, in the form of self-organizing social schemata (cultural configurations), are absorbed by the individual and serve as frames of reference (categories in the Kantian sense) through which he assimilates social reality and to which reality they help him to accommodate his behavior (Piaget 1948: pp. 195–325). The truth about learning and acceptance of new rules may lie in between the two positions outlined above; it probably consists of a combination of both. While reward and punishment technique definitely help to install new law and perpetuate it in power through external means, once so established the participation of individuals in the relations regulated by such laws is maintained through internal mechanism of Piaget's reciprocal justice.

Some of the cognitive schemata, built up in the individual minds through past participation in social life of the group, define a set of broad cultural values that, according to Wallace, form component parts of the cultural ethos, national character, or modal personality structure. These values, in turn, will influence the formulation of culturally defined needs and wants of the members of a given society and serve as criteria of acceptability of newly introduced laws (Wallace 1965: pp. 129–130). What happens, however, if laws are introduced that run counter to the established values and Piaget's cognitive schemata? An eccentric authority or an outside authority (e.g., a conqueror) may easily introduce such laws and enforce them by means of punishments for violations and rewards for conformity. It is clear that people, in face of a substantial external pressure, will accept the rules as guiding principles for their relationship patterns. However, it is equally clear that we have to distinguish two types of acceptance: a private acceptance of the rules and public conformity with them, which is manifested through persistence in the "legal behavior" even in the event that the source of induction is removed, and public conformance with private rejection of the enforced rules, manifested by the fact that the behavior persists only as long as the enforcing agency is in control of the situation (see esp. Festinger 1953: pp. 233–234). While the former type of acceptance pertains to laws that agree with the people's basic values, the latter occurs when laws alien to the people's "morals" are effectively enforced.

Festinger and Hovland, Janis, and Kelley regard the desire of the individual to remain as a member in the group (in which new laws are enforced) as a basic motivational drive for a *private* acceptance of the rules (Festinger 1953: p. 235; Hovland, Janis, and Kelley 1968: pp. 144–147). This desire, according to Festinger, is not necessarily shaped only by a positive valuation of the group membership. It is equally affected by a restraining force which prevents a man from leaving the group, by his negative evaluation of the situation outside the group and realization of hardships resulting from being an outsider, and by the sheer volume of the influence exerted upon him. In their enthusiasm for the importance of group membership valuation these mentioned authors (with the possible exception of Festinger) seem to imply a belief in the exclusive role of this factor for internalization. They claim that "a person internalizes the norm of a group to the degree that he finds positive attractions in holding membership in it." Thus the "inner factor" of his conviction regarding the rules and norms as proper and desirable, which characterizes them as internalized, seems to result almost exclusively from the subject's positive valuation of his membership in the group (Hovland, Janis, and Kelley 1968: pp. 144–147). Such an "exclusive position" stands in contradiction to empirical evidence reported by many ethnologists and with my findings in New Guinea and elsewhere. Its adequacy is further shaken by the following statements of the authors, who admit that "frequently, however, attitudes and behavior prescribed by an external authority or group become 'internalized,' i.e., genuinely accepted by the person and adhered to even in the absence of surveillance" (Hovland, Janis, and Kelley: 1968: p. 282).

Bruno Bettelheim shows how inmates of a Nazi concentration camp internalized the values of their oppressors and torturers, although they certainly had the least possible desire to remain in the group of political prisoners (1943: pp. 417–450). The motivation for the internalization of these values and standards is explained as a prisoner's desire for self-consistency or for a highly integrated self-image, which is threatened by his enforced, initially "hypocritical" behavior. Since the ruthlessly enforced behavior may not be changed, it is the values of the prisoners that have to undergo a modification (Hovland, Janis, and Kelley 1968: p. 282). In other cases the cause of internalization of new standards for behavior is the individual's affection for the person in authority who proclaims and/or enforces the rules (Hovland, Janis, and Kelley 1968: p. 282; Kohlberg 1963: p. 307).

The value of group membership as the cause and motivation for internalization has been seriously challenged by other authors. They argue that this evaluation results in the process of identification rather than in internalization and private acceptance. Private acceptance is the product of the process of internalization, induced by social influence, a force that effects change in a person's cognition, attitude, or behavior and that has its origin in another person of the group (Raven 1965: p. 371). Private acceptance produced by internalization, however, is but one of several types of acceptance of social influence. According to the level on which these acceptances occur Kelman distinguishes three qualitatively different processes: compliance, identification, and internalization. They differ in terms of "the nature of the anticipated effect, the source of the influencing agent's power, and the manner in which the induced response has become prepotent" (Kelman 1966: p. 142).

The first of these processes, *compliance,* is an overt acceptance induced by expectation of rewards and an attempt to avoid possible punishment—not by any conviction in the desirability of the enforced rule. Power of the influencing agent is based on "means-control" and, as a consequence, the influenced person conforms only under surveillance.

The second of the processes, *identification,* is an acceptance of a rule not because of its intrinsic value and appeal but because of a person's desire to maintain membership in a group or relationship with the agent. The source of power is the attractiveness of the relation which the persons enjoy with the group or agent, and his conformity with the rule will be dependent upon the salience of these relationships (Kelman 1966: pp. 141–143). The drive to maintain the relationships often results in a global identification, an acceptance of all rules for behavior that are required for maintenance of the relation. According to developmental theory, the relationship itself is attractive, because value is placed upon the presence and responsiveness of the agent. The role learning theory views identification as a general disposition of the influenced person to imitate the authority, and the psychoanalytic theory conceives of identification as a total "introjection" or "incorporation" of the parent, or in our case authority, into the personality of the individual "as an 'integral object.' " If the rules are violated, the transgressor exhibits guilt reactions, of course for different reasons than in the case of internalization. Although most intriguing in argument and logic, most of these theories explaining identification are, unfortunately, not documented empirically (Kohlberg 1963: pp. 296–307).

A special type of identification has been labeled "defensive." Anna Freud referred to it as "the identification with the aggressor." Although an individual may initially hate the agent as an oppressor and even torturer, identification with this person does take place, and positive feelings toward the tyrant do develop. This is because the individual tries to resolve the anxiety stemming from expected frustration and punishment by mastering the object of the frustration and identifying with it. The conflict between suffering and one's own values is resolved by acceptance of the values of the authority. If one is identified with a force of which one is afraid, one can no longer be hurt by it (Mowrer 1950: pp. 592, 614). The most striking examples of this type of defensive identification have been recorded by Bettelheim from the Nazi concentration camps (1943).

The last type of influence, *internalization,* which is the focus of our attention, results in the acceptance by an individual of a rule or behavior because he finds its content intrinsically rewarding. Essentially it is a "transformation of outer conformity into inner conformity" (Hovland, Janis, and Kelley 1968: p. 281). The content is congruent with a person's values either because it has been so from the start of the "influence," or because his values changed and adapted to the inevitable. Thus the result of the process may be called "intrinsically motivated conformity" (Kelman 1966: p. 142; Kohlberg 1963: p. 277). The source of power that feeds this process is the subject's conviction of the desirability of the prescribed conduct which he assumes irrespective of his feelings toward the group or the authority and his immediate surveillance (Kelman 1966: pp. 142–143; Hovland, Janis, and Kelley 1968: p. 144). Bertram H. Raven, who defined influence as "kinetic power," or we may say as application of power, classifies influence according to the type and source of the power being applied. In his scheme, which erects a basic dichotomy between socially independent and socially dependent influence (the influence originates in the first instance in the content of the behavior without any obligation to authority; in the second it is prescribed by the experimenter—the authority; the internalized laws pertain to the latter category as being induced by a "socially private-dependent influence." By the term "private" is meant a continuation of the dependent influence irrespective of whether the influenced person believes that his behavior can be checked by the authority. In the case of "public-dependent influence" the inducement to conformity rests squarely with the follower's concern with the authority's ability to observe his behavior. (Raven 1965: pp. 372–376)

The private-dependent influence is, in turn, subdivided into three subcategories, of which the "expert power" and "referent influence" types bear little relevance to the problem of internalization of laws. The third subcategory, on the contrary, deals with a set of obligatory prescriptions that have the nature of "oughtness" for people's beliefs, behaviors, attitudes, and opinions. It consists of general norms that contain internalized values. "*Legitimate influence,* then, is based on the influencee's acceptance of a relationship in the power structure such that the agent is permitted or obliged to prescribe behavior for him and the influencee is legitimately required to accept such influence" (Raven 1965: p. 375). Of course, one type of influence does not preclude an occurrence of another that may appear as "secondary" when favorable conditions have been created by the preceding type (Raven 1965: p. 376).

Internalization of a rule for behavior does not necessarily mean that such a rule is always maintained in actual behavior. There are situations in which the individual either breaks the rule on the spur of the moment, without much thinking, or he consciously compromises a moral (internalized) conviction for an immediate, and (to him) strong enough reward. However, unlike a case of simple overt compliance, breaking an internalized rule elicits an anxiety directly, "independent of either external punishment or social cues which portend punishment" (Aronfreed 1964: p. 195). The individual's psychological response to such a transgression, which an eth-nographer may register as evidence of internalized rule (Kohlberg 1963: p. 278), has been identified in our culture as guilt, in some others as shame.

The social psychologist naturally has been more preoccupied with the guilt response. The psychoanalytical theory views guilt reaction as a tech-nique (which is not necessarily conscious) for reducing anxiety caused by the expectance of punishment. It is conceptualized as an inward turning of aggressive drives, as self-punitive reaction, which is a product of an equation of self with the blaming responses of others (Kohlberg 1963: pp. 286–288). Consequently, compliance with an internalized standard may be interpreted as a "defense against guilt," an objectionable conception, according to Kohlberg. He argues that once such a conceptualization is accepted, any response to a transgression of internalized rule has to be regarded as guilt, which makes the concept too broad and thus useless. In his opinion guilt response most often takes the form of self-criticism, consisting of compo-nents of previously experienced punishment, rather than confession and reparation, which may but need not be manifestations of guilt feeling. The nature of guilt is a "conscious, developmentally advanced, self-critical (and self-controlling) response" (Kohlberg 1963: p. 294).

A cognitive attribute of guilt, the ability to pass a "moral" judgment by the individual experiencing guilt feeling, is held by Aronfreed as a diag-nostic criterion of that concept. Although he argues that not all responses to violations of internalized conduct require a higher degree of cognition and adoption of moral standards (Aronfreed 1964: p. 194), the concept of guilt response should be reserved for a cognitive reaction "compounded of the anxiety aroused by transgression and the evaluative perceptions which come through the filter of moral cognition" (Aronfreed 1964: p. 216). Supporting this definition are Kohlberg's findings which show that "moral internalization relates closely to the cognitive development of moral concepts" (Kohlberg 1963: p. 321). The drive that motivates a transgressor toward experiencing guilt is striving for anxiety reduction. Guilt response (self-criticism), which includes a component of formerly experienced or customarily expected punishment, becomes preferred to the anticipatory anxiety. Self-criticism or self-punishment brings apparent relief to the violator (Aronfreed 1964: pp. 195–197).

To conclude this highly theoretical social-psychological inquiry we may state that, at least in our culture, rules and standards for behavior are recognized by some social scientists as being psychologically internalized if, when violated, they elicit a response of guilt feeling, manifested by self-criticism. Unfortunately, in the field situation that an anthropologist experiences, recognition of internalization on this basis is wholly impractical. First, not all internalized rules are violated during the relatively brief research of an ethnologist, and second, even if violated, self-criticism is apt to be a private reaction that the researcher is unlikely to witness. Consequently, the observational approach is patently insufficient in this situation. One is again reduced to the traditional method of questioning informants and trying to elicit the subjects' reactions to a suggested violation of the rule in question (see also Festinger 1953: p. 247). The intensity and kinds of reactions, which certainly vary from culture to culture, may be used by fieldworkers as indices of the degree to which the informant has internalized a given rule. I have used this approach in the study of internalization of a new incest rule among the Kapauku Papuans. My attempt, which is described later in this chapter, demonstrates the practicability of the procedure and the significance of its results for scientific analysis and prediction.

As a striking example of psychological internalization I am summarizing Bruno Bettelheim's study of internalization of Gestapo rules, and values underlying these by political prisoners in Buchenwald, the Nazi concentration camp. Political dissidents were collected here from the territories occupied by Nazi Germany before and during World War II. According to my father, who was taken to this camp in 1939, the great majority of the prisoners were well educated, democratically minded people who had tacitly or actively opposed Nazism. One would expect that such prisoners, even under extreme brutality, would successfully resist any influence exercised upon them by their hated jailers. Instead of a rebellion and successful resistance to the influence of the SS guards, the goal of the camp institution, "to break the prisoners as individuals and to change them into docile mass from which no individual or group act of resistance could arise" (Bettelheim 1943: p. 418) was, surprisingly enough, not only achieved (usually within five years of internment) but actually far surpassed.

New prisoners resisted SS influence and pressure successfully, for a while. Slowly, however, the problem of survival, the brutal treatment, and the incessant exposure to the enforcement of the oppressors' values began to manifest its influence upon the thinking and the value system of the prisoners. They stopped talking about their former life and social status and began to accept their degradation. Eventually, "a prisoner had reached the final stage of adjustment to the camp situation when he had changed his personality so as to accept as his own the values of the Gestapo" (Bettelheim 1943: p. 447). Thus the old prisoners obeyed even the most whimsical rules of the Gestapo, often boasting of being as tough as their torturers. Although the goals and values of the Gestapo were clearly opposed to their interests, the prisoners accepted them as proper, firmly believing that "the rules set down by the Gestapo were desirable standards of human behavior" (Bettelheim 1943: p. 450). The Gestapo themselves found this fantastic accomplishment hard to believe. They had thought it was impossible that the prisoners would be won over to the Gestapo's values after being subjected to ill treatment for so long. The internalization of the values was not limited to verbal expressions only; the prisoners began to behave like their jailers, and some of them, when in charge of other prisoners (the notorious *Kapo*), behaved worse than the Gestapo (Bettelheim 1943: pp. 447–448). Bettelheim's findings are corroborated by the experiences of my father and his friends who suffered severely at the hands of their "well-adjusted co-prisoners," who even tried to change their appearance in the image of their tormentors and arrogated to themselves old pieces of SS uniforms. "If that was not possible, they tried to sew and mend their uniforms so that they would resemble those of the guards. The length to which prisoners would go in these efforts seemed unbelievable, particularly since the Gestapo punished them for their efforts to copy Gestapo uniforms" (Bettelheim 1943: p. 448). Even love for the cruel masters was developed, so deeply were the new laws and values of the "Nazi superman" internalized.

This example makes it clear that authority can break down "entrenched" customs and cultural norms and replace them by new laws and values, given enough time, inducement (rewards and punishment), and isolation of the subjects from contrary influences. It also shows that internalization of rules may occur without any desire on the part of subjects to "remain as members of the group." Indeed, internalization of values occurred here in the face of a desperate attempt to leave the group membership. The learning theory, with its emphasis on reward and punishment, seems to be more applicable to this situation.

These measures have also been successfully adopted by modern communist dictatorships, whose populations are indoctrinated, coerced by a system of secret police and prison camps, and isolated by the iron curtain of massive border armaments.

SOCIETAL INTERNALIZATION

When interest is shifted from the individual to the society we cease to emphasize the psychological aspect of internalization. Interest in the individual's feeling of how proper a response (or law) may be in a given situation, and how unthinkable an alternative would be, gives way to interest in how many members of the society (or of a societal subgroup) have psychologically internalized a given law. Any increase in the number of those members may be called social internalization. When we distinguish between laws internalized by a majority and those by a minority of the group members, I believe we obtain a meaningful difference between customary and authoritarian laws. The exact nature of the quantitative difference in terms of the number of supporters which appears to be an objective and precise criterion of the two categories of law, is marred, of course, because psychological internalizations differ in the degree to which the various subjects have actually internalized the law in question. This makes the counting difficult, and standards (relative to the culture investigated) have to be set up by the ethnologist in order to determine the degree of psychological internalization for each individual.

A given law is consequently a dynamic phenomenon. In Figure 4 the changing laws are represented by arrows. Movement *a* from *A* to *C* means that an originally authoritarian law was supported by more and more individuals until finally it entered the customary category and became socially internalized. The opposite direction represents the process of extinction of a law *c* by the progressive loss of supporters. The speed of these movements may differ—a law may become almost static for a period of time (*d* and *e*) or fluctuate within a given range between the two foci (*f*).

A new law may originate in two ways. First it can enter the legal field from the realm of custom (*g*). This happens when the authority recognizes a custom as the basis for legal decisions. For example, it was the custom not many years ago among the Kapauku of New Guinea that an adulterous woman was executed by her husband. An outdated Kapauku explicit abstract rule still reflects that situation and demands capital punishment for an adulteress (Pospisil 1958a: p. 168). However, the men realized in time that it was not profitable to kill their women because their cost in shells was high. Consequently, the actual punishment was changed to beating or wounding an adulteress. An informant explained that rich men, because they had plenty of shell money, could afford to continue the old custom, but even they finally changed to the present way. This change of custom, first opposed by the rich, was finally upheld in legal decisions of the Kapauku authorities and was implemented in all four "recent" adultery cases I recorded in 1954–1955 (Pospisil 1958a: pp. 168–170). Thus what started as a more economical practice among the poorer husbands became a customary law by being incorporated into legal decisions by the Kapauku headman.

The law that originated as a custom recognized by the authority is generally popular and customary, but with the passage of time it may lose support and grow increasingly authoritarian, favored by only a minority. Many "outmoded" Western laws that are supported by a few conservatives and which may finally be abolished by legislation belong in this group.

Law may also be directly created by the decision of an authority or by transformation of a political decision into a law. In both cases the law is originally authoritarian. In the latter, a political decision becomes law because the authority has provided it with the intention of universal application, by, for instance, proclaiming that the same decision is intended to be applied in all similar cases in the future. An authoritarian law created in this manner may gain acceptance among the people and finally become customary. It may also happen that the authority will abolish a law by no longer using it as the basis for legal decisions. If this happens and the customary law is dropped as unimportant, the practice which had been legalized will continue to exist as a custom for a period of time at least.

The ethnological literature usually contains only sporadic hints or brief statements concerning the process of internalization of new laws. Ethnologists have not elaborated on or analyzed the process because of a lack of interest and awareness rather than an inherent difficulty in obtaining the pertinent data. Most of the available statements pertain, as one would expect, to the acculturation situation, in which the reaction of the population to the imposition of European types of laws is discussed. The most spectacular of these laws are those that create a new type of administrative authority and that we can label "constitutional."

In Truk the U.S. Civil Administration introduced an election law intended to curb the autocratic power of the chiefs by enabling the electorate to vote them out of office. In 1950 this law was still basically authoritarian and the election a foregone conclusion because

> *it probably will be many years before it becomes genuinely*
> *integrated into the thinking of the Trukese as a truly available*
> *sanction they can apply freely. At present they are hesitant to*
> *use their power, and will generally re-elect a man whatever his*
> *record may be, unless the administration has previously formally*
> *deposed him and is simply asking for a replacement. (Gladwin*
> *1950: p. 20)*

The Navaho showed much greater progress in internalization of the laws imposed upon them in 1923 which created a tribal council with economic, administrative, and judicial powers, thus uniting local bands into a new social entity and a politically organized tribe. Although this was originally completely foreign to them, the Navahos "are commencing to grasp the need for thinking in tribal terms," and they actually resented in 1946 that their council had not become independent from the Indian Service (Kluckhohn and Leighton 1947: pp. 101–103). Even in those early days the Leightons could claim that "the idea of reservation-wide tribal government is finding acceptance and it will probably grow in flexibility and responsiveness as time goes on" (Leighton and Leighton 1945: p. 49). The effectiveness and reception of the constitutional law creating the tribal council can also be seen in the internalization of the laws that the body has passed. Its statute prohibiting early marriages had already in 1948 raised the average age at which young people entered into matrimony (Leighton and Kluckhohn 1948: p. 78). Also, its adoption of the white man's laws concerning inheritance, giving preference to the individual's own children over his maternal nephews and nieces, was easily internalized not only because of the influence exercised by the new political body but also because it solved a father's conflict between his love for his own children and his duty to his maternal clan (Kluckhohn and Leighton 1947: p. 57).

A quite advanced case of internalization of a white man's constitutional law imposed upon the natives is recorded by Hogbin among the Malaita Islanders of the Solomons. As part of their colonial administrative apparatus the British created the post of *maekali,* appointed chiefs, who presided over areas that combined the territories of several formerly politically independent groups led by *ngwane-inoto,* informal native headmen. The new officials were charged with some administrative functions pertaining to the economic and social life of the natives, as well as with the task of settling local disputes. By presiding over formerly hostile groups and settling their disputes the newly appointed chiefs helped to pacify the area. While the older people still nostalgically remembered the glorious days of local raids and killings, some of the young people were "of the opinion that it is an advantage to have a headman to settle the disputes. . . . A handful of my most intelligent informants were able to realize the value of an external authority" (Hogbin 1939: p. 158). Although after a death "by sorcery" people complain against the new authority and the British law prohibiting vengeance, "the young men are too appreciative of the greater security they now enjoy to complain much, even if they do have to curb their rage" (Hogbin 1935: p. 28). They say, "Now it is different. We can travel all the time and think about our affairs. We know that our lives are not in danger." And even, "Old Aningali, himself a murderer on many occasions, also agreed that the peace of today is preferable to the uncertainty of the past" (Hogbin 1939: p. 157).

Aside from laws creating new administrative machinery, the influence of the colonial governments and Western law have been often felt in the sphere of criminal law, especially in cases of homicide and sorcery, and in the realm of civil law where it modified property rules and relations of the sexes. Among the Yaghan Indians of Tierra del Fuego the missionaries imposed laws prohibiting murder with the result that "since the Word of Christ has sounded throughout those regions, savages, among whom vengeance is an unwritten law, have been found forgetting injuries and offering signs of peace to their offenders." These people, who "had robbed and massacred so many shipwrecked and helpless crews, had only a few years afterwards traveled more than a hundred miles to ask aid at Ooskonia for nine shipwrecked men" (Gusinde 1937, vol. 2: p. 325). Similarly, the people of the Ulithi island of Micronesia internalized the Christian laws prohibiting sorcery to such a degree that Lessa suspected that very few persons still resorted to this practice (Lessa 1950: p. 113).

In the realm of civil law, Western legal thought, attempting to elevate the status of females and curb the often unlimited power of the father, had already influenced China before the advent of the People's Republic. Although the new laws giving the women equality with men in terms of familial privileges, responsibilities, and rights of inheritance still tended to be ignored, considerable progress was made toward their acceptance and internalization by the population. Also, emancipation of the children from the oppressive *patria potestas* was so much advanced by the law that traditional parents who tried to maintain their dominance over their children were less able to do so (Levy 1949: p. 309). Moreover, arranged marriages by a close senior relative and the institution of the go-between were so effectively challenged by Western-inspired laws that already in 1922 Sing Ging Su could state that the Chinese people were rapidly adjusting themselves to the new law which required only the parents' consent to their children's marriage: "The general tendency of the Chinese people is to follow the new law implicitly, and the custom of employing a go-between is fast disappearing" (Sing Ging Su 1922: pp. 58–59).

Similar initial progress in internalization of laws that guarantee equality in inheritance of males and females has been reported for the modern Quechua society of Peru where, "despite all objections and prejudices to the contrary, the laws do protect female inheritance and the Indian begins to accept the inevitable" (Mishkin 1946: p. 456).

Progress in internalization of imposed civil law was recorded among the Palauans by H. G. Barnett in 1949. The Japanese, the former masters of the territory, had demanded of the natives a "decent dress" rather than their traditional loincloth. The natives have accepted and internalized this standard partially, in the sense that although they still prefer the loincloth at home or at work, "they wear shorts, and all feel they need them when they go to town or go visiting" (Barnett 1949: p. 2).

The Araucanian Indians of Chile went even farther in internalizing foreign laws introducing private and individual ownership of land. These laws, imposed by the Chilean government, went so far as to make the individual independent of *loñko,* the former head of the extended household and the past titular holder of the land, thus destroying the cement that held together the old type of social structure. Instead of turning to the *loñko* for assigned plots of land, the people favor the government courts of law which nowadays have to carry the burden of settling the numerous disputes over land titles (Titiev 1951: p. 146).

We occasionally find in anthropological literature references to internalization of new authoritarian laws designed by the natives themselves. Roscoe tells us about a Bakitara king who killed his brother, being jealous because the queen mother had given him an amulet which she had denied to the monarch. To avoid similar problems in the future the king passed a law that banished brothers of the Bakitara ruler from the capital for all time. This ruling became internalized—a customary law of that African society (Roscoe 1923: pp. 80–81).

The idea that a native "legislator" may effect changes that alter the whole sociopolitical structure of a tribe has often been scoffed at by Durkheimean-minded anthropologists (see esp. Leach 1959: p. 1097). Nevertheless such a process has been well documented in several instances. I shall

describe three examples, two from the literature on the Ontong Java Polyne-
sians and Mongol tribesmen and one from my own research among the
Kapauku Papuans of West New Guinea. The first two will be briefly reported,
but I shall present in detail the process of internalization of a change of incest
laws among the Kapauku, not only analyzing the role of the individual and
his decisions in a tribal society but also demonstrating the use of the traditional interview technique as a quantitative method for the study of internalization, an old method that may prove important in predicting legal as well
as sociopolitical changes in a given society.

The Ontong Javanese

Before the establishment of a kingdom that united all Ontong Java
islands in the nineteenth century, the sociopolitical structure of the people
was characterized by autonomous joint families consisting of blood relatives
who traced their descent through males from a common ancestor. The
oldest male functioned as its headman in directing economic activities cen-
tering around the coconut groves, coordinating the religious ceremonies,
settling local disputes, and representing the unit among outsiders, especially
in cases of revenge for wrongs perpetrated by outsiders on members of the
joint family. This unit, then, was the strongest and politically most inclusive
organized group. While law and order prevailed within it, outside relations
were characterized by armed clashes or political negotiations (see esp.
Hogbin 1961: p. 110). Although the headman's power was not absolute,
being checked by passive resistance from his constituents, his jurisdiction
was quite broad. In the nineteenth century, prior to contact with the white
man, this sociopolitical situation began to change. A succession of rulers
seized power over all the islands of Ontong Java and established themselves
by abolishing the autonomy of the families and unifying them under their
influence, only to be murdered after relatively brief periods of tenure in their
new position. Finally, Avio secured a "king's position" for himself and his
descendants.

Although completely foreign to their culture at the beginning, the new
political institution and the constitutional and other types of law surrounding
it were slowly internalized by the people. During Ke-ulaho's rule the process
progressed so far that individual complaints were customarily brought to the
attention of this authority, who was expected to rule on them and secure
eventual compensation or revenge. King Uila, his successor, already "was
in a position to intervene when any break of the peace occurred, and he
generally regulated the rights of private retaliation" (Hogbin 1961: p. 227).
The internalization of the new constitutional setup and the king's law,
backed by and in conformance with the public opinion, had a manifold
effect upon the Ontong Java society (Hogbin 1961: p. 230). It brought
internal peace, substituted law and legal self-redress for feud, unified the
tribe politically, and emancipated to a great degree families and fishing

groups from the former political subservience to the joint families' headmen by curbing the latter's powers.

The Mongols

Probably one of the greatest innovators and "revolutionaries" in human history was Temuchin, later known as Genghis Khan (1162–1267), a member of a nomadic Mongol tribe. He conquered numerous lands and built an empire whose extent has never been surpassed, and he deeply influenced the culture of his fellow tribesmen by perfecting military techniques, setting up a new type of administrative organization, introducing writing, creating an effective postal system, and developing an attitude of religious tolerance. His son and heir to the title of Kha-Khan, Ogadai, further improved the administration by limiting the power of governors, by separating the civil and military services, and by setting up official records and archives. Genghis Khan's innovations had a truly revolutionary effect on social organization. They altered profoundly the tribal organization based upon patriclans which had enjoyed political autonomy and often complete independence. Temporarily, during the traditional local wars or collective hunts, several clans (*gentes*) united themselves into a loose union presided over by a tribal council of clan leaders who elected a leader called the "khan." Obedience to the khan was pledged only for the duration of the conflict or hunt, although some of these tribal leaders managed to extend some of their political influence beyond a war period.

This system of loose conglomerates of politically and economically autonomous *gentes,* called tribes, was welded by Genghis Khan into a durable political union in which he assumed permanent, uncontested, absolute power. To make his organization more effective and to weaken the old clan solidarities, he segmented the Mongol society into a hierarchy of units composed of ten, hundred, thousand, and ten thousand households, thus cutting across former affiliations and disrupting the age-old clan system. Each of these units had its leader—however, no longer an independent chief but a feudal lord, vassal of the almighty Kha-Khan. This profound revolution in the Mongol social organization was well summarized by Hudson as follows:

> The development of the feudal fiefs and military units had a shattering effect on the old Mongol gentes and tribes and on the social structure of all the peoples who were brought within its scope. In the formation of the divisions of the "ten thousand," and "thousand," and "hundred" many units were composed of contingents drawn from various tribes and gentes. The organization of the "thousands" and the distribution of the feudal fiefs culminated in the disintegration of a whole series of Mongol tribes, as for example the Tatars, Merkits, Djadjirat, Naiman, and Kerait, the remnants of which were in most cases

*scattered among the various fiefs and "thousands." (Hudson
1938: p. 97)*

Most of the reforms of Genghis Khan were in the form of laws that
became part of the legal code, called *Yasak* (or *Yassa*), of the Mongol
Empire. The code was compiled and engraved upon iron tablets by Tatatungo, the Keeper of the Seal of Genghis Khan, and the man who introduced
Uighur writing into the growing Mongol Empire (Prawdin 1940: p. 80). He
was commanded by his ruler to be always at hand to record the khan's
decisions that would, as decrees, become law. At the same time the Kha-
Khan appointed Tatatungo's disciple Shigi Kutuku as supreme judge to administer the law contained in *Yasak* and to keep records of his decisions
(Prawdin 1940: p. 90). Thus the famous Mongol legal code was initiated. It
grew into a substantial book of which 36 fragments are preserved in the
literature (Riasanovsky 1937: pp. 83–86). The total work contained, according to Riasanovsky, five types of provisions: those concerning civil administration, the military, criminal law, private law, and special laws pertaining to
the customs of the steppes. The sources upon which Genghis Khan drew
while promulgating his *Yasak* rules were the customary Mongol tribal law,
the Chinese law, and, most importantly for us here, his own innovations that
had little or no precedent (Riasanovsky 1937: p. 34). Although originally the
Mongol law was ruthlessly applied to all subjects and conquered peoples,
as time went on and the empire comprised numerous sedentary and civilized
peoples, it became applicable primarily to the military and to the nomadic
components of the empire (Riasanovsky 1937: p. 33).

Although the sources of Genghis Khan's regulations included old
Mongol customary laws and legal principles, one should not assume that
Yasak only codified them. Rather, the old principles, or derivatives thereof,
were employed in Genghis Khan's decision and rule-making process. The
results themselves, being applied to different situations and social groups,
were certainly innovations in their own right. For example, it is true that the
principle of mutual help and comradeship was an old one among Mongols.
However, this principle, pertaining originally to the clan organization
(gentes) was applied by Genghis Khan to the new decimal hierarchical
sociopolitical structure that cut across the old boundaries of allegiance. Also,
the harsh death penalty for violation of the new law may be considered an
innovation (Prawdin 1940: p. 69; Riasanovsky 1937: p. 150).

Although Riasanovsky seems constantly to emphasize the customary
nature of Genghis Khan's decisions, he himself admits that at least 5 of the
36 fragments of *Yasak* were completely new, unprecedented legal innovations. Fragment 5 dealt with bankruptcy and provided a death penalty for
a miscreant who found himself in this financial predicament for the third
time. Fragment 20 introduced taxation, and fragment 10 exempted scholars
and religious peoples from paying taxes. The last two fragments (18 and 25)

that Riasanovsky considers pure innovations deal respectively with rigorous inspection of the equipment of troops and with the institution of the postal system (Riasanovsky 1937: pp. 83–85, 95, 153, 154, 157). In addition to these Riasanovsky also admits that the law providing a death penalty for adultery "stood in contradiction to the views of the Mongols on adultery and to their customs" (1937: p. 146). Of all of these and other provisions of *Yasak* he says that they "arose from the reforming activity of their great conqueror, from his attempt to create a world empire" (1937: p. 194).

In my opinion many more rules of *Yasak* were new to the Mongol culture and originated as authoritarian laws. For example, the law prohibiting plunder during a battle, as described by Prawdin, was certainly an innovation and authoritarian in nature (1940: p. 58), and the constitutional laws instituting absolute power over all the Mongols and forbidding not only freedom of political decision but also, under death penalty, unauthorized consultation with a foreign ruler were certainly foreign to Mongol customs (Prawdin 1940: p. 101). That the principle of absolute power and loyalty was part of the Mongol customs as they pertained to the clan or, only during wartime, to the tribe, does not, as Riasanovsky seems to imply (1937: p. 156), negate the fact that their application on the supratribal and even supranational (empire) levels of the new political organization was an important, unprecedented innovation and certainly authoritarian and not customary in nature.

Similarly, Genghis Khan's decimal system of political, administrative, and military segmentation which disrupted the clan system was also a novelty because it superseded the clan structure and applied to the totality of sociopolitical organization of the Mongols—not only to the military during the wartime—thus disrupting even the larger tribal segments of the Mongol society (Riasanovsky 1937: pp. 154–155; Hudson 1938: p. 97; Prawdin 1940: pp. 77). This form of the decimal organization became internalized and persisted in Asia, according to Riasanovsky, into the fourteenth and fifteenth centuries (1937: p. 258).

As a whole, *Yasak* was so effectively imposed upon the subjects of Genghis Khan that it became internalized by the nomads of Central Asia and continued to exercise great legal influence not only after the death of its creator but long after the collapse of the Mongol Empire (Riasanovsky 1937: p. 33). Its significance was felt even in the nineteenth century when its provisions influenced the Mongol Code of 1815, compiled under Chinese rule. There the whole sector of private law employed basically the same principles expounded in *Yasak* (Riasanovsky 1937: p. 66). Prawdin comments upon its internalization during the reign of Tamerlane as follows:

> *But it is a remarkable fact that after the decay of the Mongolian Empire, one-and-a-half centuries after Jenghis' death, Tamerlane, the new great conqueror, recognized that he owed his own*

> *ascent to his having strictly followed the* Yasak *of Jenghis Khan;
> and three hundred years after Jenghis, Baber, the Great Mogul,
> established his realm in Hindustan upon the foundations of the*
> Yasak. *(Prawdin 1940: p. 91)*

Indeed, *Yasak* and the influence of Genghis Khan had been so much part of the ''morals'' of the Central Asian peoples that the nomadic rulers of Central Asia found it necessary to rule not in their own right but in the name of a descendant of Genghis. Accordingly, ''almost every Emir kept a tame Jenghiside in his province, who bore the shadow-title of Khan. In this Khan's name the local chieftain ruled, and in this Khan's name he made war against his neighbors'' (Prawdin 1940: p. 412). It was, however, not only the local chiefs who found it obligatory to comply with *Yasak* and did not dare to rule by themselves. Even the great and all-powerful despot Tamerlane assumed only the title of Great Emir. ''He appointed as Khan a descendent of Jenghis, Syurhatmish, ruling in that worthy's name, which appeared on the coins minted by Tamerlane.'' This was all necessary because ''the tradition of Jenghis Khan was still alive in the soul of every nomad'' (Prawdin 1940: p. 435). As his empire continued to grow Tamerlane changed his titles many times, ''but he remained all the time a true follower of the *Yasak,* and bridled his ambitions, for though he ultimately assumed the title of Sultan, he never took that of Khan. When his puppet-Khan Syurhatmish died, Tamerlane appointed as successor Syurhatmish's son Mahmud'' (Prawdin 1940: p. 438). Some precepts of *Yasak* were so internalized by the people that even when they ceased to function as the law of the land they continued to be observed as customs. Accordingly, one of the consequences of Genghis Khan's law, by which a horse thief was punished by death, ''is the custom which prevailed to our own day in remote parts of Mongolia and Turkestan, that a runaway camel is not suffered to drink from a strange well, so that, being tortured by thirst, it shall find its way back to its own master'' (Prawdin 1940: p. 93).

No matter how internalized *Yasak* became, its power began to vanish with the collapse of the Mongol Empire, and in time a slow but irreversible process of extinction set in. The fundamental cause of the collapse was, first, the lack of education of the Mongol nomads, who could not keep the subjected sedentary and civilized populations in check. Second, the state apparatus was constantly being weakened by the vanishing but still important solidarity of the nomadic tribes and clans (Prawdin 1940: pp. 217–219). As a result ''the effectiveness of the Great Yassa, as a general compulsory Code for all the tribes did not continue long. At the end of the thirteenth century, its importance began to decline, this process being precipitated by the collapse of the Mongol State . . .'' (Riasanovsky 1937: p. 33). Although *Yasak's* influence had persisted, as we have seen above, for centuries, some of its precepts marked a fast decline. For example, rules guarding the power of the central authority became neglected after only a generation marked by internal dissension of the constituency of the empire (Prawdin 1940: p. 367). Also, *Yasak*'s brutality of sanctions declined rather rapidly, so that "the penal provisions of the Mongol-Oirat Regulations of 1640 were considerably milder than those of the Great Yassa. Capital punishment, so often prescribed by the Yassa was almost completely lacking in the latter Code" (Riasanovsky 1937: pp. 102, 203).

The Kapauku Papuans

As a last legal innovation that became internalized and effected profound changes in a native culture, I present the history of an incest regulation, decreed and enforced by a Kapauku Papuan headman called Ijaaj Awiitigaaj. The following material forms a chapter in a book on anthropology of law (*Law in Culture and Society,* edited by Laura Nader)[1] in which I have emphasized the role of the individual as a legal innovator in a tribal society. Nevertheless, the nature and importance of the process of internalization and its measurement are here adequately documented.

One of the unfortunate effects of sociology upon some social anthropology has been that the individual's role in the social and cultural history of the various tribal societies is not considered. This divorce of the individual from his society has given rise to the well-known cultural descriptions and social analyses in which a native innovator has no place, in which the "group as a whole acts, decides, and changes," being equipped by various writers not only with a structure and existence that is termed "superorganic" or "supraindividual," but also with such amazing faculties as "group mind" and "group will." Human society somehow has been promoted to an organism in its own right. It is not surprising, therefore, that my account (1958b) of a Papuan innovator who initiated changes in social structure became controversial and drew the following categoric refutation: "the operations of his primitive legislator had no effect whatsoever on the social structure" (Leach 1959: p. 1096).

Since almost anything of any significance in the history of science has been at one point or another controversial, criticism and the resultant controversy can be considered beneficial. Fortunately, many contemporary social anthropologists, who have somehow escaped orthodox sociological influence, do allow for the importance of the individual in shaping tribal cultures. Hoebel made his position on the native innovator quite clear when he wrote: "In the primitive world volitional inventiveness is truly a rare occurrence. Conscious tinkering with the social structure or with gadgetry

[1]Reprinted from Laura Nader, editor, *Law in Culture and Society* (Chicago: Aldine Publishing Company, 1969); copyright © 1969 by Wenner-Gren Foundation for Anthropological Research, Inc. Reprinted by permission of Aldine•Atherton, Inc.

improvement is not the order of the day. Most primitive inventions are nonvolitional" (1949: p. 470). By this statement he allowed for a possibility of cultural change due to an individual's volitional effort. Since many societies have been studied for a relatively brief period (one or two consecutive years), and since many of the investigators have been heavily influenced by the early sociological dogma that divorces the individual from the "social processes," it follows that there are very few accounts of volitional innovations. This account is intended to contribute to the growing literature on this topic and to present the history and analysis of a legal innovation made by a Papuan headman and to relate its subsequent fate and effects upon the Kapauku Papuan society during the nine years that followed my original investigation in 1954.

During my first research among the Kapauku Papuans of West New Guinea, conducted in 1954 and 1955, I recorded a case of a dramatic modification of the laws of incest and a series of subsequent changes in the social structure of a Papuan community. The modification of the incest laws was initiated by Awiitigaaj, the headman of the village of Botukebo. I had the opportunity to record the pertinent history and motivations of this man and to observe the attitude of his tribesmen toward the innovation, published in an article (Pospisil 1958b) in which I interpreted the modifications of the laws of incest and the subsequent changes in the social structure of the village as an example of a rare volitional invention made by an influential individual in a tribal society. I also proposed a hypothesis for the social acceptance of this unprecedented innovation, and made several predictions about changes that would follow. My interpretation was criticized and it was claimed that what I had actually observed was a normal, unexciting, and necessary process of fission which is present in any segmentary society (Leach 1959: p. 1096).

In 1959 I returned to the Kapauku to verify my predictions. The results of this endeavor were presented to the Annual Meeting of the American Anthropological Association in Philadelphia in 1961. I went to New Guinea for the third time in 1962 to restudy the Kapauku and test my theories of political change and those specific predictions which I had made in 1961. The results of my investigations made in 1959 and 1962 and my interpretations of the structural changes that had occurred in the social relations of the people of the village of Botukebo are reexamined here.

The general characteristics of the Kapauku culture have been already given in Chapter Three on "Attributes of Law." In the same chapter I discussed the distinctive features of the native headman and the nature of his leadership and decision-making process. In Chapter Four ("Legal Levels and the Multiplicity of Legal Systems") I analyzed the societal structure of the Ijaaj-Pigome Confederacy and used the data on the laws of incest as an example of my theoretical points. Let me now discuss in greater detail the history of the change of the incest law, engineered by a Kapauku headman.

The story of the legal change in the Botukebo village, which affected ultimately the whole Ijaaj-Pigome Confederacy, started in about 1935. In those days Awiitigaaj, the wealthy, courageous, and shrewd headman of Botukebo, fell in love with his beautiful third paternal parallel cousin, who unfortunately belonged to his own sib. Kapauku law is very explicit about the matter of incest. It categorically states *keneka bukii daa,* which means "to marry one's sibmate is tabooed." Nevertheless, Awiitigaaj did not hesitate to break the taboo and elope with the girl. The infuriated relatives of the couple pursued the lovers, and the girl's father, Ugataga, who was a coheadman of the Ijaaj-Jamaina sublineage and lived in the neighboring village of Kojogeepa, ruled that both his daughter and her seducer must be executed by arrow according to the Kapauku customary law. His decision was upheld by the head of the Ijaaj-Pigome Confederacy.

This situation was accepted as a challenge by the fugitive Awiitigaaj, who was well versed in native law, politics, and intrigue. Although he was the first man in the Kamu Valley to conclude such an incestuous marriage, he knew that in the neighboring Pona Valley some individuals, who belonged to the Adii sib, had broken the incest taboo in a similar way and had managed to survive. He hid in the bush, assuming that the girl's father would soon realize the futility of pursuit and in time, after his temper cooled off, might be willing to forego the punishment and accept a handsome bride price. After all, figured Awiitigaaj, Ugataga was a clever businessman and politician; he would see the personal disadvantage of killing his daughter and forfeiting a bride price—he would end up with no daughter and no money —a very hard prospect for even a very moral Kapauku. It was much more likely that Ugataga would show great anger in public and make exhausting expeditions into the forest until he tired out the patrilineal relatives and bored the other tribesmen. If he eventually gave up the search and accepted the inevitable, he would preserve the public's high opinion of his morality, the life of his beloved daughter, and the prospect of an unusually large bride price. Thus reasoned Awiitigaaj, any sensible Kapauku headman of the status of Ugataga would act. The acceptance of the bride price would make the marriage formally valid and would legally absolve him. The only problem seemed to be to avoid detection by his patrilineal kin who were searching the forests. To accomplish this, Awiitigaaj cleverly utilized the behavior patterns that require maternal relatives, especially mother's brothers, to protect a fugitive from Kapauku justice; these relatives supplied him with food and with information about the plans and movements of the searching parties of his paternal kin.

The patrilineal relatives of the two fugitives diligently combed the forests, ostensibly to catch the incestuous couple. Actually, however, they played the required role of moralists, thus reaping admiration and respect from the residents of the surrounding, but not involved, communities. In the evenings in front of a large audience of their neighbors they talked about their dilemma—having to do justice and, by this very act, killing their close relatives. As time passed, the pursuers tired of the game, and so did their audience. Actually, the noninvolved witnesses of the manhunt played the most important part in this affair: they were the ultimate umpires who were expected to decide when enough effort had been expended in hunting the fugitives and when the requirements of morality and justice had been satisfied. Indeed they constituted what the Durkheimean enthusiasts would call "the group mind, or public opinion." The guilty couple's maternal relatives on one side and the couple's patrilineal relatives on the other were scrutinizing the mood of this noninvolved audience. Both groups of adversaries waited for the moment when the bystanders would get tired of the futile game and suggest a settlement. Finally this day came, and headmen of two of the noninvolved confederacy lineages began publicly to demand an end of the hunt and a peaceful settlement. Although Ugataga desired this most, he knew better than to show eagerness. Like Caesar refusing the laurels of emperorship, he continued to reject the idea of peaceful conclusion of the affair. "Morality and not the money of the prospective bride price," as he put it "is the important issue." Thus his prestige as a man of high morality grew with every refutation of the overtures. However, even in this game there is a limit between the image of a very moral individual and a stubborn fool. Ugataga knew this limit, and, constantly reverting to temper tantrums manifested by the Kapauku mad dance directed against the fugitives, properly and finally began to give in. Thus, I have been informed, his brilliant performance as an indignant and vengeful father slowly changed to that of a subdued man, "crushed by public opinion" and by his futile attempts to administer justice. Finally, at the suggestion of Awiitigaaj's maternal relatives, who acted as go-betweens, he very reluctantly gave in to "the public pressure" and asked Awiitigaaj's paternal relatives for a bride price.

Legally speaking, this act implicitly recognized the incestuous marriage. For his financial demand he was able to enlist the support of his own sublineage as well as that of the head of the Ijaaj-Pigome Confederacy. Awiitagaaj seemed to have won the case. However, being a sly individual, he had an additional scheme in mind. Through intermediaries he let it be known to his patrikin that he, contrary to the general opinion, was actually poor and insolvent, which meant that the burden of payment of the bride price would fall fully upon the purses of his brothers, paternal uncles, and patriparallel cousins. As he hoped and expected, this ploy resulted in the inevitable: his paternal relatives refused to pay the price and continued to insist on the death penalty for the couple. The infuriated girl's father and his sublineage lost control of their emotions and attacked Awiitigaaj's relatives with sticks. By this act of violence, which inflicted bleeding wounds upon several of the seducer's kin, Awiitigaaj and his relatives were absolved, in conformance with well-established Kapauku customary law, from payment of the bride price. A Kapauku may legally either accept payment of damages (in this case bride price) or avail himself of the pleasure of corporally punishing the offending party—but he may not do both.

Release from their financial obligation induced the beaten relatives of Awiitigaaj to accept the settlement and recognize the incestuous union. The happiest man, of course, was Awiitigaaj, whose scheming genius had accomplished the seemingly impossible. Not only did he manage to go unpunished and keep his incestuous bride as his wife, but he was also absolved from the usually onerous payment of the bride price, for which his patrilineal relatives had to pay with bleeding scalps, a couple of fractured noses, and bruised bodies. Although they were beaten, and the girl's father suffered the loss of the bride price, Awiitigaaj gained the woman, was absolved from the payment for her, and successfully broke an established taboo. This clever manipulation of individuals and groups of relatives, and utilization of the knowledge of the Kapauku law, brought him deservedly (in Kapauku eyes) prestige and recognition and enhanced his political influence and fame.

All of this having been accomplished, one thing still remained to be corrected. As a suglineage headman and a well-to-do Kapauku businessman, Awiitigaaj could ill afford to be regarded as a violator of law. Therefore, to clothe his action with an air of legality, he promulgated a new law which stated that it was permissible to marry within the same sib, lineage, and even sublineage as long as the couple were at least second cousins. This new boundary of incest which he laid down was easily understandable. Another Kapauku law of incest specifies the prohibition of marriage between any first cousins, even if they do not belong to the same sib. Thus Awiitigaaj, while breaking one law of incest, upheld another one and applied it to paternal kin, formerly covered by the sib exogamy rule. When asked in the presence of other Kapauku about his motives for changing the laws of incest, he gave this explanation: "To marry a *keneka* [a sibmate of the same generation] is good as long as she is a second paternal parallel cousin. In the old days the people did not think of the possibility, but now it is permissible. Adii people [members of a Kapauku sib who live south of the Kamu Valley] have started this change [incest violation] and so I thought we were the same as they and I introduced the new custom. I married my cousin only after I became *tonowi* so that other people either were afraid to object or they agreed with me. To marry *keneka* is not bad, indeed it is nice; in this way one becomes rich."

While hearing this justification of his action, given in the presence of other people, it was immediately obvious to me that I was listening to a political speech rather than to an honest explanation of Awiitigaaj's motives. Later, when we were alone, I received the following confidential statement: "Why did I marry my relative? Well, I will tell you but don't tell the others. I liked her; she was beautiful." As to his new incest regulation, he had the following comment accompanied with a sly smile and a friendly dig in my ribs: "Please don't tell the others. They wouldn't like me and I would lose influence. As far as I am concerned it would be all right if first cousins were to marry. To marry your own sister is probably bad, but I am not convinced even of that. I think whoever likes any girl should be able to marry her. I set up the new taboo in order to break down the old restrictions. The people [Kapauku] are like that. One has to tell them lies."

The successful breaking of the incest taboo by a headman of a large sublineage established a precedent which, in the course of time, brought about far-reaching change in the law and societal structure of the entire Ijaaj-Pigome Confederacy (see Figure 3 p. 109). Following his own precedent, Awiitigaaj later married three second paternal parallel cousins from his own sublineage and village. As time went on, more and more young men followed the example of the innovator until in 1954 seven of fifty-two Botukebo married couples were living in "incestuous" unions. One more man married "incestuously" before my departure in 1955; four incestuously married women of the Enona sublineage of the Ijaaj sib had died prior to 1955; four Ijaaj-Enona women married men of the related Ijaaj-Jamaina sublineage (two) and Ijaaj-Notiito lineage (two) and resided outside the village of Botukebo; one woman married an Ijaaj man of the Bibigi village and therefore resided beyond the boundaries of the Ijaaj-Pigome Confederacy; and one Enona sublineage man with his incestuously married wife moved to the village of Magidimi. There were therefore actually 18 incestuous unions concluded within the Ijaaj-Enona sublineage between 1935 and 1955. Furthermore, within this period one additional incestuous marriage occurred between a man and a woman who belonged to the related Ijaaj-Jamaina sublineage, bringing the total of the incestuous unions to 19. If we assume that my timing of the marriages prior to my first research in 1954 (based on genealogical evidence and age computation) is correct and that, consequently, 295 marriages were contracted in the Ijaaj-Gepouja lineage during that twenty-year period, the 19 incestuous unions represent 6.44 percent of the total.

On the basis of a popularity test that I submitted to all adults of the Botukebo village (Ijaaj-Enona sublineage) in 1954, I found that 57.5 percent of the Botukebo people accepted, 37.5 percent rejected, and 5 percent were indifferent to the newly promulgated law of marriage that violated the old incest taboos. The acceptance and rejection of the new regulation, of course, varied in intensity, motivation, and content from individual to individual. The innovator of the new law, Awiitigaaj, privately defended almost complete freedom of choice of a spouse. Ijaaj Imopaj, who married his second paternal parallel cousin, offered this comment: "All people should be permitted to marry as they wish. However, it is bad to marry one's first paternal parallel cousin. I would beat my younger brother if he tried to commit such an outrage."

A Botukebo man whose sister married her third paternal parallel cousin accepted that marriage but raised strong objections to any union closer than that of the fourth degree of collaterality. Another covillager objected to any marriage within the same sib: "It is bad. I would never marry my sib sister. I would beat my son or younger brother if he should try to marry his sibmate." There was also one old man in the village who proclaimed that he would shoot his son with an arrow if he were to marry a girl from his own sib. Although there was quite a variety of opinion among these men of Botukebo (Ijaaj-Enona sublineage), all of them admitted the possibility that a close relative of theirs might commit such a violation of the established prohibition of intrasib marriage. As a contrast, Enaago of the Dou sib (who comes from a lineage that belongs to another political confederacy), who had recently married a brotherless Botukebo girl and went to live in her parents' house, was unable to conceive that his close paternal relative could commit such a crime. In his mind there was no alternative, not even an illegal one, to the old incest taboo. Typically, his reaction to my question about the propriety of the sexual behavior of the Botukebo Ijaaj people was highly emotional and reflected what might be called incest horror: "Bad, bad, a sib sister is never a spouse. They are all bad. Their vital substance will deteriorate, and they will all die of their crimes."

However, in spite of the opposition, acceptance of the new legislation of Awiitigaaj spread from his own sublineage to the rest of the Ijaaj-Gepouja lineage and also to the politically allied but genealogically unrelated Ijaaj-Notiito lineage of the confederacy. Finally, both lineages accepted, with some modifications, the new incest regulations. Consequently, the law of incest in the Ijaaj-Pigome Confederacy became complicated and, to a casual observer, bewildering: In the Ijaaj-Enona sublineage marriages between second paternal parallel cousins became permissible, but in the rest of the related Ijaaj sublineages and in the Ijaaj-Notiito lineage only a marriage between third paternal parallel cousins, and preferably between those who came from different sublineages, was regarded as legal. These rules stood in sharp contrast to the laws of the Pigome and Dou lineages. Pigome intrasib marriages remained prohibited and were punished by severe beating with a stick. The Dou proved to be the most conservative and resistant to the innovation: In accordance with the old tradition, its authorities continued to insist on the death penalty for offenders against the intrasib marriage taboo.

Perplexed by the complexity of incest regulation in the Ijaaj-Pigome political confederacy the reader might well wonder how the legal discrepancies among its various subgroups could be reconciled under a unified headship. Ekajewaijokaipouga, the confederacy headman from 1950 to 1958, had publicly rejected the old rule of sib exogamy, and his successor Jokagaibo, who ascended to that position in 1958, was even "incestuously married." These men had to rule over lineages whose authorities punished violations of the incest taboo by beating or execution. The solution to this problem is found in the organizational principles of the Kapauku societal structure (patterned segmentation of the society into constituent subgroups)

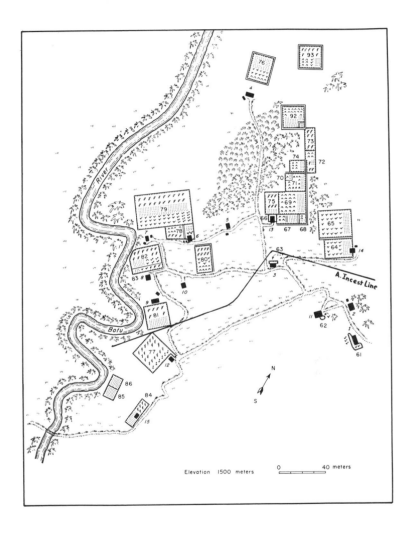

FIGURE 5. Botukebo Village and Gardens, 1954

and the rules of jurisdiction. One of the basic rules of the Kapauku legal procedure is that an individual is tried by the headman of the group to which he and his colitigant belong. Since in the confederacy there is only one lineage of either the Pigome or Dou sibs, a couple could commit incest only if both were members of the same lineage in one of these sibs. Consequently, the lineage headman of the Pigome or Dou people, rather than the confederacy leader, always adjudicates such violations. Because by a rule of the Kapauku jurisdiction there is no appeal from a verdict, the decision rendered by either of the two lineage headmen is final. The same principle of jurisdiction applies within the Ijaaj-Gepouja and Ijaaj-Notiito lineages. Since second paternal parallel cousins have to belong to the same sublineage of the three that compose the Ijaaj-Gepouja lineage, the law of incest in these three subgroups can have different content: although the Ijaaj-Enona sublineage permits second cousins to marry, the other two sublineages permit no closer marriage than that of third cousins. The latter regulation is also true of the Ijaaj-Notiito lineage. In none of these groups is incest violation carried to the confederacy headman for adjudication.

With the increase of intrasib marriages appeared an additional phenomenon: By 1955, of 18 marriages in which at least one party was a member of the Ijaaj-Enona sublineage of Botukebo, nine (50 percent) of the unions were concluded between partners not only from the same sib but also from the same village. Awiitigaaj, with his political genius and his need to establish his incestuous innovation on a more convincing moral basis, seized upon this new trend toward village endogamy. For reasons of prestige, as well as to refute the incessant criticisms and accusations of immorality and criminality hurled at him by his domestic opponents and his external enemies, he decided to render his new incest law more appealing by making it more formal and complex. By drawing a line through the community, he divided the village of Botukebo into two halves to which he assigned the names *weejato* and *auwejato* (see Figure 5). The line was so cleverly drawn that in each half of the village resided adult members of the Enona sublineage who were as far related as first cousins (but not beyond). Awiitigaaj spoke in favor of marrying across this line into the other "incipient moiety." Moreover, he even managed to induce one of the villagers, whose place of residence did not fit in with his scheme, to move his house across the newly established incest boundary.

In his legislative enthusiasm he did not stop at this point but advocated a new and revolutionary compact settlement pattern. He proposed to change the Botukebo village from a loose and completely irregular cluster of houses into a lineal village, in which the houses would stand in a single line, divided in the middle by a wider gap representing the incest boundary line. One of the new moieties was supposed to occupy the southern, the other the northern half of the settlement. By a linear village, he thought, the moiety structure would be even more accentuated. His argumentation and public speeches never failed to attract a favorably inclined audience. Because I knew Awiitigaaj's persuasiveness and influence, and his wealth and the network of extended loans that tied him to many important village debtors, I wrote in 1958: "We may expect that in the near future Botukebo village will be linear, with a main street in front of the houses" (1958b: p. 835). In the same article I made three other predictions. First, I viewed the abrogation of the sib exogamy rule as a serious blow to the cohesiveness of the Ijaaj-Pigome Confederacy. Since I knew that the marital ties uniting the four lineages into a political confederacy represented the mainstay of this alliance, I expected that with more marriages occurring within the sibs (represented here by their lineages) the important affinal bond would be weakened and the *esprit de corps* of the political union would vanish. A fragmentation of the confederacy appeared to me to be a possibility. Unfortunately, with the Dutch pacification of the Kamu Valley in 1956, it was not possible to test this hypothesis. Because of the variety of political and economic factors brought into existence by the acculturation process, the original system of confederacies had fully disintegrated by 1962, when I undertook my third field study of the Kapauku people.

I also predicted that the decrease in the number of intraconfederacy marriages, that would slowly abrogate the affinal relationships that provided one of the main channels for regional understanding and for peaceful settlement of interconfederational disputes, would eventually lead to a perceptible increase in local hostilities and open wars. Again, the pacification of the area prevented a test of this hypothesis.

Third, with village endogamy I visualized a trend to an elevation of the status of women. Under a lineage or even village endogamy, the married women would no longer be strangers marrying into another locality where they would have to depend entirely on their husbands' affection and justice. An intravillage marriage provides women with relative independence, immediate support from their consanguineal relatives in disputes with their husbands, and ultimately with a greater influence over their spouses. We may even speculate further and view such lessening of emphasis on the male line as a situation favorable to a change from patrilineality to a bilateral social organization. As in the two previous instances, pacification interfered with this natural process, enhanced the security and prestige of women, and made them less dependent upon the whims of their consanguineal or affinal kin.

Fortunately, the advance of Western civilization did not also make it impossible to test my explanation of the nature of the sociostructural change in the Ijaaj-Pigome Confederacy and my predictions of the changes in the village plan and residence pattern, as will be seen.

Professor Leach was very critical of my interpretation of the social change in Botukebo. He states, "Pospisil's primitive legislator . . . did not change the law but only its application" (Leach 1959: p. 1097). Moreover, he rejected the claim that the headman Awiitigaaj made a volitional innovation in promulgating a new law of exogamy and in creating moieties in his village. He maintained, "all that has really happened here is that one major segment of the society, which was formerly exogamous, has split up to form two segments, each of which is now exogamous" (1959: p. 1097). And later he states, "The existence of a fission process of this kind is a necessary mechanism in any segmentary structure; its operation signifies the continuity of structure and not its breakdown" (1959: p. 1097).

In my rejoinder of 1960 I pointed out that Awiitigaaj had indeed changed the native law and not merely its application. The traditional law states literally: *keneka bukii daa,* which means "to marry a *keneka* [sibmate of the same generation as Ego] is forbidden [tabooed]." Since Awiitigaaj promulgated a law by which a *keneka* became eligible as a spouse (if he or she was at least a second cousin of Ego, or a more distantly related sibmate), he broke the law of sib exogamy and substituted a new one for it. Thus what actually happened was a change of law and not merely of its application.

Leach's second criticism of my analysis arises from what appears to be superficial reading. First, to make his interpretation of the changes consistent with the data, he promated the Ijaaj-Pigome political confederacy to a "maximal lineage" (1959: p. 1096), although I devoted an entire chapter (Pospisil 1958a: pp. 64–94) to the Kapauku confederacy, showing that it is not a consanguineal group but a purely political union of several lineages that belong to unrelated and nonlocalized sibs. Furthermore, he equates sib with a lineage that seems, in his interpretation of the Kapauku culture, to be a localized segment of the confederacy. After thus having "engineered" the data of the Kapauku society, he proceeds to correct the findings and claims that what actually happened was simply that "one of the major exogamous lineages had grown too large for convenience and fission in this major segment took place" (1959: p. 1096).

Of course, I must agree that every segmentary society employs the fission process as a necessary mechanism of change. Indeed, the Kapauku have such a mechanism; fission occurs there along political, economic, and residential lines. A group that separates from its parental societal segment usually settles a new area and becomes a member of a different political confederacy. Nevertheless, *it retains the old sib exogamy.* Thus the fission in Kapauku society has nothing to do with the regulation of marriages and the rules of exogamy.

Figure 3 (p. 109) demonstrates this point. On it can be seen that the only localized consanguineal groups of the Kapauku are the lineages and sublineages; the subsibs and sibs represent nonlocalized, traditional social units, whose members live in lineages that are scattered throughout the vast Kapauku territory. As stated above, the rules of incest pertain primarily to the nonlocalized and traditional sibs and not to their segments, the localized patrilineal corporate groups which are, of course, logically also exogamous.

Consequently, if a localized sublineage or lineage divides into two segments because of population pressure, such a split has nothing to do with the incest regulations themselves. This is so because the most inclusive exogamous unit is not the parental sublineage or lineage but the more inclusive nonlocalized sib to which the two newly split societal segments still belong. A process of fission that is due to population pressure results logically in the creation of a new localized sublineage rather than a new exogamous sib. On the basis of this argument Leach's interpretation of structural changes in the Botukebo village is definitely incorrect, lacks any factual support, seems to be based on a superficial reading, and is contradicted by a mass of ethnographic, demographic, and case material.

Having dealt with the nature of the change initiated by Awiitigaaj we can now inquire into the reasons for the social acceptance of this innovation. At the outset of the discussion we may dispose of Leach's interpretation of the reasons for the split of the Ijaaj-Enona sublineage. He claimed that, due to the fact that one of the major exogamous lineages had grown too large for convenience, fission in this major segment took place (1959: p. 1096). That this interpretation does not stand the test of empirical evidence is obvious from the following facts: the Ijaaj-Jamaina sublineage of the same confederacy is much larger than the one in question and has not undergone fission because of size. Nor did the large villages of Jotapuga, Ugapuga, and Mauwa in adjacent confederacies split, although each of them was more than three times as large as Botukebo. It is obvious that population pressure had nothing to do with the division of the village of the Ijaaj-Enona sublineage into incipient moieties.

In several tribes of New Guinea, abolition of the rules of exogamy and incest followed a marked depopulation trend (Bureau for Native Affairs 1957: pp. 15, 21). Although a sharp decrease of population was without question the reason for changes of incest regulations in those tribes, this solution is not applicable to our case, since the Ijaaj-Enona sublineage, and also the more inclusive Ijaaj-Gepouja lineage, have increased remarkably, rather than diminished, during the last 120 years.

Lowie (1920: pp. 157–162) and Murdock (1949: p. 137) regarded particular techniques of food production, types of residence, and rules of inheritance responsible for changes in forms of social organization. Although this statement is unquestionably correct for many tribal societies, it does not apply to the situation in Botukebo. If we bear in mind the remembered history of social change of this village and if we compare the culture patterns of the members of the Ijaaj-Enona sublineage with those of the rest of the inhabitants of the Kamu Valley or with those of the peoples of surrounding Kapauku regions, it is unquestionably clear that none of the factors mentioned can be considered responsible for the willingness of the Ijaaj-Enona people to accept Awiitigaaj's new legislation. In all these regions division of labor, techniques of food production, type of residence, and rules of inheritance are the same as in Botukebo, yet, according to several old informants of mine, there has been no change comparable to that I recorded in Botukebo. One possible exception is provided by a few members of the Adii sib who lived in the Pona Valley, south of the Kamu. However, far from being legalized behavior, the incestuous intrasib unions of these clansmen remained violations of the prevailing law. No headman comparable to Awiitigaaj elevated these exceptions to the status of legal rules. Finally, the recorded sequence of events in Botukebo shows that the incest violation and the subsequent changes in the law, as well as the development of "incipient moieties," preceded rather than followed the alterations in residence patterns.

In my original article I considered that social acceptance of the modified incest taboos had a political basis (Pospisil 1958b). Members of the Ijaaj and Pigome lineages were latecomers into the Kamu Valley. Approximately 120 years ago, after a natural drainage of the valley had occurred and its floor became suitable for cultivation, ancestors of the two lineages migrated from the adjacent Mapia and Paniai regions. They settled in the southeastern part of the Kamu Valley and claimed the vacant, flat, and only recently dried fertile land and slowly desiccating swamps. Their newly acquired territory was surrounded by political confederacies whose members looked with envy and hostility upon the usurpers of the land, who were regarded as thieves of the territory. Inevitably, battles ensued and the Ijaaj-Pigome Confederacy became intermittently involved in wars with their numerous neighbors. Marriage, as a consequence, presented a serious problem. Because the Ijaaj people far outnumbered their small Pigome and Dou lineage allies, in order to comply with the rules of sib exogamy, they had to marry the women of their hostile neighbors. In times of war such unions did not prove to be felicitous. The wives from the neighboring political units were of questionable loyalty. Many of them betrayed the war plans of their husbands to the enemy, or even deserted them, and their desertions became further causes of war. Of eleven wars in the Kamu Valley during the twenty years preceding 1954, five were fought because of desertion of wives from hostile confederacies whose members then refused to refund the bride price. Even when an Ijaaj girl was married to a traditional enemy, matters were not rosy for the newcomers. The brothers, fathers, and paternal parallel cousins of those girls were never sure of receiving the full amount of the stipulated bride price. Often their hostile in-laws managed, under the threat of violence, to obtain a substantial reduction from the originally agreed sum.

While war and political negotiations prevail at the interconfederational level, law and order are enforced within a confederacy. Consequently, an intraconfederacy and intrasib marriage virtually eliminates the possibility of causing war and eventual economic losses. In such a case no killing and violence results from a divorce, because a full return of the bride price is legally guaranteed. Similarly, it is very difficult to cheat on the amount of

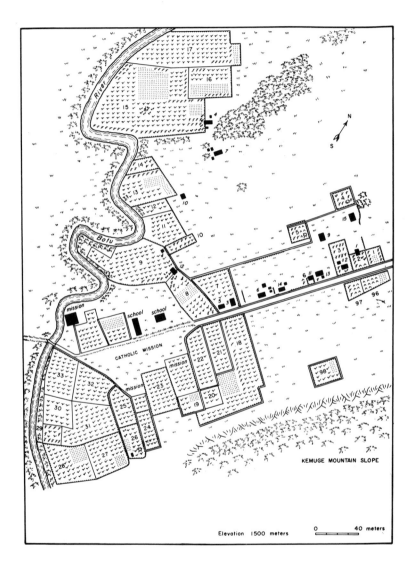

FIGURE 6. Botukebo Village and Gardens, 1959

bride price in an intraconfederational marriage. The headmen who administer the law are committed to keeping order within this political unit and
would regard such an action as a dangerous crime. Because of the political
problems, which made an interconfederacy marriage for an Ijaaj man most
insecure, and because of the fact that not enough women were available for
the Ijaaj men in the allied Pigome and Dou lineages, sib endogamy appeared
to be the logical answer to this particular political situation. This contention
is further supported by the fact that the Pigome and Dou people, who found
enough wives in the much more numerous Ijaaj lineages, firmly maintained
the traditional rules of exogamy and were utterly disinterested in the legislative products of Awiitigaaj's jural genius.

This political interpretation of the acceptance of the modified laws of
incest received additional convincing confirmation during my research in
1959. Since my first fieldwork in 1954–1955 the Kamu Valley has been
brought under administrative control by the Dutch government and the
whole region pacified. If my interpretation of 1958 was correct, this pacification and enforcement of law and order across the old boundaries of political
confederacies must have removed the cause for social acceptance of Awiitigaaj's innovations. Although the moiety system could meanwhile have been
formalized in terms of residence, there should have been some signs of
weakening observable within the new system. On the contrary, if an increase
of population were the cause of the abolition of sib exogamy (although this
proposition is contradicted by my structural analysis of the Kapauku society,
as presented above), the pacification of the area, introduction of modern
medical care, and the resulting acceleration of the population increase
should have not only upheld the moiety system and the concomitant legal
changes made by Awiitigaaj, it should even have intensified them. Indeed,
in 1959 my prediction of the changes in the residence patterns of the people
of the Ijaaj-Enona sublineage as well as in the village plan of Botukebo
materialized as postulated, on the basis of a questionnaire submitted in 1955.
My statement of 1958 that we could expect in the near future that Botukebo
village would be lineal, with a main street in front of the houses, became
literally true, as is apparent from Figure 6.

A survey and a systematic inquiry into the attitude toward Awiitigaaj's
innovation revealed that in 1959 as many as 55.32 percent of the adult and
adolescent males of the Ijaaj-Enona sublineage opposed the innovation and
regarded it as unjustified and even immoral. An additional 2.12 percent
would offer no opinion about the case; 10.64 percent gave Awiitigaaj's
changes only a qualified support ("I myself would not marry a *keneka,* but
would not punish others if they did"), and only 31.91 percent of the males
fully supported Awiitigaaj's legislation at that time. This represents quite a
loss of support, compared to the year 1955 when 57.5 percent of the
Botukebo men fully and wholeheartedly supported the new regulations of
incest and the resulting changes in the social structure.

In 1959 even Awiitigaaj, who was still publicly defending his legislative actions, in private seemed uncertain about the justification of his legal actions, probably because he already had ten wives and at his advanced age had lost interest in collecting additional specimens of female beauty. By 1959 his legislation indeed appeared to be unjustified and unnecessary when under the Dutch rule an Ijaaj man could safely marry a girl outside his own sib and confederacy. In spite of the decrease of popular support for laws allowing intrasib marriages, in 1955–1959 four of a total of fifty-nine marriages of the Ijaaj-Gepouja lineage members were concluded between partners belonging to the same (Ijaaj) sib. Thus the percentage of "incestuous" intrasib marriages had actually slightly increased, to 6.8 percent of the total. However, this does not affect my interpretation of the change, because three of these intrasib marriages were concluded *prior* to the pacification of the Kamu Valley area in 1956.

In 1961 I predicted, on the basis of these as well as other findings, that if the pacification of the Kamu Valley continued, sib exogamy would again be emphasized in the Ijaaj-Pigome Confederacy, the village plan would revert to an irregular pattern, and the moiety system, created by Awiitigaaj, would be abolished (Pospisil 1961). The formal aspects of Awiitigaaj's innovation would logically disintegrate as an immediate reaction to the failing popularity of his new law. The law itself, however, would persist longer, because the leaders—a minority of influential men such as Awiitigaaj, Ekajewaijokaipouga (the former confederacy headman), and Jokagaibo (the confederacy's headman since 1958)—were committed to it and could not tolerate that their marriages, or those of their close kin, be pronounced illegal or even criminal. The vested interest of the several leaders would thus keep the intrasib marriages permissible as long as these leaders kept their status, in spite of the adverse opinion of their followers.

The changes postulated in my paper of 1961 had indeed materialized by the time of my third research in 1962. Because of the impact of the pacification of the valley, and the stubborn support of the abolition of the taboo on intrasib marriages by the leaders and their immediate close kin and friends, the opinions of the natives concerning the support or rejection of Awiitigaaj's innovation became sharply defined. The category of individuals with no opinion and that of people who gave only qualified support to the legal change in 1959 (both comprising 12.76 percent of the adolescent and adult males of Botukebo) had disappeared by 1962. The former qualified or unqualified support of the abolition of the intrasib incest taboo diminished from 42.55 percent (in 1959) to 34.14 percent by 1962, all of which was unqualified. Consequently, a full 65.86 percent of adolescent and adult males of the Ijaaj-Enona sublineage wholeheartedly rejected abolition of the incest taboo and advocated its reinstatement. Of course, against the powerful clique of the headmen, the supporters of the intrasib marriage taboo proved still ineffective. Thus it happened, paradoxically enough, that

in spite of popular disapproval, three more intrasib marriages were concluded in the Ijaaj-Enona sublineage between 1959 and 1962. Indeed,
Ekajewaijokaipouga, who had formerly only advocated intrasib marriage,
but did not practice it, in this period selected a sibmate as his sixth wife.

In contrast to the persistence of the official recognition of intrasib
marriages as legal, the formalistic accessories of Awiitigaaj's legislation disintegrated very fast indeed. Since these were not regarded as crucial and their
abolition would not adversely affect intrasib marriages, Awiitigaaj did not
insist on a compulsory perpetuation of the moiety system and his lineal
village residential pattern. As can be seen in Figure 7, in 1962 his compact
lineal pattern disintegrated, and the community reverted to the old irregular
traditional Kapauku settlement. The moiety segmentation of the village was
not only disregarded but openly rejected by the majority of the Botukebo
residents; indeed, most of the younger people had virtually forgotten it.

This, of course, may not be the end of the story. The acculturation
situation, created by the arrival of the Indonesian administrators and Western missionaries, may provide new support for the abolition of sib exogamy.
While the Catholic missionaries may succeed in destroying the idea that
intrasib marriages are incestuous by proclaiming it an outmoded and sinful
pagan superstition, the Indonesian government officers, through their pacification activity, will certainly abrogate the death penalty for intrasib marriages—indeed they may punish the executioners as murderers. Enforcement of the native prohibition of intrasib marriages will consequently
become not only a religious sin but also a legal delict. Thus, ultimately, sib
exogamy may disappear from the Kapauku culture. When that time comes,
it will not occur as a consequence of Awiitigaaj's legalistic change but
because of the advance of civilization.

No matter what the ultimate outcome is, the data collected over a
period of nine years testify to the importance of the individual's role in legal
change and structural transformation of a tribal society. Therefore, in spite
of Leach's criticism and possible displeasure of some orthodox social anthropologists, I feel justified in reiterating my conclusion of 1958: "a volitional invention among primitives may not be as exceptional as has been
often assumed" (1958b: p. 837). Furthermore, the collected material documents the importance of the analysis of law for understanding basic changes
in the social structure of tribal societies. In this respect the importance of the
role of the techniques of food production, of technology in general, and of
rules of residence might have been overstated in the anthropological literature. Indeed, precise and systematic exposition of native law (so often lacking in anthropological analyses) may bring the study of the various types of
social structure into a new perspective and supply answers which are sought
in vain in those aspects of human culture that have been traditionally ex-
plored.

As far as Awiitigaaj's legislative activity is concerned, his accomplish-

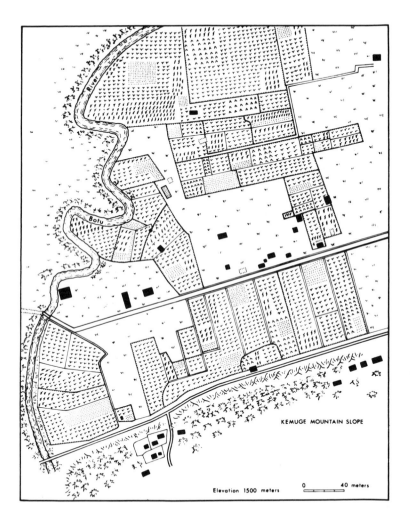

FIGURE 7. Botukebo Village and Gardens, 1962

ments, in addition to enabling a documentation of a purposive legislative attempt among a tribal people, show an interesting case of radical legal innovation of authoritarian nature, which, as time passed, slowly became internalized. Because of the pacification program enforced by the Dutch administration, the internalization process was halted and reversed. In 1959 what was already a "customary law" began to lose popular support, an extinction process set in, and pressure for reinstatement of sib exogamy became felt.

My final prediction is that this process will reverse its course again. This time, however, the abolition of sib exogamy rules will be due to externally imposed laws not to native legislation. That we do not have more cases like these in the literature is not because "primitive" people are qualitatively different from us. The reason lies in the brevity of the usual anthropological research, in the disinterest or lack of sophistication of the research worker in the area of law, and, perhaps most significantly in the fact that most anthropologists have studied "pacified natives" whose legal ways and political institutions have already been ruthlessly disrupted by the imposition of Western civilization. As this case shows, the process of internalization can be studied with an adequate degree of precision among tribal peoples. It yields data which allow for a reasonable degree of prediction—the heuristic value of any kind of science.

CHAPTER
SEVEN
JUSTICE

The popular Western conception of the main function of law has been "to mete out justice." The generally accepted view, as Lloyd observes, is "that law must be assimilated to justice and that law without justice is a mockery, if not a contradiction" (1966: p. 104). In many societies law is considered so closely related to justice that the ministry supervising the courts is called Ministry of Justice rather than Ministry of Law (France, Germany, Czechoslovakia, Zambia, etc.), and the courts themselves are regarded as institutions of justice rather than law.

Among the Lozi the king, as a supreme judge, was looked upon as a symbol of justice (Gluckman 1967: p. 329). Indeed, in precommunist Czechoslovakia the American cliché "law and order" is regarded as very odd, because what is important is achievement of justice through the administration of law, law itself being a means for achieving the "just" end. Until I came to the United States I had never heard the phrase "he is a law-abiding citizen." It is generally realized that law may be immoral or inhuman, and therefore blind compliance with it is nothing to be proud of. One has only to remember that Hitler himself was a law-abiding citizen and that most of the atrocities committed during his rule were strictly legal.

We may even go farther and speculate that in some sense justice is universal to all cultures. Accordingly, Allen states that "it needs no dialectic to maintain that there is in man a fundamental sense of justice which no law dare flagrantly transgress" and that man has to interpret law through his sense of discriminatory justice (1927: pp. 199, 232). To Aristotle, justice, inherent in man's conscience, was constant and universal while law, although derived from it, was changeable and appeared imperfect (Allen 1927: p. 233).

If we look beyond the Western cultural sphere we do find well-conceptualized ideas of justice provided with appropriate terms. To Koreans justice was synonymous with virtue (Hahm 1967: p. 40); Kapauku Papuans called it *uta-uta* ("half-half")—recalling the Western idea of symbolizing justice as a balance; the Lozi of Zambia call it *tukelo,* and their judges "are reluctant to take the view that theirs is only a court of law and not a court of justice or morals'' (Gluckman 1967: pp. 166, 177). Terms such as *uta-uta,* the French revolutionary *égalité,* and our *equity* suggest that the essence of justice is, or at least should be, equality of all members (citizens) of a society, but when one examines the cultures of the world one quickly finds that equality as a principle of universal justice is a myth.

Gluckman, for example, makes a statement to this effect about the Lozi (1967: p. 217). Plato, who thought that justice applied to things as well as to people, held that everything, including a person, has its proper sphere and that justice means conforming to that sphere—that every person is inherently adapted to a specific function (specific job) and a departure from this function (defined by custom) meant injustice (Lloyd 1966: p. 106). This, of course, represents another extreme position, namely, basic inequality. Lloyd presented the problem much more adequately. His position is applicable not only to Western civilization but also to non-Western states and tribal societies. His basic observation is that equality pertains not to all people indiscriminately but to persons ''classified as belonging to the same category,'' such as adults, minors, mentally sick, citizens, fathers, males, and nobles. Formal justice, to Lloyd, means ''equality of treatment in accordance with the classification laid down by the rules'' (1966: p. 107). It is obvious then that because rules change from society to society, and so do their categories of people, justice will not have a single, universal substantive denominator.

Since justice is a very complex category of concepts, and different ideas of substantive as well as procedural nature have been associated with it, it is obvious that the term is applied to a diversity of types of social phenomena. In his classification of legal thought Max Weber was actually classifying types of justice systems. When we look at his classification as summarized by Rheinstein (1967: pp. XLII–XLIII), it is apparent that Weber was guided primarily by *a priori* logical categories rather than by a scheme of types whose heuristic value was derived from, or subsequently tested on various legal systems, especially of non-Western origin. His basic dichotomy distinguishes irrational systems of thought (i.e., concepts of justice not guided by general rules) from rational systems (i.e., concepts of justice guided by general rules).

Although this dichotomy by itself seems unobjectionable, its subdivisions and especially their classification into the two basic categories certainly are. This is because Weber neglected the basic difference between the justice of the fact and the justice of the law (see Llewellyn and Hoebel 1961: p. 304). While factual justice inquires into the specific factual background of a dispute in trying to determine whether the defendant's or the plaintiff's statements are true (so that they could be used for an objective formulation of the *obligatio*), the justice of law pertains mainly to the question of whether the law (be it an abstract rule—*lex*—or a principle incorporated in a judicial precedent) is just in itself, and how far its provisions may be applicable to the factual background of a specific dispute to be adjudicated. In Weber's classification this basic qualitative dichotomy is overridden. As a consequence it happens that his "irrational" category is subdivided into irrational-formal "guided primarily by sacred traditions [beyond the control of human reason] without finding therein a clear basis for the decision of concrete cases" (Weber 1967: p. 351)[1] i.e., employing ordeals, oracles, etc., and "irrational-substantive" guided by reaction to the individual case in a nonformalistic intuitive way, such as the *Khadi* justice (Weber 1967: pp. 351, 352). In this way Weber grouped together a category concerned with factual justice (irrational-formal) and a category of "the justice of the law and adjudication" (his irrational-substantive category).

The second part of Weber's dichotomy does not fare much better. It is again divided into formal and substantive subcategories. The first is further subdivided into "extrinsical or empirical justice," which refers to the facts of the precedents and to interpretation of the facts of the case to be adjudicated (Weber 1967: pp. 351, 352, 354), and into a "logically formal" justice, which expresses its rules by the use of abstract concepts that constitute a complete consistent system without internal contradiction—in Weber's words, which uses "rational adjudication on the basis of rigorously formal legal concepts" (1967: p. 351).[2] The substantive subcategory on the other hand, has no subdivisions. It incorporates those systems of "rational" legal thought (justice) guided by ideological (ethical, moral, or religious) principles (values) that are external to the field of law itself (1967: p. 351). As a result, the second part of Weber's dichotomy is a category that combines as subcategory a type of "the justice of the facts" (empirical justice), with two other subcategories derived from the sphere of "the justice of the law" (Weber's logically formal and rational substantive categories).

Because my cross-cultural research revealed that the basic categorization of justice into that of the facts and that of the law (as discussed by Llewellyn and Hoebel 1961: p. 304) is heuristically valuable by lending itself to meaningful applications to the diverse systems of justice, I reject Weber's basically philosophical conceptualization in favor of the formal, more anthropologically oriented dichotomy. A most intriguing evidence of the cross-cultural applicability of the latter dichotomy of justice is the fact that the Kapauku Papuans themselves make a similar distinction. The establishment of the factual evidence for a legal case (justice of the fact) they call *boko petai* (literally "to seek the vital substance"), while the dispensation of legal justice in the adjudication of a specific case they call *boko duwai* (literally

---

[1]". . . welche in erster Linie sich an geheiligte Traditionen bindet, den konkreten aus dieser Quelle nicht eindeutig entscheidbaren Fall aber erledigt . . ." (Weber 1922: p. 662)

[2]"Der 'rationalen' Rechtsfindung auf der Basis streng formaler Rechtsbegriffe. . . ." (Weber 1922: p. 662)

"to cut the vital substance"). Both activities were, of course, part of litigation and the primary tasks of the *tonowi,* the Kapauku legal authority.

JUSTICE OF THE FACTS

In order to do justice to a legal case the authority has to make an effort to establish the objective factual basis of the dispute in order to formulate an *obligatio* that will become part of his decision. He has to investigate the nature of the controversy and the claims made by the plaintiff and the defendant. This is usually the easier part. It is much harder to establish objectively the facts relevant to the case, and it is usually difficult to decide the truth of the conflicting claims of the litigants—to find out what actually happened and whether the plaintiff has a case or not. This requires ingenuity, and experience on the part of the judge, and also his integrity and impartiality and a serious attempt at objectivity in the evaluation of the evidence (for tribal societies see esp. Pospisil 1958a: pp. 285 ff.; Llewellyn and Hoebel 1961: pp. 306 ff.; Gluckman 1967: p. 97). He often has to be suspicious of all the evidence, probe it carefully, and in his cross-examination appear to assume that the witnesses are lying and that both the defendant and plaintiff are possibly guilty of wrongdoing at least to some extent (Pospisil 1958a: p. 286; Gluckman 1967: p. 96). It is often claimed, and is probably often true, that in tribal societies many of the facts are general knowledge, which helps the judge in a way that his colleague in civilized society might envy (Llewellyn and Hoebel 1961: p. 306). Nevertheless one should not overestimate this general knowledge and assume that an authority in a tribal society faces a relatively easy task in establishing evidence. As we shall see, his problems are often as complex as those of a modern Western judge.

Establishing the factual basis of a legal case may take a secular (empirical and logical) and/or a supernatural form (nonempirical and often nonlogical). The secular establishment of evidence almost universally employs the questioning of witnesses. The judge, although suspecting that he is being lied to, probes carefully and looks for inconsistencies in the statements, compares them with the testimony of other witnesses and with the already established facts (Pospisil 1958a: p. 285; Llewellyn and Hoebel 1961: pp. 306–307; Gluckman 1967: pp. 111, 138). Both tribal and civilized people differentiate clearly between direct evidence and hearsay and also between a firm and specific statement and a vague assertion (Pospisil 1958a: p. 285; Llewellyn and Hoebel 1961: p. 307; Gluckman 1967: p. 393). As Gluckman writes about the Barotse: "Hearing and seeing the quarrel and the fight are good, hearing about them is not" (1967: p. 93). Also the personality of the witness and his relation to the defendant are almost universally considered important for establishing credibility. American or European lawyers would be astonished at the "irrelevant" questions about the diligence of a witness, the care with which he works his fields, and his behavior in his household, topics which are discussed at length at a Kapauku "court hearing." Nevertheless this is part of an important activity which, as I would put it, establishes for the judge a "credibility profile" of the witness. In 3 of the 132 legal cases I collected the Kapauku rejected testimony because it was either vague or given by individuals with dubious reputation (Pospisil 1958a: p. 285). As in our civilization, an unrelated witness is regarded as more valuable and objective than a close relative of either of the litigants (Pospisil 1958a: pp. 285 ff.; Gluckman 1967: pp. 93, 405).

It is usually claimed that a trial in a civilized or tribal society starts with the judge's cross-examination of the witnesses (Gluckman 1967: pp. 82, 93). However, I suspect that like the Kapauku many other tribal authorities have an additional important means to arrive at the truth of the case. This technique, at least among the Kapauku, almost always preceded the formal questioning of the witnesses: the authority arrived at a scene of dispute and patiently and quietly, without uttering a word, listened for hours to violent quarreling, accusations, and claims of the litigants and their witnesses. Only after a significant lapse of time would the headman begin a systematic and more formal cross-examination. Thus he has an advantage over a judge in a formal court hearing of the Barotse or Western society: He can compare cautious testimony of the witnesses and litigants, elicited by his formal questions, with statements made in the heat of the initial arguments when truth often slips unwittingly from the lips of a witness in a rage.

Testimony is also scrutinized by judges by means of what Gluckman correctly called the stereotyped behavior of a "reasonable man" or "reasonable adulterer, thief, etc." (1967: pp. 83, 136, 137). The culture is likely to impose certain standardized reactions upon liars, adulterers, and thieves that are so stereotyped that the judge "knows" who is lying or who behaves like a typical wrongdoer. As Gluckman more specifically puts it: "She behaved as a woman in adultery should behave," or as he points out, among the Lozi only a whore, charged with illicit sex relations, would boldly look at the judge (1967: p. 136). By this test of "reasonableness" and customary interpretation of actions the judges impute not only guilt but also intention and motivation (1967: p. 153). Although the Kapauku do not have a special term for a "reasonable man" as the Lozi do, nevertheless their references to "typical, customary, prudent and moral behavior" in a given situation, and their use of the repetitive tense aspect (see above in Chapter Three) amount virtually to the same phenomenon.

Witnesses, of course, may be of different kinds. In our society we have voluntary witnesses and those who have to appear *sub poena*—people forced onto the witness stand against their will. If the reader recalls my discussion of the Kapauku authority and their concept of freedom, it is only logical to conclude that the Kapauku do not employ witnesses who are forced to testify. Of the 132 legal cases collected during my first research, in 39 most of the necessary evidence was established by voluntary witnesses. As in our civilization and in other tribal societies (Llewellyn and Hoebel 1961: pp. 306–307; Gluckman 1967: p. 107) the Kapauku also secured evidence from counterspies (in one case), paid informers (in one case), and experts and special investigators (in one case).

A special type of testimony is a confession by a defendant. It can be volunteered, induced, or secured by force—a special type of the last would be torture. The latter method as the reader may recall, is an art especially employed in more advanced civilizations, by medieval inquisitions that used crude mechanical means, or by the modern brainwashing methods of dictatorships that rely on delicate psychological and chemical methods with such masterful results that the accused publicly confesses to everything his tormentors desire (e.g., political processes in the Nazi Reich and in the Soviet Union and her satellites). The courts of many tribal societies have also resorted to torture (of course, only of the crude physical type) with desired results (Gluckman 1967: p. 401), although certainly not matching the fantastic confessions of Communists like Kameniev or Zinoviev.

Among the Kapauku, a confession, although never elicited by force, was often volunteered by the defendants, who sooner or later, in accordance with the accumulation of direct or circumstantial evidence, admitted their faults or crimes. Admission of guilt did not have to take the form of an overt confession. Not responding to an accusation or escaping from the confederacy territory was regarded as proof that the charge brought to the "court" by the plaintiff was correct. In my 132 legal cases, 25 defendants openly confessed, 3 did not respond to accusations, and 5 escaped from justice. As a contrast, an emotional and repetitive denial of charges by an accused Kapauku is considered a testimony, and sometimes it becomes so convincing that the prosecution is halted. There are, of course, also cases when little formal quizzing of witnesses or confession is needed—when the crime was committed in the presence of an authority or when the defendant was caught *in flagrante delicto* by several individuals (25 cases in my Kapauku sample; Pospisil 1958a: pp. 285–286).

Instances unfortunately do exist in which direct evidence is not available. In these cases circumstantial evidence is usually secured through investigation of the scene of the crime, inspection of the *corpus delicti,* inspection of the disputed property (e.g., of garden boundaries, trees, crops, pigs, artifacts), or through investigation by experts of the tracks that a criminal left in mud or in soft ground. Since most of the tribal people, especially in the tropics, go barefooted, spoors may be read by experts whose findings are as reliable as our dactyloscopy (Llewellyn and Hoebel 1961: pp. 306–308; Gluckman 1967: pp. 105–107). In my Kapauku sample there were 17 cases in which such types of circumstantial evidence had to be secured (Pospisil 1958a: p. 286).

One more method of securing facts remains to be discussed. It is a category to which the courts of some societies resort in case of a special type of alleged crime or in others, when it is felt that secular (empirical and/or logical) evidence is impossible to obtain. This nonrational but usually formal procedure "makes use of supernatural powers" which are believed to reveal the factual proof. It usually takes the form of an ordeal, oracle, or self-curse. Ordeal, a submission of the accused to pain or danger over which, it is believed, the supernatural has control, is most common in Africa and some parts of Asia. In some societies, such as the Azande of the upper Nile (Evans-Pritchard 1937: pp. 261–262) and the Akamba of central Africa (Lindblom 1916: pp. 155–164), it is used quite commonly, whereas in others such as the Kuba of the Republic of Congo, Ibo of Nigeria, or Lozi of Zambia, it is limited to only a few specific crimes such as sorcery or witchcraft (Vansina 1965: p. 114; Forde 1965: p. 91; Gluckman 1967: p. 97). It often involves swallowing some sort of poison (fruit containing strychnine, for example), licking red-hot iron, extracting objects from boiling water, or walking through fire. Nonvomiting and blisters are often interpreted as the revelation of guilt. Ordeal as well as the self-curse often do work objectively, as Lindblom states, in the sense that the guilty or the lying individual either confesses or refuses to undertake the ordeal, or is betrayed by his fear to the medicine man who through practice has become an expert psychologist (1916: pp. 162–163).

Oath, a solemn calling upon a deity or a spirit to witness that truth is spoken, or self-curse, a solemn exhortation of the supernatural to punish the speaker, usually in a specified way, if he lies, has much broader application and is used more widely than ordeal. The self-curse or oath may be a simple utterance (as among the Lozi; Gluckman 1967: p. 101), or a formal swearing on a specified artifact such as a spear (as among the Acholi of the Nilotic Sudan; Seligman 1932: p. 129) or a sacred object (as among the Akamba of central Africa; Lindblom 1916: pp. 155–156). While both self-curse and oath are believed to bring down supernatural punishment upon a liar, oracle functions only as a medium through which the supernatural reveals the truth; in itself it does not adversely affect the accused (see, for example, Seligman 1932: pp. 527–530, for the Azande of the upper Nile). In many tribes employing supernaturally evoked evidence, it is sharply distinguished from the secular evidence, the latter often being considered more reliable (as among the Cheyenne; Llewellyn and Hoebel 1961: pp. 227, 307). The reader should be cautioned, however, against an opinion that supernaturally derived evidence is necessarily an attribute of a primitive society. Whereas in the Western civilization we still employ oath (and the charge of perjury), the secularly oriented Kapauku rely exclusively upon secular evidence.

To summarize, then, justice of the facts deals with the factual background upon which a decision is going to be passed; it is a question of how adequate and objective the fact finding of the court was and, in my terminology, how far the actual facts (as they objectively existed) match those assumed to be true which enter into a jural decision in the form of an *obligatio;* or in Lloyd's words, how far is the imputation of guilt or innocence "contrary to the fair assessment of the evidence" (1966: p. 115). The factual justice, of course, does not deal only with the statements of the parties to the dispute and those of the witnesses, but also with the problem of fairness and impartiality or corruption (through bribes, intimidation, expectation of favors) of the deciding authority (judge, court, chief, headman, etc.).

JUSTICE OF THE LAW

Whereas justice of the facts inquires into the factual background of the case in order to establish objective truth, justice of the law deals with much more complex and subtle problems. Formally it tries to enforce the principle of impartiality—of "treating like cases in the same way"; in other words it deals with the problems of adjudication. It also turns against principles of the positive law, whether they appear in the form of explicit abstract rules or abstractions implicit in precedents, and asks whether the principles themselves are just.

Justice in Adjudication

Problems of justice of this type center around impartiality and the humane application of law. It is the so-called formal justice which deals with the first of the two problems. Impartiality in application presupposes existence of legal principles (derived from rules or precedents) of a general (abstract) character, which are categorically applied by the judge to relevant, alike cases—the very idea of treating like as like (Lloyd 1966: pp. 108–109). If this type of justice is violated it results in the case being decided contrary to the pertinent legal principle, either because its relevancy was ignored on purpose (owing to corruption of the authority) or because the factual base of the case was misunderstood and the decision was based on another, not pertinent principle intended for another kind of situation. To do justice to a case in a formal way the judge must dispassionately and rationally scrutinize the evidence and use his legal skill to apply to it the proper provision of law. It is interesting to note that, psychologically speaking, males should make much better (just) judges then females. Kohlberg's experiments show that boys are "more rules- or justice-oriented," whereas girls react more emotionally out of personal sympathy and are not so ready to think in terms of abstract principles (1963: p. 311). If Kohlberg's findings can be generalized then the various cultures including our own civilization should be indeed happier to have gentlemen than ladies as judges.

Llewellyn and Hoebel distinguish between primitive and legal justice. By primitive justice they mean "the 'rightness' of a claim which rests on going practice," while a legal justice (in my terminology here "formal justice'') to them signifies "a claim which rests on demand for repetition in a new case of what was done officially before" (1961: p. 305). If I reflect upon the "most primitive" people that I have investigated I have to confess that they were not interested in "primitive justice" at all because they did not regard "going practice"—the actual behavior of the majority of people—as normative. Furthermore, they did not even hold in esteem the formal type of justice, if by this we mean their insistence that their rules should always be applied indiscriminately to the pertinent cases. Quantitatively I have demonstrated that of 176 disputes, in only 87 did the decisions conform to the abstract rules (Pospisil 1958a: p. 286). If, however, by formal justice we mean what Llewellyn and Hoebel identified above as legal justice, then such a concept is indeed relevant. Argument about a precedent was always to them pertinent and meaningful and ignoring it was *peu* ("bad").

The second problem of what I call justice in adjudication deals with a consideration of a particular case per se; one may call it a humane consideration and interpretation of law, "tempered to the individual case." In the juristic literature this type of justice has often been called "equity." Justice has usually been achieved in the various societies "by conferring a certain discretionary power to interpret the laws in the spirit of equality rather than insisting on their strict letter" (Lloyd 1966: p. 111). Thus equity, although always "a vital factor in law" (Allen 1927: p. 236), is a sort of antithesis to formal justice "by shaping itself to the individual case." From this point of view many decisions based upon formal justice may be deemed unjust and vice versa (Lloyd 1966: p. 117).

In our Western civilization equity, next to the doctrine of Natural Law (discussed above under "Form of Law," and also below), assumed an important role in the field of judge's justice. Whereas the doctrine of Natural Law remains a theory chiefly affecting only the legislative process, "equity in its relation to the common law, realized concretely in practice that supremacy which natural law claimed abstractly over the positive law" (Stone 1950: p. 228). Rules of equity, then, were applied directly to legal cases, and their sole function was propagation of justice. Equity was conceived as a "set of principles, invested with a higher sacredness than those of the original law, and demanding application independently of the consent of any external body" (Maine 1963: p. 27).

In ancient Rome administration of equity was first in the hands of the praetor who through his *cognitio* (power to issue *decreta* to the judge) intervened in certain cases, deciding these on the basis of justice rather than formally according to the precedent or statute. Later in the development of the Roman Empire, the emperor's decision became the source of equity. In neither case, however, was there a formal equity court distinct from the regular court of law. Centuries later, equity law developed in England where, until 1875, it constituted a "body of rules existing by the side of the original civil law, founded on distinct principles and claiming incidentally to super-

sede the civil law in virtue of a superior sanctity inherent in those principles"
(Maine 1963: p. 27). Unlike Rome, until 1875 equity rules in England were
administered by special judicial bodies called Courts of Equity. Both in Rome
and in England the ultimate source of equity was considered to be the
conscience and reasoning of the ruler, whether an emperor and his official
praetor or the king and his official chancellor (Buckland 1911: pp. 9–11;
Maitland 1936: pp. 3–7; Stone 1950: p. 228; Maine 1963: pp. 64, 68).

As has been stated above, in ancient Rome it was already felt that
ordinary law, although capable of maintaining order, was inadequate to do
justice to all cases. There were circumstances, such as a minor's loss of a
right, due to his lack of experience, or a loss due to fear of the defendant
(*metus*), or because of fraud of the opponent (*dolus*), or loss of a right due
to a pardonable absence of the party, which the ordinary law (to be specific,
the *intentio* part of the *actio*—the procedural formula applied to a given
case) did not take into consideration. The judge, well aware of the injustice
which his decision would create, was nevertheless powerless and had to
follow the "letter of the law"—the formal procedure of the *actio*. To allevi-
ate such circumstances and do justice to the given case the party to the
dispute had recourse to the magistrate *cum imperio* (and to his *cognitio*—
power to intercede in the name of equity in a legal process) in the form of
a *postulatio,* a petition. In this formal petition the party requested, on the
basis of recognized equity, that the effects of the civil action be set aside in
order that true justice be done. The most usual requests involved *restitutio
in integrum* (restitution to the former legal status, prior to a legal act whose
justice but not legality, was questioned), or *missio in possessionem* (award-
ing possession of property to a litigant). In these cases the praetor did not
preside over a special court of equity; he simply issued a *decretum* to the
iudex (judge) who implemented its provisions in his decision-making process.

Thus civil law and the provisions of Roman equity were administered
in their final stage by the same person, the regular judge. Later, the Roman
emperor administered equity himself and in this activity displayed remarkable freedom when, in name of justice, he "both disregarded legal principle
and overruled his legal advisers" (Buckland 1911: p. 12; also Gaius 1932:
pp. 19–20; Papinianus 1932: p. 18; Paulus 1932: pp. 16, 18, 21, 22; Ulpianus 1932: pp. 15–19, 22; Sommer 1933: pp. 63–65; Maine 1963: pp.
54–66). Although some praetors and emperors did create equity themselves,
in most instances principles of Roman equity had their ultimate origin in the
opinions of the famous jurisconsults (Buckland 1911: p. 8).

Affected by the Roman tradition, the British legal system recognized
the problems of justice and equity as being of paramount importance in the
administration of law (Bryce 1901: p. 599). Actually, this problem was
regarded so significant that the British went farther in this respect than
classical Rome and established special Courts of Equity. These courts slowly

evolved from the agenda of the chancellor, the prime minister of the king. The chancery had not only the duty to issue writs to plaintiffs so that court action could be initiated, but the chancellor himself had to deal with many petitions to the king for his justice. During the fourteenth century the delegation of the king's judicial power to the chancellor became so notorious that people addressed their petitions directly to the chancellor. As in Rome, these petitions for equity were based upon the claim that justice in the particular cases could not be obtained through the normal legal procedure because it did not take into consideration problems like poverty or the low status of the party to the dispute, his youth or old age, his illness, his opponent's influence and treachery, and so on. Gradually a formalized procedure developed whereby the defendant was called *sub poena* to the chancery and had to answer under oath questions pertaining to the content of the petition. Although the chancellor originally dealt also with common law, he had to abandon this practice and specialize on equity provisions related to uses (later abolished by Henry VIII), trusts, breach of confidence, frauds, and accidental loss of documents.

Until the end of the sixteenth century the chancellors were usually bishops, and their judicial agenda was therefore, in content as well as procedure, heavily influenced by the canon law. Later, "with the idea of a law of nature in their minds, they decided cases without much reference to any written authority, now making use of some analogy drawn from the common law, and now of some great maxim of jurisprudence which they have borrowed from the canonists or the civilians" (Maitland 1936: pp. 8–9). Toward the end of the sixteenth century the procedure, power, and competence of the Court of Chancery became solidified and in James I's time the rulings of the chancellor's court superseded those of common law. However, the chancellor in his verdicts did not annul decisions of the regular courts on the basis of their nonvalidity; he maintained only that for reasons particular to the case, the enforcement of the common law judgment would be unjust—not equitable.

By the eighteenth century barristers began to specialize in practicing before the chancellor, and thus a chancery bar formed itself. Administration of justice through rulings of specialized courts of equity continued until the end of the third quarter of the nineteenth century when, through the Judicature Acts of 1873 and 1875, they (as well as other traditional courts) were abolished and equity became the affair of regular judges, who began to administer its provisions together with common law. If provisions of the two systems clash, the Judicature Act (1873, 25th section) claims explicitly that "the rules of equity shall prevail" (Maitland 1936: p. 16). However, equity has always been regarded in theory as well as in practice as complementary to and not conflicting with common law; it has not been a legal system of itself. Rather, equity was an addendum to the British law, a formalized vehicle of justice (Maitland 1936: esp. pp. 17–19).

There are, of course, avenues to justice in a specific legal case other than through the formalized rules and procedures of equity. Since not all situations that may arise in actual life are treated in legal rules and precedents or, even if so, because alleviating or aggravating circumstances are not anticipated by the legislator or are not present in the various precedents, a blind application of legal principles might do unreasonable harm to either party to the dispute. Therefore, judges have to have some secure and predictable way to adjudicate questionable cases equitably. One solution to this problem is to apply the standard of "the reasonable man." Norms of general reasonableness, particular to specific cultures and referring to the ideals of the social status and of the roles of the parties to the dispute, are applied by the authorities to the adjudicated cases, and the actual behavior of the parties is assessed against and judged by these standards (Gluckman 1967: pp. 134, 159). These norms, to be sure, are not deposited in any codex. Rather, they are part of the "common sense" of the people.

Gluckman points out that among the Lozi there are actually two standards for behavior. One is that of *mutu yangana,* "the sensible man," and the other is that of *mutu yalukile,* "the upright man" (1967: pp. 125–126). While the standard of the upright man is an ideal toward which people should strive, the standard of the sensible or reasonable man is the minimum of correct behavior expected of everyone and, of course, demanded by law (1967: p. 128). Consequently, a Lozi man behaves legally if his behavior falls between the minimal permissible standard of a reasonable man and the ideal standard of the upright (moral) man. Gluckman considers that this idea of the reasonable man is indigenous among the Lozi and suspects that it is widespread in other tribal societies (1967: p. 161). To check on this claim in my own field experience I have to agree that the Kapauku did have two marginal standards; their *me enaa* (a good man) may be compared with the Lozi upright man, and their repetitive-obligatory tense aspects (marked by a verbal suffix -*ja*) is their minimal permissible standard—the action of their "reasonable man." *Kou dani ko te tija, kou dani peu* ("this way one does not [should not] act, this way it is wrong") is a phrase which one hears in almost every sentence of a Kapauku headman adjudicating a dispute.

In many modern civilizations, as well as tribal societies it has been recognized that *summum ius* meant ultimately *summa iniuria,* and, consequently, justice of an individual case has been made possible either through looseness in the abstract rules (in which case the judge is permitted to legislate) or by a virtual absence of rules. Looseness in the codes of abstract rules is achieved by including in the text words whose meaning may change from time to time and from case to case. Examples of this means of achieving justice are the ambiguous terms found in legal codes of continental Europe or the law of the Lozi (Gluckman 1967: pp. 202, 313): "with due care," "negligence," "in due time," "reasonable doubt," "reasonable person," et cetera. Thus the German, Austrian, and Czechoslovakian law, for example, although employing rigor in the rules and definitions of their concepts, defined some concepts so "relatively" that a judge could inject justice into a given case. Also, the rigidity of the rules has been modified by the incorporation into the codices of a series of precisely defined alleviating and aggravating circumstances. As a contrast, classical Romans and Cheyenne Indians, who did not employ many abstract rules, achieved through their "intuitive juristic precision" both well-integrated and flexible systems (Llewellyn and Hoebel 1961: pp. 310–313).

In the emphasis upon justice in individual cases, societies may, of course, reach quite an extreme, an anomalous situation in which "law" becomes unpredictable and thus actually ceases to qualify for its title. In other words, too much equity and consideration of hardship may lead to legal uncertainty and general insecurity in a society (Lloyd 1966: p. 111), or at least justice "may blur down into mushy sentimentality" (Llewellyn and Hoebel 1961: p. 308). Law and justice do not fare much better if the courts are influenced by public opinion, based in irrational feelings "instigated or guided by party leaders or by press" (Weber 1967: p. 356).

Consideration of the offender as a "whole person"—as an individual bearing a specific status which should not be ignored (and evidence thereof, although in appearance irrelevant to the delict, should not be disregarded) —is admitted as evidence without serious handicap to the predictability of law among peoples such as Kapauku, Cheyenne, and Lozi (Pospisil 1958a: pp. 254–255; Llewellyn and Hoebel 1961: p. 303; Gluckman 1967: p. 95). In Korea, however, with its Confucian legal tradition, the idea of justice for the individual became exaggerated to the point of being detrimental to law. "The Koreans did not think it feasible or proper to apply legal rules to everyone without regard to his particular worth and circumstances. They knew no two situations could be identical—Koreans rather followed the Confucian way of taking a man's status and merits into account" (Hahm 1967: pp. 40–41). Their judges were neither bound by precedent nor by abstract rules. This emphasis upon the particular nature of a given case and refusal to apply more categorical abstract legal principles led consequently to a general decadence of law and respect for it. In Hahm's words: "If the people cannot calculate in advance with some certainty what the court will do in a given situation, no one can be expected to rely on such justice" (1967: p. 41). Although consideration of the particulars of an individual case and a just solution tailored to it is certainly desirable, "an extreme form of 'particularistic justice' that obtained in Korea resulted in ultimate negation of justice itself" (Hahm 1967: p. 41).

Justice of the Principles of Law

Aside from the questions of "factual justice" and those of "justice in adjudication," a much more fundamental problem has intrigued legal scholars probably from the birth of Western civilization in Mesopotamia. The question arises whether the principles of law (contained in the enforced rules or abstracted from legal precedents—decisions) per se are just. In other words, the focus of attention and inquiry shifts here from adjudication of a particular case to the legal precepts, and ultimately to the legal system as a whole. What happens is that "the modern view recognizes positive law alone, but seeks to find in it and through it the permanent ideal concept of justice" (Berolzheimer 1929: p. 9). Since this field of inquiry into justice seems to be the most glamorous and, at the same time, allows for creative thinking and even for speculation, it is not surprising that it became the favorite of philosophers and social scientists. One may, of course, avoid all the philosophizing by embracing the extremist position of Hobbes and claim that the "standard of justice is the law itself"—that whatever it provides is ipso facto just (Hobbes 1907: p. 178), or one may take a completely relativistic position and dissolve the question of justice by stating that an unjust law is "a law, which, valid in itself, conflicts with the scale of values by which we choose to judge it" (Lloyd 1966: p. 117).

Of course, most philosophers and social scientists have not been satisfied with "solutions" as simple as these and have inquired into the matter of the justice of the principles of law in two ways. One group of scholars tried to concentrate upon the content of the legal precepts and thus investigated what has been called "substantive justice"; the other group deemed this approach fallacious and concentrated upon the legal process, thus creating a field of "procedural justice." Both groups tried to find some universally valid principles of justice that would either serve as a measure of the validity of positive law or make justice into an analytical concept with cross-cultural applicability. That this might be feasible was encouraged by some parallels of concepts pertaining to justice, such as, for example, those described for the Lozi by Gluckman (1967: p. 205).

Substantive Justice. Substantive justice has been defined by Lloyd as "that scale of values which, on whatever basis, we choose to accept as providing the criterion by which we judge all human rules of conduct, whether legal or non-legal, as being good or bad, just or unjust" (1966: p. 118).

Natural Law. Traditionally, in Western civilization the thinking, philosophizing, and writing on substantive justice has been dominated for millennia by one single theory—that of Natural Law. Until the time of Bentham no matter what school of philosophers and jurists contemplated the elusive problem of just law and correct adjudication of legal cases, the basic tenets of this theory have consistently been accepted as self-evident and incorporated into the words of the juridical scholars to such an extent that the present-day anthropologist may rightly regard the theory of Natural Law as constituting the folk theory of justice of Western civilization. Protagonists of the status quo in political life used these tenets in support of their threatened position only to be confronted by revolutionaries utilizing the same ideas for their diametrically opposed aims. Thus the established Church used the doctrine of Natural Law in a conservative sense through the writings of Thomas Aquinas (especially *Summa Theologica*), while "in its revolutionary phase natural law was in the hands of opponents of the established order" (Stone 1950: p. 220), who regarded as a " 'self-evident' fact that men were inalienably endowed with the rights to life, liberty, and pursuit of happiness" (Stone 1950: p. 229). In this way Natural Law formed, for example, the ethical and ideological basis for the French, American, and even socialist revolutions (Barker 1957: pp. xlvi–xlix). In such revolutions, according to Gierke, Natural Law

> served as a pioneer in preparing the transformation of human life; it forged the intellectual arms for the struggle of new social forces; it disseminated ideas which, long before they even approached realization, formed admittance into the thought of influential circles, and became, in that way, the object of practical effort. (Gierke 1957: p. 35)

In conservative times, on the other hand, after revolutions had evened out differences between social change and established political ideologies, Natural Law worked as a conservative force, adjusting its ideals to the existing institutional structure and thus providing a justification for its perpetuation.

As discussed earlier, the conception of Natural Law most likely originated in the Near East, from which it was brought to Greece. It finally became part of the Western *Weltanschauung* (world view), and as such it was presumed to inject stability into the ever-changing world—an inherent purpose into the progression of history. This world view held that the universe together with human society was dominated by intrinsic laws, laws that produced harmony in Nature and that emanated from things—animals, man, and human society—at the point of their fullest development. All disturbances of this harmony were regarded as violations of this law and ascribed to deviations caused, in the field of jural law, by the legal personnel administering the particular positive laws of the various countries. According to Aristotle, one should distinguish the latter laws from that which is common and "according to nature," which statement, according to Barker, implies "the idea of a common law which is natural to all humanity" (1957: p. xxxiv). This Natural Law has been regarded as immanent in the constitution of man, a potentiality which unfolds and reveals itself with his final development. Thus Natural Law is thought of as growing with the ever-increasing civilization of man and remaining perpetually adequate and applicable (Barker 1957: p. xxxv).

Specifically, the Stoics believed that Natural Law had as its origin the reason common to all men (Barker 1957: p. xxxv), a reason that later was believed by Cicero to be unchangeable and eternal. It is an application of this reason to the commands and prohibitions of positive law which formulates the tenets of Natural Law (Cicero 1967: p. 128; 1745: p. 41). In the Roman conception Natural Law, as a principle of "humane interpretation" of positive law by iudex and jurisconsult, was conceived as timeless, universal, and greatest at the culmination of man's development—as a recovery of a lost perfection—the natural state of man (Maine 1963: pp. 44, 68). In the later theorizing of the medieval church Natural Law was also supposed to have been fully developed at the moment of mankind's creation, and since that time human regulatory institutions had deteriorated in the sense that the positive law enacted in the various Western societies progressively deviated from the God-given wisdom incorporated in true human reason (Barker 1957: p. xxxvii).

For Thomas Aquinas *lex naturalis* was not created by man's thought but *discovered* by "man's divine faculty of reason, as it soared to apprehend the purpose of God's will and the rule of His Reason" (Barker 1957: p. xxxviii). Even in modern times this emphasis upon discovering Natural Law through pure and correct intuitive contemplation and through proper application of "man's reason" to the "social nature of man" has been adhered to by many lawyers (Stone 1950: p. 221). Strangely enough, even some anthropologists subscribed to the ideas of human nature and to something which approaches Natural Law when in 1966 they voted for an antiwar resolution which claimed that "These methods of warfare [e.g., use of napalm, bombing] offend human nature" (American Anthropological Association resolution of 1966). To Thomas Aquinas, then, Natural Law was man's participation in the eternal law created by God (*lex aeterna*). It contrasted with actual positive law which should aim at carrying out in detail the principles of Natural Law (Berolzheimer 1929: pp. 98–99).

The emphasis upon pure human reason, common to all mankind, as a source of Natural Law contributed to a historical legal phenomenon in Europe known as "reception of Roman Law." As outlined in Chapter Two this reception began in the twelfth century at the northern Italian universities and was practiced by the Glossators, who confined themselves to the resurrection of the Justinian Code and to the explication of its original text. Because Roman Law represented a true gem of legal reasoning and consistency which was far superior to European local laws at that time, its precepts were regarded as reflections of Natural Law and thus applicable to the European legal situation. Indeed, the next Romanistic legal school of Commentators made a valiant attempt to adapt Roman Law to the contemporary conditions of Europe, which resulted in a body of practical law that was supposed, because of its rational superiority, to supersede the varied local laws of the states of medieval Europe. Because it gradually became the property of most of Europe, the claim for its universal nature was strongly reinforced (Barker 1957: pp. xl–xli). The reinterpreted Roman Law fused with local legal traditions and social situations to such a degree that it tended to produce workable, consistent, and well-reasoned legal systems which ultimately became the famous codes of Prussia (1749), France (1804), Austria (1811), and Germany (1900). Even after World War I, newly created national states like Czechoslovakia retained as their civil law the Romanistic Austrian codification. In all these basic legislative achievements it was implicitly assumed that the codes reflected and were actually based upon Natural Law, that they incorporated some absolute, universal, and eternal human wisdom.

During this Romanistic era of European legal history the "natural light of human reason" replaced slowly but irreversibly "the creative act of God" as the putative source of Natural Law in the arguments of jurists. Conceptualization of state was no longer based upon the understanding of God's will but rather placed upon a contractual basis of free and equal rational individuals who surrendered some of their rights to this common institution. This kind of original contract was even postulated as a historical fact, although no historical evidence could be marshaled to support such a claim. A tribal society was also viewed as based upon such an agreement, although in this case a tacit form was assumed (Gierke 1957: esp. pp. 107–110). We may say that during the seventeenth and eighteenth centuries the theory of Natural Law was definitely divorced from theology and became secularized. Moreover, the doctrine emancipated itself slowly even from Roman civil law so that jurists began to regard themselves as bound only by their own reason. Since their reasoning was primarily based upon the ideas, principles, and juristic manner of thinking of the Romanistic tradition, their reasoning de facto remained shackled by Roman Law in spite of assurances to the contrary.

There was, however, an important sociological difference between the pure Roman tradition and modern European jurisprudence. Although in ancient Rome the theory and interpretation of law were conducted almost exclusively by lawyers, in modern Europe the protagonists of legal thought and argumentation were mainly academic people, university professors, and philosophers, such as Grotius, Pufendorf, Hobbes, Locke, Spinoza, Kant, Fichte, and Rousseau, to name just a few. As time progressed, the basic tenets of Natural Law rested not only upon the idea of free and equal individuals viewed as moral persons but also upon a newly developed concept of "the pursuit of human happiness" (Stone 1950: p. 232; Barker 1957: pp. xlii–xlv). Thus the doctrine slowly shifted ground and gradually declined in the face of subsequent legal philosophies.

Although the philosophic superstructure over the basic tenets of Natural Law changed with time and place, its main function remained the same. Since it was regarded as an ideal and just law, eternal, forerunner of all positive legal systems of the various nations, and unaffected by local cultures and changes of times (Berolzheimer 1929: p. 6; Stone 1950: p. 226), it functioned as a "criterion for judgment whether positive law is just," as a criterion to which positive law of a specific country must conform (Stone 1950: pp. 226). In its position as a measure for existing law it bound also the sovereign and the state authorities (Stone 1950: pp. 219, 227), it imposed itself upon the legislator in providing justification for the legal future (Gierke 1957: pp. 35–36), and in the opinion of legal scholars rendered positive law that deviated from its maxims null and void (Barker 1957: p. xlvi). Positive law in general was then regarded as a necessary evil that should be tolerated only if it conformed to the principles of Natural Law (Stone 1950: p. 225).

The impact of the theory of Natural Law has not remained limited to local legal systems of the various nations and states. Since it was conceived as a basis for the law of all peoples, it became a philosophical-theoretical formulation upon which a juridical system regulating interstate and international legal problems could be built. Indeed, this possibility was already conceived and exploited by Roman lawyers, who were confronted with a practical problem which grew out of the transition from Rome as a city-state to the *Imperium Romanum,* of adjudicating disputes between parties who were not *quirites* (Roman citizens). In charge of such disputes was the office and the court of *praetor peregrinus,* most of whose agenda consisted of ordering relations of foreign merchants through a system of legal principles called *ius gentium.* This legal system, equated with the Law of Nature by Gaius and Justinian's *Institutes* (but contrasted with it by Ulpianus) ambitiously presumed to reflect human juridical thinking underlying legal systems of all the known tribal and state nations of the Mediterranean world (as Maine contends—1963: pp. 48–50). However, in actuality it was based upon principles and theoretical traditions of *ius quiritium* (Roman civil law) that was deprived of its particular national features and its rather rigid formality. The end result of this process of generalization was a skillful adaptation of the law of a city-state to that of an empire composed of peoples with different cultures (Sommer 1933: pp. 13–14; Stone 1950: p. 217; Barker 1957: p. xxxvii). Originally this law regulated relations among merchants who were not Roman citizens, and also between them and Roman citizens. Thus it stood in formal opposition to *ius quiritium,* law used by Roman citizens only, whose provisions, such as *mancipatio* and *usucapio,* were reserved to the *cives Romani* (Roman citizens) and denied to *peregrini* (foreigners). Of course, as the *Imperium* grew and many foreign tribes were incorporated within its borders, this distinction slowly diminished until it completely disappeared when all residents within the *Imperium* became Roman citizens during the reign of Justinian. The theory of Natural Law played a dual role in the Roman Empire. It provided a foundation for the development of *ius gentium,* from whose concrete commercial provisions it was always, as *ius naturale,* differentiated by being a general legal idea; by having its principles incorporated into the praetorian edict, it became a means of securing a measure of justice by superseding the Roman civil law (Maine 1963: p. 54; Barker 1967: p. xxxvii).

Similarly, in the seventeenth and eighteenth centuries in Europe Natural Law provided a base for the development of international law. On the basis of this theory it was assumed that not only the relations between individuals within a state but also the relations between independent states themselves were, and ought to be, governed by Natural Law. The reason why public rather than civil international law was first affected by this theory was that while the public law lacked a solid basis upon which to build a generally acceptable body of legal principles and solutions, the exponents of civil law could always rely upon international acceptance for solution based upon the highly regarded Roman law (Gierke 1957: p. 38; Maine 1963: p. 51). In this domain of public law, followers of the Natural Law doctrine "came more and more to regard their ultimate task as consisting in the discovery of a rational ideal, which, if it could never be fully realized in actual life, was none the less to be made the object of a constant effort at approximation" (Gierke 1957: p. 40).

It was theorized that in old times no status and no social groups existed, that "men were originally free and equal, and therefore independent and isolated in their relations to one another"; states in their turn, represented by their authorities, were regarded as "moral persons" or "social persons," and as such to be subject, like the individuals, to the principles of Natural Law derived from the contemplation of the nature of man and his just and natural reasoning (Gierke 1957: p. 97). Thus the argument of the scholars, such as Hugo Grotius (1583–1645) and S. Pufendorf (1632–1694), who were engaged in application of the theory of Natural Law to international conditions, embraced for their conceptualization a purely secular philosophy and justification in which "natural law is unrelated to the will and existence of God" and derives purely from the rational and social nature of man (Berolzheimer 1922: pp. 115, 130; also Gierke 1957: p. 36). Of course, in order to make their theories palatable to the public authorities of their times these scholars paid formal lip service to the theological argument by contending that "natural law issues in the last resort from 'the author of nature, God' " (Stone 1950: p. 222).

> *The law of nature is a dictate of right reason, which points out that an act, according as it is or is not in conformity with [the social and] rational nature [of man] has in it a quality of moral baseness or moral necessity; and that, in consequence, such an act is either forbidden or enjoined by the author of nature, God. (Grotius 1925: pp. 38–39)[3]*

---

[3]"Jus naturale est dictatum rectae rationis, indicans actui aliqui, ex ejus convenientia aut disconvenientia cum ipsa natura rationali ac sociali, inesse moralem turpitudinem, aut necessitatem moralem, ac consequenter ab auctore naturae Deo talem actum aut vetari, aut praecipi." (Grotius 1751b: p. 8)

Since Natural Law derived from the ideal nature of man, whose main feature was supposed to be peaceable sociableness (Pufendorf 1934: pp. 146–147), and from his proper reasoning process, it was logically the only source for a meaningful and universally applicable international law, bound by neither place nor time.

Unlike international law, the positive laws of particular societies differed from one another and were also subject to change in time, owing to their not being derived from man's pure reason but from the will which was the property of only a particular people (Grotius 1751a: p. 17). While Grotius and especially Pufendorf relied primarily upon the *a priori* method of discovering natural law through pure contemplation, later exponents of the doctrine (following the old Roman praetorian claim that *ius gentium* was derived by way of abstraction from concrete legal systems of the various peoples) have embraced the *a posteriori* procedure, relying upon empirically determined principles common to the various meticulously investigated legal systems. These principles, determined by either of the two methods, were believed to be collatable into a systematic code of law which, unlike the positive legal codes of particular nations, could enjoy almost eternal application (Grotius 1751a: pp. 17–18).

The theory of Natural Law with its major tenets played the leading role in the theory of justice in Western civilization. It indeed became so entrenched in our legal thinking that it became part of our folk concept of justice; it affected even legal scholars, who clearly realized its shortcomings, into assuming that some of its basic assumptions were not those of the West only but were somehow common to humanity. Accordingly Barker states: "Social thought, as it operates in time, is indeed a basis of justice; but the mind of man will always demand that the core of justice shall be beyond time and space" (Barker 1957: p. l). Although this may appear to be logically true, empirically it does not stand the test of cross-cultural examination. For example, the Kapauku Papuans, being basically relativistic in their *Weltanschauung,* certainly do not assume that their own concept of justice (*uta-uta*) is an expression of a universal and absolute truth. Indeed, they explicitly state that the canons of justice are related to the various people who formulated them. In this way they try to argue for a judicial independence from civilized juridical thought imposed upon them by their colonial masters.

Although it is true that modern legal philosophy has explicitly discarded the conception of a universally valid Natural Law, nevertheless lawyers in their actual thinking and actions do apply its principles, as we have witnessed in the Nürenberg trials. In our anthropological context we have to agree with Stone on the nonapplicability of the doctrine of Natural Law as a tool for scientific comparison; we have to concur that once "the spell of a common intuition is broken the standard appears suspended in mid-air devoid of any apparent basis in reality" (Stone 1950: p. 235).

Immanuel Kant (1724–1804). The traditional ideas of the absoluteness and universality of Natural Law as well as of its source, the reason of man, certainly made a profound impression upon Kant's theory of ethics. In the older tradition of this school he embraced the *a priori* argument for identifying Natural Law and justice on the basis of pure reasoning and ignored the later emphasis upon *a posteriori* empirical identification of Natural Law which abstracted it from the various existing legal systems. However, unlike his predecessors, Kant rejected the notion that Natural Law would be derived through purely intuitive contemplation of a conflict situation by legislators or judges. Pure reasoning and Natural Law to him had to emanate from something much more objective and determinate, something which absolutely could not be exposed to any sensuous stimulation, to any feeling which a jurist might have about an act or relationship, because such a feeling was certainly not universal but varied from one person and situation to another and was determined by many particular factors (Kant 1887: p. 13). Pure ethical reason and Natural Law had to be guided by a very fundamental *a priori* (and therefore noumenal) and explicit postulate, universal to all mankind. A prerequisite for arriving at and applying such a principle to human actions was the universal existence of free will and the equality of all men. In Kant's words, "There is, indeed, an innate Equality belonging to every man which consists in his Right to be independent of being bound by others to anything more than that to which he may also reciprocally bind them" (1887: p. 56).[4] Indeed, "the conception of Freedom is a conception of pure Reason" (1887: p. 28),[5] the two ideas being indivisible. A man cannot use his "innate reason" when he is not completely free to do so. Furthermore, since man's nature and innate reasoning are essentially moral (1887: esp. pp. 17, 56) there cannot be morality without free will, because the latter is a prerequisite for the exercise of pure reasoning (1887: p. 30). Thus, Kant reasons, every man has an innate right "which belongs to everyone by Nature, independent of all juridical acts of experience,"[6] an innate right to equality and free will which is neither acquired through, nor dependent upon any juridical act. It is the reason and not a statute of positive law that "commands how we ought to act" (1887: pp. 55, 17).[7]

The basis for the commands of how we ought to act as differentiated from how we "have to act" of positive law are not left by Kant to the

---

[4]"Die angeborne Gleichheit, d.i. Unabhängigkeit nicht zu mehrerem von Anderen verbunden zu werden, als wozu man sie wechselseitig auch verbinden kann." (Kant 1797: p. xlv)

[5]"Der Begriff der Freyheit ist ein reiner Vernunftbegriff. . . ." (Kant 1797: p. xviii)

[6]". . . welches, unabhängig von allem rechtlichen Act, jedermann von Natur zukommt." (Kant 1797: p. xliv)

[7]". . . gebietet wie gehandelt werden soll." (Kant 1797: p. x)

imagination and intuition of the individual. There is a determinate principle, a common postulate implicit in any pure and therefore moral and just reasoning, to which all these commands must conform. This basic, universal, and absolute postulate of morality and justice is Kant's categorical imperative: "Act according to a maxim which can be adopted at the same time as a Universal law" (1887: p. 34).[8] In other words, an action is moral or a legal principle is just if, and only if, that action or principle can be made universal without self-contradiction. In reverse, a legal provision is unjust and immoral if, when made into a universally applicable rule, it cancels itself because its inherent inconsistency contradicts itself. As is obvious, the content of the imperative is based upon Kant's democratic postulate of basic equality of all free-willing people. All moral actions and therefore all just laws and legal decisions *have to* be based upon or derived from this imperative. The imperative is noumenal and therefore it is binding in itself; it is *a priori* without any reference to an external purpose of phenomenal cause. Because it is basic to a rational morality innate to all people it is therefore binding on all rational beings everywhere and for all time. It is thus truly categorical, not dependent upon any "if," any condition of phenomenal nature. Pragmatic argument, which makes an act moral because of the nature of its consequences, and a utilitarian argument emphasizing the maximization of human happiness as a measure of morality and justness, are obviously out of place in the Kantian conceptualization—they are utterly irrelevant. Decisions to act because of, and according to, the categorical imperative are made by a moral and free will which is the only kind true to rational man.

Thus "there is, also, the natural quality of JUSTNESS attributable to a man as naturally of *unimpeachable Right (justi)*" (Kant 1887: p. 56).[9] Legal justice, however, does not always involve ethics, because "whatever is juridically in accordance with External laws, is said to be JUST (*Jus, justum*); and whatever is not juridically in accordance with external laws is UNJUST (*unjustum*)" (1887: p. 32).[10] Consequently, not all the "juridically just" law is morally or ultimately just, because external laws, namely those for which "external legislation is possible" are of two kinds (1887: p. 33): "Those External Laws, the obligatoriness of which can be recognized by Reason *a priori* even without an external Legislation, are called NATURAL LAWS. Those Laws, again, which are not obligatory without actual External Legislation, are

---

[8]". . . handle nach einer Maxime, welche zugleich als ein allgemeines Gesetz gelten kann." (Kant 1797: p. xxv)

[9]". . . mithin die Qualität des Menschen ist . . . die eines unbescholtenen Menschen (*justi*)." (Kant 1797: p. xlv).

[10]"Was nach äusseren Gesetzen recht ist, heisst gerecht (*iustum*), was es nicht ist, ungerecht (*iniustum*)." (Kant 1797: p. xxiii)

called POSITIVE LAWS."[11] The distinction between the two is obvious. Whereas Natural Law ultimately is absolute and noumenal in its nature (*Ding an sich*), positive law is relative in time and place and therefore phenomenal. The rights which the two types of laws create have, of necessity, different origins. Thus "Natural Right rests upon pure rational Principles *a priori;* Positive or Statutory Right is what proceeds from the will of a Legislator" (1887: p. 55).[12] In other words, positive law is valid because it reflects the authoritative will of the legislator or judge (legal authority), while Natural Law derives its validity from the pure reasoning natural to all men—from their "free will." I may go even farther and say that Kant would logically assume that while positive laws can be legislated—created in particular societies by their authorities—Natural Laws can be only discovered and made explicit because they exist already *a priori.*

From the above discussion it is clear that I have to agree with Stone's statement that "Kant's 'natural law' is merely a criterion of justice quite distinct from the positive law to which the criterion is to be applied" (1950: p. 243). On the other hand, I have to qualify Stone's statement that "Kant does not regard natural law as superior to positive law in the sense that positive law is only valid insofar as it conforms to natural law" (1950: p. 243). It is true enough that, in the phenomenal world, the world of power relations, positive law, according to Kant does derive validity from authority. However, that does not make it equal to Natural Law, which is of noumenal order, of an order which Kant regarded as superior, as ultimately true. Thus Kantian Natural Law is a measure of justice, absolute and ultimate, a measure that ought to be applied to all law; moreover it is a measure that any rational individual (and therefore moral individual), thinking freely and truly, actually does apply. The question arises, of course: How does the individual apply the measure in practice? Although Kant's concept of the categorical imperative could be used by scrutinizing a given precept for its consistency with universal applicability, another basic and sometimes more accurate measure of Natural Law may concentrate upon its reaquirement of freedom and equality for all men. A law is, then, just if it exercises minimal restraint of the freedom of individuals in a society in which all are equal, or in reverse, as elaborated by Fichte (1796), if it secures maximal liberty for equals. In this form Kantian philosophy heavily influenced British law and the United States

[11]"Unter diesen sind diejenigen, zu denen die Verbindlichkeit auch ohne äussere Gesetzgebung *a priori* durch die Vernunft erkannt werden kann, zwar äussere, aber natürliche Gesetze; diejenigen dagegen, die ohne wirkliche äussere Gesetzgebung gar nicht verbinden (also ohne die letztere nicht Gesetze sehn würden) heissen positive Gesetze." (Kant 1797: p. xxiv)

[12]". . . Naturrecht, das auf lauter Principien *a priori* beruht, und das positive (statutarische) Recht, was aus dem Willen eines Gesetzgebers hervorgeht." (Kant 1797: p. xliv)

Declaration of Independence and Bill of Rights (for detailed discussion see
Stone 1950: pp. 246–254).

No matter how influential the philosophies of Natural Law and Immanuel Kant were, it is obvious that both employed values that were relative
in time and place—by the latter I mean, of course, Western civilization. A
cursory look at the value systems of non-Western cultures reveals that the
ideas of equality and individual freedom, for example, are not universal—
that substantive justice, absolutely conceived, is a myth. This was already
obvious in the eighteenth century in the writings of Montesquieu. Although
it is true that some tribal peoples, for example, the Kapauku, value equality
and individual freedom highly, it is equally true that the Nunamiut Eskimo
are not concerned about either. Their dependence upon a skilled hunter is
of paramount importance for survival, and freedom to them is a luxury they
cannot often afford. Tirolean peasants, although militantly concerned about
individual freedom, recognize in their local (village) law that equality is not
practical. Status, such as that of the parish priest, mayor, or *Bauer* (farmer),
means in practice inequality for the lower classes of *Häusler* (individuals
owning a house but fields too small for independent farming), *Knechte*
(farmhands), or *Hirte* (shepherds). Similarly, the Korean "concept of justice
never included elements of freedom, equality, and the sovereignty of law as
its constitutive parts" (Hahm 1967: p. 40), and Lozi justice accepted as one
of its basic assumptions a hierarchy of social statuses rather than an
egalitarian doctrine (Gluckman 1967: p. 217). Thus we may conclude that
justice cannot pertain to some absolute, universal system of values—it cannot determine with universal validity whether freedom or slavery or serfdom
is just. In Lloyd's words "justice is little more than the idea of rational order
and coherence and therefore operates as a principle of procedure rather
than of substance" (1966: p. 110).

Procedural Justice.   With this quotation we can now turn to our last
category of justice. The eighteenth century, which saw Kant formulating his
theories and his reactions to the doctrine of Natural Law, produced also
another far more radical and basic reaction to that dominant legal doctrine.
This reaction stressed utility (and happiness) as a measure of the morality of
an act, and was well represented in philosophy by the writings of David
Hume.

Jeremy Bentham (1748–1832).   Bentham was undoubtedly influenced by Hume's philosophy and, impressed by the convincing argument
of Montesquieu about the relativity of law and justice and consequently by
the futility of substantive justice, he embraced utilitarianism as his philosophy of morality and legal justice. Like Kant he rejected the emphasis of
scholars of Natural Law upon intuition as a basis for revelation of canons of
justice. But unlike Kant he abandoned the belief in absolute justice and

morality unrelated to any particular culture. To him, as to Montesquieu, the content of justice was relative to a particular culture in which it existed— relative in time and space. Therefore justice could not emanate from a universally uniform human reason, and the essence of just law was not an expression of a universally moral and reasoning man. Just law was rather a command by an authority, a command which had to be enforced to curb the excesses of individuals and thus to assure maximum of happiness to as many members of a society as possible.

In essence, while the principle of just law (the achievement of maximum of happiness and pleasure) was held to be universal, the content of just law could vary from society to society. In this relative setting the task of law was to maximize the pleasure of individuals (good) and decrease their pain (evil) and thus prove its utility (Bentham 1876: p. 2). The latter concept, in Bentham's words,

> expresses the property or tendency of a thing to prevent some evil or to procure some good. Evil is pain, or the cause of pain. Good is pleasure, or the cause of pleasure. That which is comfortable to the utility, or the interest of an individual, is what tends to augment the total sum of his happiness. That what is comfortable to the utility, or the interest of a community, is what tends to augment the total sum of the happiness of the individuals that compose it. (1871: p. 2; also 1876: pp. 3, 4, 7, 323)

Consequently, the law's production of a more or less subjective feeling of happiness (pleasure) and its maximization in a community (its utility) is Bentham's ultimate principle of justice which "neither requires nor admits of any other regulator than itself" (1876: p. 23). In this way his conception of justice could be truly relative in time and space and, at the same time, universally applicable. The principle of utility Bentham regarded as the foundation of morals, "the only safe rule of legislation" (Hildreth 1871: p. iii), the embodiment of the Public Good and "the foundation of reasoning" of any legislator (Bentham 1871: p. 1). To Bentham, ascetism, a self-denial of personal pleasures, was an antithesis to utility and justice, and those who followed it had "a horror of pleasures . . . they found morality upon privations, and virtue upon the renouncement of one's self" (1871: p. 4; also 1876: p. 9). Public happiness as produced by law (its utility) was the only criterion of justice, and equality, liberty, and good morals were the only means to achieve the ultimate end of justice—they were never ends in themselves (1871: p. 14). If he admitted that they were, he would have violated Montesquieu's conception of law's relativity, which he obviously adopted as one of his own basic assumptions about law and justice.

Bentham's theory of justice, if read *in abstracto*, sounds logical, practical, and convincing. His measure of justice is a result of a calculus, a sum of balances of "all the values of all the pleasures on the one side, and those of all the pains on the other" for every individual of the society in which the law in question is enforced (1876: p. 31). In other words, to determine the degree of justice of alternative modes of action and to make the "just" selection, one has to "calculate their effects in good and evil, and prefer that which promises the greater sum of good" (1871: p. 87). Unfortunately, when the author tried to demonstrate the applicability of his theory he fell into the trap of ethnocentrism. Instead of refraining from identifying the pleasures and pains and leaving the nature and significance of these to be determined for every culture and time separately, he became involved in a lengthy and often simplistic enumeration and evaluation of these, obviously based on his common sense (1871: pp. 20–32; 1876: pp. 29–42). Having recognized individual differences in perception of pains and pleasures, he postulated differing sensitivity to objective acts in various categories of people (characterized by sex, age, health, etc.) and circumstances affecting it (1876: pp. 43–69; 1871: pp. 33–43). The inventory of these categories and kinds of sensitivities is, of course, culturally biased, and we may even suspect that because of its nonempirical derivation inadequate even for the England of Bentham's day.

In addition to this theoretical inconsistency, producing an unwieldly, intuitive, and ethnocentric inventory of people's pleasures, pains, and sensitivities, Bentham's theory suffers from insensitiveness to individual variability (rather than cultural variability) in terms of values and preferences. Also, its basic assumption that man's main motivation is a search for pleasure is not so self-evident as it appears. As Stone puts it, "In actual life pleasure comes rather as an incident to the search for other things than as an intended result of the search" (1950: p. 288). Notwithstanding the criticisms and the fact that Bentham's theory cannot be used cross-culturally, its effect on English law was certainly beneficial, eliminating many of its past cruelties and inequities.

Until the time of Bentham the pivotal factor in the consideration of justice was concern for the individual. The nineteenth century of Europe did not, of course, dwell only on individualism and the laissez-faire role of the economy, state, and law—it produced as a reaction several strains of socialism, in whose doctrines the importance of the individual was either submerged in that of the collective (society, state, commune, or what have you) or eliminated altogether. Concern with the welfare of the society as a whole became the vogue of the time, and the conceptualization of justice of this epoch was dominated by this concern. Although some of these socialistic conceptualizations, when put into practice later in the twentieth century, deteriorated into a dictate of the "nation" (e.g., the national socialism of the Nazis) or of the "working class" (communism), which usually meant the command of a single dictator, (be it Führer or chairman), there were other social theories which, while emphasizing the importance of the collective, did not lose sight of the individual and his rights.

Rudolf von Ihering (1818–1892). To the theories which did not require the sacrifice of the present for the future or of the individual for the collective belonged the social utilitarianism of Ihering. He emphasized, like Bentham, the importance of utility (in terms of pleasure and pain resulting from achievement of purpose) for the conceptualization of justice, but he opposed the traditional divorce of law and justice from other social phenomena. This led him inevitably to the rejection of individualism in favor of social utilitarianism and into the recognition that law, also the most evolved and effective tool for enforcement of conformity, was but one of several other means of social control within a society. Although he rejected intuitive or metaphysical measures for justice, he did not commit the error of the Marxists and the followers of Durkheim—he did not embrace the idea that law and justice were defined and their history determined by suprain-dividual (or "superorganic" if we want to use Kroeber's term) forces that man could not change. To use Stone's phrase, he did not subscribe to "legislative impotence." He emphasized social considerations as paramount, but he did not emasculate law and did not transform it into a sort of mystical, inhuman "social" entity (Ihering 1904: pp. 66–67). Social life, of which law was a part, he viewed as "working together for common purposes, in which everyone in acting for others acts also for himself, and in acting for himself acts also for others" (1913: p. 67).[13] The source of law for Ihering then was social and individual purposes, both defined and capable of being realized or modified by human effort. Since he was also influenced by Darwinian evolutionism he viewed the development of society and its law in its perspective over time and thus did not find it necessary to condemn Natural Law as a heresy. He actually regarded it more as a sucessful tool of law in the past for solving problems of the evolving European community.

Ihering considered man capable of affecting his destiny, as a rational individual whose action is guided by a purpose formulated by his will. To him the force "which moves the human will is interest" (1904: p. 38). These interests, in turn, are determined by the contemplation of pleasures and pains (1904: p. 26). Such utilitarian motivations are not only egoistic in nature (discussion of egoistic purposes 1904: pp. 46–58). According to Ihering man is also motivated by self-denial, by an ethical self-assertion: "It is the feeling on the part of the agent of the ethical destiny of his being, i.e.,

---

[13]". . . ein Zusammenwirken für gemeinsame Zwecke, bei dem jeder, indem er für andere, auch für sich, und indem er für sich, auch für andere handelt." (Ihering 1904: p. 66)

his feeling that existence was given to him not merely for himself, but also for the service of humanity" (1913: p. 45).[14] Thus Ihering's theory presupposes a universal existence of "social morality" (my expression) for man. Although the above quotation suggests Ihering's belief that completely altruistic motivations underlie the formulation of social purposes, the actual implementation of these is certainly strenthened by the rewards which morally acting individuals derive from acting ethically and in harmony with the purposes of others—and at the same time they realize their own aims. In other words, aside from the purely ethical considerations, man realizes social goals because he is conscious that in such a social harmony his own egoistic purposes will thus best be promoted.

This harmonious achievement of individual and social purposes is especially realized in the society's subgroups—associations such as clubs, churches, and companies. Thus associations are, so to speak, evolutionary steppingstones for social purposes. They originate with individuals and grow larger and become associational (and thus social). The association finally "is the pioneer which levels the roads for the State—what is now association is after thousands of years the State" (1913: p. 230).[15] Thus social purposes concern the life of the society, be it an association or, ultimately, a state (1904: p. 45).

Social control within a society is directed toward controlling individual purposes, bringing them into harmony with each other, and thus adjusting them to, or even transforming them into, social purposes. Law, as a type of institutionalized social control, is the most effective means of achieving social purposes (and crime is the disregard of such purposes). Its establishment and maintenance, as the sum of principles of regulated and disciplined coercive force (principles that lie behind statutes and decisions; Ihering 1866: pp. 44–47) is not only one of the state's functions, but according to Ihering is the state's main and paramount purpose. Moreover, law is not only the main characteristic of the state (1904: p. 32), it is also the force which created the state (1913: p. 240). Law evolves "as the politics of force" in human society: it becomes its measure, an "accessory element belonging to it." Finally, at the state level, law becomes dominant and force a mere accessory to it. However, even at this stage of the "rule of law," force need not remain in second place. During *coups d'etats* or revolutions it becomes supreme and radically changes or even lays down new law (1904: pp. 193–194). Thus law in times of political stability secures conditions of social life, while in times of political upheavals it is formulated by political force

[14]"Sie ist das Gefühl des Subjekts von der ethischen Bestimmung seines Daseins, d.h. davon, dass ihm letzteres nicht bloss für sich, sondern zugleich im Dienste der Menschheit verliehen ist." (Ihering 1904: p. 45)
[15]"Der Verein ist der Pionier, der dem Staat die Wege ebnet—was heute Verein, ist nach Jahrtausenden Staat. . . ." (Ihering 1904: p. 239)

and its underlying newly formed individual and social purposes. It is realized through its enforcement. This realization in enforcement is the criterion of law. Thus even when not formally recognized in the learned literature, enforced and effective customary law *is* law. On the contrary, whatever is not enforced, and thus does not effect social control, cannot be law (1866: p. 49). Accordingly, Ihering defines law as "the sum of the conditions of social life in the widest sense of the term, as secured by the power of the State through the means of external compulsion" (1913: p. 380).[16]

Of course, as he observes, "law is not the highest thing in the world, not an end in itself" (Ihering 1913: p. 188).[17] Above it stand the social purposes of the society. If through enforcement law realizes and secures these as fully as possible and with the least amount of friction, then it is just —then it is "socially useful" and should be upheld because then it serves the society as a whole (*dem Ganzen;* 1905: pp. 164–166). In other words, the criterion of a just law is its capacity to adjust conflicting individual egoistic purposes, upholding those which are not in conflict with social purposes and furthering them so that with the least amount of injury and pain their maximal realization can be achieved. Since this process of adjustment deals with aims determined by the cultural values and individual desires of various people, and because these desires change with the evolution of societies, justice is necessarily relative in space (from society to society, from subgroup to subgroup) and in time. Only after the content of the purposes has been determined for the society in question and for time can the justice of a legal precept be computed by the calculus in which satisfaction of the social purposes would supersede that of the individual ones.

Although the substantive (content) relativism of justice is commendable and the various purposes for a given culture and time could be determined by an anthropologist, their evaluation—deciding which should take precedence over others—would certainly be highly arbitrary and subjective. Even to decide concretely which purpose is individual and which social would not be a realistic undertaking. For these reasons the social utilitarian theory of justice is of little value in comparative social science.

Rudolf Stammler (1856–1938). Although I have criticized Ihering's theory for its inapplicability, Stammler's theory of justice is open to much broader criticism. It is not only impractical but, in François Gény's words, "there is in his whole work a vagueness that is extremely painful" (1925: p. 548). Nevertheless, because Stammler's theory contains some very impor-

---

[16]". . . der Inbegriff der mittels äusseren Zwanges durch die Staatsgewalt gesicherten Lebensbedingungen der Gesellschaft im weitesten Sinne des Wortes." (Ihering 1905: p. 399).
[17]"Das Recht ist nicht das Höchste in der Welt, nicht Selbstzweck. . . ." (Ihering 1904: p. 194)

tant observations on a comparative concept of justice which is applicable to diverse cultures (observations I found useful for analyzing the Kapauku Papuan legal phenomena), I consider it necessary to include his work in the present discussion.

Like several of his predecessors and contemporaries Stammler was influenced by the philosophy of Immanuel Kant. He not only embraced the necessity of free will of individuals as one of the pillars upon which to rest his concept of justice, but he also separated justice from positive law by making justice a universal concept and a measure of the law, and by claiming that positive law did not have to derive its authority from consideration of ethics or justice. Like Kant's categorical imperative, the justice of a given rule to Stammler meant the possibility of its universal application. As a consequence, the philosophy of law, whose main subject is justice, has to deal with those aspects of law that have universal validity and, therefore, "pure legal thinking" should be devoid of concrete material (Stammler 1925: pp. xx, xxiv). Like Kant he emphasized the indispensability of free-willing individuals whose purposes are stated and adjusted by a free-willed legislator. Thus he theoretically opposed the social determinism of people like Durkheim and supported the codification efforts in Germany and in Prussia. There was, however, one important point of departure from Kantian conceptualization. Unlike his great predecessor, Stammler did not believe that the role of just law was a mere adjustment of the behavior of individuals to one another. He stated that individual claims and actions have to be in agreement with the fundamental idea of a legal society (1925: p. 11).

Law then, to Stammler, had a dual role: it had to harmonize the purposes of all the members of a given society and adjust them to each other and, at the same time, make them compatible with the basic purpose of the society as a whole (Stammler 1902: p. 33; Stammler 1925: p. xxvi). As a basic prerequisite to these legal processes Stammler postulated "a community of men willing freely, as the final expression which comprehends in unitary fashion all possible purposes of persons united under the law" (1925: p. 153).[18] Only in such a community, which he calls the social ideal, can just law exist, a law which would correctly readjust conflicting claims of litigants. Indeed, the litigants themselves with their claims are supposed to be brought mentally into a "special community" which they share, in which their claims can be adjusted in agreement with the purpose of the society as a whole (community of men willing freely; Stammler 1902: p. 196), with the highest law of the social ideal (1902: p. 281). Thus law in essence is, he says, a social volition: "a volition superadded to or superimposed upon the isolated volitions of the various individuals, which combines the purposes

[18]". . . Gemeinschaft frei wollender Menschen; als letzter Ausdruck, welcher alle möglichen Zwecke von rechtlich Verbundenen einheitlich zusammenfasst." (Stammler 1902: p. 198)

of all and makes those of one serve as a means for those of the other" (Stammler 1925: p. xxx). It differs from morality which deals with the motives and desires of the individual (Stammler 1902: p. 53). A rule of law is then an external regulation of human conduct and as such it becomes just only if it *"agrees with the fundamental idea of law in general"*—the legal expression of the basic purpose of the whole society in question (1902: p. 15).

From what has been said so far it is obvious that Stammler thought justice has no absolute content, that in this contentual sense it is *relative* and changes from society to society (according to the differently formulated fundamental purposes) and in time. However, it is *absolute* in the sense of its method, which is supposed to be universal in judging the ever-changing positive law (Stammler 1902: pp. 118, 182). The method regards as just law (or rule) that one which represents "the unity of the methodical adjustment of individual purposes in accordance with the one final purpose of the community" (1925: pp. 152–153).[19] In other words "the content of the rule of conduct is just when it corresponds in its specific character to the thought of the social ideal" (Stammler 1925: p. 153)[20] Thus a just law is only a positive law that possesses the above methodologically objective qualities; although all positive laws may be regarded as attempts at justice, only some attain this ideal (1902: pp. 17–25). Those which do have to incorporate the following four principles of just law, which are held to be logical extensions of the ideas of "the free-willing individuals" composing a community at large and the "special community." The principles of "respect" demand that "the content of a person's volition must not be made subject to the arbitrary desire of another"[21] (thus assuring the freedom of will of the individual from compulsion and whim of another individual) and that "every legal demand must be maintained in such a manner that the person obligated may be his own neighbor"[22] (thus assuring that the execution of the demand will not go beyond such a point that the obligated will cease to be a member of the community of the free-willing individuals; 1925: p. 161). Two additional principles of participation ensure that the obligated individual will not be excluded from the common social life and will not be deprived of legal protection and rights that belong to him as a free-willing member of the community (1925: p. 163).

[19]". . .die Einheit des methodischen Abwägens von Einzelzwecken nach einem Endzwecke der Gemeinschaft. . . ." (Stammler 1902: p. 197)

[20]". . . Der Inhalt einer Norm des Verhaltens ist richtig, wenn er in seiner besonderen Lage dem Gedanken des sozialen Ideales entspricht." (Stammler 1902: p. 198)

[21]"Es darf nicht der Inhalt eines Wollens der Willkür eines anderen anheimfallen." (Stammler 1902: p. 208)

[22]"Jede rechtliche Anforderung darf nur in dem Sinne bestehen, dass der Verpflichtete sich noch der Nächste sein kann." (Stammler 1902: p. 208)

As one reads Stammler one has to agree with the complaints and criticisms of Gény (1925: p. 548) and Stone (1950: p. 325) about the stylistic vagueness of his exposition and his philosophically circular arguments. However, what I found anthropologically important and useful in Stammler's theory, while analyzing the conception of justice among the Kapauku Papuans, was not his particular and specific statement about the principles of legal justice but his valuable and cross-culturally applicable idea of relativity of the content, but absoluteness of the method of justice. While the content has to be described in folk concepts relative to the cultures investigated, the method of justice (specifically the idea of comparing two sets of sociolegal phenomena for consistency) may well be elevated upon the niveau of a meaningful analytical concept of cross-cultural applicability. I shall return to this problem at the conclusion of this chapter.

Josef Kohler (1849–1919). The emphasis upon the study of cultural values in modern anthropology of law may be ultimately traced to the pioneering work of Kohler, a professor of law at the University of Berlin, an exponent of comparative legal history, an expert on several branches of substantive law (especially criminal, bankruptcy, and patent law), and a scholar interested in legal ethnology, history, and folklore. Because of his broad education and wide interests, philosophy of law to Kohler was not an isolated, autonomous discipline but an integral part of the culture in which it appeared. Consequently, like some of his predecessors and contemporaries, and especially Stammler, he embraced the study of the society as a whole in order to understand the nature of such social institutions as law and justice. He also recognized the necessity of relativity because of the variation of law and canons of justice through time and space. Actually, according to Kohler, law has to change constantly in order to keep up with the needs of the society, although it often lags behind (Kohler 1914: p. xliii).

Society, together with its leading philosophies, values, and notions of just law, he conceived as in a permanent flux. Underlying this historical process was a law of progress, an inevitable unfolding of an idea, an evolution of constantly higher and higher culture, so that in the course of history "man becomes more and more godlike in knowledge and mastery of the earth." Thus Kohler accepted the basic historical orientation of Hegel, together with his dialectic historical method by which progressive changes were viewed as a chain of theses, giving rise to antitheses (implicitly included in the former), and their recombination and reconciliation into syntheses which, in turn, became theses to other contradictions to be reconciled. Thus contemporary ideas, according to Kohler, are actually products of the past and causes for future development: "Only when based on this foundation can the requirements of the law be recognized as the requirements of the advancing culture which the law is to serve" (Kohler 1914: pp. 26–

27).[23] As a consequence, he rejected the idea of unchanging Natural Law and Marxian monistic materialism and its economic determinism (1914: pp. xliv, 10).

In this advancement, however, the path of developing human culture and civilization was, according to Kohler, not always as logical and predictable as Hegel would have it. The illogical elements of the cultural evolution are the chances due to effects of environment, natural and cultural, and the ignorance of man and of his basic psychological and mental processes (Kohler 1909: pp. 18–19). Accordingly, in some eras the rational element dominates over the chances represented by feelings, emotions, and political and religious fanaticism, which signify a time of critical reasoning (1909: pp. 23–24), and at other times the emotions dominate the cultural milieu, thus marking ages of illogical behavior and decadence (1909: p. 26). In this uneven path of historical progress, law, as "the standard of conduct which, in consequence of the inner impulse that urges man toward a reasonable form of life, emanates from the whole, and is forced upon the individual,"[24] should constantly be an expression of progress, a framework for it, by delimiting the individuals' rights vis-à-vis the values of the civilization. Law is then "the law of the group, not of the individual" (Kohler 1914: p. 51).[25]

As a group phenomenon a just law has to reflect the values shared by the group, values which the society expects the law to uphold and enforce. These values, called by Kohler *Rechtspostulate* (postulates of law) and translated by Stone as "jural postulates" (1950: p. 337, meaning actually postulates for law) are not abstractions from legal rules and decisions. Actually they derive from outside of law; they are indeed an ethical property of the society as a whole and are supposed to be incorporated into legal decisions and, enforced, to bring law into harmony with the society's evolutionary, progressive change (Kohler 1909: p. 38). "Thus every culture has its definite postulates of law, and it is the duty of society, from time to time, to shape the law according to these requirements" (1914: p. 4).[26] They are the measure of justice, directions that the legislator and judge should follow. Being extralegal phenomena, these values must probably be discovered by

[23]"Nur auf diesem Untergrunde lassen sich die Erfordernisse des Rechts erkennen, als die Erfordernisse der immer fortschreitenden Kultur. . . ." (Kohler 1909: p. 17)

[24]"Das Recht aber ist die Norm des Verhaltens, die sich infolge des innerlichen Triebes nach vernünftiger Lebensgestaltung von der Gesamtheit auf den Einzelnen aufdrängt." (Kohler 1909: p. 39)

[25]". . . das Recht ist ein Recht der Gruppe, nicht ein Recht des Einzelwesens. . . ." (Kohler 1909: p. 34)

[26]"Auf diese Weise hat jede Kultur ihre bestimmten Rechtspostulate, und Aufgabe der Menschengesellschaft ist es, jeweils das Recht nach diesen Erfordernissen zu gestalten." (Kohler 1909: p. 2)

a social psychologist, or I may say, a social anthropologist (Kohler 1909: p. 23).

To conclude the argument, one might say that law, according to Kohler, is just and therefore good if its precepts are an expression of the jural postulates derived from the ehtical part of the culture, a part which changes with the rest of that culture. If this were so, one would be led to the conclusion that an investigation of the people's values and expectations would reveal Kohler's jural postulates. However, this is not so. There is an important qualification to this procedure and to the claim that these postulates are the property of the society as a whole. They are such, Kohler would agree, only if they reflect the canons of progress—if they reflect the rational and not the emotional attitudes of the people. In an emotional era, when the masses rely more on their feelings than on reason, thus causing stagnation or even decadence, a just law would hardly reflect these negative trends. In such times lawyers should stand against the people and their illogical demands and should oppose and, if need be, even alter the prevailing trends in favor of progress. A just and farsighted legislator should "soften the pathological tendencies"[27] and thus reduce the pain they might otherwise bring about; it is not the masses but only the brilliant and highly trained intellectuals who can formulate the ethical principles that should serve as the source of jural postulates (Kohler 1909: pp. 26, 33). The legal cowards who float with the trend of stagnation or decadence are "ringleaders in human follies and mad pranks";[28] in their hands law would lead (as it often has in history) to "wildest orgies and most cruel persecutions" (1914: p. 40).[29] Thus just law's function is "to secure and increase the progress of culture by so molding the rights and the universal cultural values which it protects that the hampering elements are removed and the upward tendencies are supported and strengthened" (1914: p. 60).[30]

While advancing progress the law in decadent times should nevertheless be made comprehensible to the masses, and thus of necessity it should be "as far as possible in accordance with its own uncultured state";[31] but

[27]". . . die krankhaften Züge der Entwicklung begütigen. . . ." (Kohler 1909: p. 26)

[28]". . .die Rädelsführer menschlicher Verirrungen und Torheiten." (Kohler 1909: p. 26)

[29]". . . wahnwitzigen Orgien und zu den grausamsten Zerfleischungen. . . ." (Kohler 1909: p. 26)

[30]"Aufgabe der Rechtsordnung ist aber endlich die Sicherung und Steigerung des Kulturfortschritts durch eine solche Gestaltung der subjektiven Rechte und der zu schützenden Gesamtkulturgüter, dass hierdurch die hemmenden Elemente entfernt und die aufsteigenden Bestrebungen getragen und gehoben werden." (Kohler 1909: p. 40)

[31]"Sie wird natürlich nach einem Rechte drängen, welches der Unkultur möglichst entspricht. . . ." (Kohler 1909: p. 38)

constantly, of course, the aim must be to return to a progressive trend which will lead the society out of its cultural slump (Kohler 1914: p. 58). This concession to decadence is necessary not only for comprehension by the ignorant masses but also and especially because law cannot remain the property of the courts and legislators—it has to mold and be incorporated into the people's activities. Because of this necessity even "coarse legal forms" at such unfortunate times are permissible and justified (1909: p. 87).

Although this theory of justice is admittedly vague because of its value judgment, the question of who is actually progressive, and how to determine the quality of progress at a given time, Kohler's contribution to anthropological theory of legal justice lies in his relativistic method, his cultural orientation, and especially in his conception of justice as a system of values derived from the ethics of the people, a system of values—or jural postulates, that can be used as a measure of legal justice. If we subtract the notion of "progress" from his scheme, we obtain a useful, cross-culturally applicable analytical concept of justice.

Roscoe Pound (1870–1964). Another protagonist of jural postulates as the basic measure of justice was Roscoe Pound, a professor at Harvard and dean of the Harvard Law School for twenty years, a legal philosopher whose culturally oriented ideas of law and justice heavily influenced modern legal anthropologists such as E. Adamson Hoebel. Like Kohler's conception, Pound's jural postulates were abstracted from actual interests or claims that the people in a given culture (or civilization) had asked the law to recognize and protect. Like Kohler's theories, Pound's jural postulates were legally oriented values, derived from the matrix of the culture external to law itself, and their contents varying in time and space (Pound 1942: pp. 108–109). In other words these culturally relative jural postulates, in Stone's words, were "postulates *for* law" and "not postulates *of* law" (1950: p. 360).

The basis of Pound's philosophy of justice rests on James's pragmatic recognition that human claims are valid by the fact that they are actually made and that, consequently, the aim of ethical philosophy should be satisfaction at all times of as many claims as possible (James 1897: pp. 195 ff.). Thus the first step toward a valid theory of just law (for a given society at a given time) would be a collection and tabulation of de facto interests that the members of a society demand the law to recognize. From these concrete demands the "jural postulates," as a next step, should be abstracted. The question, of course, arises: Which interests should be used and which should be discarded from the jurist's consideration? This discrimination is necessary because in a given culture demands will be made that are incongruent to the point of contradiction. In this evaluative selection Pound seems to follow two principles. First, those interests which are numerically overwhelming should be preferred; the broader and more common an interest is, the greater its significance as a value to the society, as raw material for the derivation of jural postulates. Law itself, according to Pound, always involves the force of a politically organized society which coerces the antisocial residuum of its membership (1942: pp. 33, 43, 58, 108). Thus just law should be definitely based on the values (interests) of the majority of the society's membership. Adherence to this principle is only logical when one recalls the pragmatic basis and Pound's major tenet that a just legal measure should "adjust relations and order conduct with the least friction and waste" (1942: pp. 110 and 65; 1965: p. 47). There seems to be, however, one more criterion for selection of interests as legally important.

Second, like Kohler, Pound also injects value judgment into his definition of the main function of law by demanding that just law further civilization by increasing man's control over natural environment and man himself (1942: p. 132). Unlike Kohler, however, he does not deal with the problem of what should be done in times of obvious decadence when the interests of a majority of the people are detrimental to the progress of the civilization. Kohler gives explicit preference for upholding the principle of progress even if it means recognition of interests of a brilliant minority and a disregard for the majority's decadent tendencies, but Pound avoids the issue. I am not at all sure what his jural postulates would look like in times of decadence, when the two principles of Pound's just law would obviously clash. Be that as it may, in times of progress, which Pound assumes to be typical of most of history, it is the jurists who "work out the jural postulates, the presuppositions as to relations and conduct, of civilized society in the time and place, and arrive in this way at authoritative starting points for legal reasoning" (1942: p. 112). In this activity the jurists rely for adjustment of interests on past experience as well as on reasoning in formulating the relevant postulates. However, even in times of progress and, strangely enough, in times of its greatest impact, when it achieves a momentum that causes the society and its cultural values to change with such speed that they are in constant flux, abstraction of jural postulates becomes a serious problem. Because of the swiftly changing cultural matrix a constant derivation of new postulates is impossible. In such times, Pound argues, the jurists cannot wait "until the social order has settled down for a time in a condition of stability in which its jural postulates can be recognized and formulated" (1942: pp. 133–134). In such times courts must rely only upon the pragmatic principle of "satisfying as much of the whole body of human wants as we may with the least sacrifice" (1965: p. 47), without the benefit of postulates that would be a more secure measure of justice.

If we take the two problematic historical situations (decadence and too swift progress) as exceptional, in normally progressive times the broadly abstracted jural postulates, the principles for human conduct (see for example Pound 1942: pp. 113–118), will serve as criteria for selecting a scheme of de facto interests—generalization of the concrete tabulated claims—which are compatible with these principles. Pound elaborates on this

scheme and divides the interests into three classes (1942: pp. 70–80): individual (e.g., domestic, health, economic interests), public (interests of political or governmental institutions as property owners), and social (claims and
values of the society such as general security, general health, security of
social institutions). This scheme of interests should be used, he says, by
judges as a tool for arriving at a just decision. A conflict is viewed as a clash
of interests of the parties to the dispute (1942: pp. 66–67). The judge is
expected to analyze the situation, identify the interests, and check these
against the scheme. Those that agree with a generalized prototype contained
in the scheme should receive the support of the law, and a decision must
be selected that causes least disturbance to the scheme as a whole (Pound
1942: p. 357). As Stone puts it, a judge should be "evaluating the conflicting
interests as against each other *in terms of the scheme of interests as a whole
*" (1950: p. 362). Thus, in the last analysis, legal decisions are just when they
uphold those interests that are congruent with, or are an expression of, the
jural postulates (Pound 1942: pp. 112–113).

As far as I can judge, the most significant aspect of Pound's theory of
justice was an elaboration on the nature of jural postulates, already conceptualized by Kohler. Pound's injection of pragmatism into the scheme presents a logical and practical problem when it is confronted with his principle
of progress in times of cultural decadence. Unlike Kohler, Pound has not
attempted to resolve this dilemma. From the practical point of view Pound's
theory presents an additional difficulty. For an anthropologist to ascertain
jural postulates on the basis of selection from a multitude of de facto claims
(even if he succeeded in collecting a representative sample of these) is
virtually impossible because sheer numerical frequency in the sample cannot
determine whether a claim is important enough to be recognized by law.
This is so because values always imply a hierarchy of importance, irrespective of the frequency at which they are called upon by the litigants.

Justice in Terms of Institutional Jural Postulates. Of course, there is
a much safer source for workable jural postulates—values exterior to the
legal field itself, values that the people expect their law to enforce. These
certainly do not form the basis for *all* the claims made in a society; they are
expressed in the *just* claims. Obviously then one must derive these values
from a matrix other than Pound's de facto claims. Kohler's postulates came
close to the solution and Stone defined these basic jural postulates as "generalized statements of the tendencies actually operating, of the presuppositions
on which a particular civilization is based . . . they are ideals . . . directives
issuing from the particular civilized society to those who are wielding social
control through law within it" (Stone 1950: p. 337). Hoebel makes these
lofty concepts more workable and thus changes them into a possibly cross-
culturally workable anthropological tool. He shows that these postulates
have to be distilled on the one hand from the explicit statements about

self-evident truth made by informants (I may add of only those informants that are thought to be knowledgeable as well as highly moral) and on the other hand, as I would put it, from the analysis of the basic cultural institutions themselves in which they are embedded as covert guiding principles (Hoebel 1954: p. 13 ff.). In his book Hoebel (1954) demonstrates how these jural postulates can be identified for various specific tribal societies (Eskimo, Ifugao, Comanche, Cheyenne, Trobriand Islanders, Ashanti). The enumeration of each set of postulates is always preceded by a careful analytical sketch of the society.

If I were to propose a method of determining just law I would go a step farther. I would combine Hoebel's jural postulates (set of values derived from the society's basic morality and institutions) with the "legal values" isolated by Smith and Roberts, who abstracted these from actual legal decisions (1954: pp. 124–148). A comparison of Hoebel's jural postulates and Smith and Roberts's legal values could determine whether the various decisions are just or unjust. One would combine, then, basic cultural values with what Rheinstein may call *ratio decidendi* (1967: p. xlviii)—principles abstracted from legal decisions, principles that actually permeate law. It is assumed that the jural postulates are, through the education of the judges and legislators, built into the legal system. Of course this is only an assumption of justice which lends itself to the suggested test. In some civilizations, such as that of the United States, some of the most crucial basic jural postulates are made explicit in the Constitution and thus formally incorporated, through the rulings of the Supreme Court on the constitutionality of laws and judgments, into the judicial system itself. As long as these statements on "basic rights" are not just powerless exhortations, as is the case in France (Lloyd 1966: p. 121) or in the Soviet Union and her satellites, the explicitly stated jural postulates become certain, obligatory, and are systematically enforced through the legal process. Thus justice is supposed to cease to be a virtue of the few and becomes a must of all legal personnel.

Justice Measured by Internalization. There is still one more possibility of conceptualizing legal justice in a cross-culturally applicable way. It derives again from the principles of the precedent—of legal case decisions. However, rather than measure this justice by comparing decisions with jural postulates, one may measure it by my concept of "social internalization." While the above legal procedural concept of justice depends upon objective criteria such as basic cultural values, in the case of internalization we measure justice by counting individuals' feelings about a given legal principle (law). Almost all the above types of procedural justice (except jural postulates) may be interesting and important philosophically (ethics), but from the sociological point of view, recording the opinions and feelings of the members of the group, aside from the jural postulational theory of Hoebel, is relevant.

In my book on the Kapauku law (1958a) I compared the internalization of 132 legal decisions with the appropriate abstract rules and arrived at the following results: 76 decisions were regarded as "just" (internalized by the majority of the members of the investigated confederacy) and corresponded to their pertinent abstract rules; in 35 cases the decisions were regarded as just but did not correspond to the abstract rules; eight cases were terminated by "unjust" decisions which corresponded with the abstract rules; and the remaining 13 cases were, according to my informants, adjudicated in an unjust way which differed from the pertinent abstract rules. We may then conclude that an overwhelming majority of decisions were, in terms of their internalization (and in the opinion of the majority of the Kapauku), just.

I have mentioned Gluckman's interesting account of the Lozi dichotomy between the standard of behavior of a reasonable (sensible) man and that of the upright man. A man among the Lozi behaves legally if he meets the minimal standards of the sensible man. Interestingly, the Kapauku also have two comparable standards of behavior—the legal one, being expressed by the obligatory-repetitive tense aspect and the moral standard of behavior to which they refer as a "good [nice] behavior" or of whose violation they are ashamed of. Although legal conduct is enforced by law, violation of morals alone cannot constitute a reason for convicting anyone. For example, morality requires the father of a newborn baby to distribute food to the guests who attend the birth ceremony but to abstain from it himself. However, he cannot be punished for not complying with this canon. Similarly, although it is permissible according to the law to marry the wife of a relative who has deserted her husband, one feels ashamed (ego) to do so because it is considered immoral (peu).

When I compared the data on procedural justice of "internalization" with moral considerations as they pertained to the 132 cases, I obtained the following results. There were 4 cases with just decisions that, however, were regarded as immoral; in 4 decisions the verdicts were considered unjust but moral; and in the rest of the 124 decisions the presence or absence of morality coincided, in the evaluation of the majority of my informants, with those of justice. When I compared the morality considerations in the 132 decisions with the corresponding abstract rules (leges) I found 76 cases with moral decisions that corresponded to the abstract rules, 31 cases with moral decisions that did not correspond to their rules, 9 cases with immoral decisions that corresponded to abstract rules, and 16 cases with immoral decisions that did not correspond to abstract rules.

Among the Kapauku I found the procedural justice measured by the degree of internalization relevant and meaningful. From our discussion of changes of laws, it is obvious that all customary laws, from the point of view of "internalization justice," are also "just" laws. We may conclude this discussion by the interesting finding that like the Lozi, the Kapauku differentiate rules (*leges*) from precedents, and legality from justice and from morality. It is my opinion that procedural justice may become a meaningful, analytical, cross-culturally applicable concept if justice were conceptualized as either the conformity of the values of legal principles with basic jural postulates (Hoebel 1954: esp. pp. 13 ff.; Smith and Roberts 1954: pp. 124–148) or as a degree of social internalization (Pospisil 1958a: pp. 281–282).

CHAPTER EIGHT
FORMAL ANALYSIS OF SUBSTANTIVE LAW

All the topics discussed so far have dealt with procedural law and concepts and problems related to this field. This chapter is an exception to this policy and discusses a method by which the substantive laws of the various peoples of the world might be analyzed and compared. It is expected that utilization of this method of formal analysis will not only yield an insight into the structure of the various legal systems but will also enable (as in kinship organization) generalizations about the content and structure of the legal systems and empirically derive a series of types of legal systems that will show a relationship to (or even a correlation with) the various types of social organization. As a graduate student in Murdock's class on social organization I conceived of such a possibility. I tried to test it in a term paper by correlating statistically in 132 societies the types of descent (meaning genealogical principles of membership in social groups) with residence and with types of laws of inheritance. Not to my surprise the correlation of descent with the laws of inheritance was much higher than that between descent and the rules of residence (Pospisil 1954).

In the following sections I try to show the workability of the project by applying a method of formal analysis to three legal subsystems. The first two are taken from the law of the Kapauku Papuans of West New Guinea and deal with land tenure and laws of inheritance respectively. The third subsystem is taken from a Western civilization—the laws of inheritance of the Austrian Tirol. By this selection (all based on my own research) I shall demonstrate the applicability of an objective, cross-cultural, formal analysis of systems of substantive law to any society—whether tribal or civilized.

KAPAUKU PAPUAN LAWS OF LAND TENURE[1]

In any society the legal rules concerned with land tenure are the most important, after laws of inheritance, with respect to social structure. Despite this importance, and in spite of several outstanding accounts of land tenure in particular societies, the contributions to a legal theory of land tenure have not been entirely satisfactory. It seems to me, for the present at least, and contrary to the opinion of Herskovits (1960: p. 350), that the problem lies more in the lack of a precise, formal, and cross-culturally applicable comparative method than in any absence of philosophical considerations. In this chapter this methodological problem is investigated through an application of various methods of formal analysis drawn from the fields of ethnoscience and linguistics, and there is proposed a type of analysis, with cross-cultural applicability and comparative significance, that is expected to permit an exact inquiry.

To demonstrate the use and merits of the various methods I shall apply them first to the Kapauku Papuan laws of land tenure. This West New Guinea Highlands society was selected because I possess a firsthand and reasonably full account of their law, and because the laws of land tenure of these Papuans are sufficiently complex and conceptualized to serve the purpose. It must be emphasized that this analysis pertains only to the Kapauku *ideal* land tenure, the abstract rules of which are the mental property of most adult males. A few general remarks concerning these rules follow.

First, the actual behavior of the Kapauku is generally consonant with their ideal abstract rules, and those decisions over disputed cases I have collected show a remarkable conformity to the ideal.

Second, Kapauku rules of land tenure contradict Herskovits' generalization about Melanesian communities that they "admit the ownership of produce rather than of the garden where it is grown" (1960: p. 358). Kapauku rules clearly refer to land which is owned individually and may be

[1]This discussion is reproduced with minor changes by permission of the American Anthropological Association from "A Formal Analysis of Substantive Law: Kapauku Papuan Laws of Land Tenure" by Leopold Pospisil in *American Anthropologist,* vol. 67, no. 5, October 1965, pp. 186–214.

sold, leased for shell money, or loaned by the owner. Consequently, contrary to Herskovits (1949: p. 283), the title to Kapauku land does not rest on its use.

Third, since Kapauku legal rules against trespass apply not only to gardens but also to fallow land (grassland and secondary forest) as well as to partly exploited virgin forest, brooks, and small lakes, they contradict Herskovits' generalization that "the recognition of trespass as an offense thereupon merely becomes evidence of a recognition of the right to own crops" (1960: p. 358).

Fourth, Kapauku rules of land tenure cannot be classified easily as belonging either to the "status" or the "contract" type of the dichotomy postulated by Sir Henry Maine (Bohannan 1963: p. 222), although they clearly exhibit both principles. Several categories of persons of this Papuan society find their rights to land defined by their status, but land is also the subject of a variety of well-defined contracts through which not only the title to the usufruct but also to the land itself may be transferred.

Finally, Kapauku rules of land tenure as here defined do not cover laws concerning various types of contractual dispositions with regard to land. Some economists or anthropologists probably would prefer to call the category of laws discussed here "land owernship." In accordance with my European legal training I choose to keep tenure of the various rights to land and to its fauna and flora separate from laws governing contractual agreements concerning these rights; these I prefer to treat and analyze together with other contracts.

Methodological Problem

The law of Western society traditionally is analyzed as an autonomous, logically consistent legal system in which the various rules are derived from more abstract norms. These norms, arranged in a sort of pyramid, are derived from a basic norm or a sovereign's will. Such analyses present a legal system as a logically consistent whole, devoid of internal contradictions, whose individual norms gain validity from their logical relationship to the more abstract legal principles implied ultimately in the sovereign's will and in a basic norm. Another analytical approach to substantive law justifies various legal dispositions in terms of canons of justice emanating from various philosophical approaches and tenets lying outside the field of law proper. In contrast, "sociological jurisprudence" tries to analyze the various legal systems as parts of larger sociological matrices of the societies in which they exist, and inquires into the relationships of the legal systems to other social phenomena. Unfortunately, these approaches are not intended to provide structural analyses, adequate for cross-cultural comparison, of the essential principles operating in particular legal systems. Nor could my goal be achieved by traditional legal analysis of specific rules into their component rights or duties, for it fails to present the total structure of a legal system and does not abstract its important structural features. Even an elaborate system of precisely defined legal analytical concepts, supposed to have universal applicability, is not applicable (Hohfeld 1923).

For an analysis to present the structure and distinctive features of the total field of inquiry, we turn to formal methods already applied successfully in cultural anthropology. Specifically in my mind are the taxonomic approach used in folk classifications by Conklin (1962a) and the componential analysis used in the fields of structural linguistics and kinship terminology by Goodenough (1956) and Lounsbury (1956). Both methods are well known for conciseness of expression, precision of analytical inquiry, and elegance of design. The taxonomic approach rather simply parallels taxonomies in botany or zoology, where the various taxa are arranged hierarchically according to their degree of inclusiveness so that a higher-level taxon includes several subordinate-level taxa (see Conklin 1962a: esp. pp. 128 f). Componential analysis is applied to a complete matrix of kinship terms, defined in the well-known kin-type notation (Br, FaBrSo, etc.). This procedure allows the abstraction of distinctive semantic components responsible for grouping particular kin types into the respective "named categories." According to the kind of contrast implied, the semantic components are grouped into several dimensions representing specific values. The goal of this analysis is a set of symbolic notations capable of defining the various kin terms by specific combinations of the contrastive components. The procedure is usually concluded by a statement (often diagrammatic) about the semantic relationship among the terms and principles which structured the paradigm (Wallace 1962: esp. p. 352). Since segments of a legal system (contracts, laws of inheritance, and the like) form a closed universe similar to that of a kinship terminology, the universe composed of the Kapauku rules of land tenure is here analyzed componentially. Unfortunately, despite their similarities, sets of kin types and systems of legal rules exhibit several differences which give rise to three serious problems concerning the universe, the components, and the purpose.

Problem of the Universe. Whereas a given kinship terminology represents an objectively well-structured universe, any functionally related set of rules that form a segment of a legal system (rules of inheritance, for example) and, therefore, any system of rules of land tenure, contains nothing comparable to the "objectively defined kin types" universally present in all systems of the same type. Instead, the legal rules (which may be regarded as analogous to kin terms) composing the systems must be defined in terms of rights, their subjects, and their objects (all three of which may be regarded as analogous to kin types), which do not form a logically necessary universe as kin types do. Some of the rights may even be unique to a given legal system. Kin types are defined genealogically and objectively, representing a universal set, but legal rights are determined through cultural selection from a vast number of possibilities.

Moreover, unlike kinship terms, individual legal rules are not covered by words whose semantic values we must elucidate. If there are no terms to be analyzed for semantic content, what should be selected as a matrix? We could take the individual rules (the legal utterances) as the units to be examined and show how they differ, in terms of content components, one from the other. Although this might bring out some interesting contrasts and attributes of the rules, it would not even approach a legally meaningful analysis. There are, of course, other possibilities. One need not take the whole of legal rules as units, but take segments of these, and arrange them into meaningful matrices. In this way one may analyze componentially the various rights and duties contained in the rules in terms of dimensions based upon the types of subjects and objects of those rights. One may also analyze componentially the subjects of the rights in terms of the rights themselves and in terms of objects of those rights. The choice of the matrix to be analyzed and of the types of dimensions often depends on the cultural bias of the legal system to be investigated. For the Kapauku rules of land tenure, I concluded (through trial and error) that the most meaningful analysis might be achieved by using the various land and water categories incorporated in the Kapauku rules as the investigated universe. These not only form a logical matrix, grouping all the Kapauku physical environmental formations into segments without residuum, but, furthermore, they are provided with Kapauku terms which, when considered together with the more inclusive environmental categories, form a folk taxonomy. If taken into consideration only on the lowest level, they form a paradigm whose semantic as well as legal meaning may be investigated fruitfully. This matrix is analyzed in terms of the various physical and economic features explicitly recognized by the Kapauku, as well as in terms of the pertinent legal dispositions primarily responsible for the existence of this matrix.

Problem of the Components. This problem logically follows from the preceding discussion and pertains especially to the analysis of the matrix of the land categories (as they appear in the Kapauku rules of land tenure) in terms of the pertinent legal dispositions. It arises because the matrix of the Kapauku land and water categories is not being analyzed, in this case, by components abstracted from its segregates (terrain classes), but by features which are extrinsic, being derived from the matrix of legal dispositions (consisting of entitled parties and their rights). These components are not implicit in the analyzed matrix in the sense that genealogical features are implied in a set of kinship terms. Because they cannot be extrapolated from the analyzed matrix but derive from another domain, and consequently differ from the genealogical components, I shall call them "correlates."

Problem of the Purpose. Wallace states that the primary purpose of the componential analysis of kinship terminology is "to define the taxonomic system itself—that is, to explicate the rules by which the users of the terms group various social and genealogical characteristics into concepts" (Wallace 1962: p. 352). He further argues that it is basically a semantic problem and "as a semantic problem it is of cognitive and logical interest" (1962: p. 352). Some writers, enthusiastic about the cognitive role of the componential analysis of kinship terminologies, seem to have gone almost as far as to claim an exclusive validity only for those analyses based upon distinctive features which the natives themselves hold (esp. Hymes 1964: p. 118). Although there is little controversy about the semantic purpose of the kinship terminological analysis, several writers express serious doubts with respect to the cognitive purpose of the methodological procedure. Burling, for example, points out that Goodenough, one of the two originators of the componential terminological analysis, "suggests an intricate distinction between 'lineal,' 'ablineal,' and 'co-lineal' to help in the ordering of English kin terms," and that these components scarcely approach anyone's cognitive system (Burling 1964b: p. 121).

To this and several other well-taken criticisms I add two of my own. First, I cannot quite understand why, if an inquiry has a purpose other than cognitive, one has to analyze a kinship terminology in terms of native components, even if these are made readily available by the informants. Scientific inquiry uses as its tools concepts, categories, apparatus, and procedures designed or selected by the scientist and not by the subjects he studies. Even if the purpose of the analysis is cognitive, one studies the native categories and cognitive processes as facts, as phenomena presented by the native informants; one does not necessarily adopt these categories for one's own cognition. In order to understand Kapauku thinking, and their cognitive categories, one does not have to think like a Kapauku.

The second of my criticisms is directed against the procedure advocated for arriving at the natives' cognition. Even if we accept the assumption (certainly erroneous) that all peoples could provide us, through explicit utterances or drawings, with statements about their cognitive categories, it still does not mean that these statements necessarily reveal the cognitive processes. It has long been recognized that there is often a significant discrepancy between what people think they do and what they say they do, and between what they say they do and *actually* do. These differences most probably are responsible for the difficulty Frake had in getting an agreement about "the term to be used in a given instance of predicting naming" (Hymes 1964: p. 118, see also Frake 1962), whereas he had little trouble in getting the natives to spell out the "cognitive" disease components. Be that as it may, I am not making any claims here about native cognition. Even in the following section in which I present a Kapauku folk taxonomy and folk components (as given to me by my informants), I do not consider that the two analyses reveal Kapauku cognition. Actually, I show subsequently that the natives are in error in claiming that their "folk components" are responsible for the categorization of the land and water into specific categories.

The purpose of my analysis of the Kapauku terrain types in terms of their legal attributes, which follows, is to show how the various classes of land and water are mutually distinguished in legal respects (by different rules pertaining to them) and how they are correlated with the components of the several legally significant dimensions. Through this procedure I attempt to arrive at a concise structural and descriptive presentation of the field of Kapauku laws of land tenure, point out its essence in terms of the most significant legal features, and clarify the Kapauku concept of land ownership.

Analysis of the Kapauku Terrain Types in Terms of Economic and Physical Attributes

The Matrix.   The universe chosen to be the object of my analysis is a set of terrain terms used in the Kapauku rules of land tenure and applied to the 14 categories into which the natives classify their natural environment according to its physical and biotic features. These categories fully comprehend the matrix of the Kapauku land and water environment and together constitute what the natives call *uwoje-makije,* the world. The Kapauku conception of the world also includes *maikaida,* the ocean, and *epa maida,* the solid bowl of the blue sky which, they believe, overhangs land and water, but these two categories are not included in the analysis because neither is of economic or legal significance (no rule applies to them) nor are they actual parts of the native habitat. The terrain classes, presented in an order which proved important in their "folk taxonomical" and componential analyses, in addition to their contrasting physical characteristics are of economic and legal significance.

> 1. *Bugi,* the garden. This term is assigned to any type of land actually under cultivation. It combines gardens of the valley floor, under intensive complex or shifting cultivation and used for several crops in succession (Pospisil 1963a: pp. 102–126), with mountain swiddens whose extensive shifting cultivation method limits the gardener to a single crop, after which the area is left fallow for seven to twelve years (1963a: pp. 90–102). The mountain swiddens are used exclusively for extensive cultivation of sweet potatoes, with some *Amaranthus* green intercrop; the valley gardens present a very different appearance. Some of their plots are under intensive, complex cultivation consisting of an elaborate pattern of raised, composted beds and drainage ditches, and are planted with sweet potatoes and *Amaranthus* greens. Other valley gardens are swiddens, which are subject to an intensive shifting cultivation producing on their unworked soil surface such crops as sweet potatoes, taro, some yams, several varieties of greens, sugar cane, a cane with edible efflorescence (*Saccharum edule*), bananas, beans, squash, cucumbers, and gourds (1963a: pp. 103–122). All these cultivated plots the Kapauku call *bugi.* Because they are fenced in, I call them gardens.

2. *Juwuuda,* the yard. Always, in front of a Kapauku house and sometimes around it, there is an uncultivated area covered with ankle-deep mud or with grass growing on solid ground which, during rainless days, serves as a meeting place for adults, a workshop for male and female artisans, a playground for children and adolescents, an outdoor kitchen, a "courtroom," or a site for performing the various magical rites and other more secular ceremonies. Irrespective of its size and its position vis-à-vis the house, such an area is called *juwuuda.* Economically as well as legally it forms a special category distinct from any other Kapauku terrain type.

3. *Geiga,* fallow grassland. Despite their rich soil, compost enrichment, and crop rotation, Kapauku gardens on the flat, wet floor of the Kamu Valley require a period of rest. During the fallow period an abandoned garden site is swiftly overgrown with tall grass and reeds. Over a period of time some willow-like trees may appear on higher ground. Although not exploited agriculturally during the fallowing period, a *geiga* type of terrain is by no means economically unimportant. During a dry spell the natives fire-hunt there by setting the dry vegetation afire and following the fire line as it moves with the wind. They collect the roasted carcasses of the birds, rodents, marsupials, and reptiles that could not escape the blaze or the suffocating smoke. During a rainy period followed by a flood this area offers the native bow-and-arrow hunter numerous stranded rats and birds and a few marsupials. Also, at such a time, insects floating helplessly in the water are collected by the Kapauku women who deposit them in tubular bamboo containers and later steam them by pushing the containers into hot ashes. Trapping of various animals in these areas is practiced all year round.

4. *Gapuuga,* fallow bush. Because of the incline and the thinner and poorer soil, Kapauku gardens on the mountain slopes require a long period of fallowing after a single crop. An abandoned garden plot is first overgrown by weeds and grass, then by bushes, and later by a fast-growing secondary forest in which willow-like trees and then oaks predominate. This area of bush and secondary forest is referred to as *gapuuga.* It is exploited by hunters and trappers of the various mammals and birds, and by gatherers who, irrespective of the weather, collect the various edible greens, insects, bird eggs, and reptiles, and harvest tall branches whose inner bark is suitable for making the string used in netting bags and fishing nets. Like *geiga,* this type of environment is temporary in the sense that it alternates with *bugi,* the garden type.

5. *Gamouda,* exploited virgin forest. Kapauku classify as *gamouda* all the virgin forest land which has been stripped earlier of most of the

rattan vines and canoe and plank trees. It is thus conceptually distinguished from the unexploited virgin forest called *buguwa*. The term *gamouda* itself suggests the "partial exploitation" of the area by being derived from the verb *gaamai*, "to split off planks," to which the suffix *-ida*, connoting "place where something happens," is added. Accordingly, the economic importance of this type of land still consists in providing the natives with some of the valuable tree trunks from which planks are hewn or dugout canoes made. The area may also still have some rattan vines, an excellent and durable binding material for house and fence construction. Otherwise, the natives use *gamouda* as hunting and trapping grounds and as a place where most of the *deno*, the edible varieties of fern, is collected.

6. *Buguwa,* virgin forest. The distinction between this class of forested land and *gamouda* is that the virgin forest still possesses a considerable supply of plank and canoe trees and rattan vines, which make the area a suitable workshop for a canoe builder or a carpenter. Because of its plentiful large game, consisting of several species of marsupials (kangaroos, wallabies, bandicoots, etc.), wild boar, python, and the large cassowary bird, *buguwa* is a source of protein food and monetary income for groups of hunters and lone trappers, and offers a pleasant diversion for the solitary Kapauku hunter who pursues game as a sport instead of a serious economic enterprise. The virgin forest also provides excellent seclusion for the sorcerer whose black art requires open space but who also demands secrecy.

7. *Ita,* path. There are two types of paths in the Kapauku territory —temporary and permanent. The temporary footpaths usually lead through fallow land and belong to the owner of the plots which they cross. Since they represent nothing more than stamped-down grass, their direction frequently changes with the desire of the relatively few individuals whom they serve. When a plot owner decides to cultivate his area, the path must alter its course. Although Kapauku refer to these lines of communication as *ita,* they also explain that they are not actually *maagodo ita,* "real paths." According to the informants, the correct (and not loose) application of the term *ita* should be limited to the permanent paths with surfaces exempt from cultivation that are held in common ownership by all the members of the local sublineage through whose territory they pass. These trails are open to all travelers, from any political confederacy. The heavily worn surface is dotted with deep mudholes and puddles, studded with slick boulders and tree roots, and in times of heavy rain it forms a bed for a muddy stream of water which rushes downhill through the depressed area. If a path crosses a swamp, the middle portion may be so worn down that there are many bottomless holes filled with what I would call "quick-mud." For these reasons the English word path does much

more than justice to these treacherous lines of communication the Kapauku call *ita.*

8. *Begadimi,* mountain summit. This agriculturally unproductive land with its leached yellow clay, loose gravel, and numerous limestone outcrops, located on the summits of sharp ridges and mountains, is covered by grass, moss, herbs, some bushes, and a few old crooked trees. In terms of economic importance the area offers only a few birds and mammals to a hunter and some rats to a trapper. The term *begadimi,* which is applied to this type of terrain, is a polysememe. In a noneconomic context it may be used for any mountain top, irrespective of its vegetation cover (e.g. grassland, virgin forest, or rocky cliffs). However, when one has in mind the land's economically important features (as in our case) it is limited to a grassy mountain summit and contrasts with those mountain summits covered with forests (termed *buguwa*), or consisting of rocky cliffs (termed *bago*).

9. *Bago,* crag. Although for brevity's sake and as a label the word crag may be allowed for the Kapauku term *bago,* "rocky mountain peak or wall" is a more precise definition. This class of terrain includes all the upper reaches of high mountains, whose surface consists mostly of stone cliffs and exposed bedrock, and whose sheer height prevents any cultivation in those crevices and depressions which retain some soil. In the Kamu Valley the top of Mt. Deijai, on the northern rim of the Kamu Valley, is the nearest example of such a terrain category. Although the local sublineage in whose territory any part of the *bago* lies "owns" the area and possesses an exclusive right to trap there, practically speaking it is wasteland, and its meager resources are not exploited at all. In the Kapauku rules of land tenure the term *bago* is also extended to caves and precipices which in nonlegal context have special terms.

10. *Takapaka,* swamp. A swampy area that cannot be improved by the Kapauku system of drainage ditches, that remains moist most of the time, and that floods after only a slight rainfall, is called *takapaka.* It is usually overgrown with some reed and a carpet of either tubular swamp grass which the Kapauku call *dudupugu,* or of leafy grass called *widime* (Cyperaceae, *Gahnia sieberiana,* Kunth). There are islands of more elevated ground on which there may be a few old trees. The area is unfit for cultivating even those crops requiring a great deal of moisture. This kind of agriculturally unproductive land covers approximately one half of the entire floor of the Kamu Valley. Despite its lack of agricultural significance, the swamp is by no means economically unimportant. It provides an excellent fishing ground for the Kapauku women who catch its numerous waterbugs,

dragonfly larvae, tadpoles, and an occasional crayfish. It is also an important hunting ground for the Kapauku males who comb this area for ducks, herons, mud hens, and muskrats. Groups of women with torches roam the swamp on starry nights, collecting its abundant frogs, thus providing their households with a rather steady supply of animal proteins. Because of its importance in fishing, hunting, and gathering, Kapauku do not regard *takapaka* as a wasteland.

11. Dego-uwo, brook. The Kapauku classify all unnavigable streams as brooks. To qualify as a "river" the stream must be wide and deep enough to permit the Kapauku woman not only to push her canoe through it but also to turn it around. Actually this means that a brook must not be wider than one length of a Kapauku canoe (i.e., under 6 meters). Brooks are usually considered the property of the local sublineage, unless, of course, they form a boundary between two landholdings of two such segments of the Kapauku society. If this is the case, then they are owned in common by the neighboring sublineages, even though the two groups may belong to different or even hostile political confederacies. The economic importance of a brook is limited to sporadic fishing and catching frogs.

12. Pekuu, small lake. The swampy, flat floor of the Kamu Valley, a naturally drained ancient lake bed, is dotted with many lakes, all of which the Kapauku classify as "small" lakes or *pekuu.* These are invariably located within a territory of a lineage or sublineage and are regarded as the property of either the local nonsubdivided lineage or of that subdivided lineage of which the local sublineage is a segment. Although they are the property of such lineages, they are accessible for fishing purposes to all members of the political confederacy to which the unilineal kinship group belongs. These lakes, containing a fair supply of crayfish and a large population of waterbugs, dragonfly larvae, and tadpoles, are important fishing grounds for the women. None of the lakes is accessible to outsiders, the fishing rights being carefully guarded by the husbands of the fisherwomen as well as by the leader of the local lineage. The lake may also serve the males as a hunting ground for ducks or white herons.

13. Uwo ibo, large lake. This, or another term *"ibo pekuu,"* is reserved for large lakes with shores owned by lineages and sublineages which belong to many different political confederacies. In the Kapauku territory only three lakes qualify for this category: Tigi, Tage, and Paniai, which lie from south to north in this order, and are behind the mountains to the east and northeast of the Kamu Valley. These waters are regarded as "international" so that anyone, even non-Kapauku Papuans and whites, can "legally" fish and hunt there. The lakes offer the Kapauku fisherwomen abundant crayfish and frogs, and the Kapauku hunter large water birds such as ducks and herons.

14. Onee, river. As stated above, Kapauku regard as rivers only those streams in which a native canoe can be turned easily. All streams smaller than this are by Kapauku definition not navigable and are therefore not classified as *onee* even though a canoe could be used on them. On the other hand, rapids in a river do not disqualify it as *onee,* especially if the stream is wide and navigable above and below the rough water. In addition to its function as a communication and transport route, a river provides numerous crayfish and frogs. Occasionally ducks or herons may settle in a river bend and offer good hunting. Because of its importance in communication, a river does not belong to anyone, thus attaining an "international legal status" like the large lake.

The Folk Taxonomy. The fourteen land and water categories are, strictly speaking, folk categories into which the Kapauku have arbitrarily classified their natural environment according to its physical and economic features. This set of categories is used by a Kapauku speaker in legal context —the categories appear in the Kapauku rules of land tenure from which I have abstracted them. With the exception of the imaginary solid bowl of sky and the remote ocean, the categories adequately classify all the varieties of land and water formations which compose the Kapauku *uwoje-makije,* the world. However, the legal classification of the "Kapauku natural world" includes several additional, more abstract, categories which are superordinate to the fourteen described above and are interposed (through the process of lexical inclusion) between the fourteen terrain types and the highest level of inclusiveness, the "world." Thus all these categories, which appear on four distinct levels of inclusiveness, are related by hierarchic lexical inclusion and form a true folk taxonomy (Conklin 1962: p. 128). The hierarchical arrangement of the various folk taxa is represented in Figure 8, which reveals that this Kapauku folk taxonomy complies with some additional "regular" taxonomic requirements as specified by Conklin (1962: p. 128). Its highest level of inclusiveness is occupied by only one maximal taxon, *uwoje-makije,* which includes all the subordinated taxonomic classes of the system, taxonomic categories on the same level are all mutually exclusive. Of the fourteen basic terrain classes only one belongs to more than one level: *ita,* the path, has contrastive value at the bottom level, and it also contrasts at the next higher level of inclusiveness with the more abstract categories— *mude,* agricultural land; *pijaijda,* wooded area; *peu-maki,* bad land; and *uwo,* water. The taxon *uwo,* in turn, belongs to the second level of inclusiveness as well as to the third, where it contrasts with *maki,* land.

Of the more abstract categories, the taxon *mude* is most interesting.

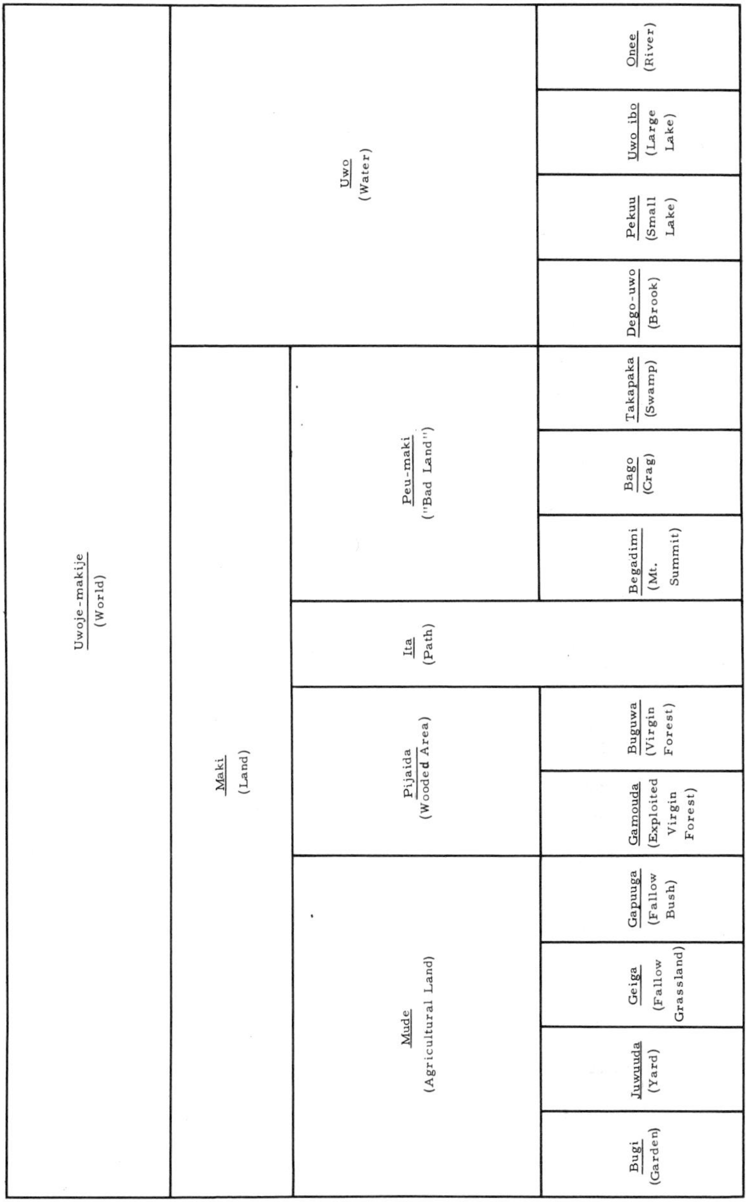

285

FIGURE 8. Kapauku Taxonomy of the Economically Important Terrain Types

The word is a polysememe. In the Kapauku legal taxonomy of terrain types it means "agricultural land": in another legal context, in which the speaker tries to distinguish between land ownership and titles to various rights to land which have been contractually passed to persons other than the owner, *mude* may be translated as "subsoil." This second meaning becomes obvious when one inquires into a land tenure of *bugi,* a garden plot leased by the owner to another individual. Accordingly, to the question *"Meime mude ipuwe?"* (Who owns this *mude?*), the answer is the name of the landlord. On the other hand to the question *"Meime bugi ipuwe?"* (who owns this *bugi?*), the reply is the name of the individual who leased the land and made the garden on it.

Analysis in Terms of Kapauku Components. Since it is the Kapauku who divide their environment into fourteen classes and, in turn, group these into categories on a higher level of inclusiveness, the Kapauku criteria for distinguishing the different classes of land and water require elucidation. During my research in 1962 I inquired about this matter and learned from the natives that the classification is based on distinction made between the various physical features of the terrain categories. The distinctive features identified by my informants allow me to make a componential analysis of the fourteen legally relevant terrain types in terms of their "folk components." This analysis differs in several respects from the above-described taxonomy. Whereas the taxonomy includes all the legally relevant terrain categories, irrespective of their degree of inclusiveness; the following componential analysis presents a paradigm—which employs a matrix consisting of only the fourteen terrain types that are of the same degree of inclusiveness, are in contrastive distribution, and appear in the taxonomy on its lowest level. The primary objective of the taxonomy was a presentation of all the legally relevant terrain categories in a vertical arrangement to show the hierarchical relationship of the categories in terms of their lexical inclusion. (Categories of the same degree of inclusiveness appeared on the same level.) On the contrary, the objective of the following componential analysis is to elucidate the contrasting features responsible for the Kapauku terrain classification into the fourteen types.

The English labels of the folk components are loose translations and have been chosen to permit a logical, systematic analysis. To preserve their authenticity, additional translations of the distinctions made by the Kapauku informants are given if the English label departs from a proper translation. It is clear, however, that, aside from the few loose English labels, we are dealing here with what Burling called "God's Truth" (1964a: p. 27). I feel justified in calling these Kapauku criteria of differentiation components because they define the native terrain classes, have a contrastive function, and especially because their summaries constitute the significata of the various classes. One aspect of the following analysis will not please the "purists" in the anthropological school of componential analysis; for the structure of the analysis is not binary. However, since kinship terminological analyses do employ dimensions with more than two value-components (e.g., generation dimension), this lack of elegance may perhaps be excused.

Componential analysis of the types of terrain in terms of the Kapauku criteria discloses six dimensions of contrasting components defining the fourteen terrain classes in terms of their physical and economic features which the natives have recognized as significant.

1. Nature of surface (land versus water). This dimension applies to all the classes of terrain types and divides them into two major categories: land, which includes the first ten, and water, which includes the last four. The dichotomy contrasts *bugi, juwuuda, geiga, gapuuga, gamouda, buguwa, ita, begadimi, bago,* and *takapaka* with *dego-uwo, pekuu, uwo ibo,* and *onee.*

2. Cultivation significance (agricultural land versus potentially cultivable, versus exempt from cultivation, versus unfit for cultivation). This dimension applies only to the first ten land types and classifies them into four categories. The land that is cultivable (irrespective of whether it is actually under cultivation or is lying fallow) the Kapauku call *mude,* which can be translated loosely as "agricultural land." It comprises *bugi* (garden), *juwuuda* (yard), *geiga* (fallow grassland), and *gapuuga* (fallow bush). The next component of this dimension I have called "potentially cultivable" despite the fact that the Kapauku describe this category as *pijaida,* which means literally "wooded area." The Kapauku term is a misnomer. It is true that *pijaida* is composed of *gamouda* (exploited virgin forest) and *buguwa* (virgin forest), but it is equally true that this category contrasts in the taxonomy with *mude* which includes the class *gapuuga* (fallow bush), which often is a secondary forest—another type of wooded area. When I pointed this out to my informants they readily explained the difference between *mude* and *pijaida* and thus also between the first two components of this dimension: the first category was already subject to the cultivation process, whereas the second was potentially cultivable (exact translation: "could be made into a garden"). The third component of this dimension is cultivable land that is permanently exempt from cultivation (in the informant's words: "landowners relinquished it for path"). The fourth and last component I call "unfit for cultivation," which expresses quite well what the Kapauku mean by their term *peu-maki,* "bad land." The four components of this dimension contrast *bugi, juwuuda, geiga, gapuuga,* with *gamouda, buguwa,* with *ita;* and with *begadimi, bago, takapaka.*

3. Degree of vegetation disturbance (complete versus substantial, versus very slight). This dimension applies only to the first six land classes and distinguishes them on the basis of the degree of surface disturbance and removal of natural vegetation. The Kapauku regard three degrees of disturbance as significant; these constitute the three components of this dimension. The natural vegetation may be either "completely destroyed" and removed as in the case of a garden (*bugi*); or it may be merely "substantially disturbed" by the removal of only some types of trees and bushes, as is the case of a yard around a Kapauku house (*juwuuda*) and exploited virgin forest (*gamouda*); or the vegetation may be only "slightly disturbed" as is the case of fallow land (*geiga, gapuuga*) and virgin forest (*buguwa*). Kapauku verbalize quite explicitly these distinctions between the exploited virgin forest and the virgin forest. However, when they distinguish garden, yard, and fallow land, they state the different functions the garden, fallow land, and yard serve in addition to the degree of vegetation disturbance. Since functional considerations were not specified in the dichotomy made between exploited virgin forest and virgin forest, I gave preference to the dimension dealing with the degree of disturbance of natural vegetation over one that dealt with the land's function. This dimension, then, contrasts *bugi* with *juwuuda* with *geiga* and *gapuuga; gamouda* with *buguwa.*

4. *Type of vegetation* (grass and reed versus trees, versus swamp grass, versus little vegetation). This dimension applies only to five land classes which it contrasts on the basis of their natural vegetation. Accordingly, *geiga* (fallow grassland) is characterized by its grass and reed cover, *gapuuga* (fallow bush) by its shrubbery (in the very early fallowing stage) and secondary forest (in the rest of its fallowing cycle), *begadimi* (mountain summit) by its short grass growth, *bago* (crag) by its scarcity of vegetation and prevalence of exposed cliffs and bedrock, and *takapaka* (swamp) by its swamp grass which requires fairly constant flooding of the ground. This dimension contrasts *geiga* with *gapuuga; begadimi* with *bago,* and with *takapaka.*

5. *Size* (small versus large). When one knows the Kapauku quantitative world outlook and their obsession with counting and size, it is not surprising to find that they give precedence to the size rather than to the kinetic quality of water. This dimension dichotomizes between "small waters," which includes brooks (*dego-uwo*) and small lakes (*pekuu*), and "large waters," consisting of large lakes (*uwo ibo*) and large rivers (*onee*). What the Kapauku regard as large or small is explained above in the description of the four water classes. This dimension contrasts *dego-uwo, pekuu* with *uwo ibo, onee.*

6. *Kinetic quality* (stream versus static). This dichotomy is applied to the "classes of water" and distinguishes between streams and lakes. The dimension contrasts *dego-uwo* with *pekuu; uwo ibo* with *onee.*

289

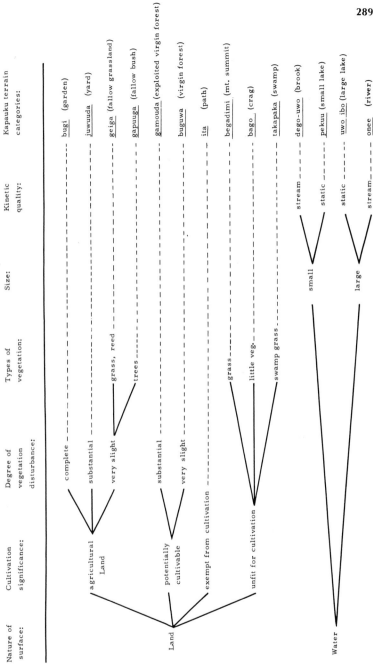

FIGURE 9. Componential Analysis of Kapauku Terrain Types in Terms of their Physical and Economic Attributes

The structure of the analysis of terrain types in terms of their "folk components" is presented in Figure 9, where the components of the six dimensions are related with the fourteen land types.

The fourteen land and water categories were designed and labeled by the Kapauku themselves and contrasted in terms of distinctive features (components) which the natives hold important; they may be regarded as part of the Kapauku culture—as folk data. However, it would be going too far to claim that organizing these folk data into a sequential arrangement and a diagram offers a "folk-componential analysis." Although the basic concepts and their interrelationships derive from the natives, the overall organization of the figure is mine, for informants certainly did not conceive such a systematically organized total image. Their ideas about the contrasts were consistent but limited to the various unassembled dimensions and levels. Thus the pieces of the mosaic were there, with the uneven edges of a jigsaw puzzle; it remained for me only to assemble them.

It is worth noting that the first two dimensions of the componential analysis match exactly the two corresponding abstract levels in the "folk taxonomy." Accordingly, the components "land" and "water" correspond to the taxa *maki* and *uwo,* and the components "agricultural land," "potentially cultivable," "exempt from cultivation," and "unfit for cultivation" correspond to the taxa *mude, pijaida, ita,* and *peu-maki.*

Analysis of the Kapauku Terrain Types in Terms of Their Legal Attributes

Kapauku say that the division of their natural habitat into the fourteen classes is due to the need to distinguish in their legal rules the various land and water environments according to their observable and important physical attributes, but this statement is hardly accurate. My doubts about the sole emphasis upon distinctive physical features in this classification are justified and are documented by the fact that many other types of land, conceptualized by the Kapauku and provided with proper terms, have not been incorporated into this legally important folk taxonomy and paradigm. For example, the Kapauku neglect such important environmental features as *mugu* (a precipice), *bijo* (a cave), and *mogo* (huge boulders), and tacitly identify these with *bago* (high, rocky mountain peak), despite the obvious physical and environmental differences. The reason for this is not that there is a striking physical similarity among these features but that all these terrain types carry the *same economic and legal significance.* In other words, in spite of what the Kapauku *say* they do, this system of terrain classes actually is designed for economic-legal purposes and is used only in a legal context. The discrepancy between their statements and facts, instead of leading us to "God's Truth," leads to what in Burling's terminology could be called, "folk hocus-pocus" (Burling 1964a: p. 27). In the subsequent discussion I shall concentrate upon the relationship of the fourteen terrain categories to their economic-legal significance and try to reveal something culturally more significant than would be a folk taxonomy and an analysis by "folk components."

Analysis in Terms of Contrastive Legal Correlates. Since various legal rights pertain to the fourteen terrain types, and since this particular set of land and water categories is used in discussions pertaining to land tenure problems, I consider it justified to assume that the features responsible for the classification into contrastive classes are legal principles contained in the rules governing Kapauku land tenure. This being the case, then, in contrast to the folk-analytical approach, the contrastive features are not inherent in the terrain concepts themselves. Consequently, I am not able to abstract contrasting characteristics from the fourteen land and water categories. I must avail myself of principles inherent in another matrix (namely, laws of land tenure), thus making the classificatory features extrinsic to the matrix to be analyzed. The legal principles that form the essence of the land tenure rules will constitute my dimensions, and the specific values thereof will serve as the "contrastive correlates." As explained in the section Methodological Problem, the word "correlates" signifies that these features are not derived from the analyzed matrix and differ in this respect from the components used in the current componential analyses. Because of their extrinsic nature, I feel justified in distinguishing these criteria of differentiation from the components in spite of the fact that, like the components, they represent the principles responsible for the classification, have contrastive function, and their summaries constitute the significant features of the various classes. The following analysis is binary with a single exception: the sixth dimension has three instead of two correlates.

Analysis in terms of contrastive legal correlates of the fourteen land and water categories discloses seven dimensions of contrastive features sufficient to define the categories in terms of principles of the Kapauku rules of land tenure.

1. Kind of ownership (individual versus nonindividual). This dimension divides all fourteen classes of terrain into two major categories: plots of the first six classes of land are always owned by a Kapauku individual, whereas land and water areas of the eight remaining classes are owned by a group of people (sublineage, lineage, or the whole Papuan public). Kapauku conceptualize "ownership" in terms of legal power, which *ipuwe,* the owner (or owners), holds with respect to *mude,* the subsoil of a piece of land or a stretch of water. In practical and analytical terms as we shall see later, Kapauku ownership of land and water means a bundle of specific rights held exclusively by *ipuwe,* the owner (or owners). The dimension contrasts *bugi, juwuuda, geiga, gapuuga, gamouda, buguwa,* with *ita, begadimi, bago, takapaka, dego-uwo, pekuu, uwo ibo, onee.*

2. *Relative degree of legal exemption of terrain areas from the control of sublineage members* (less exempt versus more exempt). Unlike the preceding dimension this applies only to the last eight categories of land and water owned in common by groups of people. Within these eight categories the two correlates of this dimension dichotomize between those classes owned and controlled exclusively by the members of the local sublineage, and those which the local sublineage must share with a larger grouping, such as the lineage or general public (which includes members of any Papuan tribe). The dimension contrasts *ita, begadimi, bago, takapaka, dego-uwo,* with *pekuu, uwo ibo, onee.*

3. *Degree of limitation of the right to trespass, navigate, fish, and gather* (limited to special individuals versus no limitation). This dimension differentiates those land and water types on which the rights to trespass, navigate, fish, and gather plants and animals belong to members of the local group (sublineage or lineage) and those classes that have no such legal limitation and are open to anyone for travel, fishing, and gathering. The dimension contrasts *bugi, juwuuda, geiga, gapuuga* with *gamouda, buguwa; ita, begadimi, bago, takapaka* with *dego-uwo; pekuu* with *uwo ibo, onee.*

4. *Scope of people entitled to fell secondary trees* (owner versus sublineage). This dimension is limited only to the first six of the land and water categories. It contrasts those land types with second-growth trees (as distinguished from the old virgin growth) which are regarded as the exclusive property of the individual owner of the plot, with those land types with secondary trees (usually up to fifteen years old) which are the property of the local sublineage, whose members are legally permitted to fell the secondary trees growing on this type of land irrespective of the desires of the owners of the plots. As a rule, the right to fell secondary trees is extended to the members of the whole sublineage only on land types with usually few secondary trees such as garden, yard, fallow grassland, or virgin forest. On the contrary, on land where secondary trees are abundant or even form a forest (fallow bush and exploited virgin forest) the right of felling is reserved to the individual owner of the plot. This dimension contrasts *bugi, juwuuda, geiga* with *gapuuga; gamouda* with *buguwa.*

5. *Relative importance of laws that regulate gathering of frogs* (important versus not important). As in the preceding dimension, this dichotomy applies only to some of the land and water categories. It distinguishes those types of land and water where catching frogs is

"legally important" in the sense that the right of gathering is legally restricted to a specific group of people (e.g., the local lineage), and those types of terrain where the right of gathering frogs is free to all and is not subject to any legal regulation whatsoever. The last category combines land types where the frogs are either completely absent or exceptional (e.g., path, mountain summit, crag) with water areas that are "intertribally owned" (e.g., large lakes). In this dimension the reader may well wonder about the rationale that limits frog-gathering on intertribal (navigable) rivers to members of a local lineage, and permits it to anyone, free from any restriction, on intertribal lakes. The reason behind this is that one can collect frogs from a boat or while wading in the shallows of a large lake, but on a river, because of the current and deep water next to the bank, one can collect frogs only by trespassing on the adjacent banks of the local lineage. Consequently, in order to make the rules concerning frog gathering compatible with those regulating trespass, gathering of frogs on intertribal waterways is limited to the local lineage members. This dimension contrasts *ita, begadimi, bago* with *takapaka; uwo ibo,* with *onee.*

6. *Relative scope of people entitled to fell old trees* (inapplicable versus smaller, versus larger). This dimension pertains only to six land classes among which it distinguishes those on which there are no old (first-growth) trees from those where old trees may be felled by a "smaller" category of people, from those where old trees may be cut by groups of a more inclusive membership than in the preceding category. It should be remembered that the correlates of this dimension are relative to each other, not absolute. That is, in the contrast between garden on one hand and yard and fallow grassland on the other, "smaller" means the individual owner and "larger" refers to members of the local sublineage. In the contrast between path and mountain summit, "smaller" means members of the local sublineage and "larger" means any Papuan, irrespective of his tribal affiliation. In comparing the regulations pertaining to tree cutting, it is surprising to find that the felling of old trees in a cultivated garden is the exclusive prerogative of the garden owner, but young trees may be cut by any member of the local sublineage. The Kapauku had a logical explanation for this puzzling regulation: unless the tree is a fruit tree (which would not be part of the natural environment anyway and therefore not subject to the discussed regulations), secondary and old trees are always a liability in a garden. However, one can cut down a small secondary tree without much difficulty and damage to the growing crops, but felling an old tree is a major undertaking that always effects some degree of destruction to the crops. Consequently, such an operation should be reserved to the discretion of the garden owner. This

dimension contrasts *bugi* with *juwuuda, geiga; ita* with *begadimi,* with *bago.*

7. *Relative size of the group entitled to hunt nonrats* (smaller versus larger). This dimension pertains only to two land classes, which it contrasts on the basis of the relative size of the groups of people entitled to hunt animals (other than rats) therein. In a yard only members of the local sublineage are allowed legally to shoot marsupials and birds, but in the fallow grasslands this right pertains to all the members of the whole local lineage. This dimension contrasts *juwuuda* with *geiga.*

The overall structure of the analysis of the terrain types in terms of contrastive legal correlates is presented in Figure 10, in which the seven legal dimensions with their specific values form seven vertical columns, and the horizontal levels summarize legal provisions pertinent to particular land types. The top horizontal level consists of the identifications of the seven dimensions, and the last vertical column contains the fourteen land classes.

Figure 10 demonstrates how the classification of the fourteen types of the Kapauku environment is accounted for by the contrastive correlates, which represent values of the seven dimensions derived from the matrix of the rules of land tenure. Although this analysis in terms of legal determinants of the land and water categories is in itself interesting, and shows that the set of the fourteen terrain terms actually constitutes a part of a "legal dictionary" of the Kapauku, from the purely substantive legal point of view it does not prove too satisfactory. Because it focuses on the fourteen land and water classes and not on the various rights and duties which relate to them, the analysis lacks a full account of the Kapauku system of rules of land tenure. As with any componential analysis, it concentrates exclusively on those values of the land tenure dimensions that have contrastive significance at a given point. It omits all those regulations which, at a given point, do not contrast one property class with another. For example, although a Kapauku rule states explicitly that the individual owner possesses the exclusive right to hunt marsupials and birds in his own garden, this right is not specified in the analysis. Because it is unimportant in the contrastive sense, it is omitted from the tabulation of the contrastive correlates. The too general nature of the seven dimensions is another legal weakness of the above analysis. For example, the dimension of the "relative scope of people entitled to fell old trees" is meaningless from a legal point of view. If our interest is legally oriented, we want to know if the owner is an individual or a precisely defined group. To these vital questions this analysis gives no answer, and because of these limitations it is desirable to apply another method that tabulates in a very specific way the total field of the Kapauku laws of land tenure.

Analysis in Terms of Legal Correlates.   In the preceding analysis the emphasis was upon the terrain categories, and the purpose was to delimit

295

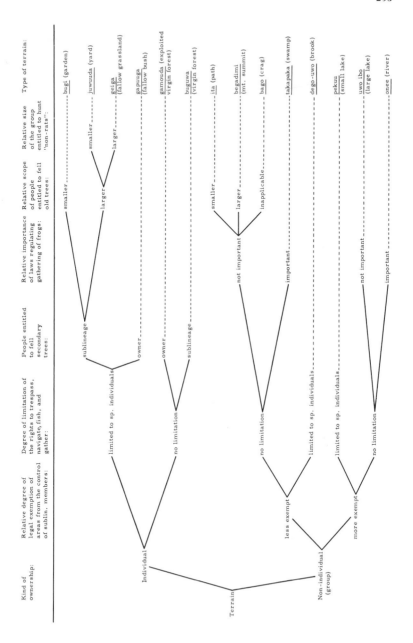

FIGURE 10. Analysis of Kapauku Terrain Types in Terms of their Contrastive Legal Correlates

the distinguishing legal principles responsible for their existence. Now the primary emphasis is placed upon the principles themselves and their relationship to the terrain categories; only secondarily are we interested in their function as contrastive criteria. To achieve the goal of complete exposition of the content and structure of the Kapauku rules of land tenure, we must depart from several rules governing the traditional componential analysis. First, since specific dispositions of rules pertaining to particular rights to land do not constitute simple dichotomies (three or more "values" belonging to a single "right dimension"), a binary analysis cannot be employed. Second, since the purpose is to analyze the relationship between legal dispositions and terrain classes, I shall include in the analysis, in addition to the legal specifications with contrastive value (legally contrastive correlates of the terrain classes), any other legal disposition pertaining to any terrain class that is not contrastive in nature. Consequently, these "new correlates" are different from those of the preceding analysis. Because this method uses correlates which are not necessarily contrastive, and because these correlates do not constitute features implicit in the matrix to be analyzed but are drawn from another, functionally related, matrix, I propose to call this method "analysis in terms of legal correlates" (omitting the word contrastive). Third, as a result of these alterations the nature of this analysis itself is quite distinct from the preceding one. Rather than analyzing one matrix, it actually relates three: the terrain types, the various rights pertaining to land and water, and the set of types of entitled parties. The matrix of the terrain types (the objects of the rights) are "analyzed"; the matrix of the various rights are used as a set of analytical dimensions, and the matrix of entitled parties (the subjects of the rights) are utilized as specific values (correlates) of the dimensions.

Analysis of the Kapauku land and water categories in terms of legal correlates employs eight dimensions, whose correlates define the fourteen categories in terms of specific rights and types of entitled parties and present all the Kapauku rules of land and water tenure in a concise, encyclopedic outline at the same time. Because of its different nature and purpose, this method presents eight instead of six dimensions, in the form of specific rather than generalized rights, with correlates that precisely specify the types of the entitled parties.

1. *Right of ownership* (individual versus sublineage, versus lineage, versus everyone). The Kapauku term for ownership of land is *mude ipuwe* (exact translation: "party entitled to the subsoil") and for ownership of water it is *uwo ipuwe* ("party entitled to the water"). As has been pointed out so often in anthropological literature, the term ownership in itself is unsatisfactory and misleading. It is actually a bundle of specific rights which an individual holds with respect to land, water, or an object. Since these rights differ from society to society it is mandatory that the ethnographer enumerate precisely the specific

297

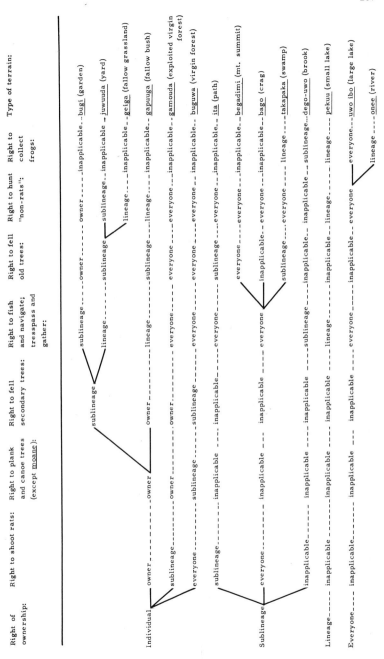

FIGURE 11. Analysis of Kapauku Terrain Types in Terms of their Legal Correlates

rights that the owner enjoys. Among the Kapauku the owner's rights to land and water differ from one terrain class to another. However, there is a bundle of specific rights that any owner (individual, sublineage, lineage, or the general public—"everyone") possesses with respect to his (their) property that may pertain to any of the fourteen terrain classes. If any of these rights is exercised by someone other than the owner (*ipuwe*), this happens only on the basis of a contractual agreement between the two (contrariwise, the other rights, not listed in this "ownership" dimension, may limit the owner without such an agreement). These specific rights, or the concept of "general land and water ownership," constitute our first dimension. This type of Kapauku ownership consists of the following rights: exclusive right with regard to a piece of land or water to negotiate a contractual agreement (sale, lease, barter, *servitus,* etc.), right to cultivate, right to trap, right to cut *moane* trees (best material for canoe construction), right to hunt by means of fire (burning dry grasslands), and right to collect indemnity for damage done to the terrain by others. The dimension of "right of ownership" applies to all fourteen terrain types and distinguishes among them on the basis of "individual" ownership (garden, yard, fallow grassland, fallow bush, exploited virgin forest, virgin forest), sublineage ownership (path, mountain summit, crag, swamp, brook), lineage ownership (small lake), and everyone's ownership (large lake, river). Consequently, this dimension contrasts *bugi, juwuuda, geiga, gapuuga, gamouda, buguwa,* with *ita, begadimi, bago, takapaka, dego-uwo,* with *pekuu,* and with *uwo ibo, onee.*

2. *Right to shoot rats* (inapplicable versus owner, versus sublineage, versus everyone). Unlike the preceding dimension, this one does not apply a legal regulation to all the Kapauku terrain categories for the reason that there are no rats in the water categories. In Figure 11 the word "inapplicable" signifies no legal disposition because of scarcity or absence of the object of the particular right in the given environment. However, because an absence of legal regulation does carry a contrastive value, it must be included as a value in this analysis. The present dimension distinguishes types of water without any legal disposition (*dego-uwo,* brook; *pekuu,* small lake; *uwo ibo,* large lake; *onee,* river) from types of land on which the right to hunt rats is restricted exclusively to the individual owner (*bugi,* garden; *juwuuda,* yard; *geiga,* fallow grassland; *gapuuga,* fallow bush), from those land categories where the right is held in common by all members of the local sublineage (*gamouda,* exploited virgin forest; *ita,* path), and from land where hunting rats is permitted to everyone (*buguwa,* virgin forest; *begadimi,* mountain summit; *bago,* crag; *takapaka,* swamp).

3. Right to plank and canoe trees (inapplicable versus owner, versus sublineage). This dimension includes rules pertaining to the allocation of the right to plank and canoe trees (except *moane*) growing on the various types of land. It contains three different types of values. "Inapplicable" indicates an absence of any legal regulation and pertains to: *ita,* path; *begadimi,* mountain summit; *bago,* crag; *takapaka,* swamp; *dego-uwo,* brook; *pekuu,* small lake; *uwo ibo,* large lake; *onee,* river. The second reserves to the individual owner of the plot the exclusive right to the plank and canoe trees growing in his *bugi,* garden; *juwuuda,* yard; *geiga,* fallow grassland; *gapuuga,* fallow bush; and *gamouda,* exploited virgin forest. The last asserts common ownership for all local sublineage members of the valuable trees that grow in their virgin forest (*buguwa*).

4. Right to fell secondary trees (inapplicable versus owner, versus sublineage). Among the Kapauku the right to "second-growth trees," for all practical purposes, is reserved to the individual owner of the grove. Sublineage members may share in felling only those secondary trees that grow on those types of land where they are very scarce, such as in cultivated gardens, yard, fallow grasslands, or virgin forests. In the last category one finds second-growth trees only in those small and rare areas where an old giant tree has fallen, taking with it surrounding trees and vegetation; but wherever large groves of secondary forests are found, such as in the fallow bush and exploited virgin forest, the right to harvest the trees belongs exclusively to the individual landowners. The dimension, then, distinguishes classes of land and water with no related legal disposition pertaining to the felling of secondary trees (*ita,* path; *begadimi,* mountain summit; *bago,* crag; *takapaka,* swamp; *dego-uwo,* brook; *pekuu,* small lake; *uwo ibo,* large lake; *onee,* river) from those in which felling of secondary trees is reserved to the individual owner of the plot (*gapuuga,* fallow bush; *gamouda,* exploited virgin forest), from those in which this prerogative belongs to all the members of the local sublineage (*bugi,* garden; *juwuuda,* yard; *geiga,* fallow grassland; *buguwa,* virgin forest).

5. Right to fish and navigate, trespass and gather (sublineage versus lineage, versus everyone). From the legal point of view, there are several interesting points with respect to this dimension. First, it is obvious that among the Kapauku the right to navigate automatically includes the right to fish, and the right to trespass gives the entitled person also the right to collect wild plants and animals (except frogs). If we regard navigation as a kind of trespass on water, then one is led to the conclusion that, in the legal sense, the Kapauku regard fishing and gathering as equivalent activities, the first pertaining to water, the second to land. Another interesting aspect of this dimension is that it

does not have values which are labeled "inapplicable" and "owner."
In other words, there is no category of the Kapauku environment not
subject to a specific legal disposition with respect to this dimension
(right); neither is there any category in which this right is restricted to
the individual owner of the plot. Accordingly, this dimension distinguishes classes of land and water where the rights to fish, navigate,
gather, and trespass belong collectively to all members of the local
sublineage (*bugi,* garden; *dego-uwo,* brook) from classes where these
rights are shared by all members of the local lineage (*juwuuda,* yard;
geiga, fallow grassland; *gapuuga,* fallow bush; *pekuu,* small lake),
and from classes where these rights are extended to everyone
(*gamouda,* exploited virgin forest; *buguwa,* virgin forest; *ita,* path;
begadimi, mountain summit; *bago,* crag; *takapaka,* swamp; *uwo ibo,*
large lake; *onee,* river).

6. *Right to fell old trees* (inapplicable versus owner, versus sublineage, versus everyone). In the exploited virgin forest and virgin forest
those old hardwoods unsuitable for canoes or planks belong in the
category of "old trees." The canoe and plank trees form a separate
category to which special legal dispositions apply. In addition to the
hardwoods in the two types of virgin forest, this category also includes
old trees (usually twenty-five years and older) growing sporadically in
other types of environment such as garden, yard, fallow grasslands,
fallow bush, path, mountain summit, and on small elevated areas in
the swamp. In the first three of these categories, and on the islands
in the swamps, one usually finds the old casuarina trees and what the
Kapauku call *onage* (*Dodonaea viscosa,* Jack); in the other environments the old trees are mostly oaks (*Quercus,* sp.). This dimension
distinguishes classes of land and water without legal provision for the
felling of old trees (*bago,* crag; *dego-uwo* brook; *pekuu,* small lake;
uwo ibo, large lake; *onee,* river) from classes whose old trees may
be cut only by the owner of the plot (*bugi,* garden), from classes on
which this right is reserved to the members of the local siblineage
(*juwuuda,* yard; *geiga,* fallow grassland; *gapuuga,* fallow bush; *ita,*
path; *takapaka,* swamp), from classes where the right to harvest old
trees is explicitly free for all without any restriction (*gamouda,* exploited virgin forest; *buguwa,* virgin forest; *begadimi,* mountain summit).

7. *Right to hunt "non-rats"* (inapplicable versus owner, versus
sublineage, versus lineage, versus everyone). The objects of this right
are all types of animals hunted with bow and arrow or club except
the common rat (*Rattus,* sp.). Accordingly, in this category belong all
types of birds, marsupials, and rodents except the rat, wild boar, bats,
and two species of python. Other small animals, such as lizards, frogs,
and invertebrates, are gathered or fished for rather than hunted, and

their acquisition is subject to other legal regulations. The dimension distinguishes classes of environment in which the native law makes no provisions for this hunting right (*dego-uwo,* brook) from classes of land and water where the right is reserved for the individual land-owner (*bugi,* garden), from classes where the right is extended to all members of the local sublineage (*juwuuda,* yard), from classes where the right is allocated to all members of the local lineage (*geiga,* fallow grassland; *gapuuga,* fallow bush; *pekuu,* small lake), from classes where the native law specifically gives permission to everyone to hunt (*gamouda,* exploited virgin forest; *buguwa,* virgin forest; *ita,* path; *begadimi,* mountain summit; *bago,* crag; *takapaka,* swamp; *uwo ibo,* large lake; *onee,* river).

8. *Right to collect frogs* (inapplicable versus sublineage, versus lineage, versus everyone). By collecting frogs the Kapauku mean systematic gathering on a large scale, rather than occasionally catching one or two. For this reason, catching tree frogs, encountered only occasionally in wooded areas, gardens, and grasslands, is excluded from this regulation. The Kapauku law refers here to the organized frog-catching expeditions of the women who go out at night, equipped with flaming torches, and scoop the frogs in large quantities into nets made especially for this purpose. The dimension distinguishes classes of environment for which the law makes no provision because of absence of a substantial number of frogs (*bugi,* garden; *juwuuda,* yard; *geiga,* fallow grassland; *gapuuga,* fallow bush; *gamouda,* exploited virgin forest; *buguwa,* virgin forest; *ita,* path; *begadimi,* mountain summit; *bago,* crag) from a class where the right to collect frogs is restricted to the members of a local sublineage (*dego-uwo,* brook), from classes of land and water where the right is extended to the membership of the local lineage (*takapaka,* swamp; *pekuu,* small lake; *onee,* river), from the class of large lakes in which everyone is permitted to collect these amphibians (*uwo ibo,* large lake).

The total picture and the structure of the analysis of the Kapauku rules of land tenure is presented in Figure 11 in which the vertical columns represent the eight dimensions (identified by headings) and their specific values (expressed in terms of the identification of the entitled parties); the horizontal levels summarize the legal dispositions with regard to the fourteen Kapauku terrain categories that are identified at the end of each horizontal line and that form the last vertical column. In other words, the vertical columns list all the various kinds of allocation of a particular right with respect to the fourteen different land and water classes; the horizontal lines present all the legal provisions pertaining to a given category of terrain with respect to the eight clusters of rights which I have used as dimensions for the analysis. This tabulation of legal correlates of the fourteen terrain classes accomplishes two purposes simultaneously: by not limiting itself to those factors that distinguish one class of terrain from the other (as the preceding analysis does), and by listing all the specific correlates (whether contrastive or not) in each dimension for every one of the fourteen classes, it gives a concise and full account of the Kapauku laws of land tenure. In spite of this emphasis upon an encyclopedic presentation, this analysis also readily makes available all features having a contrastive value by connecting in Figure 11 contrastive correlates with the correlates of the preceding dimension by solid lines.

In addition to effecting these two objectives, the analysis in terms of legal correlates—by bringing together all the rules of land tenure and abstracting from them the various rights—fixes attention upon several important characteristics of the Kapauku land-tenure system which would otherwise remain obscure in the body of the rules. First, it is significant that the analyzed matrix is composed of the legally important classes of land and water, distinguished by the natives on the basis of their economic-physical characteristics. It classifies the Kapauku land-tenure systems as a type basically different from, for example, the European systems, in which the physical features of land do not play such a decisive legal role but where other considerations such as the kind of acquired title to the land, or its size and location, become legally relevant. Second, the classification of the various rights into the eight dimensions suggests a "legal equivalence" of those rights in the same dimensional category. Accordingly, the rights of the fourth dimension show that, from the legal point of view, the right to walk on and the right to navigate on, as well as the right to gather and the right to fish, are legally equated and constitute two sets of analogous behavior on land and on water.[2]

The most important of the aggregates of rights is the first dimension,

[2]This analogy may induce the reader to assume that I have "legally equated" and subsumed under the same dimension those rights that are in complementary distribution (e.g., trespassing on land being complementary to navigation on water). Consequently he may wonder why the eighth dimension has not been fused with the third or the fourth, since it stands in complementary distribution with either one of the two. Although for the sake of elegance this may be easily accomplished without much change in the structure of the analysis, I have refrained from doing so because I have not equated the various rights on the basis of complementary distribution. Only those rights have been subsumed under the same dimension that "overlapped" at least in one instance, presenting the same positive disposition toward at least one category of terrain. Accordingly, for example, in case of the fifth dimension the Kapauku rules state that *everyone* may gather (insects, bird eggs, plants, etc.) and trespass on a swamp territory during a spell of dry weather, and navigate and fish there when the water level is high. Because of this same disposition with regard to the swamp (which sometimes is a dry land, and at other times an area covered with water) the two sets of rights have been included into the same dimension. The same procedure has been followed in "legally equating" the rights that appear in the first, third, and seventh dimensions.

labeled "right of ownership." Here we have an exact definition of the Kapauku ownership right to any land, irrespective of its type. Before I applied this analysis to the Kapauku laws of land tenure I was not aware of this significant bundle of rights (despite the fact that I knew quite well the individual rights separately) and thus I failed to discuss it in my monograph on the Kapauku economy (Pospisil 1963a). Third, the analysis in terms of legal correlates also shows the relative legal importance of the various rights which, in turn, suggests their importance in the native economy. For example, the group of rights which form the "ownership dimension" certainly are held as the most important because, without exception, they belong exclusively to the person or group of persons whom the natives call *mude ipuwe* or *uwo ipuwe,* "owners of land" or "owners of water." The legal and economic importance of the rights to hunt rats (as opposed to the right to hunt other animals), to collect frogs (as opposed to the right to gather other small animals and plants), to cut plank and canoe trees (as opposed to the right to cut the many other varieties of old trees) is demonstrated because the objects of these rights have been singled out and legally treated by separate rules. Since the Kapauku are notorious individualists (1963a: pp. 402–404), the relative importance of the various rights can be determined simply from the diagram: the more important a right is, the more frequently (with respect to the fourteen land and water categories) it is allotted to the individual owner; or, if individual ownership is legally excluded because of the terrain type (e.g., any of the water types), to the type of group of the smallest inclusiveness.

KAPAUKU PAPUAN LAWS OF INHERITANCE[3]

In the literature," observes Murdock, "two primary modes of inheritance are commonly distinguished, namely, patrilineal and matrilineal. They are differentiated according to whether the preferred heir traces his relationship to the deceased through males or through females" (1949: p. 37). On the following page of the same book Murdock stresses the importance of exactness in the analysis of social systems and complains about the study of the rules of inheritance: "In actuality, the complexity of inheritance rule is such as to make the simple dichotomy of patrilineal and matrilineal highly inadequate for satisfactory analysis." In the following text he points out the various factors that obviously play a significant role with respect to inheritance, but which the dichotomy neglects. Accordingly, ethnographic exposi-

---

[3]This section is reproduced with minor changes by permission of the American Anthropological Association from "A Formal Analysis of Substantive Law: Kapauku Papuan Laws of Inheritance" by Leopold Pospisil in *American Anthropologist,* vol. 67, no. 6, December 1965, pp. 166–185.

tions employing the patrilineal versus matrilineal dichotomy generally obscure or even omit such considerations as that some parts of the property may be destroyed, that proprietary rights of "the two sexes may exert a significant influence upon inheritance," that some articles may be regarded as belonging exclusively to the sex that uses them and inherited only by persons of the same sex, that "distinct rules of inheritance may prevail for different types of goods," and that "all the relatives of a given category may share alike, or a preference may be shown for the eldest or the youngest" (1949: p. 38). This lack of exact inquiry in the laws concerning inheritance was much too frequent until recently, despite some outstanding exceptions (such as Llewellyn and Hoebel's *The Cheyenne Way,* 1961) and despite many scholars of anthropology like Murdock and, before him, Lowie (1920: p. 157), who claimed that the transmission of property rights was important (along with the mode of residence) for establishing the various principles of unilineal descent. After Murdock's legitimate complaint was registered, other anthropologists helped correct this anomalous situation and have supplied much more adequate and exact data on inheritance. In one respect this section tries to contribute to this accumulation of precise knowledge by describing the rules that govern the disposition of inheritance among the Kapauku. However, the study of the laws of inheritance and, indeed, the realm of substantive law lack not only a solid body of comparative and exact ethnographic data from various cultures, but also a precise analytical method. Such a method should be capable of breaking down particular systems into their significant components and of abstracting from the bodies of rules the legal principles that, first, would enable scholars to define the essence of the various systems and that, second, could be classified into categories of comparative value. The main purpose of this, and of the following analysis of Tirolean laws of inheritance, is to deal with the methodological problem and to show that the formal analysis described in the previous section may permit exact inquiry and cross-cultural applicability not only in the field of the laws of land tenure but also in the laws of inheritance and, consequently, in any other legal universe one might choose. As in the previous analysis I am confronted here with three problems: the universe to be analyzed, the components, and the purpose. As far as the first problem is concerned, in the Kapauku rules of inheritance I was led to the conclusion that the most meaningful analysis might be accomplished by choosing the objects of the rules (classes of property left by the deceased) as the matrix, to be analyzed in terms of the pertaining legal dispositions responsible for the existence of the "property classes." As in the analysis of the laws of land tenure, the second problem deals with the fact that the features (i.e., the legal dispositions of the classes of property) by which the matrix of the inherited types of property are analyzed are derived from another matrix and are consequently extrinsic. Because this extrinsic nature prevents an extrapolation of these legal dispositions from the analyzed matrix of the inherited property classes, I call the features correlates rather than components. For the problem of the purpose, I intend to show how the various property categories are mutually distinguished legally and how they are correlated with the various values (correlates) of the several legally significant dimensions. Through this procedure I hope to arrive at a concise structural and descriptive presentation of the domain of the Kapauku rules of inheritance, to give its essence in terms of the most significant legal features, and to avoid the use of such ambiguous and sweeping labels as, for example, patrilineal inheritance and primogeniture.

Property Classes

Kapauku rules of inheritance classify the various items of a deceased person's property into seventeen categories. Although the individual rules of inheritance fall into types, each of which is applied to several but not to all the property classes, a unique combination of the rules is applied to a given property class (which in the kinship-terminological analysis would correspond to summaries of the distinctive semantic features that define the various significata). Thus every class of property described below is subject to a set of regulations which in some respect is different from those of any other class. The property classes are presented in an order that proved to be important in their analysis.

1. *Iron and stone machetes, axes, knives, and salt of the deceased male.* This class combines the most valuable tools of a Kapauku man with his salt supplies. The stone tools are manufactured by grinding and polishing suitably shaped pebbles found usually in riverbeds. Some of the artifacts of highest quality and value are made of dark-green serpentine quarried in the Highlands northeast of the Kamu Valley. *Maumi,* the stone ax, is petaloid in shape, ovate in cross section, and is inserted by its rounded butt into a hollowed end of a short piece of wood and held in position by several rattan loops. Sometimes the hollowed piece of wood is replaced by several flattened wooden pieces lashed together by the rattan loops. This assembly is then inserted into a perforation in a hard wood handle about 75 centimeters long, thus forming an ax. Needless to say, the actually valuable part of this implement is the polished celt. *Jabo,* the stone machete, is usually made of a hard, dark stone (jadeite, chert) or of slate, about twenty centimeters long. The tool is an elongated ellipse or a willow leaf shape, highly polished and used without a handle. *Ipa,* the stone knife, resembles *jabo* in every respect except that it is much smaller. *Jika,* the introduced steel ax; *mawai,* the introduced steel machete, and *putewe,* the introduced steel knife have been "legally equated" (a Kapauku version of legal fiction) with their stone counterparts and are subject to the same inheritance regulations. *Diga,* the

native salt, comes to the Kamu Valley through trade from the Moni Papuan country (salt springs) in the form of *kemo,* elongated stone-hard bundles weighing approximately two kilograms, wrapped in banana fronds and tied with rattan. Because of their relative scarcity and the usually high demand, they are as valuable as the precious tools and deserving of the same treatment by the laws of inheritance.

2. *Pigs and debts from pig trade.* The pig constitutes part of the focus of the Kapauku culture. It furnishes the natives with the necessary proteins and provides the only means of acquiring wealth. Since wealth is the highest goal for which every Kapauku strives and the prerequisite for attaining political and legal leadership as well as economic and social security, it is easy to understand why the animal has attained its focal position in the native culture and why, together with debts and credits from its trade, it forms a separate class, subject to a special combination of inheritance regulations.

3. Ususfructus *of land.* This property right, unless excepted by the testament, belongs to the heir of the land. However, at the death of an individual who has rented gardens, the usufruct of these lands forms a separate part of the estate. Also, separate provisions are made for usufruct in connection with the guardian of a minor heir.

4. *Tabooed currency in possession of a wife of the deceased.* Currency of the Kapauku consists of *mege,* specially processed cowrie shell; *dau,* glass beads introduced into New Guinea by the white man; *pagadau,* strings of introduced small glass beads; and *dedege,* necklaces made of small *Nassarius* shells. Cowries constitute the main type of the means of exchange and, according to their size, shape, and age, are divided into several types of different values, corresponding to our money denominations. In order to ensure a good future for his sons, a conscientious Kapauku businessman sets aside a certain part of his income as inheritance for his male offspring in the form of *daa mege,* tabooed cowries, *daa dau,* tabooed beads, etc. The taboo placed on the currency is imposed by the Kapauku owner and bars him as well as anyone else except the heirs (or, the guardian of an heir who is a minor) from using it under pain of a supernatural death to the violator. Such currency is either held by the owner and deposited in a cache, or it is turned over to one of his wives for safekeeping. In this class of property is included only such tabooed currency as is in the possession of the owner's wife, at the time of his death.

5. *Land.* Some of the types of terrain into which the Kapauku classify their natural environment are not owned by individuals and thus do not become part of the estate. For example, not all *uwo,* water types (*dego-uwo,* the brook; *onee,* the river; *pekuu,* the small lake;

uwo ibo, the large lake), and *peu maki,* bad land (*begadimi,* grassy mountain summits; *bago,* stony cliffs; and *takapaka,* swamps) are individually owned. On the other hand, every type of *mude,* cultivated land (*bugi,* gardens; *juwuuda,* yard; *geiga,* fallow land covered with reed and grass; and *gapuuga,* fallow land overgrown with secondary forest and bush) and *pijaida,* wooded virgin areas (*gamouda,* partially exploited primary forest; and *buguwa,* virgin forest) that is suitable for eventual agricultural exploitation is owned individually in the Kamu Valley and belongs to this class of property, being subject to the same legal provisions with regard to inheritance.

6. *Tabooed currency in possession of the deceased male.* This category of property is listed in class 4, except that at the time of death it is in the owner's personal possession, usually hidden in the house or in the numerous limestone cliffs that cover the upper reaches of the slopes surrounding the Kamu Valley.

7. *House, women's huts, and canoes.* Kapauku build their homes of planks, reed, and thatch. With no exceptions, all their houses have a rectangular floor plan, plank walls, an elevated floor, and a thatched, gabled roof. A usual *owa,* house, comprises one or two common men's dormitories and several small women's quarters (Pospisil 1963a: pp. 257–259). Since every married woman is, ideally, entitled to her own room, which she shares with her children, a Kapauku house-owner is often forced to build *tone,* single-room structures, each intended for one married woman and her progeny (Pospisil 1963a: p. 260). With respect to inheritance the disposition of all these buildings is regulated by the same set of rules. The most valued parts are the hewn planks of which the walls are made. Only an heir who lives in the home at the time his relative died is likely to continue to live there without taking it apart. Other heirs, not coresident, usually dismantle a structure and take possession of the planks, which they use as building material for their own homes, or which they sell. The Kapauku dugout canoe, which is also included in this class of property, is a simple hollowed-out tree trunk. Its value rises with the size of the craft (1963a: pp. 285–286).

8. *Dogs, chickens, men's net carrying bags, men's necklaces.* In this class of property are included the Kapauku domesticated animals except the important pig, and the artifacts that constitute the native objects of art. The Kapauku excel in net making, and their fine products are probably the best of their kind in the whole of New Guinea. By employing three different netting techniques the natives make several types of utilitarian and ornamental bags (Pospisil 1963a: pp. 267–273) like *jameka agija,* the man's net carrying bag, which is

rectangular, provided with a strap handle, and often decorated by yellow or red orchid-stem wrapping. Fine specimens sometimes have as high a value as one or two precious old cowrie shells (one old cowrie buys about four pounds of pork). Other types of men's net carrying bags include *mitu ute,* a net purse decorated all over with yellow orchid wrapping; *ute pugeukwa,* a narrow tubular shell container; *detaa agija,* the most precious net shoulder bag, provided with two rows of boar tusks and a cassowary bird bone spinner; *amaapa,* a net breast bag with an elongated rectangular body and a strap, worn on the chest with the strap running under the arm and around the neck; *dageebai,* a hairnet; and *tamau,* a net bag similar to *amaapa,* but worn around the neck by old men. The Kapauku men's necklaces consist of netted bases to which animal teeth and shell are attached (1963a: pp. 274–277). The several types include *dodi ego gope,* dog-tooth necklace; *keege ego gope,* cuscus-tooth necklace; and *dedege gope,* Nassarius shell necklace. A man may also possess and wear *wotiimo gope,* a *Melo hunteri* shell necklace, which he manufactures, but which usually is worn by a woman.

9. *Bows, arrows, charm stones, tools, and men's utensils.* This category includes men's artifacts of lesser value. The most important or these are *boote,* palm bows. The class includes other types of bows made of hardwoods; a great array of native arrow types (see Pospisil 1963a: pp. 231–235); black charm stones with white veins (1963a: pp. 278–279); a variety of such tools as rat-tooth chisels, bone needles and awls, flint scrapers, whet and grinding stones, bamboo knives, fire saws, claw and python-jaw surgical instruments, and earth knives (1963a: pp. 278–281, 287–289); utensils such as tobacco containers of bamboo, red-ocher containers, wooden combs, racks for drying tobacco leaves, and bagworm-cocoon containers (1963a: pp. 270, 281–282). Their small value is reflected in the relative lack of concern of the laws of inheritance, which impose no restrictions on the testator, guardian, or main heir as to their use and disposal. Excluded from this category are children's bows and arrows, utensils, and tools that are not considered worth any legal concern or regulation.

10. *Free currency from a deceased male.* This category of Kapauku money contains articles identical with those described in classes 4 and 6. The only difference between them is that this currency has not been set aside by the owner and provided with a protective taboo; it was used until the owner's death as fluid capital for financing his economic and political ventures and as a source of cash for the purchase of consumer goods.

11. *Iron and stone machetes, axes, knives, and salt of the deceased female.* A Kapauku woman may own any of the stone and

steel tools, as well as salt, that have been described in class 1. She usually receives these items as gifts from her husband, from male consanguineal relatives, or from friends. The fact that she, rather than a male, is the owner of this property at the time of her death requires special legal provisions, and the items form a separate class with respect to the rules of inheritance.

12. Free currency from a deceased female. A woman usually owns beads and dedege and *pagadau* necklaces which she uses as money. Should she acquire cowrie shells, she is expected to turn them over to her husband or close male relatives as loans. They, in turn, are required by law to repay the debts, not in the same kind of money, but in beads or the two types of necklaces. Consequently, this category is different from class 10 in that it does not include cowries and that the late owner was a woman rather than a man. These differences, of course, require special legal treatment with respect to inheritance.

13. Average-sized ako *necklaces and women's net bags.* An *ako* necklace is exclusively a woman's decoration; it is never worn by a man. It consists of vertically arranged slices of polished *Conus* shell fastened to a braided base made of inner-bark string. It is fastened with a string around the neck and it hangs between the breasts (Pospisil 1963a: 276–277). Unlike the man's net carrying bags, the woman's bags are not decorative and are purely utilitarian. Accordingly, they have lower value. They include *jagamoka agija,* the woman's net carrying bag, which except for a lack of decoration resembles the man's, and various small net bags called *ute,* used as receptacles for crayfish, sweet potatoes, insects, frogs, and so forth (Pospisil 1963a: pp. 268–269).

14. Large ako *necklaces.* These are the most precious decorations of a woman and vary in value according to the size of the *Conus* shell pieces. Structurally they are identical with the common *ako* necklaces described above. Because of their markedly higher value the laws of inheritance make special provisions for their disposal after the death of the owner.

15. Fishing nets and jato *net bags.* As in the preceding four classes of property, articles of this category belong to a Kapauku female. However, unlike the preceding classes, the fishing nets and *jato* net bags are considered a purely feminine concern and are inherited in the female line. The nets are of several well-defined types, the largest and most valuable of which is *udeebai,* the common net for catching crayfish. It is oval in shape and is fitted into a frame made from a flexible branch of the *Acalypha* tree, its larger diameter approximating

120 centimeters. *Tobaabai,* a tadpole-fishing net, is of the same shape and structure, differing from the former net only in size, being about 90 centimeters in diameter. In addition to these two nets the Kamu Kapauku women use the much smaller *tanoobai,* dragonfly larvae fishing net and *igimiteebai,* water boatman (a waterbug) fishing net, both densely netted especially in the center; circular in shape, about 50 centimeters in diameter; and fitted into a frame made from a flexible branch (Pospisil 1963a: pp. 223–225). The last type of net, *dogeebai,* used as a dipper, is for catching frogs; it is teardrop in shape and fitted into a flexible frame so that it forms a scoop of approximately 50 centimeters length (1963a: p. 227). Children's fishing nets are regarded as toys and are not subject to legal inheritance regulations. The last article of this class, the *jato* net bag, serves not only as a large carrying device for transporting sweet potato shoots, firewood, and other bulky burdens, but it also forms a sort of a garment, being suspended from the woman's head and hanging down her shoulders and back; it looks like a cloak (1963a: p. 268).

16. Bride price. The Kapauku bride price is composed of two different parts: *kade,* the less important part, which consists usually of introduced cowries, beads, and necklaces; and *one,* the major payment composed of valuable types of currency and pigs (Pospisil 1963a: pp. 323–324). Only the latter constitutes a heritable debt or credit. An average *one* amounts to 120 Kapauku cowries, three *dedege* necklaces, and one large male pig. The bride price varies with the groom's wealth rather than with the quality of the bride; a rich man is expected to pay more and thus to show his "generosity." The importance of the bride price and its relationship to a living woman (either the bride or her daughter) merits, according to the Kapauku law, a special regulatory consideration with respect to its inheritance.

17. Penis sheaths, belts, armlets, wigs, noseplugs and earplugs, skirts, and rain mats. All the articles in this class are regarded by the Kapauku as close personal property of the deceased, indeed, almost as part of his body. Because of respect for the deceased and fear of the evil spirit who is believed to have caused his (her) death, these articles of clothing and body ornaments are not separated from the corpse. They are either abandoned with it in a grave, dead house, or on a scaffold, or they are burned together with the body, if the deceased happened to be an executed criminal or a slain enemy.

Analysis in Terms of Contrastive Legal Correlates
In the following analysis the seventeen described classes of property will constitute the universe subjected to the analysis. As in the preceding section, the features responsible for the distribution of the various property

items and their classification into contrastive categories are not attributes inherent in the content of the classes. Consequently, we are unable to abstract common contrasting characteristics from the various classes themselves, as we can in a componential semantic analysis of kin terms. Instead, we have to use legal rules of inheritance and segments thereof (all cultural data) that are the explicit cause of the Kapauku property classification. The legal principles that form the essence of these legal principles will serve as contrastive correlates. Because of the extrinsic nature of the correlates, I feel justified in calling these criteria "correlates" and thus distinguishing them from the traditional "components" of intrinsic nature as used in the current componential analyses of kinship terminologies. In respect to function, my extrinsic correlates parallel the traditional components. Accordingly, they are the principles responsible for the classification and can define it; they have the contrastive function, and their summaries constitute the significata of the various classes. The binary structure of the analysis will be pleasing to the purists in the anthropological school of componential analysis; however, a less pleasing aspect of this procedure is that the last three dimensions do not have contrastive importance for all the classes. Unlike the preceding ones, these dimensions deal with "relative importance" rather than with absolute attributes, which makes them inapplicable to those classes in which they cannot play a contrasting role. Since kinship terminological analyses also use such dimensions, perhaps the lack of elegance may be excused here.

Analysis of the categories of property left by a deceased Kapauku discloses seven dimensions of distinctive legal features (correlates) which are sufficient to define the seventeen classes of property in terms of principles of the Kapauku rules of inheritance:

1. *Inclusion in estate* (included versus excluded). This dimension applies to all properties of the deceased and groups them into two major categories: sixteen classes of property that are designated for inheritance and thus become part of the estate, and one class of property that is relinquished with the corpse. The dichotomy contrasts 1–16 and 17.

2. *Kind of determination of the main heir* (normal patrilineal sequence versus other types of sequences). This dimension applies to the sixteen classes constituting the estate and distinguishes the classes of property that pass to a main heir (determined according to a "normal Kapauku patrilineal sequence" of available heirs, and those classes of property that are to go to heirs determined on the basis of another principle. The normal Kapauku patrilineal heir sequence requires that the main heir be the eldest son of the deceased male or female. If there are no sons the eldest son of the eldest deceased son inherits, and if there are no patrilineal descendants, the eldest living

brother is the heir. In the absence of the latter, the eldest son of the eldest brother inherits. In the absence of first fraternal nephews or their male progeny (main heir determined again on the principle of primogeniture within the generation), the father inherits. If the father is dead, the father's eldest brother inherits. If all paternal uncles are dead, the eldest son of the father's eldest brother becomes the exclusive heir, and so on. The dichotomy contrasts classes 1–10 and 11–16.

3. *Degree of participation of co-heirs* (participation versus no participation). This dimension applies to all classes constituting the estate. It contrasts those classes of the deceased individual's property in whose inheritance the siblings of the main heir participate, with those classes inherited exclusively and totally by the main heir alone. The dichotomy contrasts classes 1–7 and 8–10; classes 11–12 and 13–16.

4. *Appeal to guardian's morality by the rule* (appealed to versus no appeal made). As in the dimensions described above, this dichotomy is applied to all classes that constitute the estate; and contrasts classes of property whose inheritance by a minor heir is regulated by rules that make an appeal to the minor's guardian's moral obligation to share the estate with the heir, with those classes whose inheritance by a minor heir is not subject to rules making such an appeal (not relying on morality of the guardian). The dichotomy contrasts classes 1–2 and 3–7; classes 8 and 9–10; classes 11 and 12; classes 13–14 and 15–16.

5. *Relative freedom in testament* (testator less restricted versus testator more restricted). Unlike the dimensions above, this dichotomy applies to only thirteen of the classes of property that form the estate. It distinguishes those classes that cannot be freely disposed of by the testator (he has to respect limitations imposed upon him by the Kapauku law) and those classes that may be willed with little restriction. The dichotomy contrasts classes 1 and 2; classes 3 and 4–7; classes 9 and 10; classes 13 and 14; classes 15 and 16.

6. *Relative equality of distribution among co-heirs* (more equally distributed versus less equally distributed). This dichotomy, with an application limited to only four property classes, distinguishes the classes of property that are divided more equally among the co-heirs (the main heir and his full siblings of the same sex) and those classes whose major portion must go to the main heir. This dichotomy contrasts classes 4, 5 and 6, 7.

7. *Relative importance of the identity of the possessor of the various parts of estate for their allocation* (more important versus less important). This dichotomy, which subdivides the four classes di-

chotomized by the preceding dimension, distinguishes those classes of property whose allocation depends on the identity of the possessor of the property at the time of death of the owner (thus it is important whether the deceased had the property in his personal possession or whether he had entrusted it to his wife) and those classes whose allocation does not depend on such an identity. This dichotomy contrasts classes 4 and 5; classes 6 and 7.

The structure of the analysis of the categories of property left by a deceased Kapauku may be presented in outline form with the sequence of these dimensions of distinctive legal features (correlates) indicated by successive indentions.

I. Included in estate
  A. Normal patrilineal sequence
    (A) Participation of co-heirs
      1. Appealed to guardian's morality
        (1) Testator less restricted   1. Iron and stone machetes, axes, knives, and salt of a deceased male

        (2) Testator more restricted   2. Pigs (and debts from pig trade)

      2. No appeal made to guardian's morality
        (1) Testator less restricted   3. *Ususfructus* of land
        (2) Testator more restricted
          a. More equally distributed
            (a) Identity more important   4. Tabooed currency in possession of wife of the deceased

            (b) Identity less important   5. Land
          b. Less equally distributed
            (a) Identity more important   6. Tabooed currency in possession of the deceased male

            (b) Identity less important   7. House and women's huts

    (B) No participation of co-heirs
      1. Appealed to guardian's morality   8. Dogs, chickens, men's net bags, men's necklaces

(Continued)

ANTHROPOLOGY OF LAW **314**

2. No appeal made to guardian's
morality
   (1) Testator less restricted

   (2) Testator more restricted

B. Other types of sequences
  (A) Participation of co-heirs
    1. Appealed to guardian's morality

    2. No appeal made to guardian's
    morality

  (B) No participation of co-heirs
    1. Appealed to guardian's morality
      (1) Testator less restricted

      (2) Testator more restricted
    2. No appeal made to guardian's
    morality
      (1) Testator less restricted

      (2) Testator more restricted
II. Excluded from estate (abandoned with
corpse)

9. Bows, arrows, charms, tools, men's utensils
10. Free currency from a deceased male

11. Iron and stone machetes, axes, knives, and salt from a female

12. Free currency from a deceased female

13. Common *ako* necklaces and women's net bags
14. Large *ako* necklaces

15. Fishing nets and *jato* net bags
16. Bride price

17. Penis sheaths, belts, armlets, wigs, noseplugs, and earplugs, skirts, rain mats

The preceding analysis of the property classes in terms of correlates derived from the rules of inheritance depicts the contrastive features that account for the classification; it points out the basic reasons for having different classes of property. From the legal point of view, however, it leaves much to be desired. First, because it focuses on property categories and not on disposition of these through laws of inheritance, it does not offer a full statement of rules of inheritance. It concentrates exclusively on those values of the legal dimensions which have, at a given point, contrastive function, omitting all those regulations which, at a given point, do not contrast one property class with another. For example, although a Kapauku rule states that pigs (class 2) ought to be shared to some extent (under a moral penalty of ostracism) by the main heir and his co-heirs, no notation of this rule appears in the analysis above. It is absent because it does not carry a contrastive function. In other words, the preceding analysis concentrates exclusively upon the bare minimum that must be known in order to distinguish between the categories of the Kapauku estate from the legal point of view. Second, all dimensions except the first are too general to give a full statement of the legal desiderata. Because of these serious limitations another method is required to present (in outline but in a specific enough form) the whole picture of the Kapauku laws of inheritance.

Analysis in Terms of Legal Correlates

In order to arrive at a complete exposition of the content and structure of the Kapauku precepts of inheritance we must depart from additional rules governing traditional componential analysis and even sacrifice some of them. Since, as contrasted with the more general dimensions in the preceding analysis, values of the various specific legal dimensions are usually not dyadically arranged (three or more values often belonging to a single dimension), the presentation will not employ a binary analysis. Furthermore, since now the intention is to present and analyze the full relationship between the legal dispositions and the property classes, we shall not be limited to only those specifications that have a contrastive function among the categories of the estate. On the contrary, we shall include any legal disposition pertaining to any class of property left by the deceased, irrespective of its contrastive value. As a consequence the correlates of this type of analysis are different from those of the preceding section.

As in the analysis of the laws of land tenure, the focus in this method shifts from the analysis of a matrix to the analysis of the relationship of two or more matrices (one matrix being correlated with segments of another), and since it transfers its emphasis from the minimal contrastive exposition to a full, so to speak, encyclopedic analysis, I propose to differentiate it from the former analysis and to call it "analysis in terms of legal correlates" (leaving out the word contrastive). The correlates employed below will include not only those that are related to the analyzed matrix by grouping the latter's cultural segregates into functionally related classes, but also those that in spite of their relationship to specific segregates of the related matrix have no such contrastive function.

Analysis of the categories of property left by a deceased Kapauku discloses five dimensions of legal correlates that are sufficient to define the seventeen classes of property in terms of the Kapauku laws of inheritance and simultaneously to present the rules of inheritance in a concise outline form (see Figure 12). Because of its different nature, this method introduces two major changes into the outline of the legal principles and property categories in the preceding discussion. First, because it does not adhere to a binary categorization of features, it enables presentation of the Kapauku laws of inheritance in five rather than seven dimensions of correlates. The former sixth dimension (relative equality in distribution among co-heirs) has been fused with the third dimension (degree of participation of co-heirs), and

316

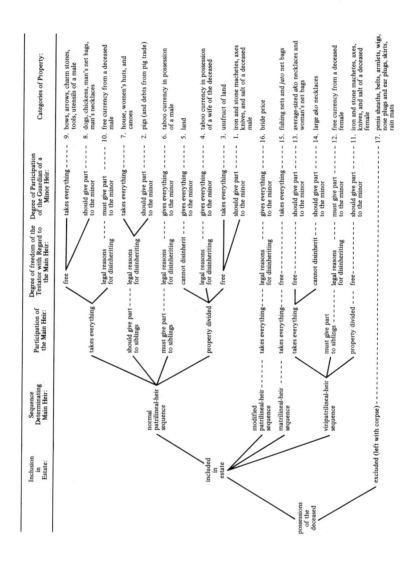

FIGURE 12. Analysis of Kapauku Laws of Inheritance in Terms of their Legal Correlates

the seventh dimension (relative importance of the identity of the possessor of the various parts of the estate for their allocation) has been eliminated and its specifications incorporated into the categories of property of the deceased. Second, because of these structural-analytical changes, the order of the sequence of the various property categories must be altered.

1. Inclusion in estate (included versus excluded). This dimension is identical with No. 1 in the preceding analysis. It applies to all Kapauku classes of property and differentiates classes designed for inheritance from a class of property abandoned with the corpse. The dichotomy contrasts classes 1–16 and 17.

2. Type of sequence of determination of the main heir (normal patrilineal sequence, versus modified patrilineal sequence, versus female matrilineal sequence, versus viri-patrilineal sequence). This dimension applies to the first 16 classes that constitute the estate and distinguishes among classes of property whose main heir is determined through four distinct types of heir sequence.

The "normal patrilineal sequence" has been described above in the paragraph dealing with the second dimension of the preceding analysis.

The "modified patrilineal sequence" (which applies in case of inheritance of bride price) resembles the normal patrilineal sequence in that the selection of the heir follows the male line. However, within this rule there are certain important modifications in the preferential selection of the main heir. It is always a brother who is first in line for the right to the bride price. Which of several surviving brothers receives it depends upon whose turn it is to collect—the eldest brother takes the bride price of his eldest sister, the next brother collects the payment for the second sister, and so on. In the absence of surviving brothers the right passes to the eldest son of the eldest (deceased) brother. In the absence of brother's sons and their male progeny (male primogeniture is strictly followed at each successive step of selection) the bride price is collected by the father. If the father is dead, the eldest son of the father's eldest brother becomes the exclusive heir. (Here the reader should note that the father's brother is bypassed in the heir sequence.) If there are no patriparallel cousins, the eldest son of the eldest patriparallel cousin inherits, and so on.

The "female matrilineal sequence" requires that the main heir be the eldest daughter of the deceased woman. If there is no daughter or female progeny, the articles of property are inherited by the deceased woman's eldest sister. If no sister exists, the eldest daughter of the eldest sister inherits. If there are no sister's daughters or female descendent of them, the articles become the property of the mother of the deceased woman. In absence of the mother, the mother's eldest sister inherits, and so on.

The "viri-patrilineal heir sequence" designates the eldest son of a deceased woman as her main heir. If the woman had no male progeny, her husband inherits. In his absence the subsequent main heirs are selected on the basis of the normal patrilineal sequence, which in this case equates the husband with the deceased woman and traces the patrilineal sequence from him. This dimension distinguishes the first ten classes of property, which are inherited by an heir determined through the normal patrilineal sequence, from the following classes: class 16, whose heir is determined on the basis of the modified patrilineal sequence; class 15, which should be inherited by an heir selected according to the female matrilineal sequence; and classes 11–14, which are required by law to be inherited by an heir determined according to the viri-patrilineal heir sequence.

3. *Degree of participation of the main heir* (takes everything, versus morally obligated to give part to siblings, versus legally required to give part to siblings, versus property division among co-heirs). This dimension of correlates differentiates classes of property inherited by the main heir (classes 8–10, 13–16); classes of property inherited by the main heir, who is morally (but not legally) obligated to share with his full male siblings (classes 2,7); classes of property inherited by the main heir, who is required by law to surrender parts of it in favor of his full male siblings (classes 6, 12); and classes of property which are required by law to be equally divided among the main heir and his siblings (classes 1, 3, 4, 5, 11).

4. *Degree of freedom of the testator with regard to the main heir* (testator is free, versus testator may disinherit for legal reasons, versus testator cannot disinherit the main heir). This dimension contains three correlates of legally prescribed behavior. It distinguishes classes of property that may be disposed of freely by the testator without any restrictions with regard to the main intestate heir (classes 1, 3, 8, 9, 11, 13, 15) from classes of property of which the main heir may be deprived by testamentary disposition if certain legally specified reasons are fulfilled (e.g., beating or verbal abuse of the testator by the prospective main heir without a socially recognized reason, neglect of the testator by the prospective heir in disease or old age; classes 2, 4, 6, 7, 10, 12, 16) and from classes of property in whose testamentary disposition the intestate main heir may not, under any condition, be deprived of his legal share (classes 5, 14).

5. *Degree of participation of the guardian of a minor heir* (takes everything, versus morally should give part of the property to the minor heir, versus legally has to give a part of property to the minor heir, versus has to give everything to the minor heir). This dimension includes rules that determine the extent of the participation of a guardian of a minor (usually his or her father's brother) in the distribution

of the estate. This dimension contains legal correlates of four different kinds. One states that certain classes of property (3, 7, 9, 15) become inalienable property of the guardian and the minor heir has no right to request their return. Another correlate requires, under the penalty of a moral sanction, that the guardian return at least part of the property left by the deceased to the minor heir (classes 1, 2, 8, 11, 13, 14). The third correlate of this dimension requests, under penalty of law, that part of certain kinds of inherited property be shared by the guardian with the minor heir upon his coming of age (classes 10, 12). The last correlate specifies that certain classes of property be kept by the guardian during the childhood and adolescence of the minor and, upon the latter's coming of age, be fully surrendered to the main heir (classes 4–6, 16).

The structure of this analysis of the Kapauku laws of inheritance may best be presented in the form of Figure 12 in which the vertical columns represent the different correlational values (correlates) of the five legal dimensions (of correlates), and the horizontal levels summarize legal provisions pertinent to the particular segments (classes) of property left by a deceased Kapauku. The top horizontal level represents an outline of the five dimensions of correlates; the last vertical column is composed of the identifications of the seventeen property categories. Consequently, if read in columns from top to bottom the tabulation gives, precisely and concisely, all legally relevant information about a particular category of legal principles (dimension of legal correlates). If read horizontally, the tabulation presents, line by line, all the legal inheritance regulations that pertain to given categories of property.

Since the "analysis in terms of legal correlates" relates legal precepts with the appropriate categories of property and gives a specific correlate in each dimension for every one of the categories, it does not limit itself to only those features that distinguish legally one category from the other. That does not mean, however, that the distinctive legal features are not included, or are not readily available from the tabulation. On the contrary, the correlates that contrast one property category with another can be readily recognized by the fact that they are connected with the correlate of the preceding dimension by a solid line. Thus the tabulation of correlates accomplishes two tasks; it gives concise and full account of the Kapauku field of the laws of inheritance and it also identifies all those correlates that have a contrasting function. As exact comparative data on inheritance accumulate it may prove possible to use the existence or absence of the various dimensions of correlates and their particular values (correlates) for a typology of systems of laws of inheritance. Thus, the categorization of the systems of inheritance may achieve, or at least approximate, the exactness of the classification of kinship terminologies and discourage the use of such misleading overall labels as patrilineal, matrilineal, primogeniture, ultimogeniture, and the like.

Moreover, the method presented has another value: it is a convenient analytical tool for extracting the basic legal attributes of the system under investigation. In this respect Kapauku regulation of the disposition of the property of the deceased exhibits several important characteristics. First, with respect to the different parts of an estate there are several types of "main heirs," determined on the basis of the four different "heir sequences." Second, the Kapauku inheritance system is strongly biased in favor of the male and of the patriline in determination of the main heir. Accordingly, the "normal" and the "modified" patrilineal sequences of selection of the main heir trace the line of the successive possibilities through the males, differing only in relatively minor points in the succession of the surviving male relatives. Even the third type, the "viri-patrilineal heir sequence," favors only male relatives of the deceased woman. If she has no sons of her own, her property goes to her husband or, in his absence, follows the normal patrilineal heir sequence among her husband's relatives.

The third major characteristic of the Kapauku inheritance system is the emphasis placed upon the firstborn in the sibling group of the kin type selected by the various heir sequences to provide the main heir. In the literature, this principle has been called primogeniture. However, the term itself is not specific enough to describe precisely the social reality. First, we must specify whether we deal with male or female primogeniture. The analysis in terms of legal correlates shows that both of these subtypes are present in the Kapauku inheritance system, the former employed in the three types of patrilineal heir sequence, the latter applied in the female matrilineal sequence. However, the two subtypes of primogeniture principle are still not sufficient to designate precisely the main heir. Since the Kapauku are polygynous, a logical question arises: Do we mean the absolutely eldest son (e.g., the eldest surviving son of the deceased male), or do we mean the eldest son of the first wife of the deceased? In the Kapauku it is the eldest son of the deceased male who becomes the main heir, irrespective of whether his mother was the first, second, or last wife of the deceased. I propose to call this principle of heir determination "absolute male primogeniture" (as contrasted with absolute female primogeniture) and suggest that the term absolute primogeniture (without sex specification) be reserved for a type of inheritance or succession in which the firstborn child, irrespective of sex and of the identity of the other parent, is designated the main heir. The other types of primogeniture which make the selection dependent upon the identity of the other parent I propose to call "relative." In addition to the absolute male primogeniture in inheritance from a male, and in several instances from a female, the Kapauku also employ absolute female primogeniture with respect to inheritance of fishing nets and *jato* net bags from a deceased female.

Another interesting characteristic of the Kapauku system of inheritance is that, although most of the property is taken by the main heir, the economically most significant parts of the estate have to be shared, in various degrees according to the type of property, with his full male siblings, the co-heirs. Accordingly, land, tabooed currency in possession of the wife of the deceased, and important tools made of stone and steel are equally divided among the main heir and his brothers. Also, a portion (usually about 30 percent) of other economically important items (e.g., tabooed currency in possession of the deceased male and free currency from a deceased female) has to be, according to the Kapauku rules, surrendered to the co-heirs.

Several Kapauku rules are concerned with the testamentary freedom of the testator. The Kapauku testament *bogai mana* (the dying words) is verbal and is regarded as an ethical duty of the dying man. Most testaments simply restate rules of intestate inheritance, thus eliminating possible uncertainties and trouble in dividing such possessions as land, currency, and the like. However, disinheritance occasionally occurs. When this is done for legal reasons (e.g., because of beating or verbal abuse of the testator by the prospective heir without a socially recognized reason, or neglect of the testator by his heir in disease or old age) disinheritance (i.e., the testament that contradicts the rules of intestate inheritance) is enforced by members of the family as well as by political authorities. In this event currency of all kinds, bride price, pigs, houses, and canoes may be willed to relatives other than the main, "legally undeserving," heir. If the testament is unjust it can be invalidated, and the rules of intestate inheritance enforced. Only two property categories are completely subject to the provisions of the laws of intestate inheritance: the economically most valuable property of a male (his land) and of a female (her large *ako* necklace). These are exempt from testamentary disposition and are inherited irrespective of an heir's behavior toward the deceased individual.

The Kapauku law of inheritance is also concerned with the welfare of an orphan who is a minor. A juvenile main heir has a legal right to stay in his father's brother's home, to be fed and brought up there. His paternal uncle becomes his guardian and is expected to take over completely the role of the father and preserve for him the property he will inherit when he comes of age. A boy, however, may choose to stay with another person, such as his mother and her new husband or his mother's brother, who then functions as a foster parent and is rewarded for his care by *mune* (payment for bringing up a child), which is delivered by the foster son when he comes of age and sponsors a *tapa* ceremony. A foster parent of a girl should be reimbursed from the bride price paid at the time of her marriage. But no matter where the boy makes his residence his father's brother remains the nominal guardian and is obligated to help him buy a wife when the young man is ready to start his own family. For this care and responsibility the guardian is remunerated by the Kapauku law that allows him to participate in the boy's inheritance from his father. He receives all the deceased man's weapons, charms, tools, utensils, houses, and canoes and is allowed to cultivate the land of the estate free of charge until the minor grows up. Also, most of the domesticated animals (pigs, chickens, and dogs), free currency, precious stone and iron tools, necklaces, and net bags become his property. However, Kapauku law provides for the economic future of the minor heir by specifying that all tabooed currency, all land, and bride price payments owed to his father should be inherited exclusively by him. In addition to the legal provision, a religious taboo imposed upon the currency protects the minor against an unethical guardian by threatening the latter with a curse of lethal disease should he violate the law.

TIROLEAN LAWS OF INHERITANCE

In order to provide comparative material and to document the feasibility of using a formal analysis cross-culturally even in most modern civilized societies, I present the following analysis of the Tirolean laws of inheritance. The statutes being analyzed are contained in two codes of law in use in the Tirol: *Das Allgemeine Bürgerliche Gesetzbuch* (Civil Code of 1963, originally compiled in 1811 and subsequently changed by new legislation; Kapfer 1963a) and *Tiroler Höfegesetz* (a collection of statutes pertaining to *Höfe,* or farms of Tirol, dating from 1900; Kapfer: 1963b). In particular, the analysis includes 91 statutes from the Civil Code of 1963 (§§531–551 and 727–796) and 14 from the Tirolean Farm Codex (T.H.G. §§1–2 and 15–26). The provisions of the Tirolean Farm Codex were recognized as legally binding, as far as *Höfe* are concerned, by statute §761 of the main Civil Code. My analysis enables condensation and full analysis of the complex mass of 105 statutes, many of which have several sections, in a relatively brief and systematic way that documents its applicability to legal systems of varying complexities, belonging to tribal cultures as well as civilizations.

For the sake of comparison with the preceding Kapauku material I shall concentrate on substantive laws of "legal" inheritance (i.e., inheritance regulated by law rather than by the last will of the deceased). Laws concerning testament, bequests, and inheritance contracts (*Erbvertrag;* for these divisions see §533) are therefore omitted. Consequently, the analyzed law concerns situations when there is either no last will or not a legally valid one; or when not all property has been disposed of in a last will; or when an "unavoidable heir" *(Noterbe)* has not been dealt with at all or only inadequately in the last will (in which case he has a right to sue for his legal share; §729); or, finally, when the heirs cannot or will not inherit (§§727–728, T.H.G. §26). What follows is actually an analysis of two matrices abstracted from the rules, as they relate to each other: the matrix of the allotments of the inherited property, and the matrix of legal conditions under which these allotments are realized. The classes of the former are analyzed by the legal provisions of the latter.

Classes of Inherited Property

The rules of the two Austrian codifications (*leges*) classify the allotment of inherited property into eighteen categories. Although the individual dispositions of inheritance represent types, each of which is applied to one or several (but not to all) of the property allotment classes, a unique combination of these dispositions (which in its function would correspond to summaries of the distinctive semantic features that define the various significata in kinship-terminological analyses) is applied to a given property class. As a consequence, every class of inherited property described below is subject to a set of regulations which in some respect is different from those of any other class. The classes of inherited property allotments are presented in an order that proved to be important in their analysis.

1. Parentela *portion*. This is an allotment of inheritance, received by the main intestate heir(s), which amounts, in the case of a single heir, to either the whole estate or, if there are several heirs, to a share of it which is equal to those of allotments inherited by other main co-heirs. In other words the inheritance is equally divided among the co-heirs who share the same degree of consanguineal relationship with the deceased. The actually received allotment of a descendant intestate heir must be reduced (*Anrechnung*) by the gifts he (she) has received from the deceased as dowry, as help in establishing a business or in setting up an office, or as payment of his (her) debts (§§788, 790, 791). This *Anrechnung* (accountability) may be excused by the parents, but only to the extent that it is used for upkeep and education of the beneficiary's minor siblings (§792). If one of the descendants has received so many gifts that their value is higher than the estate, he need not return anything, but he gets nothing more (§793). The value of the gifts of mobile objects is that of the time of the death of the benefactor; the value of immobile gifts (real estate, etc.) is that of the time of the gift (transfer of the property; §794). The share of a deceased heir (who died prior to the decedent) is allotted equally to his heirs; in their absence it accrues equally to the shares of the co-heirs of the deceased heir (§§732–734).

2. *One-quarter of estate*. One-fourth of the actual (market) value of the estate is allotted to the spouse together with the husband's movables. If there are children as co-heirs, only those movables that the spouse needs are added to the allotment (§§757–758). The value of the estate is determined by officially appointed appraisers (*Sachverständige*) and approved by the pertinent court. There are usually two such appraisers in a Tirolean village, appointed from among the local farmers.

3. *One-half of estate.* As little as half the actual value of the estate, or as much as the whole estate, is allotted to a spouse under specific conditions (§757).

4. Hof. In this class of property are included all farms (i.e., *Geschlossener Hof,* farmland and a farmhouse that belongs to it) whose description and area are entered in the *Höfeabteilung des Hauptbuches* of the *Grundbuch* (farm section of the main land register; T.H.G. §1). Any changes in farm property (through enlargement, diminution, sale, gift, or division by inheritance) have to be authorized by the *Höfebehörde* (office for farms) (T.H.G. §2; for rules regulating changes and disposal of this property see T.H.G. §§3–8; for regulations concerning pertinent legal process and the official administration of the *Hof* affairs see T.H.G. §§9–14).

5. *Choice* Hof. If the estate left by the deceased comprises more than one farm, the main heir has a choice of one. If the individual farms are so small that each or at least two of them cannot feed at least five people, then, at the request of the main heir (*Anerbe*), the pertinent court of law, upon hearing the opinion of the farm office may allow unification of two small farms, provided that unification will not violate diverse hypothecary rights pertaining to the farms, that it will not exceed the legal size limit of support for twenty people (T.H.G. §3), and that one can expect substantial economic or cultural advantages from the unification (T.H.G. §23, sec. 1–3).

6. Hof parentela *portion.* This portion of inheritance of a *Hof* estate type of property follows the same rules, as to relative size, allocation, and *Anrechnung* (inclusion of gifts) as outlined for class 1 above. However, an important difference from the non*Hof parentela* portion lies in the fact that the co-heirs are not main heirs and therefore do not inherit the same *absolute* amount of property as the "main co-heir"—the *Anerbe.* In other words, the single, and always single, main heir receives the whole *Hof,* and the co-heirs do not receive property of equivalent value. What happens is that the farm and its inventory are appraised by the court of law (on the basis of an estimate submitted by experts and by the *Vorstand*—the community administration body) not according to their market value but according to a formula that enables the main heir to pay off the *Hof parentela* portions to his co-heirs within three years (T.H.G. §§18, 19) and also operate the farm on a reasonably profitable basis. The appraisal is based on the productivity of the farm, and as a rule it is much lower than the market value. The allotments of the co-heirs, which are legally regarded as debts of the *Anerbe,* are expressed as a percentage of the "appraised" value of the *Hof* estate. All disputes arising from the allotments, which must be paid within three years of the transfer

of the title, or from the division of the inheritance, are to be settled by the pertinent court of law. If, within the three-year period the farm is sold, the co-heirs should be paid immediately (T.H.G. §21). Further, if the farm is sold within six years of the death of the benefactor, the co-heirs are additionally entitled to a proportionate part of the difference between the appraised value of the *Hof* and the actual sale price, of course, after the value of improvements made by the main heir (*Anerbe*) has been subtracted (T.H.G. §24).

7. *Other* Hof. If a *Hof* property consists of several farms, the co-heirs, in the *parentela* sequence of preference, may have their second, third, etc., choices of the other farms left after the main heir has made his choice (T.H.G. §23; see class 5 above).

8. *One-quarter of* Hof *estate.* This allotment to the heir equals one-fourth the value of the "appraised" *Hof*. Since the appraiser's value is lower than the market value, this inheritance allotment is much lower than that labeled one-quarter of estate (see class 2 above; T.H.G. §§18–21; 24; also §757).

9. *One-half of* Hof *estate.* As little as one-half of the appraiser's value of the *Hof* estate or as much as the whole estate is allotted to a spouse under specific conditions (see above class 3; T.H.G. §§18–21, 24; also §757). As in the case above, this allotment is different from that of class 3.

10. *One-half of* Hof. One-half of the actual *Hof* is allotted in this case to the heir (T.H.G. §22, sec. 1–2).

11. *Co-owned choice* Hof. If the estate is composed of several farms of which the surviving spouse co-owns at least two, he has a choice of one of these co-owned *Höfe* and receives his deceased spouse's half of the *Hof* he has selected (T.H.G. §23, sec. 4).

12. Pflichtteil-*half of estate*. *Pflichtteil,* which may be translated as a compulsory portion of the estate (§764), is allotted to the *Noterbe* —an "unavoidable heir" who has been neglected in the provisions of a testament. In this case a consanguineal descendant of the testator, for whom the testator did not provide at all (tacitly omitted, §776), or only inadequately (less than his *Pflichtteil*), has a right to one-half the allotment from the estate that he would have received as an intestate heir (§785). Every portion of inheritance or bequest that the testator left to the *Noterbe* has to be counted as *Pflichtteil,* or part thereof (§774). Also, every illegally disinherited *Noterbe* or a child of the testator about whose existence he (she) did not know, has a right to this allotment (§775), the latter receiving as much as that *Noterbe* who received the smallest portion from the testator's will. If an unavoidable heir, omitted because the testator did not know he existed

or because he was born after the will was made, happens to be the only *Noterbe,* his *Pflichtteil* comprises the whole estate with the exception of those bequests that are made to public or religious institutions or for services rendered to the testator; however their total may not be larger than one-fourth of the estate (§778).

In order to gather the *Pflichtteil* for the omitted *Noterbe,* all beneficiaries are assessed in proportion to their appropriation from the estate (§783). In determining the *Pflichtteil,* the value of all movables, real estate, rights, and credits (minus debts) must be reckoned for the estate. If a controversy arises over an evaluation, the *Noterbe* may request a sale of the property in question (§784). Bequests and liabilities imposed by the last will are to be disregarded (§786). In addition, a descendant *Noterbe* may request that gifts received from the deceased during his life (except those given prior to the birth of *Noterbe,* those that did not diminish the substance of the estate, those of moral obligation, and these given to others than *Noterbe* in two years prior to the death of the benefactor) be reckoned as part of the estate for the purpose of determining his *Pflichtteil* (§785). Of course, the *Noterbe* has to include in this account all such gifts and bequests to himself, by which his own *Pflichtteil* will be diminished (§787). He (she) must also include dowry and gifts received toward establishing his business or achieving office or payment of debts (§788). An ascendant *Noterbe* has to diminish his *Pflichtteil* only by those gifts that were not part of his legally guaranteed support (§789). The determination of the value of the property of the estate follows the same rules that pertain to *Anrechnung* and *Sachverständige* (see property classes 1 and 2).

13. *Pflichtteil-third.* As in testament omitted or partially omitted (receiving less than his *Pflichtteil*), *Noterbe* has a right to one-third of the allotment from the estate that he would have received as an intestate heir in case the deceased has left no testament (§766; for the nature and determination of the *Pflichtteil* see property class 12).

14. *Hof Pflichtteil-half.* The amount of *Hof Pflichtteil* in this category amounts to one-half the portion of the appraised *Hof* estate that the heir, omitted in the testament by the deceased, would have received had no testament been made—in other words one-half the amount in class 6 above. If this heir is a minor, he should receive the cost of upbringing in addition. Also, the *Hof Pflichtteil* entitles the *Noterbe* to return to the *Hof* and receive necessary support from the estate in case of economic emergency—if he cannot subsist by himself because of health, or lack of funds, or unemployment (*Notfall;* T.H.G. §25).

15. *Hof Pflichtteil-one-third.* The amount of *Hof Pflichtteil* in this category amounts to one-third the portion of the appraised *Hof* estate that the heir, omitted in the testament by the deceased, would have

received had no testament been made—in other words one-third the amount noted in class 6. As under class 14, the inherited amount is augmented by necessary education and support in the case of a minor or the heir's *Notfall* (T.H.G. §25).

16. Decent support. The beneficiary of this allotment (*Anständiger Unterhalt*) has a right to support and, if he is a minor, to an upbringing that is commensurate with his status (§§789, 792, 796).

17. Necessary support. The beneficiary of this allotment (*Notwendiger Unterhalt*) receives only such support as is necessary or indispensable for living. This support does not take into account either the status or the value of the estate and is certainly much lower than the decent support mentioned above. Both types of support are determined by the pertinent court (§795).

18. All. In the absence of heirs (testamentary or intestate) the state receives the estate (§760).

Analysis in Terms of Contrastive Legal Correlates

In the following, the eighteen types of allotment of property from an individual's estate are subject to a feature analysis in terms of legally recognized conditions governing their allocation to the legal (nontestamentary) heirs. As in the preceding analysis of the Kapauku laws of inheritance, the features responsible for the distribution of the various allotments from the estate and their classification into contrastive categories are not attributes inherent in the content of the allotment classes. Instead, I have to use as classificatory criteria segments of rules of the two Austrian legal codes which state the conditions under which the eighteen various types of estate allotment are awarded to different types of recipients. The legal conditions that form the essence of the inheritance rules may be grouped, according to the nature of the principles which they contain, into eleven dimensions, of which they constitute their specific values—contrastive correlates of the property allotment. As in the analysis of the Kapauku laws of inheritance I feel justified in calling these criteria correlates because of their extrinsic nature. Unlike in that analysis, however, I am not forced to surrender the binary opposition method in order to present a complete exposition of all the Austrian-Tirolean dispositions pertaining to the laws of legal inheritance. Indeed, here I am able to use a contrastive exposition, and express through it an encyclopedic analysis of the field. As a consequence, the following analysis in terms of contrasting legal correlates will adhere to a binary categorization of features, and it will fully analyze the Tirolean laws of inheritance in terms of eleven dimensions composed of twenty-two contrasting features—conditions governing the allocation of the eighteen types of property allotment.

The order of the dimensions, as they appear in Figure 13 (p. 333), is not a result of free choice. As the analytically minded reader will observe, the sequence of the first three dimensions is a fixed one—it cannot be altered because the binary values of each of the following dimensions are comprised in one of the values (condition types) of the previous dimension, while they are irrelevant to (and actually both excluded from) the opposite value (e.g., an heir, whether disinherited or not, has to be a member of the previous and more inclusive heir category only—he is certainly not "the State of Austria"). The sequence order of the last four dimensions is similarly fixed. As a contrast, the order of the four intervening dimensions (nos. 4–7) is interchangeable. My (commutable) sequence of the four dimensions has been chosen mainly for elegance.

One more point should be made concerning the sequence of the contrastive values within a given dimension. Here the much more frequent and "normal" type of condition precedes the less frequent and somehow less normal or even abnormal type of condition. For example, one would consider the intestate heir (*gesetzlicher Erbe*), in the absence of a testament, as more likely than an unavoidable heir (*Noterbe*) who has been forgotten or simply bypassed in the making of a testament. Also a consanguineal heir in Tirol is a much more frequent (normal) type than an heir by marriage. Similarly, because of high fertility of the females, a descendant consanguineal heir is more normal than an ascendant one, the latter implying the deceased's lack of progeny.

1. Existence of heir (yes versus no). This dimension applies to all eighteen classes of allotments and differentiates the first seventeen classes that require the existence of a potential heir (whether or not he is legally allowed to take possession of his allotment; an individual or institution, defined as an heir by the rules of intestate inheritance or by a testament, who has survived the decedent, who may legally acquire property, or, if a religious institution, which complies with the relevant political laws; §§536–539), from the eighteenth class which assumes the absence of such an heir(s). In the absence of an heir the State of Austria becomes the recipient of the estate (§760).

2. Right to inherit (yes versus no). This dimension applies to the first seventeen classes of allotments and differentiates the first sixteen classes, which require the absence of any legal obstacles to the possession of inheritance, from the seventeenth class which assumes such obstacles, such as voluntary surrender of the right to inherit, omission from the testament (spouse only), or disinheritance on the basis of legally recognized reasons (§767). Voluntary surrender occurs through a contract with the benefactor, which takes the form of an affidavit before a notary public or a court (§551). An heir is judged unable to inherit (or may be legally disinherited, in a testament; §770) if he has committed a crime against the deceased and has not been forgiven, in which case the heirs of the heir inherit (§§540, 541); if he has influenced the dispositions of the testator (the will) by force or by ruse, or has suppressed the last will (§542); if he (as a spouse) is recognized by the court as having committed adultery or incest and was disinherited in the last will (§543); or if he left the State of Austria or its armed forces without official permission (§544).

An ascendant or a descendant may be disinherited by the testator if he abandoned the latter in an emergency situation (*Notstand*), if he was sentenced for crime to a prison term of twenty years or longer, or if he persists in leading a publicly offensive and immoral life (§768, §769). In addition to these reasons an ascendant may be disinherited if he has neglected the upbringing of the deceased (§769). All these causes for disinheritance also apply to a potential unavoidable heir (*Noterbe*) omitted from the testament, if any of these can be proved by another heir (§782). Also, if a potential heir is a notorious spendthrift and heavily in debt so that there are reasons to believe his descendants may never receive anything from the testator, the latter may bypass the heir and will his estate directly to the latter's heirs instead (e.g., to the testator's grand children, etc.; §773).

A spouse omitted from a testament who has not been divorced, or if so is not the guilty party, qualifies as an heir, but a spouse legally disinherited does not qualify. He (she) is legally disinherited if he (she) has been divorced from the deceased because of his (her) guilt, or if the deceased had begun legal proceedings for divorce and it can be proved that the surviving spouse would have been found guilty had the deceased lived long enough to complete the divorce process (§759; T.H.G.: §22, sec. 3). In all the above cases (except voluntary surrender of property through a contract) the grounds for disinheritance have to be proved by the next heir in line (§771). The revoking of disinheritance must take the form of a legal decision (§772). In these cases the heirs of a disinherited heir receive at least the *Pflichtteil* (mandatory portion) of the estate (§780).

3. *Need for support* (no versus yes). This dichotomy applies to the first sixteen classes of allotments and separates the sixteenth class from the other classes. In the sixteenth class the noninheriting, not remarried spouse (if passed over in the testament; §796), unprovided-for parents of the deceased (§154, §789), and the deceased's minor children (§792; T.H.G. §25), are regarded by law as needing support from the estate. Other heirs do not satisfy these conditions and are excluded (classes 1–15).

4. *Type of heir* (intestate heir versus *Noterbe*). This dimension applies to the first fifteen classes of allotments. It dichotomizes between them on the basis of the absence (classes 1–11) or presence

(classes 12–15) of a testament that omitted or passed over *Noterbe,* an heir(s) who may not legally be passed over in a testamentary disposition (who may be deprived of participation in the inheritance only for legally specified reasons; see dimension 2). These *Noterben* are the consanguineal, lineal descendants of the deceased (children, grandchildren, etc., whether legitimate or not), and his parents and grandparents (§§762, 763).

5. *Kind of estate* (non-*Hof* versus *Hof*). The two values of this dimension apply to the first fifteen classes and contrast those classes of allotments which have a farm as part of the estate (classes 4–11, 14–15) and those that have not (classes 1–3, 12–13). The concept of *Hof* has been described above in allotment class 4.

6. *Kind of relative* (consanguineal versus spouse). This dimension applies to the first eleven classes and contrasts classes of allotments assigned to consanguineal relatives of the deceased (classes 1, 4–7) from classes of allotments to be inherited by a surviving spouse (classes 2–3, 8–11). The spouse inherits these allotments only if there is no testament in which he (she) was omitted, and, if divorced, or sued for a divorce by the deceased, he (she) is found not guilty (§§796, 759, T.H.G. §22, sec. 3). In the following intestate inheritance (a system of potential heirs sequence) the individuals genealogically related to the deceased in the same way are treated as equals —irrespective of sex or age. Their allotments are equal (e.g., full siblings inherit allotments of equal size). Legitimate children (born to a married couple) are treated as equal to children legitimized by a subsequent marriage (when the father and mother marry after the birth of the child; §752). A child legitimized through an act of a court on the request of his (her) father (and therefore not legitimized through the subsequent marriage of his or her parents—i.e., a child legitimized into a family of his or her father who married a woman other than the child's mother) is equal to a legitimate child only as far as inheritance from the father is concerned (§753). An illegitimate (and not legitimized child) inherits only from the mother and has no rights to the father's property (§754). The parents' rights to the property of the legitimized and illegitimate children are reciprocal (§756).

The consanguineal relatives of the deceased inherit according to the *erbfähige Linien (parentela)* system. In principle the sequence of the determination of the heir(s) is almost the same as in Roman law. The intestate heir(s) is selected from the potential consanguineal candidates by following, and fully exhausting in the prescribed sequence of preference, each of the four *Linien (parentelas)* before heirs from the next *parentela* are called upon. The heir(s) is always the "closest" consanguineal relations to the decedent (§§730–731; T.H.G., §20); the first *parentela* comprises all lineal descendants, and within this *parentela* the first descending generation is called upon first. The children of ego inherit equal portions of the estate. If one of the children has died, his (her) heirs as a unit inherit his (her) portion, which they, in turn, divide among themselves equally (§§732–734, 779). On the other hand, the portion of a deceased heir who has died without progeny accrues equally to the rest of his co-heirs. If only one heir of the inheriting generation of a *parentela* is left, and the other deceased heirs have left no progeny, he inherits the whole estate, and nothing is given to the heirs of the next *parentela*.

The second *parentela* is composed first of the parents (each of whom inherits, in the absence of any progeny of the deceased, one-half the estate), and then of their descendants (siblings of the deceased, etc.), the rules for allotment of property following those applied to the first *parentela* (§§735–737).

The third *parentela* is composed of grandparents of the deceased and their progeny, inheriting as described for the preceding *parentelas*. However, one must bear in mind that the estate is divided into two halves, one going to the deceased benefactor's father's parents, the other to his mother's parents. In case of deaths within the two halves (predeceased upper-generation relatives) the portions are always allocated within the basic two branches of the third *parentela*—they do not cross over. Heirs of the decedent's paternal grandparents inherit the portion of the maternal grandparents only if in the latter *parentela* half no living progeny is left (§§738–740). If there are no surviving relations from the third *parentela,* the fourth "limited" *parentela* relations inherit, which means that only the great-grandparents of the decedent partake of the inheritance, and not their progeny. The allotment then follows the same principles as stated above, i.e., paternal great-grandparents inherit one-half, and maternal great-grandparents the other. These halves are further divided into fourths according to the grandparental links (§741). If, in addition to consanguineal heirs, there is a spouse as a co-heir, the potential consanguineal heirs are limited to the first two *parentelas* and grandparents of the deceased (§757).

These four *parentelas* exhaust the intestate consanguineal heirs. The rest of the more distant consanguineal relatives are completely excluded from intestate inheritance (§751). If one of the close relations is related to the decedent through several legally recognized lines, he inherits cumulatively all portions of the estate allotted to him through the different channels (§750; e.g., a marriage with a first cousin, in which case the spouse inherits his or her intestate consanguineal share in addition to the spouse portion).

7. *Generation direction* (descendant versus ascendant). This dimension of generation direction dichotomizes between allotments

offered to descendant (classes 12, 14) and ascendant consanguineal heirs (classes 13, 15). The determination of the main heir(s) follows the same guidelines of the *parentela* system described above (§§765, 766). All the heirs, of course, are *Noterbe* and therefore in the ascending generations the potential heirs are limited to parents and grandparents of the deceased only (§§762, 763, 781; T.H.G. §25, sec. 1).

8. *Importance of heir (Anerbe* versus co-heirs). This dimension is composed of two legal conditions that regulate inheritance of a *Hof* property in Tirol. It contrasts the allotment containing the *Hof,* which is turned over to the *Anerbe*—the main Tirolean farm heir (classes 4, 5) from classes of allotments given to his co-heirs (classes 6, 7). *Anerbe* (and his co-heirs) are determined through the principles of *parentela.* If alone, the *Anerbe* inherits the whole estate. If there are several co-heirs (e.g., siblings, deceased sibling's children, etc., as determined by the *parentela* system) then the *Anerbe* is selected from among them by the following criteria presented in the sequence of their importance: male sex has preference over female, older age over younger (primogeniture; if there are twins lottery decides), progeny of a dead son over progeny of a dead daughter, consanguineal child over adopted, legitimate (and legitimized) over illegitimate. If descendents are absent *Anerbe* comes from that side (patrilateral or matrilateral) from which the *Hof* came. An individual may be disqualified as *Anerbe* not only for reasons for disinheritance or because of disability as discussed under the second dimension, but also because of physical or psychological inability to become a farmer, because he already has another farm (unless he turns it over to the next-in-line *Anerbe* candidate), or because of employment that would keep him away from the farm. Also, a man who has been missing for at least two years is disqualified as *Anerbe.* The *Verlassenschaftsgericht* (inheritance court) decides about the disqualification of an *Anerbe* and, in case of a disqualifying verdict, turns over the farm to the next heir in line (T.H.G., §§15–17).

9. *Children as co-heirs* (present versus absent). This dimension distinguishes between classes of allotments from estates of deceased spouses that have surviving children (classes 2, 8) and those from estates of deceased childless spouses (classes 3, 9–11). If there are no intestate heirs of the first and second *parentela* and no grandparents, the spouse inherits the estate (§757).

10. *Spouse's co-ownership* (absent versus present). This dimension differentiates between the allotments to a spouse who is not a co-owner of a farm (class 9) from those to a surviving spouse who is a co-owner of the *Hof* estate (classes 10, 11; T.H.G. §§22–23).

333

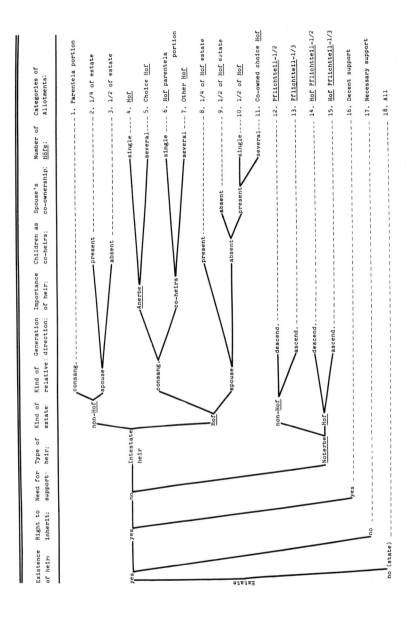

FIGURE 13. Analysis of Tirolean Laws of Inheritance in Terms of their Contrastive Legal Correlates

11. *Number of Höfe* (single versus several). This dimension differentiates between classes of allotments from estates composed of one
farm (classes 4, 6, 10) and those from estates composed of several
farms (classes 5, 7, 11; T.H.G. §§22–23).

As in the Kapauku examples, the structure of this analysis of the
Tirolean laws of inheritance may best be presented in the form of a table
(Figure 13), in which the eleven vertical columns represent dimensions of the
various kinds of legal conditions (features, or contrasting correlates) governing the allotments from the inherited estate. The latter form the last (twelfth)
column. The horizontal and diagonal lines summarize all the various legal
conditions pertinent to the particular allotments from the property left by a
deceased Tirolean. The top horizontal level identifies the eleven dimensions
of the contrastive conditions (contrastive correlates). Consequently, if read
horizontally, the tabulation presents, line by line, all the legal inheritance
regulations that must be met in order that the particular eighteen allotments
be awarded.

I was able to express the whole Tirolean inheritance field, which I was
not able to do for the Kapauku, in a diagram composed of only contrastive
legal correlates. Although Figure 13 presents the structure of the Tirolean
laws of inheritance in a system of binary oppositions, and thus preserves
some of the classical requirements of a componential analysis, it gives at the
same time a full and concise account of all the legally relevant information.

The structure of the Tirolean laws of intestate inheritance, as presented
in Figure 13, discloses some major basic sets of dichotomies. The first (type
of heir—the fourth dimension in the table) contrasts laws that are applied to
an estate left by a man who died without leaving a testament, with laws that
apply in a case when an unavoidable heir was illegally deprived of his share
by having been bypassed or disinherited. In both cases it is the legal decision
and not the last will of the deceased that determines the distribution of the
property. When one compares the two halves of this dichotomy, one finds
that the basic similarity lies in the fact that the consanguineal heirs are
determined through the principles of the *parentela* system. But there the
similarity stops. While the intestate inheritance distinguishes further between
consanguineal relations and spouses, the *Noterbe* inheritance rules disqualify a spouse completely from the inheritance and, in turn, make another
discrimination which the intestate inheritance does not employ: they distinguish between descendants and ascendants, not only in terms of the potential heir sequence but also by favoring the former with a larger allotment from
the estate. Also, when one looks at the amount of allotments, the *Pflichtteile*
of the unavoidable heirs are always less than the portions of the intestate
heirs. The second important dichotomy (the fifth dimension of "Kind of
estate") pertains to the existence or nonexistence of a farm as part of the
inherited estate (*Hof* versus non-*Hof*). Since this dichotomy is expressed in

the existence of two different legal codes one would assume that it figures as a basic and first division (dimension) in a structural picture of the Austrian system of inheritance. However, since several principles are common to both codes, this dichotomy *has to* take only the fifth place in the sequence of the various dimensions. Thus it actually becomes almost central to the whole structural field, signifying how well the two codes are logically interrelated. Also, even a cursory look at this system of laws of inheritance reveals the exceptional nature of the *Anerbe* concept. In addition to the spouse this is the only type of heir who by law does not, and even may not, share with the other consanguineal heirs in his allotment of the *Hof.* Thus it violates the *parentela* system, according to which consanguineal co-heirs should be treated as equals. The rules pertaining to the determination of the *Anerbe,* which favor male sex and primogeniture, are another violation of this system; these rules are not applied to the rest of the Tirolean regulation of inheritance.

CONCLUSION

This chapter has presented three formal analyses of legal subsystems: the first dealing with the laws of land tenure of a Stone Age tribal society, the other two with laws of legal (nontestamentary) inheritance, one taken from the same tribal society, the other from a central European civilization. All three subsystems were analyzed by a formal method that used "legal correlates" rather than the traditional "components" employed in the now numerous analyses of kinship terminologies. There is an important difference between the components used in the analysis of kin terms and the correlates that I had to use in the analysis of substantive law. In analyzing a set of kin terms, one first determines the categories of kin types that these terms denote. The kin types are expressed genealogically. Consequently, if we try to abstract from these genealogically defined types (MoBr, FaSi, etc.) features that are common to the particular classes, we are dealing with intrinsic components already implied in the definitions of the various kin types. Unlike property classes—where we have to have the knowledge of another matrix (namely, the types of disposition of the property), from which we derive the features that classify the property (which are thus extrinsic to it) —in kinship terminology it is sufficient to know the classes of kin types (the semantic meaning of the terms); we need not be interested in any associated type of behavior or other relevant, although certainly not intrinsic, cultural phenomena. The kin types of the same class provided with a kin term, are comparable to the property types that belong to a given property class, *but not* to the types of disposition of that property, which derive from another matrix. The existence or nonexistence of terms applied as labels to classes of the categorized property types is logically irrelevant to this argument.

While working on the rules of land tenure collected during my first fieldwork among the Kapauku in 1954–1955, summarized in the two monographs written before my last field research in 1962 (Pospisil 1958a: pp. 97–100, 176–184; 1963a: pp. 130–135), I became increasingly dissatisfied with the rule-by-rule presentation, which lacked conciseness, elegance, and analytical insight that would elucidate the structural principles permeating the Kapauku system of rules of land ownership as a whole. With this dissatisfaction grew also an awareness that identification of the relevant land categories accompanied all the rules. This awareness, coupled with the influence of Conklin's and Frake's articles on folk taxonomies (Conklin 1962b, Frake 1961), impelled me to conduct a thorough inquiry into the system of Kapauku land and water folk classification during my last research in the summer of 1962. The material collected then permitted me to construct a folk taxonomy and an analysis based on folk components, and also led to a conception of the Kapauku system of rules of land tenure that could be presented in a concise and analytical form. These two constructs form the content of the first formal analysis.

After describing the fourteen Kapauku terrain categories, I have presented them as a part of a native taxonomy. To show how the Kapauku differentiated one category from another, I collected native criteria of contrast and used these as components in a formal analysis. Up to this point, then, I was engaged in what Conklin and others may call "ethno-science" or, better, "folk classification." What I began to realize while still in New Guinea was that, contrary to the explicit statements of my informants and the assumptions of folk criteria, the Kapauku terrain classes were not designed out of need to distinguish classes on the basis of their economic-physical features alone. The very obvious motivations were economic-legal. In the subsequent discussion I therefore concentrated upon the relationship of the fourteen terrain categories to their economic and legal connotations. Using legal principles abstracted from the Kapauku rules as dimensions and their specific values as correlates (as contrasted with the intrinsic "components"), I have analyzed the matrix of the fourteen terrain classes in terms of their contrastive extrinsic legal features (contrastive correlates) and have shown how the legal factors contributed to the native classification of their physical environment.

However, because the analysis in terms of contrastive legal correlates shows only the legally relevant contrasts among the land and water classes, it is of limited value from the legal point of view. The legal goal is much more comprehensive. A satisfactory analysis must present all the legal dispositions vis-à-vis land and water types, organize them in a systematic way, and elucidate the important structural principles that uphold all the rules of land tenure. In other words, our emphasis had to shift from analysis of the terrain classes themselves to the legal precepts and their relationship to the former. In order to accomplish this, I departed from the rules governing the traditional componential analysis even further and derived from this a broader inquiry labeled "analysis in terms of legal correlates." It relates in one diagram three matrices whose combinations produce the Kapauku rules of land tenure: the types of right (which in the table are the headings for the eight dimensions); the subjects of the rights—the types of entitled parties (which function as the specific values of the dimensions, the correlates); and the objects of the rights—the related land and water classes (which function as the analyzed matrix).

This analysis accomplishes the following tasks which neither an analysis of the individual rules (as presented in my two monographs), nor the traditional componential analysis could even approximate. First, it presents the whole field of the Kapauku laws of land tenure in a concise form from which the reader can readily ascertain any existing legal precept concerning native land tenure. Second, it abstracts from the rules legally significant matrices whose nature sheds light on the essential legal considerations held by the members of this particular society. Sets of such legally significant matrices abstracted from legal systems of various peoples may be used, on a cross-cultural basis, for classificatory as well as comparative purposes. Third, it abstracts from the rules the various types of rights which it classifies and groups, on the basis of legal equivalence, into the analytical dimensions. This classification is so significant that it not only shows the legally equivalent rights, but it also specifies the various particular rights whose combination constitutes the legal meaning of the Kapauku concept of *mude ipuwe,* land ownership. Fourth, by grouping the various rights in a specific way the table indicates the relative importance the Kapauku law and economy place upon the various rights and upon the various land and water classes. Fifth, the matrices and the structure of their interrelation may be regarded as a kind of "legal grammar" of the Kapauku system of land ownership.

In the second analysis I have presented two methods of formal examination of substantive law: an analysis in terms of contrastive legal correlates and an analysis in terms of legal correlates, and have applied them to the rules of inheritance of the Kapauku Papuans of West New Guinea. The former method, structured in a dyadic form, takes as its domain the various legally relevant categories of the estate and analyzes them in terms of their contrastive legal features; the latter method correlates in one diagram the domains of the legally relevant categories of the estate with all the various rules that deal with its disposal. These rules, categorized by the latter analysis into several dimensions according to their main subject, state in their correlates the rights and duties of the parties concerned in the estate. They also divide the property of the deceased into parts destined either for inheritance or for abandonment with the corpse, they enunciate the principles involved in determining the main heir and his degree of participation in the estate; they set limits to the freedom of the testator; and they determine the degree of participation of the various co-heirs and of the guardian of a minor heir in the distribution of the property. Whereas the first analysis shows only the legally relevant contrasts among the categories of the estate (contrasting correlates), the second analysis presents the whole field of the Kapauku laws of inheritance in a concise diagram from which the reader can quickly ascertain any existing legal disposition of the property of a deceased Kapauku. Furthermore, this analysis abstracts from the rules the categories of the most essential legal features and presents them in a compact arrangement of the various dimensions.

The value of the "analysis in terms of legal correlates" can be readily determined by comparing my account of the rules of inheritance and the pertinent legal decisions, as presented in my monograph on the Kapauku law (Pospisil 1958a: pp. 201–208), with the present, concise, tabular analysis of the same body of data. In the former account the essential features and principles of the Kapauku regulation of inheritance are submerged in the text of the rules, and the relationships are obscured; in the latter account a cursory inspection of the tabulation not only gives the reader the essentials of the Kapauku inheritance system, but it also provides a complete account for all the legal dispositions pertinent to it.

Furthermore, the traditional "rule-by-rule" analysis, as used in my monograph, is incapable of accounting for the existence and relationship of the sixteen property classes into which a deceased individual's estate is segmented. As a contrast, the analysis in terms of legal correlates not only shows the reasons for the categorization of such property, but also presents, in a concise manner, the structure of the whole field of the Kapauku laws of inheritance by setting forth the interrelations of the categories of property with the legal dispositions and the different types of subjects of the various rights.

When compared with the system of the laws of inheritance of the patrilineal Kapauku, the inheritance laws of the bilateral Tiroleans stand in rather sharp contrast. First, except for the determination of the *Anerbe* (when male takes precedence over female) the system does not discriminate between the sexes, and the typical sequence of potential heirs takes the form of a bilateral *parentela*. There are no unilineal sequences, such as the Kapauku "normal patrilineal heir sequence" or "matri-heir sequence." Furthermore, unlike the Kapauku, the Tirolean spouse plays a prominent role in Tirolean inheritance. In every type of property (*Hof* or non-*Hof*) she or he competes with the consanguineal heirs, although the latter receive systematically preferential treatment. Among the patrilineal Kapauku, as a contrast, the wife has no right to inheritance at all, and only the husband can inherit his wife's valuable property. Inheritance of land constitutes another sharp distinction between the two systems of inheritance. While in the Tirol the oldest surviving son receives all the land in the form of the *Hof,* the Kapauku divide land equally among the male siblings, thus, strangely enough, keeping a principle of the Austrian *parentela* system which the Tirolean law itself (*Anerberecht*) violates.

Another interesting difference is the fact that with regard to inheritance the Kapauku classify property in an absolute way into categories by kind, such as currency, pigs, bows, arrows, and land. These kinds of property, then, because of their nature, are differently disposed of and go to different types of heirs. Except for the farm the Tiroleans do not make such a distinction. All the rest of their inherited property categories assume the form of allotments from the estate, a certain fraction of its total value, irrespective of what kind of property is being inherited. In other words whereas the Tirolean non-*Hof* property is all expressed in terms of its monetary value, the monetary value of inherited Kapauku property is not considered. This is so in spite of the fact that Kapauku have a money economy (cowrie shells) and that all inherited property could be expressed in terms of its monetary value, since it is as a rule freely sold in their "market," barter being an exception. One strikingly common feature of both systems is the fact that, with the exception that the state acquires an heirless Tirolean estate, all property types and allotments are inherited by individuals rather than by groups of individuals such as siblings, married couples (grandparents, for example), clan, lineage, or community.

This chapter may be concluded with a repetition of my belief that similar structural presentations of the domains of substantive legal systems of different peoples will prove to be of value in cross-cultural comparisons and in setting up a system of types (of laws of inheritance, for example) that could approximate in their significance the types established in the field of kinship terminology.

Another immediate and heuristic value may inhere in the formal analysis of law. As a law student in Czechoslovakia I had to study the hundred-odd statutes for the laws of inheritance, with their numerous subdivisions, in order to be prepared for an examination (Czechoslovakia enforced then the same Civil Law Code as Austria). In those days I would have certainly appreciated an outline which presents, for example, the whole field of the Austrian-Tirolean inheritance in a parsimonious and systematic way that, in spite of its brevity (if compared to the numerous pages in the Austrain Codex), and thanks to the elimination of duplications and abstraction of common elements from the rules as "correlates," retains all the necessary legal information. I think that in this sense anthropologists of law could be of help not only to the student of law but also to the legal profession in general.

CHAPTER
NINE
CONCLUSION

One of the characteristics of Western *Weltanschauung* is to think in terms of dichotomies, and many Western anthropologists have not escaped the cultural burden of thinking in terms of qualitatively different opposites. For them there are primitive and civilized societies, and tribal and state organizations. The differences have usually been conceptualized in qualitative terms and enunciated through crude evolutionary explanations. If civilized peoples were regarded as logical thinkers, then the "primitives" had to have prelogical mentality; since civilized people had religion backed by a deep theological philosophy, the opposite had to be true about the primitives—their religion not only lacked a philosophical base but was supposed to be dominated by magic; because contemporary Western civilization was capitalistic, the primitives had to live in communism, and so on. When anthropologists began to report on the deep individualism and wealth of the profit-oriented highlanders of New Guinea their orthodox, often Marxist-oriented colleagues became deeply disturbed. When I reported that the Kapauku Papuans (Pospisil 1963a) were not only individualistic and wealth oriented, but also used true money and the institutions of sale, savings, interest, speculation with capital gains, and true markets whose prices were dominated by the law of supply and demand, the inevitable happened. Pospisil was wrong; he was called a "formalist" and with other heretics was relegated to another dichotomy, of "substantivists versus formalists," the latter obviously the villains (Dalton 1969: esp. pp. 65–66, 79).

Law has not remained unscathed by this conceptualized dichotomization. Some anthropologists committed to nineteenth-century orthodoxy ruled that only civilized people had law and that stateless societies had none, while others contented themselves with less grandiose dichotomies and listed a series of qualitative differences between tribal (or primitive) and civilized (or advanced) law (see especially Chapter Five). To all these scholars I have committed another heresy by writing this book.

My major assumption and the explicit conclusion of my comparative studies is that there is no basic qualitative difference between tribal (primitive) and civilized law. The important attributes, functions, and processes of law are present in both these artificial segregates. Having been impressed by the arguments of Hoebel and other American realists, and convinced by subsequently collected empirical evidence from my fieldwork, I have concluded that law (*ius*) manifests itself in the form of a decision passed by a legal authority. This decision may solve a dispute, or it may advise a party before any legally relevant behavior takes place, or it may give approval to a solution of a dispute made by participants before it was brought to the attention of the authority.

This form of law has two important aspects, neither of which is possessed by abstract rules (*leges*) or actual behavior. A decision resolves a concrete dispute, which represents the behavioral aspect of it. In other words, passing of a decision is a behavior of the legal authority. A decision is also regarded as a precedent, incorporating an ideal which not only the parties to the dispute but also the judge himself and people who did not participate in the controversy are expected to follow. A decision, then, is a behavior as far as the authority's action is concerned, and an ideal insofar as it affects the followers of the authority we have in mind. The abstract rule (*lex*), on the contrary, lacks the behavioral aspect, whereas the actual behavior of the followers does not incorporate the ideal. As a consequence, while many of the rules (*leges*) are jural fossils that clutter the codes and do not exercise any social control, abstractions from actual behavior (the famous "living law") are actually in their nature sociological generalizations (sociological laws). Neither of them represents the jural law (*ius*).

In my theory, then, the legal field consists of principles abstracted from legal decisions which may or may not coincide with the rules (*leges*) or with actual behavior (sociological laws), or with both. If they do, the *leges,* which are then said to be enforced, coincide with *ius* and may be called "legal rules," and the conforming behavior may be called "legal behavior." But whether or not a rule (*lex*) or a behavior is truly legal is determined by the *ius*—the abstraction from the authority's actual decisions.

It has been pointed out that not all decisions passed in a society qualify as legal. Only those do that incorporate true *ius,* principles of social control propounded in decisions by a legal authority—the informal tribal headman, formal tribal chief, ruling oligarchy, council of elders, king, or modern judge —intended to be applied universally (to all "the same cases"), dealing with a true social relation of two parties whose interlocking rights and duties form an *obligatio,* and are provided with a sanction of physical (corporal or economic), psychological, or social nature. Because this concept applies well to our Western conceptualization of law, this term, in its limited sense of the Latin *ius,* has been accepted as a label for my cross-culturally derived phenomena of authoritative social control. The concept proves its heuristic value for social scientific analysis in that it is universal, cross-culturally applicable, and central to the existence of any functioning social group in the sociological sense of the word.

The essential feature of law implicit in the above definition of law by its form and the four criteria, is the fact that the adjudicating authority who passes a decision has to have power over both parties to the dispute or, in other words, he must possess jurisdiction over both litigants. In sociological terms this means that all the personnel (the parties to the dispute as well as the authority) have to belong to the same social group in which the authority has jurisdiction. In this sense, then, law is an intragroup phenomenon. It has been shown that every functioning group exhibits phenomena which have been categorized into a concept labeled law. As a consequence law is not just floating around in an unstructured way in a society (as is often assumed). On the contrary, it pertains to specific social groups and subgroups of a society. Furthermore, it belongs only to functioning, politically united groups. As a consequence a society segmented into politically *independent* lineages cannot and does not have an overall legal system. In this sense there is no law of the Nuer or Kapauku. That, however, does not mean that there is no law within these tribes, pertaining to the politically organized subgroups. As a matter of fact, there are as many legal systems in segmented or other types of societies as there are functioning groups, because disputes in functioning groups or subgroups cannot be allowed to continue indefinitely and unadjudicated lest they disrupt and destroy the social groups. A group, in a sense, is a group because there is a legal system that expresses and safeguards its vital pattern of prescribed behavior and induces (or in cases of violation, forces) its members to conform to it.

As a logical consequence, the multiplicity of legal systems within a society forms an overall configuration which reflects precisely the pattern of the society's subgroups or, as I have termed it, societal structure. Legal systems of groups of the same inclusiveness and type belong to the same legal level. Thus we have in any society a hierarchy of legal levels according to the degree of inclusiveness of the groups pertinent to the legal systems. The legal system of an inclusive group is applied to all members of its constituent subgroups. An individual, then, is exposed to, and controlled by, as many legal systems as there are subgroups of which he is a member. The various legal systems may, in their provisions, differ one from another to the point of contradiction. They also impose upon the individual controls of different intensity. Legal systems of those groups that exercise a maximum of social control in a society I view as forming a center of power in that society, a dynamic center that may shift its locus from one level to another. These conceptualizations help us understand why a man in one society is primarily loyal to his clan, family, village, or voluntary association and only secondarily to a state, political federation or what have you, whereas in some other societies he conforms first to the society, state, or tribal legal level and only secondarily to the legal systems of the subgroups.

Moreover, on the basis of empirical evidence this theory settles the controversy whether Nuer or Kapauku actually have law (*ius*) that exhibits the same basic features as that of civilized societies. Since all functioning groups have been found to have law in the sense of the theory presented, even a gangster's behavior is then not absolutely "illegal," because it is legal from the point of view of the gang with whose laws the gangster primarily conforms. The argument has to be concluded with the observation of the relativity of law and custom.

What appears to be custom on the society's level may definitely be law (if all the legal criteria are met) on the levels of the society's subgroups. Law as a category of social phenomena is related, after all, to the rest of the organizing principles of a society, to the patterns of its subgroups. Since there are customs that are observed without becoming laws even on the lowest (e.g., nuclear family) legal level, I have proposed to distinguish these "neutral" customs from the society's customs that are laws on the subsociety legal levels by calling the former customs and the latter "mores." Although it has been claimed by some sociologists that mores are provided with "diffused" or "social" (meaning actually nonlegal) sanctions, this diffuseness changes into something definite when one leaves the society's point of reference and descends to the subgroups.

Within the legal field I have differentiated two types of laws: customary and authoritarian. The process of social internalization has been found to be an important criterion for this distinction. Accordingly, customary law has been conceived of as being internalized by the majority of the members of the group, while authoritarian laws are found to have the support of only a minority. To be sure, both types of law are upheld by the decisions of the authority. However, while there is usually little need for excessive external force to uphold the customary law, the authoritarian law, being regarded as unjust by most of the people, needs for its enforcement the prestige and influence or even the intimidation and physical force of the authority and his supporting minority. The frequent failure to recognize the existence and nature of authoritarian law has led to misconceptions and misinterpretations on the part of Western scholars not only of the structure and function of social controls in a dictatorship but also to a misunderstanding of the basic nature of law itself. Thus I have to repeat again that jural law need not be, and often is not, an emanation of the "will of the society," that it does not necessarily reflect the values and desires of the majority of the people. If it did, we would have to regard Nazi Germany, Genghis Khan's empire, Stalin's Soviet Union, and many European medieval kingdoms as "lawless." Not even an ultraconservative Marxist would go so far as that (and he had better not if he happens to be in the Soviet Union). Once authoritarian law is recognized, the claim that tribal societies possess only "customary law" and that their chiefs do not have legal power is shown to be a myth that has been believed for too long.

Internalization has been defined as a process. A law introduced as an edict by an authority, although authoritarian at the beginning, may become slowly internalized by more and more people until it becomes customary. Or the process may take the opposite direction, and an originally customary law may lose more and more supporters until it is upheld only by the authority and his minority backers, thus becoming authoritarian. In this sense, then, legal phenomena are constantly changing as does the rest of the culture. Customs may become laws through recognition of the judicial decisions of the authority, and laws may vanish when the authority ceases to enforce them or decides cases on the basis of opposite principles.

The concepts of the process of internalization and of legal levels disclose a kind of legal relativity that is similar to the relation between the concepts of custom and law. The same law that is customary on the society level may be authoritarian when we look at it from the perspective of those subgroups whose members have not had enough time or desire to internalize it. Thus it appears that in jurisprudence and anthropology conceptualization in terms of relativity will, as in other sciences, replace orthodox thinking in terms of absolutes.

In addition to the outlined theory of law I have formulated a concept of justice and a method for analysis of substantive law. With respect to the concept of justice I favored two cross-culturally applicable theories. The first, a combination of the approaches of Hoebel and Smith and Roberts, would express justice in terms of a comparative analysis of basic jural postulates (derived from the culture and its institutions in general) and legal values (abstracted from the *ius* as implied in legal decisions). A just law would be one whose values agree with a pertinent jural postulate. The second, an application of my concept of social internalization to adjudication, would measure justice by the degree of support a legal decision receives from the members of the pertinent group.

With respect to substantive law I have designed, on the basis of a componential analysis, a method called "analysis in terms of legal correlates," that proved to be applicable to a tribal legal system as well as to one with sophisticated, codified laws. Aside from presenting a subdivision of a legal field (e.g., laws of land tenure or of inheritance) in a logical, systematic, and parsimonious way, it showed the following advantages over the traditional rule-by-rule analytical approach. First, although it presents a whole section of a legal system in a concise way and augments this by a table from which the reader can readily ascertain any legal disposition he is interested in, it does not leave out any legally important information.

Second, it identifies important and logically consistent sets of segregates (matrices) and shows their interrelations in analyzing one matrix (e.g., classes of property) by another (e.g., conditions under which these classes are inherited), matrices which in the rule-by-rule analysis are often not apparent in the text. Sometimes, as in the Austrian laws of inheritance, one can actually discover through this analysis a "new" type of allotment that in the rules was lumped together with a related but different allotment, both being provided with the same term. For example, the term *Pflichtteil,* as used in Tirolean law, covers two different types of allotments, a fact that the reader does not realize. While a *Pflichtteil* from a property that does not contain a farm (*Hof*) is calculated from the *market* value of the estate, a *Pflichtteil* from a farm property is determined by the *productivity* of the farm and the *capacity* of the main heir to pay off the co-heirs within the specified period of time. Thus the *Hof Pflichtteil* (my own compound) is certainly different from the "normal" *Pflichtteil* in that it is considerably lower.

Third, the method abstracts from the rules the various types of rights which it classifies, on the basis of their legal equivalence, into analytical dimensions. This classification itself is so important that, for the first time, it showed me the precise meaning of the Kapauku term "land ownership" (*mude ipuwe*) by defining it in terms of rights that otherwise would have remained obscure and scattered in the plethora of abstract rules.

Fourth, in the case of land tenure laws, the analytical table indicated the relative importance of the various rights, which, in turn, suggested their importance in the native economy. Because the Kapauku cherish independence and individualism highly, the relative importance of the various rights could be determined simply by the fact that the more important the right was, the more frequently, with respect to the fourteen land and water categories, it was allotted to the individual owner.

Fifth, in the Tirolean laws of inheritance the formal analysis showed well that the two pertinent legal codes (Austrian Civil Law and Tirolean Farm Law) were not only logically compatible and complementary but also integrated: the crucial distinction between the two codes, the dispositions pertaining to the non-*Hof* property (Austrian Civil Code) versus those applying to *Hof* property (Tirolean Farm Law), appeared as the fifth dimension in the analysis, the sequence of the first four dimensions being irreversible. Prior to that formal analysis I assumed that the first and the most crucial distinction (first dimension) in the whole Tirolean laws of inheritance would be that pertaining to the basic distinction between the two codes. Nothing but the formal analysis could have shown me so convincingly my logical error.

Sixth, the correlated matrices and the structure of their interrelations may be regarded as a "legal grammar" of the analyzed systems.

Seventh, it is assumed that similar structural presentations of the domains of legal systems of different peoples will prove to be important to exact structural cross-cultural comparisons of substantive law. It is suggested (by analyses of other tribal legal systems made by my students) that it will be possible to set up a set of types of substantive legal systems (of laws of inheritance, land tenure, contracts, marriage, etc.) that may approximate in their significance the types of kinship terminology or kinship organization.

Many legal thinkers, philosophers, jurists, sociologists, and even anthropologists have contributed to the growing volume of literature on the evolution (or change) of legal systems. Even some political scientists and anthropologists not trained in law have been intrigued with the evolutionary problem and have added their theories to the volume of evolutionary schemes. Yet this topic is the most difficult to tackle for the simple reason that the necessary wealth of comparative material is lacking and, as a consequence, what is usually accomplished is at its best an exercise in pure philosophizing or at its worst speculation and doctrinaire preaching. A pristine law or a pristine state that is postulated to have "evolved" once upon a time, of whose structure, function, or even basic history we know virtually nothing, is certainly not a topic whose elucidation a modern anthropologist, as a scientist, is called upon to undertake. The situation is bad enough when one turns, for example, to a comparative research of contemporary laws of inheritance. Although these data are ethnographically crucial and easily obtained in the field, there are only a few accounts available, which give us more than only oversimplified statements. If we do not have data on contemporary laws adequate for a thorough comparative study, how can we deal with the evolution of law in the past, where the historical data are far more scanty and often beyond recovery? To defend my aversion to speculative evolutionism I may reiterate that my values and preferences lie in the empirical field which I regard as central to anthropology. I have always preferred, for example, a specific and exact formal analysis of kinship terminology to a vague exegesis on the evolution of kinship terminological systems, or a meticulous analysis (with theoretical implications) of the concrete law of, for example, the Cheyenne Indians, to a sweeping theory of evolution of political systems.

BIBLIOGRAPHY

Allen, C. K.
　　1927　*Law in the Making.* Oxford, The Clarendon Press.
Aronfreed, Justin
　　1964　"The Origin of Self-Criticism," *Psychological Review,* vol.
　　　　　71, no. 3, pp. 193–218.
Barker, Ernest
　　1957　"Translator's Introduction," in Otto von Gierke, *Natural
　　　　　Law and the Theory of Society, 1500 to 1800.* (1st ed.,
　　　　　1934) Boston, Beacon Press. Pp. lx–xci.
Barkun, Michael
　　1968　*Law without Sanctions.* New Haven, Yale University Press.
Barnett, H. G.
　　1949　*Palauan Society.* Eugene, University of Oregon.
Barton, R. F.
　　1919　"Ifugao Law," *University of California Publications in
　　　　　American Archaeology and Ethnology,* vol. 15, pp. 1–186.
　　1949　*The Kalingas: Their Institutions and Custom Law.* Chicago,
　　　　　University of Chicago Press.
Bass, Bernard M.
　　1960　*Leadership, Psychology, and Organizational Behavior.*
　　　　　New York, Harper & Row.
Baudin, Louis
　　1928　*L'empire socialiste des Inka.* (Travaux et Mémoires de
　　　　　L'Institut d'Ethnologie, vol. V) Paris, Institut d'Ethnologie.
Bentham, Jeremy
　　1871　*Theory of Legislation.* London, Trübner and Co.
　　1876　*Introduction to the Principles of Morals and Legislation.*
　　　　　(1st ed., 1780) Oxford, The Clarendon Press.
Berndt, Ronald M.
　　1962　*Excess and Restraint.* Chicago, University of Chicago Press.
Berolzheimer, Fritz
　　1929　*The World's Legal Philosophies.* New York, The Macmillan
　　　　　Company.
Bettelheim, Bruno
　　1943　"Individual and Mass Behavior in Extreme Situations," *The
　　　　　Journal of Abnormal and Social Psychology,* vol. 38, pp.
　　　　　417–452.

Bohannan, P. J.
>1957 *Justice and Judgment Among the Tiv.* London, Oxford University Press.
>1963 *Social Anthropology.* New York, Holt, Rinehart and Winston, Inc.

Bruijn, J. V. De
>1953 "Korte Notities over de Verwantschapsterminologie en het Grondenrecht bij de Ekagi." Hollandia, New Guinea, Gouvernement van Nederlands-Nieuw-Guinea. Mimeographed.

Bryce, James
>1901 *Studies in History and Jurisprudence.* New York, Oxford University Press.

Buckland, W. W.
>1911 *Equity in Roman Law.* London, University of London Press.

Bureau for Native Affairs
>1957 *Anthropological Research in Netherlands-New Guinea since 1950.* Hollandia, New Guinea, Bureau for Native Affairs.

Burling, Robbins
>1964a "Cognition and Componential Analysis: God's Truth or Hocus-Pocus," *American Anthropologist,* vol. 66, no. 1, pp. 20–28.
>1964b "Burling's Rejoinder," *American Anthropologist,* vol. 66, no. 1, pp. 120–122.

Carter, Hugh
>1927 *The Social Theories of L. T. Hobhouse.* Chapel Hill, University of North Carolina Press.

Carter, Launor F.
>1953 "Leadership and Small-Group Behavior," in Muzafer Sherif and M. O. Wilson (eds.), *Group Relations at the Crossroads.* New York, Harper & Row. Pp. 257–284.

Cattell, R. B.
>1951 "New Concepts of Measuring Leadership, in Terms of Group Syntality," *Human Relations,* vol. 4, pp. 161–184.

Chapple, Eliot D., and Carleton S. Coon
>1942 *Principles of Anthropology.* New York, Holt, Rinehart and Winston.

Ching Lin Hsia, James L. E. Chow, and Liu Chieh Yukon Chang
>1931 *The Civil Code of the Republic of China.* Shanghai, Kelly and Walsh.

Cicero, Marcus Tullius
>1745 *De Legibus.* London, J. and P. Knapton.
>1928 *De Legibus,* trans. by Clinton Walker Keyes. New York, Putnam's.
>1967 *De Re Publica.* Florence, Arnoldus Mandador.

Collier, M. C.
    1966 *Local Organization among the Navaho.* New Haven, Human
          Relations Area Files.
Colson, Elizabeth
    1962 *The Plateau Tonga of Northern Rhodesia.* Manchester, Man-
          chester University Press.
Conklin, Harold C.
    1962a "Comment," in Thomas Gladwin and William C. Sturtevant
           (eds.), *Anthropology and Human Behavior.* Washington, The
           Anthropological Society of Washington. Pp. 86–93.
    1962b "Lexicographical Treatment of Folk Taxonomies," *Interna-
           tional Journal of American Linguistics,* vol. 28, no. 2, pp.
           119–141.
Cook, Edwin A.
    1965 "Manga Social Organization." Unpublished doctoral disserta-
          tion, Yale University.
Cowley, W. H.
    1928 "Three Distinctions in the Study of Leaders," *Journal of Ab-
          normal Social Psychology,* vol. 23, pp. 144–157.
Dalton, George
    1969 "Theoretical Issues in Economic Anthropology," *Current An-
          thropology,* vol. 10, no. 1, pp. 63–80.
Davis, F. James, Henry H. Foster, C. Ray Jeffery, and E. Eugene Davis
    1962 *Society and the Law: New Meanings for an Old Profession.*
          New York, The Free Press.
Dollard, John, and Neal E. Miller
    1950 *Personality and Psychotherapy.* New York, McGraw-Hill
          Book Company.
Durkheim, Émile
    1893 *De la division du travail social.* Paris, Félix Alcan.
    1895 *Les règles de la méthode sociologique.* Paris, Félix Alcan.
    1897 *Le suicide.* Paris, Félix Alcan.
    1912 *Les formes élémentaires de la vie religieuse. Paris, Librairie
          Félix Alcan.*
    1953 *Montesquieu et Rousseau.* Paris, Librairie Marcel Rivière et
          Cie.
    1960 *Montesquieu and Rousseau: Forerunners of Sociology.* Ann
          Arbor, University of Michigan Press.
    1964 *The Division of Labor in Society,* trans. by George Simpson.
          New York, The Free Press.
    1966 *The Rules of Sociological Method.* New York, The Free Press.
Dyk, Walter
    1938 *Son of Old Man Hat.* New York, Harcourt Brace Jovano-
          vich.

Ehrlich, Eugen
  1913 *Grundlegung der Soziologie des Rechts.* Munich, Duncker und Humblot.
  1936 *Fundamental Principles of the Sociology of Law,* trans. by Walter E. Mell. Cambridge, Mass., Harvard University Press.
Engels, Frederick
  1907 *Socialism: Utopian and Scientific,* trans. by Edward Aveling. (1st ed., 1892). Chicago, Charles H. Kerr and Company.
  1935 *Herr Eugen Dühring's Revolution in Science* [*Anti-Dühring*], trans. by Emile Burns; ed. by C. P. Dutt. (1st ed., 1878). New York, International Publishers.
  1959 "On Historical Materialism," in Lewis S. Feuer (ed.), *Marx and Engels: Basic Writings on Politics and Philosophy.* New York, Anchor Books. Pp. 47–67.
  1962a *Der Ursprung der Familie, des Privateigenthums und des Staats.* (1st ed., 1884) In *Karl Marx, Friedrich Engels Werke,* vol. 21. Berlin, Dietz Verlag. Pp. 25–173.
  1962b *Herrn Eugen Dühring's Umwälzung der Wissenschaft.* (1st ed., 1878) In *Karl Marx, Friedrich Engels Werke,* vol 20. Berlin, Dietz Verlag. Pp. 5–303.
  1964 *The Origin of the Family, Private Property and the State.* New York, International Publishers.
Escarra, Jean
  1936 *Le droit chinois.* Peking, Éditions Henri Vetch.
Evans-Pritchard, E. E.
  1937 *Witchcraft, Oracles and Magic among the Azande.* Oxford, The Clarendon Press.
  1940a *The Nuer.* Oxford, The Clarendon Press.
  1940b "The Nuer of the Southern Sudan," in Meyer Fortes and E. E. Evans-Pritchard (eds.), *African Political Systems.* Oxford, Oxford University Press. Pp. 272–296.
Festinger, Leon
  1953 "An Analysis of Compliant Behavior," in Muzafer Sherif and M. O. Wilson (eds.), *Group Relations at the Crossroads.* New York, Harper & Row. Pp. 232–256.
Fichte, J. G.
  1796 *Grundlage des Naturrechts.* Jena, C. E. Gabler.
Fiedler, Fred E.
  1967 *A Theory of Leadership Effectiveness.* New York, McGraw-Hill Book Company.
Firth, Raymond
  1939 *Primitive Polynesian Economy.* London, George Routledge and Kegan Paul.

Forde, Daryll
    1965   "Justice and Judgment among the Southern Ibo under Colonial Rule," in Hilda Kuper and Leo Kuper (eds.), *African Law: Adaptation and Development.* Berkeley, University of California Press. Pp. 79–96.

Frake, Charles
    1955   "Social Organization and Shifting Cultivation among the Sindangan Subanun." Unpublished doctoral dissertation, Yale University.
    1961   "The Diagnosis of Disease among the Subanun of Mindanao," *American Anthropologist,* vol. 63, no. 1, pp. 113–132.
    1962   "The Ethnographic Study of Cognitive Systems," in Thomas Gladwin and William C. Sturtevant (eds.), *Anthropology and Human Behavior.* Washington, D.C., The Anthropological Society of Washington. Pp. 72–85.
    1969   "Struck by Speech: The Yakan Concept of Litigation," in Laura Nader (ed.), *Law in Culture and Society.* Chicago, Aldine Publishing Company. Pp. 147–167.

Freuchen, Peter
    1931   *Eskimo.* New York, Horace Liveright.

Fried, Morton
    1967   *The Evolution of Political Society.* New York, Random House, Inc.

Gaius
    1932   "De in Integrum Restitutionibus" (excerpt from *Digesta,* book 4, p. 533), in Otakar Sommer (ed.), *Texty ke Studiu Soukromého Práva Římského.* Prague, Politika. Pp. 19–20.

Gartlan, J. S.
    1968   "Structure and Function in Primate Society," *Folia Primat,* vol. 8, no. 2, pp. 89–120.

Gény, François
    1925   "The Critical System (Idealistic and Formal) of R. Stammler," in Rudolf Stammler, *The Theory of Justice,* trans. by Issac Husik. New York, The Macmillan Company. Pp. 493–552.

Gibb, Cecil A.
    1966a   "The Principles and Traits of Leadership," in Paul A. Hare, Edgar F. Borgotta, and Robert F. Bales (eds.), *Small Groups: Studies in Social Interaction.* New York, Alfred A. Knopf. Pp. 87–95.
    1966b   "The Sociometry of Leadership in Temporary Groups," in A. Paul Hare, Edgar F. Borgotta, and Robert F. Bales (eds.), *Small Groups: Studies in Social Interaction.* New York, Alfred A. Knopf, pp. 658–674.

Gibson, Charles
    1948   *The Inca Concept of Sovereignty and the Spanish Adminis-tration in Peru.* Austin, University of Texas Press.
Gierke, Otto von
    1868   *Das deutsche Genossenschaftrecht.* Berlin, Wiedmann.
    1957   *Natural Law and the Theory of Society 1500 to 1800.* (1st ed., 1934) Boston, Beacon Press.
Gillin, John Paul
    1934   "Crime and Punishment among the Barama River Carib of British Guiana," *American Anthropologist,* vol. 36, pp. 331–344.
Ginsberg, Morris
    1968   "Hobhouse, L. T.," in David L. Sills (ed.), *International Ency-clopedia of the Social Sciences,* vol. 6. New York, The Mac-millan Company. Pp. 487–489.
Gladwin, Thomas
    1950   "Civil Administration on Truk: A Rejoinder," *Human Organi-zation,* vol. 9, no. 4, pp. 15–24.
Gluckman, Max
    1940   "The Kingdom of the Zulu of South Africa," in Meyer Fortes and E. E. Evans-Pritchard (eds.), *African Political Systems.* Oxford, Oxford University Press. Pp. 25–55.
    1959   *Custom and Conflict in Africa.* (1st ed., 1956) New York, The Free Press.
    1965   *Politics, Law and Ritual in Tribal Society.* Chicago, Aldine Publishing Company.
    1967   *The Judicial Process among the Barotse of Northern Rhodesia.* (1st ed., 1955) Manchester, Manchester University Press.
Goodall, Jane
    1965   "Chimpanzees of the Gombe Stream Reserve," in Irven DeVore (ed.), *Primate Behavior.* New York, Holt, Rinehart and Winston, Inc.
Goodenough, Ward H.
    1956   "Componential Analysis and the Study of Meaning," *Lan-guage,* vol. 32, no. 1, pp. 195–216.
Graburn, Nelson
    1968   "Inuariat: The Killings." Paper presented to the Symposium on Primitive Law, Annual Meeting of the American Anthropologi-cal Association, Seattle, November.
Grotius, Hugo
    1751a *De Jure Belli ac Pacis Libri Tres. Prolegomena.* (1st ed., 1625) Lausanne, Marcus-Michael Bousquet.

1751b *De Jure Belli ac Pacis Libri Tres. Liber I.* (1st ed., 1625) Lausanne, Marcus-Michael Bousquet.

1925 *De Jure Belli ac Pacis Libri Tres,* trans. by Francis W. Kelsey. (1st ed., 1625) Oxford, The Clarendon Press.

Gusinde, Martin

1937 *Die Feuerland Indianer.* (2 vols.) Modling, Austria, Anthropos.

Hahm, Pyong-Choon

1967 *The Korean Political Tradition and Law.* Seoul, Hollym Corporation, Publishers.

Hall, K. R. L.

1968 "Aggression in Monkey and Ape Societies," Phyllis C. Jay (ed.), in *Primates: Studies in Adaptation and Variability,* New York, Holt, Rinehart and Winston. Pp. 149–171.

Hall, K. R. L., and Irven DeVore

1965 "Baboon Social Behavior," in Irven DeVore (ed.), *Primate Behavior.* New York, Holt, Rinehart and Winston. Pp. 53–110.

Hartland, E. Sidney

1924 *Primitive Law.* London, Methuen and Co.

Hazard, John N.

1957 *The Soviet System of Government.* Chicago, Chicago University Press.

Herskovits, Melville J.

1949 *Man and His Works.* New York, Alfred A. Knopf.

1960 *Economic Anthropology.* New York, Alfred A. Knopf.

Hildreth, R.

1871 "Translator's Preface," in Jeremy Bentham, *Theory of Legislation.* London, Trübner and Co. Pp. iii–ix.

Hill, W. W.

1940 "Some Aspects of Navajo Political Structure," *Plateau,* vol. 13, no. 2, pp. 23–28.

Hobbes, Thomas

1907 *Leviathan.* London, George Routledge and Kegan Paul.

Hobhouse, L. T.

1896 *The Theory of Knowledge; a Contribution to Some Problems of Logic and Metaphysics.* London, Methuen and Co.

1901 *Mind in Evolution.* London, Macmillan and Co. Limited.

1906 *Morals in Evolution.* London, Chapman and Hall Limited.

1908 *Morals in Evolution,* part I. London, Chapman and Hall Limited.

1922 *The Elements of Social Justice.* London, George Allen and Unwin Limited.

1924   *Social Development. Its Nature and Conditions.* New York, Holt, Rinehart and Winston.

1927   *Development and Purpose. An Essay towards a Philosophy of Evolution.* (1st ed., 1913). London, Macmillan and Co. Limited.

1966   *Sociology and Philosophy.* Cambridge, Mass., Harvard University Press.

Hobhouse, L. T., G. C. Wheeler, and M. Ginsberg

1930   *The Material Culture and Social Institutions of the Simpler Peoples.* London, Chapman and Hall.

Hobsbawm, Eric J.

1966   "Introduction," in Karl Marx, *Pre-Capitalist Economic Formations,* trans. by Jack Cohen. New York, International Publishers. Pp. 9–65.

Hoebel, E. Adamson

1940   *The Political Organization and Law-ways of the Comanche Indians.* (American Anthropological Association Memoir 54). Santa Fe, Santa Fe Laboratory of Anthropology.

1949a   *Man in the Primitive World: An Introduction to Anthropology.* New York, McGraw-Hill Book Company.

1949b   "Introduction," in Roy F. Barton, *The Kalingas.* Chicago, University of Chicago Press. Pp. 1–5.

1954   *The Law of Primitive Man.* Cambridge, Mass., Harvard University Press.

1961   "Three Studies in African Law," *Stanford University Law Review,* vol. 13, pp. 418–442.

Hogbin, H. Ian

1935   "Sorcery and Administration," *Oceania,* vol. VI, no. 1, pp. 1–32.

1939   *Experiments in Civilization.* London, George Routledge and Kegan Paul.

1961   *Law and Order in Polynesia.* (1st ed., 1934) Hamden, Conn., Shoe String Press.

Hohfeld, W. N.

1923   *Fundamental Legal Conceptions as Applied in Judicial Reasoning and Other Essays.* Ed. by Walter Wheeler Cook. New Haven, Yale University Press.

Hollander, E. P.

1964   *Leaders, Groups, and Influence.* New York, Oxford University Press.

Hollander, Edwin P. and James W. Julian

1968   "Leadership," in Edgar F. Borgatta and William W. Lambert (eds.), *Handbook of Personality Theory and Research.* Chicago, Rand McNally and Company. Pp. 890–899.

Holleman, J. F.
    1952   *Shona Customary Law*. London, Oxford University Press.
Holmes, O. W., Jr.
    1881   *The Common Law*. Boston, Little, Brown, and Co.
    1886   "The Law as a Profession," *American Law Review,* vol. 20,
            pp. 741–742.
    1897   "The Path of Law," *Harvard Law Review,* vol. 10, pp. 457–
            478.
Hovland, Carl I., O. J. Harvey, and Muzafer Sherif
    1966   "Assimilation and Contrast Effects in Reaction to Communica-
            tion and Attitude Change," in Harold Proshansky and Bernard
            Seidenberg (eds.), *Basic Studies in Social Psychology*. New
            York, Holt, Rinehart and Winston. Pp. 186–195.
Hovland, Carl I., Irving L. Janis, and Harold H. Kelley
    1968   *Communication and Persuasion: Psychological Studies of
            Opinion Change*. New Haven, Yale University Press.
Howell, P. P.
    1954   *A Manual of Nuer Law*. London, Oxford University Press.
Hudson, Alfred E.
    1938   *Kazak Social Structure*. (Yale University Publications in An-
            thropology No. 20) New Haven, Yale University Press.
Hymes, Dell H.
    1964   "Discussion of Burling's Paper [Cognition and Componential
            Analysis: God's Truth or Hocus-Pocus?]," *American An-
            thropologist,* vol. 66, no. 1, pp. 116–119.
Ihering, Rudolf von
    1866   *Geist des römischen Rechts auf den verschiedenen Stufen
            seiner Entwicklung,* vol. I. Leipzig, Breitkopf und Härtel.
    1904   *Der Zweck im Recht,* vol I. (1st ed., 1877) Leipzig, Breitkopf
            und Härtel.
    1905   *Der Zweck im Recht,* vol II. (1st ed., 1883) Leipzig, Breitkopf
            und Härtel.
    1913   *Law as a Means to an End,* trans. by Isaac Husik. Boston, The
            Boston Book Company.
Ingstad, Helge
    1954   *Nunamiut*. London, George Allen and Unwin Ltd.
James, William
    1897   *The Will to Believe*. New York, Longmans, Green and
            Co.
Kant, Immanuel
    1797   *Metaphysische Anfangsgründe der Rechtslehre.* (1st ed.,
            1791) Königsberg, Friedrich Nicolovius.
    1887   *The Philosophy of Law,* trans. by W. Hastie. Edinburgh, T. and
            T. Clark.

Kapfer, Hans (ed.)

1963a *Das Allgemeine bürgerliche Gesetzbuch.* Vienna, Manzsche Verlags- und Universitätsbuchhandlung.

1963b "Tiroler Höfegesetz: Gesetz vom 12. Juni 1900, LGB1. für Tirol Nr. 47, betreffend die besonderen Rechtsverhältnisse geschlossener Höfe," in *Das Allgemeine bürgerliche Gesetzbuch.* Vienna, Manzsche Verlags- und Universitätsbuchhandlung. Pp. 1591–1601.

Karsten, Rafael

1935 *The Head-Hunters of Western Amazonas.* Helsingsfors, Societas Scientiarum Fennica.

Kelman, Herbert C.

1966 "Compliance, Identification and Internalization: Three Processes of Attitude Change," in Harold Proshansky and Bernard Seidenberg (eds.), *Basic Studies in Social Psychology.* New York, Holt, Rinehart and Winston. Pp. 140–148.

Kluckhohn, Clyde, and Dorothea Leighton

1947 *The Navaho.* Cambridge, Mass., Harvard University Press.

Kohlberg, Lawrence

1963 "Moral Development and Identification," in Harold W. Stevenson *et al.* (eds.), *Child Psychology.* Chicago, University of Chicago Press. Pp. 277–332.

Kohler, Josef

1909 *Lehrbuch der Rechtsphilosophie.* Berlin, Dr. Walter Rothschild.

1914 *Philosophy of Law,* trans. by Adalbert Albrecht (1st ed., 1908) Boston, The Boston Book Company.

Koppers, Wilhelm

1924 *Unter Feuerland Indianer.* Stuttgart, Strecker and Schröder.

Krech, David, and Richard S. Crutchfield

1948 *Theory and Problems of Social Psychology.* New York, McGraw-Hill Book Company.

Krech, David, Richard S. Crutchfield, and Egerton L. Ballachey

1962 *Individual in Society.* New York, McGraw-Hill Book Company.

Lang, Olga

1946 *Chinese Family and Society.* New Haven, Yale University Press.

Lasswell, Harold D.

1931 "Feud," in David L. Sills (ed.), *Encyclopedia of the Social Sciences,* vol. 6. New York, The Macmillan Company. Pp. 220–221.

Latourette, Kenneth Scott

1934 *The Chinese. Their History and Culture,* vol. II. New York, The Macmillan Company.

Leach, E. R.
   1959   "Social Change and Primitive Law," *American Anthropologist,* vol. 61, no. 6, pp. 1096–1097.
Leighton, Dorothea C., and Clyde Kluckhohn
   1948   *Children of the People.* Cambridge, Mass., Harvard University Press.
Leighton, Dorothea C., and Alexander H. Leighton
   1945   *The Navaho Door.* Cambridge, Mass., Harvard University Press.
Lenin, V. I.
   1917   *The Tasks of the Proletariat in our Revolution.* London, Martin Lawrence, Ltd.
   1935–1938   "The Agrarian Programme of Social-Democracy in the First Russian Revolution, 1905–1907," in *V. I. Lenin Selected Works,* vol. III. New York, International Publishers. Pp. 157–286.
   1943   *State and Revolution.* New York, International Publishers.
   1961   *Agrarnaya Programa Social-Demokratiyi v Pervoy Ruskoy Revolyuciyi, 1905–1907,* in *V. I. Lenin: Polnoye Sobraniye Sochinyeniy,* vol. 16. Moscow, Gosudarstvennoye Izdatel'stvo Politicheskoi Literaturi. Pp. 193–413.
   1962   *Gosudarstvo i Revolyuciya,* in *V. I. Lenin: Polnoye Sobraniye Sochinyeniy,* vol. 33. Moscow, Gosudarstvennoye Izdatel'stvo Politicheskoy Literaturi.
Lessa, W. A.
   1950   *The Ethnography of Ulithi Atoll. Final Report.* (Coordinated Investigation of Micronesian Anthropology, vol. 28). Los Angeles, Pacific Science Board, National Research Council, University of California.
LeVine, Robert A.
   1960   "The Internalization of Political Values in Stateless Societies," *Human Organization,* vol. 19, no. 2, pp. 51–58.
Levy, Marion J., Jr.
   1949   *The Family Revolution in Modern China.* Cambridge, Mass., Harvard University Press.
Lindblom, Gerhard
   1916   *The Akamba.* Uppsala, K. W. Appelbergs Boktrykeri.
Lippitt, Ronald, and Ralph K. White
   1966   "An Experimental Study of Leadership and Group Life," in Harold Proshansky and Bernard Seidenberg (eds.), *Basic Studies in Social Psychology.* New York, Holt, Rinehart and Winston. Pp. 523–537.
Lipps, O. H.
   1956   *The Navajos.* Cedar Rapids, Iowa, The Torch Press.

Lips, Julius E.
 1947 "Naskapi Law," *Transactions of the American Philosophical Society,* vol. 37, part 4, pp. 378–492.
Llewellyn, Karl N., and E. Adamson Hoebel
 1961 *The Cheyenne Way.* (1st ed., 1941) Norman, University of Oklahoma Press.
Lloyd, Dennis
 1966 *The Idea of Law.* (1st ed., 1964). Guildford, Eng., MacGibbon and Kee Ltd.
Lounsbury, Floyd G.
 1956 "A Semantic Analysis of the Pawnee Kinship Usage," *Language,* vol. 32, no. 1, pp. 158–194.
Lowie, Robert H.
 1920 *Primitive Society.* New York, Horace Liveright.
 1937 *The History of Ethnological Theory.* New York, Farrar, Straus & Giroux.
MacCallum, Spencer H.
 1964 "Law without Sanction." Mimeographed.
Maine, Henry Sumner
 1875 *Lectures on the Early History of Institutions.* London, John Murray.
 1883 *Early Law and Custom.* New York, Holt, Rinehart and Winston.
 1963 *Ancient Law.* (Reprint of 1861 ed.). Boston, Beacon Press.
Maitland, F. W.
 1936 *Equity.* (1st ed., 1909) Cambridge, Eng., Cambridge University Press.
Malinowski, Bronislaw
 1934 "Introduction," in H. Ian Hogbin (ed.), *Law and Order in Polynesia.* New York, Harcourt, Brace Jovanovich. Pp. 1–74.
 1959 *Crime and Custom in Savage Society.* (1st ed., 1932) Paterson, N.J., Littlefield, Adams and Company.
 1964 "An Anthropological Analysis of War," in Leon Bramson and George W. Goethals (eds.), *War: Studies from Psychology, Sociology, Anthropology.* New York, Basic Books. Pp. 245–268.
Marx, Karl
 1946 "Remarques sur la récente règlementation de la censure prussienne," in *Oeuvres philosophiques, oeuvres complètes de Karl Marx,* trans. by J. Molitor. Paris, Alfred Costes, Éditeur. Pp. 121–161.
 1953 *Grundrisse der Kritik der Politischen Ökonomie.* (1st ed., 1858) Berlin, Dietz Verlag.
 1959 "A Contribution to the Critique of Political Economy," in Lewis S. Feuer (ed.), *Basic Writings on Politics and Philoso-*

phy, *Karl Marx and Friedrich Engels.* Garden City, N. Y., Doubleday and Co., Inc. Pp. 42–46.

1964a *Das Kapital. Kritik der Politischen Ökonomie,* vol. III, in *Karl Marx, Friedrich Engels Werke,* vol. 25. Berlin, Dietz Verlag.

1964b *Zur Kritik der Politischen Oekonomie.* (1st ed., 1859) In *Karl Marx, Friedrich Engels Werke,* vol. 13. Berlin, Dietz Verlag. Pp. 3–160.

1966a *Pre-Capitalist Economic Formations.* (1st ed., 1857–1858) New York, International Publishers.

1966b "Letter to Zasulich, March 8, 1881," in Eric J. Hobsbawm (ed.), *Pre-Capitalist Economic Formations.* New York, International Publishers. Pp. 142–145.

Marx, Karl, and Friedrich Engels

1959a "Manifesto of the Communist Party," in Lewis S. Feuer (ed.), *Karl Marx and Friedrich Engels: Basic Writings on Politics and Philosophy.* New York, Anchor Books. Pp. 1–41.

1959b *Manifest der Kommunistischen Partei.* (1st ed., 1848) In *Karl Marx, Friedrich Engels Werke,* vol. 4. Berlin, Dietz Verlag. Pp. 459–493.

1962 *Die deutsche Ideologie* (1st ed., 1845–1846) In *Karl Marx, Friedrich Engels Werke,* vol. 3. Berlin, Dietz Verlag. Pp. 9–530.

Mauss, Marcel

1906 "Essai sur les variations saisonnières des sociétés Eskimos: Étude de morphologie sociale," *L'année sociologique,* 9e année, pp. 39–132.

Means, Philip Ainsworth

1931 *Ancient Civilizations of the Andes.* New York, Scribner's.

Meggitt, M. J.

1962 *Desert People. A Study of the Walbiri Aborigines of Central Australia.* Sydney, Angus and Robertson.

Miller, Neal E. and John Dollard

1941 *Social Learning and Imitation.* New Haven, Yale University Press.

Mishkin, Bernard

1946 "The Contemporary Quechua," in Julian H. Steward (ed.), *Handbook of South American Indians.* (Bureau of American Ethnology Bulletin No. 143, vol. 2). Washington, D.C., U.S. Government Printing Office. Pp. 411–470.

Montesquieu, C. L. J. de Secondat, Baron de la Brède et de

1750 *De l'esprit des lois,* vols. I, II. Edinburgh, G. Hamilton and J. Balfour.

1929 *Lettres persanes.* Paris, Éditions Fernand Roches.

1949 *Oeuvres complètes de Montesquieu,* vol. I, collected and annotated by Roger Caillois. Paris, L'Imprimerie Bellenand.

1951　*Oeuvres complètes de Montesquieu,* vol. 2, collected and annotated by Roger Caillois. Dijon, Imprimerie Darantière.

Moore, Stanley
1960　"Marxian Theories of Law in Primitive Society," in Stanley Diamond (ed.), *Culture in History: Essays in Honor of Paul Radin.* New York, Columbia University Press. Pp. 642–662.

Morse, H. B.
1909　*The Gilds of China.* London, Longmans, Green and Co.

Mowrer, O. Hobart
1950　*Learning Theory and Personality Dynamics.* New York, The Ronald Press Company.

Murdock, George Peter
1934　*Our Primitive Contemporaries.* New York, The Macmillan Co.
1949　*Social Structure.* New York, The Macmillan Co.

Nadel, Siegfried F.
1947　*The Nuba: An Anthropological Study of the Hill Tribes in Kordofan.* London, Oxford University Press.

Nader, Laura
1964　"An Analysis of Zapotec Law Cases," *Ethnology,* vol. 3, no. 4, pp. 404–419.

Nader, Laura, and Duane Metzger
1963　"Conflict Resolution in Two Mexican Communities," *American Anthropologist,* vol. 65, no. 3, part I, pp. 584–592.

Needham, Joseph
1956　*Science and Civilization in China,* vol. 2. Cambridge, Eng., Cambridge University Press.

Neilson, W. A. *et al.*
1940　*Webster's New International Dictionary of the English Language.* (2nd ed.) Springfield, Mass., G. and C. Merriam Company.

Nicholson, J. A.
1926　"Some Aspects of the Philosophy of L. T. Hobhouse," in *University of Illinois Studies in the Social Sciences,* vol. XIV, no. 4., pp. 1–86.

Northrop, F. S. C.
1951　"Philosophical Anthropology and World Law," *Transactions of the New York Academy of Sciences* (Series II), vol. 14, pp. 109–112.

Ovid (Naso Ovidius, Publius)
1719　*Metamorphoses,* ed. by Daniel Crespin. London, R. Knaplock.

Ovid (Naso Ovidius, Publius)
1815　*Metamorphoses,* trans. by John Dryden. New York, R. M'Dermut and D. D. Arden.

Papinianus

    1932   "De in Integrum Restitutionibus" (excerpt from *Digesta,* Book 4, p. 533) in Otakar Sommer (ed.), *Texty ke Studiu Soukromého Práva Římského.* Prague, Politika. P. 18.

Paulus

    1932   "De in Integrum Restitutionibus" (excerpts from *Digesta,* Book 4, pp. 44, 533) in Otakar Sommer (ed.), *Texty ke Studiu Soukromého Práva Římského.* Prague, Politika. Pp. 16, 18, 21, 22.

Piaget, J.

    1948   *The Moral Judgment of the Child.* New York, The Free Press.

Pospisil, Leopold

    1952   "Nature of Law." Unpublished master's thesis, University of Oregon.

    1954   "Inheritance." New Haven, Yale University. Mimeographed.

    1955   *Uta-Uta: Papuan Justice.* A 16-millimeter Kodachrome film.

    1956   "The Nature of Law," *Transactions of the New York Academy of Sciences* (Series II), vol. 18, no. 8, pp. 746–755.

    1958a *Kapauku Papuans and Their Law.* (Yale University Publications in Anthropology No. 54) New Haven, Yale University Department of Anthropology.

    1958b "Social Change and Primitive Law: Consequences of a Papuan Legal Case," *American Anthropologist,* vol. 60, no. 5, pp. 832–837.

    1958c "Kapauku Papuan Political Structure," in Verne F. Ray (ed.), *Systems of Political Control and Bureaucracy in Human Societies.* Seattle, American Ethnological Society.

    1959   "Multiplicity of Legal Systems in Primitive Societies," *Bulletin of the Philadelphia Anthropological Society,* vol. 12, no. 3, pp. 1–4.

    1961   "Structural Change and Primitive Law: Consequences of a Papuan Legal Case and Cultural Contact." Paper presented at the Annual Meeting of the American Anthropological Association, Philadelphia.

1962–1969   "Law and Informal Social Control in a Tirolean Community." (Unpublished notes and qualitative analysis of ethnographic material collected during research in Tirol, in 1962–1969). New Haven, Yale University Department of Anthropology.

    1963a *Kapauku Papuan Economy.* (Yale University Publications in Anthropology No. 67). New Haven, Yale University Department of Anthropology.

    1963b *The Kapauku Papuans of West New Guinea,* in George and Louise Spindler (eds.), *Case Studies in Cultural Anthropology.* New York, Holt, Rinehart and Winston.

    1964   "Law and Societal Structure among the Nunamiut Eskimo," in

Ward H. Goodenough (ed.), *Explorations in Cultural Anthropology: Essays in Honor of George Peter Murdock.* New York, McGraw-Hill Book Company. Pp. 395–431.

1965a "A Formal Analysis of Substantive Law: Kapauku Papuan Laws of Land Tenure," in E. A. Hammel (ed.), "Formal Semantic Analysis," *American Anthropologist,* vol. 67, no. 5, part 2, pp. 186–214.

1965b "A Formal Analysis of Substantive Law: Kapauku Papuan Laws of Inheritance," in Laura Nader (ed.), "The Ethnography of Law," *American Anthropologist,* vol. 67, no. 6, part 2, pp. 166–185.

Pound, Roscoe

1942 *Social Control through Law.* New Haven, Yale University Press.

1965 *An Introduction to the Philosophy of Law.* New Haven, Yale University Press.

Prawdin, Michael

1940 *The Mongol Empire,* trans. by Eden and Cedar Paul. London, George Allen and Unwin Ltd.

Pufendorf, Samuel

1934 *De Jure Naturae et Gentium Libri Octo.* (1st ed., 1672) Oxford, The Clarendon Press.

Radcliffe-Brown, A. R.

1940 "Preface," in Meyer Fortes and E. E. Evans-Pritchard (eds.), *African Political Systems.* London, Oxford University Press. Pp. xi–xxiii.

1952 *Structure and Function in Primitive Society: Essays and Addresses.* New York, The Free Press.

Radin, Max

1938 "A Restatement of Hohfeld," *Harvard Law Review,* vol. 51, pp. 1141–1164.

Raven, Bertram

1965 "Social Influence and Power," in Ivan D. Steiner and Martin Fishbein (eds.), *Current Studies in Social Psychology.* New York, Holt, Rinehart and Winston. Pp. 371–382.

Redl, Fritz

1966 "Group Emotion and Leadership," in A. Paul Hare, Edgar F. Borgotta, and Robert F. Bales (eds.), *Small Groups: Studies in Social Interaction.* New York, Alfred A. Knopf. Pp. 71–86.

Rheinstein, Max

1967 "Introduction," in *Max Weber: Law in Economy and Society.* (1st ed., 1954). New York, Simon and Schuster. Pp. xvii–lxiv.

Riasanovsky, V. A.

1937 *Fundamental Principles of Mongol Law.* Tientsin, China, Telberg's International Bookstore.

Rivers, W. H. R.
    1924   *Social Organization.* New York, Knopf.
Roscoe, John
    1923   *The Bakitara.* Cambridge, Eng., Cambridge University Press.
Rostow, W. W.
    1952   *The Dynamics of Soviet Society.* New York, W. W. Norton
           and Company, Inc.
Rowe, John Howland
    1946   "Inca Culture at the Time of the Spanish Conquest," in *Hand-
           book of South American Indians,* vol. 2 (Smithsonian Institu-
           tion, Bureau of American Ethnology Bulletin 143). Washing-
           ton, D.C., U.S. Government Printing Office. Pp. 183–330.
Rycroff, W. Stanley
    1946   *Indians of the High Andes.* New York, Committee on Cooper-
           ation in Latin America.
Sasaki, Tom, and John Adair
    1952   "New Land to Farm: Agricultural Practices among the Navaho
           Indians of New Mexico," in E. Spicer (ed.), *Human Problems
           in Technological Change.* New York, Russell Sage Founda-
           tion. Pp. 97–113.
Savigny, Friedrich Karl von
    1831a *Of the Vocation of Our Age for Legislation and Jurispru-
           dence,* trans. by Abraham Hayward. London, Littlewood and
           Company.
    1831b *Geschichte des römischen Rechts während des Mittelalters.*
           Heidelberg, J. C. B. Mohr.
    1840   *Vom Beruf unsrer Zeit für Gesetzgebung und Rechtswissen-
           schaft.* (1st ed., 1814) Heidelberg, J. C. B. Mohr.
    1849   *System des heutigen römischen Rechts.* (1st ed., 1840) Ber-
           lin, Veit und Komp.
Schneider, Joseph
    1964   "Primitive Warfare: A Methodological Note," in Leon Bram-
           son and George W. Goethals (eds.), *War: Studies from Psy-
           chology, Sociology, Anthropology.* New York, Basic Books.
           Pp. 275–283.
Seligman, C. G.
    1932   *Pagan Tribes of the Nilotic Sudan.* London, George Routledge
           and Kegan Paul.
Shepardson, Mary
    1963   *Navajo Ways in Government.* (American Anthropological As-
           sociation Memoir No. 96) Menasha, Wisc., George Banta
           Company, Inc.
Sherif, Muzafer
    1947   "Group Influence upon the Formation of Norms and Atti-
           tudes," in Theodore M. Newcomb and Eugene L. Hartley

(eds.), *Readings in Social Psychology*. New York, Holt, Rinehart and Winston. Pp. 77–89.

1966   "Formation of Social Norms: The Experimental Paradigm," in Harold Proshansky and Bernard Seidenberg (eds.), *Basic Studies in Social Psychology*. New York, Holt, Rinehart and Winston. Pp. 461–471.

Sing Ging Su

1922   *The Chinese Family System*. New York, Columbia University Press.

Smith, Watson, and John M. Roberts

1954   *Zuni Law: A Field of Values*. (Papers of the Peabody Museum of American Archaeology and Ethnology, Harvard University, vol. 43, no. 1) Cambridge, Mass., Peabody Museum.

Sommer, Otakar

1932   *Prameny Soukromého Práva Římského*. Prague, Melantrich.

1933   *Učebnice Soukromého Prava Římského*, vol. I. *Obecné Nauky*. Prague, Nákladem Vlastním.

1935   *Učebnice Soukromého Práva Římského: Právo Majetkové*, vol. II. Prague, Nákladem Vlastním.

Southwick, Charles H., Mirza Azhar Beg, and M. Rafiq Siddiqi

1965   "Rhesus Monkeys in North India," in Irven DeVore (ed.), *Primate Behavior*. New York, Holt, Rinehart and Winston. Pp. 111–159.

Spencer, Herbert

1893   *The Principles of Ethics*, vol. II. New York, D. Appleton and Company.

1899   *The Principles of Sociology*, vol. II. New York: D. Appleton and Company.

Spencer, Robert F.

1959   *The North Alaskan Eskimo*. (Smithsonian Institution Bureau of American Ethnology Bulletin 171). Washington, D.C., U.S. Government Printing Office.

Spengler, Oswald

1921–1922   *Der Untergang des Abendlandes*. (1st ed., 1918) Munich, C. H. Beck'sche Verlagsbuchhandlung.

Stalin, I. V. (Joseph)

1947   *Ob Osnovakh Leninizma*, in *Sochinyeniya*, vol. 6. Moscow, Gosudarstvennoye Izdatyel'stvo Politicheskoy Literatury. Pp. 69–188.

1965   "The Foundations of Leninism," in Arthur P. Mendel (ed.), *Essential Works of Marxism*. New York, Bantam Books. Pp. 209–296.

Stammler, Rudolf

1902   *Die Lehre von dem richtigen Rechte*. Berlin, J. Guttentag.

1925   *The Theory of Justice,* trans. by Isaac Husik. New York, The
        Macmillan Company.
Stark, W.
    1960   *Montesquieu. Pioneer of the Sociology of Knowledge.* Lon-
            don, George Routledge and Kegan Paul.
Steenhoven, Geert Van den
    1959   *Legal Concepts among the Netsilik Eskimos of Pelly Bay N.
            W. T.* (Report No. 59–3) Ottawa, Northern Co-ordination and
            Research Center.
    1962   *Leadership and Law among the Eskimos of the Keewatin
            District, Northwest Territories.* The Hague, Uitgeverij Excel-
            sior.
Stogdill, R.
    1948   "Personal Factors Associated with Leadership: A Survey of the
            Literature," *Journal of Psychology,* vol. 25, pp. 35–71.
Stone, Julius
    1950   *The Province and Function of Law.* Cambridge, Mass., Har-
            vard University Press.
    1965   *Human Law and Human Justice.* Stanford, Calif., Stanford
            University Press.
    1966   *Social Dimensions of Law and Justice.* Stanford, Calif., Stan-
            ford University Press.
Tannenbaum, Robert, Irving R. Weschler, and Fred Massarik
    1961   *Leadership and Organization: A Behavioral Science Ap-
            proach.* New York, McGraw-Hill Book Company.
Tessman, Günter
    1930   *Die Indianer Nordost-Perus.* Hamburg, Frederichsen De
            Gruyter and Co. M. B. H.
Timasheff, Nicholas Sergeyevitch
    1938   "Law as a Social Phenomenon," in J. Hall (ed.), *Readings in
            Jurisprudence.* Indianapolis, The Bobbs-Merrill Co. Pp. 868–
            872.
Titiev, Mischa
    1951   *Araucanian Culture in Transition.* Ann Arbor, University of
            Michigan Press.
Ulpianus
    1932   "De in Integrum Restitutionibus" (excerpt from *Digesta,* Book
            4, p. 533), in Otakar Sommer (ed.), *Texty ke Studiu Sou-
            kromého Práva Rímského.* Prague, Politika. Pp. 15–19, 22.
Valk, Marc van der
    1939   "An Outline of Modern Chinese Family Law," *Monumenta
            Serica,* monog. II. Peking, Henri Vetch.
Vansina, Jan
    1965   "A Traditional Legal System: The Kuba," in Hilda Kuper and

Leo Kuper (eds.), *African Law: Adaptation and Development.* Berkeley, University of California Press. Pp. 97–119.

Vinogradoff, Paul

1892 *Villainage in England: Essays in Medieval History.* Oxford, The Clarendon Press.

1904 *The Teaching of Sir Henry Maine.* London, Henry Frowde.

1905 *The Growth of the Manor.* New York, The Macmillan Co.

1908 *English Society in the Eleventh Century: Essays in English Medieval History.* Oxford, The Clarendon Press.

1909 *Roman Law in Medieval Europe.* London, Harper & Row.

1914 *Common-Sense in Law.* New York, Holt, Rinehart and Winston.

1920 *Outlines of Historical Jurisprudence,* vol. I. Oxford, Oxford University Press.

1922 *Outlines of Historical Jurisprudence,* vol. II. Oxford, Oxford University Press.

1923 "Introduction," in *Outlines of Historical Jurisprudence.* London, Oxford University Press.

Wagner, Gunther

1940 "The Political Organization of the Bantu of Kavirondo," in Meyer Fortes and E. E. Evans-Pritchard (eds.), *African Political Systems.* London, Oxford University Press. Pp. 197–238.

Wallace, Anthony F.C.

1962 "Culture and Cognition," *Science,* vol. 135, no. 3501, pp. 351–357.

1965 *Culture and Personality.* New York, Random House.

Wallace, Anthony F.C., and John Atkins

1960 "The Meaning of Kinship Terms," *American Anthropologist, vol. 62, no. 1, pp. 58–80.*

Weber, Max

1922 *Grundriss der Sozialökonomik,* part 3. *Wirtschaft und Gesellschaft.* Tübingen, J. C. B. Mohr.

1967 *Law in Economy and Society,* ed. by Max Rheinstein, trans. by Edward Shils and Max Rheinstein. New York, Simon and Schuster.

Wright, Quincy

1959 *A Study of War.* (1st ed. 1942) Chicago, University of Chicago Press.

Yang, Martin C.

1945 *A Chinese Village: Taitou, Shantung Province.* New York, Columbia University Press.

Zake, S. J. L.

1962 "Approaches to the Study of Legal Systems in Nonliterate Societies." Unpublished doctoral dissertation, Northwestern University.

INDEX

Acholi, 239
actio, 242
Adair, J., 45
adjudication, Inca, 114; justice in, 240, 245; Kalinga, 124; Kapauku, 111, 118, 122
adultery, Tirolean laws of inheritance, 329
Akamba, 239
Allen, C. K., 233, 241
Das Allgemeine Bürgeliche Gesetzbuch (Austrian Civil Code of 1811–1963), 322–335
ambassador, of Kalinga, 124; *see also* Kalinga
analogia legis, iuris, 22
analysis, analytical concepts, legal, 275; formal (structural), 273–339; of Kapauku laws of inheritance, 303–322; of Kapauku laws of land tenure, 274–303, 336–337; of Tirolean laws of inheritance, 322–335; *see also* formal analysis of law
Ancient Law, 143, 144, 150
Andamanese Islanders, 188
Anerbe, see main heir
anständiger Unterhalt, Tirolean laws of inheritance, *see* support, decent
anthropology, 102, 103; of law, 112
appraiser (*Sachverständige*), appointed expert, Tirolean laws of inheritance, 323, 324, 325, 326
Aquinas, Thomas, 247; and Natural Law, 248
Araucanian Indians, household, 119; internalization of law, 208
arbiter, Kalinga, 123
Aristotle, 233; and Natural Law, 247
Aronfreed, J., 202
ascendants, Tirolean laws of inheritance, 326, 331, 332, 333; *see also* formal analysis of law
Ashanti, 189
assault, physical, Kapauku, 111
associations, 99, 102, 103, 104, 105, 112, 114, 115
attributes of law, 39–96, 106, 112; attribute of authority, 44–81; attribute of intention of universal application,

78–81; attribute of *obligatio,* 81–87; attribute of sanction, 87–95; and comparative research, 39–40; as defined by Pospisil, 43–44; and definitions of law, 40–43; *see also* individual entry for each attribute
attributes of legal system, Kapauku laws of inheritance, 320–322
Austin, J., 22, 96, 179
Australian Aborigines, 79, 174, 188
Austria, 118, 119, 339; laws of inheritance, 322–335, 345, 346; *see also* Tirolean peasants
Austrian Civil Law, 346
Austrian legal codification of 1811, 28, 322–335
authoritarian, law, 193, 194, 344; leadership, 58–59; and legal cases among Kapauku, 196–197, 205
authority, 8, 125, 343; and absence of, 44–49; absolute, 60; alleged absence of, among Eskimo, 72–78; among Kapauku, 65–72; attribute of, 43, 44–81; authority types, formality range of, 61; authority types, power range of, 60; as defined by Llewellyn and Hoebel, 43; formal, 61, in Austria, 63, in Chinese Empire, 63, in the Inca Empire, 63; informal, 61 (*see also* headman); jural, 106, 107, 111, 115, 125; and leadership, 49–52, 57–58; "legal authority," 50; pact holder, Kalinga, 123–124; political, 104, 106, 120; types of leadership and, 58–63; *see also* attributes of law; leadership
Azande, 239

Bachofen, J. J., 157
Bakitara, internalization of law, 208
Ballachey, E. L., 51, 56, 58, 59, 63–64
band, leadership of, Nunamiut, 76–78; 98
Barama River Carib, 28, 188
Barker, E., 247, 248, 249, 250, 251, 252
Barkun, M., 39, 40; and definition of law, 41; and "jural community," 48, 49, 91; and law in tribal society, 48–49; and "legal universals," 41

DATE